T0354794

HEALING ACROSS TIME II

A. BETWEEN MY SOULS AND OTHER SOULS

B. FOR OUR FAMILY LINES

Lorrie Leigh

HEALING ACROSS TIME II
A. BETWEEN MY SOULS AND OTHER SOULS
B. FOR OUR FAMILY LINES

iUniverse books may be ordered through booksellers or by contacting:

iUniverse
1663 Liberty Drive
Bloomington, IN 47403
www.iuniverse.com
844-349-9409

ISBN: 978-1-6632-5625-6 (sc)
ISBN: 978-1-6632-5626-3 (e)

Library of Congress Control Number: 2023918521

Print information available on the last page.

iUniverse rev. date: 10/27/2023

CONTENTS

PREFACE

Welcome back to the story of my life as a reader, an outside observer, and, in some cases, a "fellow experiencer." Hopefully, most of you are, or will go on to become, a fellow "being healed person," and many will go on to become a fellow "helping heal family members and others person," and a "helping heal your family lines person."

This book is about healing for my Souls and the Souls of family members from previous lifetimes. One's family lines and Soul line get healed by Souls from previous lifetimes being healed.

Addressing the "Big Issue"

For those who do not believe in people living more than one lifetime, I repeat what I said in the Preface of Healing Across Time I, "I am not trying to convince anybody that that is the case. I am simply relating my experiences and what I learned from Spirit." Messages I received from Spirit regarding that:

> Mar 1, '08. [| Only part of your Spirit is incarnated at any given time. The rest of your Spirit, your Higher Self, oversees your experiences and lovingly directs you from the spirit world. Your Higher Self is one with Me, yet distinct as a Spirit. |] (HAT I p. xv)

> May 7, '08. Father God, does each portion of one's Full Soul live a human life only once? [| Y |] Since the Soul portions are from a unit, does it seem to each portion of the Soul like the experiences of the other portions happened to them? [| Y |] Does our Soul carry the memories of all our lifetimes? [| Y |] (HAT I pp. xv-xvi)

Message from Father God

Father God asked me to include this message from Healing Across Time I because it also pertains to Healing Across Time II.

I sat down for a quiet time, hoping to learn from Spirit how *Healing Across Time I* and *II* apply to clearing and healing for other people and Souls and their family lines.

Father. I await a word from You.

[| First of all, Lorrie, relax. Let your mind, body, and Spirit relax. You know from experience that what I have to say often does not match what you thought I would say.

I send forth My word, and it does not return to me void.

"So shall My word be that goes forth from My mouth; It shall not return to Me void, But it shall accomplish what I please, And it shall prosper in the thing for which I sent it." (NKJB, Is 55:11)

I sent My word out to you through the years, saying, "Write that down. Ask this question. Write down My answer. Keep track of it all. Follow the promptings of My Spirit as best you can." You did well in following My instructions.

Healing for others is contained in, inherent in, your story. Hope and healing are interwoven within your story, within the words. I, My grace, will work within each person who reads even a part of it. I will trigger hope, faith, and a desire to be free and healed within them that will bring about miracles in their life and relationships.

Each Soul has knowledge within their consciousness or subconscious of the forgiveness for others that is needed in their current lifetime and in the lifetimes that other portions of their Full Soul lived. Each of those Souls knows what curses are hanging over them and their families in their current lifetime and over the Souls that other portions of their Full Soul lived.

I will give each of those Souls the desire to release others from curses they placed on them knowingly or unknowingly. As each of them chooses in their Spirit to extend blessings and love to everyone who placed curses against them or wished them ill and asks that all uncleared curses be permanently sealed, that will take place.

I am saying, Lorrie, that you have nothing to worry about in offering your story to the world as it is written. It is My project, remember?

Forgiveness will take place between people and Souls in the family lines and the Soul line of the readers. I can't enumerate all the minutiae of healings that will take place within individuals and families, but I give you My word that a massive amount of healing will take place for those who read your story or part of it and for many other people who are connected with the reader in some way. As you are aware, when one person in a family (community, group) makes a change, it brings about a ripple effect of changes within the people and Souls that person has connections with.

So, Lorrie, not to worry! Through the years, you placed yourself, the writings, and everything in My hands many times. The flower is blooming and spreading its perfume throughout the world! Rejoice with Me, for you and others are not lost. You are found! Rest and live securely in My Arms, in My Garden. Peace! |] (HAT I p. 349-350)

Things to Know

Portions of *Healing Across Time I* and *Healing Across Time II* overlap time-wise, but if I had interwoven the stories, I would have had to keep interjecting with, "In the meantime, this was happening."

Lorrie Leigh (Lay) and Fern Shakta are pen names. I gave alternative names to everyone I mentioned.

Messages from Spirit (Father-Mother God, the Holy Spirit, and Jesus) are designated by brackets: [| ... |]

Background information regarding messages from Spirit:

I had a profound spiritual experience In my mid-forties, after which I felt drawn to spend an hour a day in quiet time, reading from the Bible and writing my thoughts about the scriptures. After I had been doing that for a while, a spirit-filled friend received a message from the Holy Spirit that after spending a short time in quiet, I should begin writing down the thoughts that would come to mind. As I began doing that, spiritual thoughts and lessons flowed easily into my mind, and I simply wrote them down.

Before I met her, Fern had attended a workshop where she learned how to discern whether the answer to questions that she or others asked the Holy Spirit was "Yes" or "No." I attended that type of workshop in 2007 and learned how to do that, too. Also, both Fern and I received understanding directly from Spirit.

Following the example of *A Course in Miracles,* I capitalized the pronouns that refer to Father-Mother God and the Holy Spirit but not those that refer to Jesus.

Portions with titles all in capital letters are the ones I consider the most important. Portions with the title in capital and small letters are continuations of my story, not subheadings of the portion preceding them. Sections, e.g., 1-A, are mini-lessons or mini-stories within the main story.

(!!!) Means a sudden insight from the Holy Spirit.

<FERN> Designates that Fern answered from the other side.

Superscript designations:

    P... Part of me: Sylvia^{P}

  MD... Me Dual Soul: Mia^{MD}

  MP... Me Prior life: Darla^{MP}

  AP... Aunt Mollie Prior life: Corrie^{AP}

  LP... Lee Prior life: Darin^{LP}

  JP... My brother Joel Prior life: Cal^{JP}

  RP... Ron Prior life: Tony^{RP}

  YS... Young Soul: Nate^{YS}

GM... Grandma/Me Prior life: Marie^{GM}

 GP... Grandma Prior life (after split): Marie^{2GP}

Dates within each section, e.g., 1-A, are in parentheses in chronological order.

Dates in the main text are not in parentheses and are in chronological order from the beginning to the end of the book. However, a few are in parentheses to keep that portion under that particular heading.

Directions for doing the clearings that I tell about are in *Healing Across Time III*.

About Praying for Healing and Clearing

As you read about one clearing after the other that I did for people/Souls (often the same ones), you might wonder whether the prayers were even helping. I assure you that some clearing and healing took place each time. It's just that more clearing was needed, or those Souls needed to choose that they wanted to be healed and have that particular issue cleared.

There were surprises for me around every corner, as there will be for you. May you enjoy, learn, grow, be blessed, and receive healing! Peace to all!

Lorrie

ACKNOWLEDGEMENT

Thank You, Father-Mother God, Holy Spirit, for prompting me to study the teachings of *A Course in Miracles*, for Your patience in teaching and encouraging me as You guided me on the path to healing and wholeness, and for sustaining me in good health. Thank You for "keeping faith in me," even though it took a long time until I became (mostly) willing to release being in control of things myself. You are awesome!

Thank you, Jesus, for your patience in teaching and encouraging me, particularly during the earlier years when I first began receiving lessons from Spirit.

Thank you, Fern, for being a loving, nonjudgmental friend, for joining me in receiving understandings from Spirit – being a "fellow listener" – for eight years. Thank you for helping me process traumatic memories and, after crossing over in August 2009, for being on the spiritual writing-editing team that has patiently assisted me with getting the writings into a suitable form for publishing. Thank you to every member of that team. God bless you, Fern and Team!

Thank you, Mandy, for the spiritual Reading you did that helped me get untangled from Darla's^MP Soul. God bless you!

Thank you, Beth Stein, for being a loving, nonjudgmental friend, offering encouragement, double-checking answers from the Holy Spirit, ministering to me, and being my spiritual sister. God bless you!

Thank you, Jennie Seil, for your love and encouragement and for being there for me. We met only a few years ago, but I immediately felt we had known each other for a long time. God bless you!

A: BETWEEN MY SOULS AND OTHER SOULS

CHAPTER 1

THE WORLD OF SPIRIT

Jan 1, '07   NETWORK OF LOVE

[| Speaking to everyone, you "haven't the foggiest" about the energy connections that exist between you and living and deceased relatives; between you and your pets; between you and the world of plants, minerals, and all living things; between you and the angels and saints; between each of you and your Creator God; between you and the whole universe.

Everything is held together and connected by a *network of love*. Love is throughout all and within all, and Love Is One. You are one with the universe, one with Me. The life within you is My life and yours at the same time. It is to be expected that if one hurts, that hurt affects all to a greater or lesser degree.

On the natural level, one might think that one person's expansion in love and openness to grace could not affect other people except to improve their relationship with that person. The world of Spirit is so different from the natural physical world, however, that very little of the natural level applies to the spiritual level in the same way. |]

The following are understandings about the *network of love* that a spiritual seeker, Lee Carroll, received from Spirit through an entity who calls himself Kryon:

The Cosmic Lattice – Part 1

(Par. 7) "We wish to tell you this night of a specific kind of energy. ...It is the missing piece of energy that you have been looking for so long. It is the energy of love. It is the energy of Spirit. It is the energy of the Universe...that we will call 'The Cosmic Lattice.'

(Par. 9) "There is no place that you can conceive of—no matter what the dimension—that is without the lattice. ...[It] is perhaps what you could call the consciousness of God and yet it is physics and it is energy and it contains conscious love.

(Par. 11) "The most distant part of this lattice knows exactly what the part that is here in this room is doing.

(Par. 21) "The Cosmic Lattice, dear ones, is what allows the mechanics for co-creation, for synchronicity, for what we have called love. The Cosmic Lattice contains the mechanics which allow for miracles on the planet."

(www.kryon.com/k_26.htm)

The Cosmic Lattice – Part 2

(Par. 12) "[The Cosmic Lattice] is a physics staple of the way things work throughout all the visible universe. We told you that light is slow compared to the communication of the lattice [which is] almost instantaneous.

(Par. 15) "[T]he cosmic lattice is indeed the very essence of the energy of healing." (www.kryon.com/k_29.htm)

Jan 3, '07   WORDS FROM A HAG

A scenario opened in thought and image: As newcomers join a family line, those who have crossed over watch for people to shove their heavy burdens of anger, anguish, and hopelessness onto: *"We had to go through this shit. Somebody else should have to, also, so they can see what it was like for us, and we can get rid of some of the garbage heaped on us!"*

Those farthest back in the line become freer by passing their burdens down to others, specifically, struggles related to sexuality. Those referred to are abused, shortchanged women who have gone before in the family line, a shadowy lot, ethereal. They passed the word along as they saw me: *"Here's a sweet, unsuspecting young thing! We can get to her! When I give the word, everybody heave!"* And they dumped a bunch of manure (contumely) on me.

Some women in the family line who suffered abuse and deprivation – having numerous pregnancies, miscarriages, and births, possibly under degrading conditions; women with alcoholic, abusive husbands – very likely breathed contumely and passed curses and bondage onto upcoming generations of women.

A hag such as in The Wizard of Oz says to me: "Not so fast, my pretty one! Do you think you're going to get away from this one? Not on your life! We are laying these things down to go to you, breathing them into you, cursing, passing them on to you. Why should we be the only ones who had to suffer? Now we'll see how you next ones can manage! Hee! Hee! Hee!"

> contumely *n.* 1 haughty and contemptuous rudeness; insulting and humiliating treatment or languages (Web p. 317)

Jan 1, '08. DREAM: I attended a service in a country church. Afterward, a man asked me, "Are you a witch? You have the mark of a witch." He motioned towards my left wrist, which had a circular age spot. I thought, "That's ridiculous!" and woke up. END.

As I was about to fall back to sleep:

HAG-TYPE WOMAN: "Not so fast, my sweetie! Let's discuss this. There is a reason that circle appeared on your skin in your dream. It's because you have what people consider "witch-type powers." You and I know, though, that your powers are natural abilities through the Holy Spirit that everybody could develop if they choose to.

"Using those kinds of spiritual abilities has gotten a lot of people in trouble through the years, especially women, but don't let that hold you back. You are meant to use those God-given abilities. Use them more instead of less.

"Those types of spiritual abilities follow down the family line to those whose Soul is willing to accept and use them for the good of all. They don't bring darkness as most people fear, but light. Those healings are meant to take place. Questions about where those abilities come from are also meant to come forth.

"You are helping teach people about the mysteries of God, the gifts of God, as they show up in people's lives. The hope is that, eventually, humankind may come to know those gifts as natural gifts that they can exercise, too, if they choose.

"Thank you for being open to using these natural gifts from God! Yes, you are carrying painful cellular memories related to the reactions of mistrustful people to the gifts you had in earlier lifetimes. You sensed several times that we "hags" from farther back are somehow family to you. That we are!

"Bless you, Lorrie, our sister! May you use your abilities as Spirit directs without fear of what people think or say."

Me: Thank you, my sister hags! I am honored to be part of the family. Thank You, Holy Spirit!

Jan 21,'08. [| Religious teachers in some traditions have long taught not to trust your feelings, that feelings have no valid place in a life of faith. They have been sadly mistaken. |]

CAME TO MIND: Whodunit. Mystery. Mischief. Misfit. Is it so?

Is "what" so? Passing it on. I didn't know the difference. END.

[| That is how it is for everyone. You pass on to your children what you learned because you do not know any different. For those following religious teachings religiously, breaking from what they learned is much harder.

Thank you, Lorrie, for being willing to think outside the box of literal interpretation to examine any concept that comes to mind because you know that truth will hold up. One person's willingness to listen trustingly to Spirit makes a huge difference for everyone. It may take time, but more will follow now that you and others have pushed the door open. Blessings! |]

Thank You, Father God! Bless You!

Feb 17,'08   The Way Many of You Feel

[| My children, you are all family! You belong, every one of you. Some of you forgot that as you spent any number of lifetimes on Earth in a fairly dense state.

4

Many of you feel scared to death. Alone. Forsaken. Neglected. Forgotten. Hounded by fear. At the mercy of fate. Abandoned by God and everyone else. Guilty. Depressed. Helpless. On the verge of going crazy. Desperate.

The list could go on and on, but wherever you picture yourself to be, I am there with you, experiencing what you are experiencing. You cannot be separated from Me, for I am All Existence, and you exist within Me. You cannot fall out of Me. You cannot run or fly away from Me.

May this assurance give you warmth for your cold feet and a gentle flow of love and peace throughout your body, mind, and spirit. I do not abandon you. Please do not abandon yourself. Whatever difficulties you are experiencing, know that *"This, too, shall pass."* Good night, Lorrie and everyone! |]

May 17,'08. Father God, You suggested that Fern and I meet with Pastor Eric. I feel very anxious when I think about him reading my written material. Am I getting in touch with an earlier lifetime in which I was mistreated for being a "witch"?

[| Things are as you described. The lockdown of your feelings didn't take place all at once. The beginning of that process was a former lifetime in which people mistreated you because of your spiritual gifts and beliefs.

When you are suffering because of some experience, you may think it would be better not to be able to feel so deeply, but you need to be able to suffer deeply to be able to rejoice deeply. It is heaven to be able to both suffer and rejoice deeply because, in so doing, you are fully being who you are, a child of God. Deep breathing will help free up your emotions. |]

Holy Spirit, the top of my head has been very achy lately. If that is related to an earlier lifetime, do I have to know what caused the pain for it to be released? [| N |] Should I release by expressing my emotions? [| Y |]

Can someone carry cellular memories from prior lifetimes of their mother? [| It can happen if their mother was (is) carrying cellular memories from previous lifetimes. |]

5

Suppose a painful cellular memory from their mother surfaces for a person. If they work through the emotions connected with the memory, does that bring healing for their mother? [| Y |] Does their mother receive healing in the lifetime in which the incident happened? [| Y |] And in the present? [| Y |] Neat!

May 27,'08   Loosening Stuck Emotions

How can fear from a previous lifetime affect me now?
[| Yes, through cellular memories. |] Is the presence of fearful cellular memories one of the reasons why I often haven't been able to respond fully in believing and trusting God? [| Y |]

Does expressing one's emotions about a traumatic experience help clear the person's whole emotional body? [| Y |]

Including stuck emotions from previous lifetimes? [| Y |]

Is getting our stuck emotions expressed so important for our spiritual well-being that our Soul will invite situations into our life that will bring about emotional release? [| Y |]

From a spiritual standpoint, is emotional release so important that it would even be worth losing one's home or a loved one to bring it about? [| Y |] Wow!

Jun 9, '08. Fern and I met with Pastor Eric to tell him about the writing task that I am (we are) working on. He prayed with Fern for a health concern and with me to help release the fear that rises within me so often. Thank You, Father God!

[| The back of the fear that had taken up residence within you has been broken, Lorrie. Choose with your will to deny yourself the secondary gain you have been receiving from feeling the adrenalin rush triggered by fear.

Your task is to recognize and stop yourself from triggering fear by thinking such thoughts as *"What will so-and-so think? What if this? What if that?"* It will take time to establish new thinking patterns, but I will help you. 'Bye! |]

Jul 14, '08   Relax!

[| My sons and daughters, please do not let hurtful experiences you have had or seen turn you against Me. I hold you to My heart with love even while you have experiences that almost drain the life out of you.

If your Soul had stayed in Heaven and you had never gone out to live a life on Earth or elsewhere, you would be doing just as much searching there as you are doing here. I, God, have gone through an evolution and continue to evolve.

"At that time, I had an unconscious image of Myself that said I had to be perfect from the beginning, and perfect meant that I had to know everything already. ...I have since... realized that God also has process or I would not be an evolving God, and that this evolution has a perfection to it that is an evolving perfection." (Original p. 120)

To be fully alive, you need to evolve, and that is:
1. Where the blissful experiences of life fit in, for you to expand to higher and wider vibration energy levels
2. Where the Soul and mind-shattering experiences of pathos and sadness fit in, for you to experience lower energy levels to develop compassion for others and
3. Where ordinary experiences fit in, to provide a stabilizing balance for your whole person.

Your Full Soul chooses the experiences that you have. It is present with you to encourage, strengthen, and cheer you on! You also have many angel helpers and guides. Peace! []

Nov 14, '08   A "BIGGIE"

[| Lorrie, remember that long line of witches (hags) who decided to dump a bunch of contumely on you so they could be free of it? Well, it got dumped all right, and you are starting to become aware that things are not in right order around and within you in the energetic realm.

The energy of other Souls should not affect your energetic field and physical being as much as it does. Some of that contumely has been cleared by releasing emotions and having others pray for you, but the gunk left behind (residue) still attracts erratic energies. That gunky energy needs to be replaced with clean energy.

When you shared that message about a long line of witches/ hags with your counselor, she understood it to represent a line of healers. You were a healer, but there are always some people who would like to have the recognition that goes with being a healer, and when that does not happen, they resort to playing tricks on those gifted with healing, including using black magic.

You wonder whether *your Aunt Mollie* was one of the people in another lifetime of yours who was jealous and turned to witchcraft to wield influence over you. *Yes, she directed witchcraft energies at you during a couple of lifetimes when she and you were nuns in the same convent.* Her Soul from those lifetimes needs deliverance from the spirit of witchcraft. Once that clearing is complete, you need prayer to neutralize and dissolve the *contact points,* the energetic connections through which you were affected at those times and are still being affected now.

Ask Pastor Eric to join you in praying for deliverance for the Souls of Mollie and her cohorts in those lifetimes from the spirit of witchcraft. Ask for a protective shield around those unwilling to release the power and energy of witchcraft to remain in place until they become willing to choose the way of good.

Mollie's Soul, from every lifetime, desires to be free and fully in the light. She has a powerful Soul and will minister in powerful ways once the gunk left over from yesteryear has been cleared. Peace! []

Thank You, Father God!

I couldn't meet with Pastor Eric at that time, so I emailed him, asking him to pray for the clearing of witchcraft energies from Mollie and her pals in those earlier lifetimes as nuns and for the clearing of witchcraft energies and contact points for witchcraft and dark energies from me. He replied that he was praying for those intentions. Thank you, Pastor Eric!

Nov 15, '08. **Are energies timeless?** [| Y |] Are the witchcraft energies that Mollie and her pals directed at other nuns and me at that convent still affecting my Soul and the Souls of the nuns from those lifetimes and at present? [| Y |] Wow!

Dec 11, '08. Pastor Eric emailed me that he has been praying for the last three weeks to clear witchcraft energies and contact points and the spirit of witchcraft from Mollie's Souls and the Souls of the other nuns who practiced witchcraft with her in those previous lifetimes. Thank you, Pastor Eric!

I did a clearing for the spirit of witchcraft and contact points for dark energies from Mollie's Soul and the Souls of the other nuns who practiced witchcraft with her. I placed a protective shield around whichever of those Souls is unwilling to release witchcraft energies, to remain in place until no longer needed.

Holy Spirit, are Mollie's Souls and the Souls of the other nuns from those previous lifetimes cleared of the spirit of witchcraft? [| Y |] Thank You! That's great!

Are the contact points for witchcraft energies cleared from me? [| N |] I emailed that information to Pastor Eric and asked him to continue praying for me for that intention, and I prayed for that intention, also.

(Two days later) Are those contact points cleared? [| Y |]

Jan 5, '09   I Meet With Pastor Eric

I am reading *Honestly* by Sheila Walsh, in which she tells about coming to terms with clinical depression, that under the depression was fear of being known and of being rejected (Walsh p. 76). I am dealing with both of those fears.

I firmly believe that Father God led me to study and accept the teachings in *A Course in Miracles*. He seems to be guiding me to share some of those beliefs with Pastor Eric, but I find it challenging to think about doing that. If I don't talk with him soon, I will begin to feel artificial, like I am just putting on a good front.

Father God, I place this in Your hands. Bless You!
[| Bless you, Lorrie! I will take care of this matter. |]

Aug 30, '09. I met with Pastor Eric, and it went well. Thank You, Father, for being with us during that time.

[| I am always with each of you. Please do deep breathing now and throughout the next few days. You have tension to release related to meeting with Pastor Eric and not feeling well. Bless you! Have a nice evening. |]

Thank You, Father God! Bless You!

Oct 24, '09. Good morning, Father God!

[| Good morning, Lorrie! Please sit quietly to relax and dismiss all anxiety. (Pause) You have noticed that you are in the habit of "calling up" anxiety to have a slight edge of excitement while you do whatever you are doing. For your own good, dissolve the roots of that habit and dismiss anxiety. You will need to watch yourself for quite some time to clear that habit. |]

Thank You, Father! This is marvelous: When we say, "Bless you!" to people (Souls), we aren't helping only them. Situations are gradually getting settled between those people and us in this lifetime and in earlier lifetimes that didn't get settled then! Healing is taking place across time!

1-A: MYSTIFYING EXPERIENCES

(Aug 30, '04)   OUT OF THE ORDINARY

My systolic (upper) blood pressure reading rises 40+ points during the daytime. What could be causing that?

Aunt Mollie died last week in the nursing home where she lived for the last eighteen months. During the two weeks before she died, Mollie said she heard somebody call her name several times, even at night. She said to the staff, "You girls have to stop calling me," but none of them had. She also heard knocking a couple of times.

I think Mollie's mother, Grandma Leigh, was calling her name and knocking to invite Mollie to join her.

(Oct 15, '04) The front windows of my car have begun making an annoying rattle when I drive on an uneven road. Sometimes, the noise will stop when I open and close the windows. The weird thing is that the windows rattle only sometimes when I drive on a bumpy road. It doesn't make sense.

Also, an annoying sound is coming from the right corner of the dashboard in my car, like a small woodpecker pecking rapidly. It seems related to bumps in the road, but there often is no sound for a day or two, and then it will be back. It didn't help to tap the vent.

It took me two years to learn what was causing those sounds, something I would never have guessed. Read on!

(Feb 14, '06)   A Pesky Pimple

This next is rather personal: Early in 2005, I developed a pimple, like a small boil, on my anal area that wouldn't clear up with taking sitz baths and applying an antibiotic salve. I had minor surgery in August '05, took a strong antibiotic for a month, and took hot sitz baths twice daily, but the pimple still didn't heal. The doctor performed a second minor surgery in Oct 2005 to clean the area well. It still didn't heal, so he sent me to a specialist.

I had a third minor surgery in Dec '05. The specialist cleared a fistula and was confident the area would heal nicely. The pimple was smaller and less sore than it had been, but it was still there. I took sitz baths for a long while to keep it from worsening.

Fern told me that she and her friend Roxie had attended a workshop at which they learned how to locate positive and negative vortexes – natural parts of the energy of the Earth – and how to put copper rods in place to nullify detrimental effects of negative vortexes on a person. She said a negative vortex where a person sleeps or spends a lot of time could cause physical problems or prevent healing.

I asked Fern and Roxie to check my apartment to see if a negative vortex might prevent my pimple from healing. They discovered a strong negative vortex located under the center of my bed! I followed Fern's suggestion to switch bedrooms. The pimple didn't clear up, but it got smaller. I figured I would just have to live with it.

I asked Fern to read the story of my life that I had written, covering from birth through 1999. A few weeks after she finished reading it, the pimple on my bottom cleared up without special treatments, and it never returned! *It appears that toxins were released from my system by telling my story, telling the secrets.*

(Feb 15, '06)   Unseen Visitors

After Fern and Roxie finished checking my apartment for negative vortexes yesterday and were ready to leave, I felt prompted to ask Fern: "Is it good for me to have so many things from Aunt Mollie: clothing, crafts, and such?"

Instead of answering my question, Fern said: [| *Mollie is here. And so is your mother.* |] (She felt very cold and understood from the Holy Spirit that those Souls were there.)

What should I do with the things from Mollie?
[| You should donate or discard everything that was Mollie's and that she gave you. It would be better not to give them to family members. After removing those things from your apartment, do clearing for negative energies. |] I will do that.

(!!!) Is Mollie causing the sounds in my car to try to get my attention? [| Y |]

That solved the mystery of what was causing the noises in my car, but I had another mystery: Why was the Holy Spirit directing me to dispose of all items connected with Mollie?

(Mar 2, '06) After having the "Mollie" items in a large copper ring for 24 hours to clear negative energies, I gave a few things to relatives and took the rest to a second-hand store.

Fern was at my place again. The Holy Spirit prompted me to ask a question. *Holy Spirit, is it good for me to have so many pictures, objects, and clothing with roses on them?*
[| No, it isn't. Give away or discard those items. |]

Should I remove photos that have roses in them? [| Y |]

(!!!) *Am I being directed to remove all rose items because of a connection with a lifetime in which I was a nun named Rose of Lima?* [| Y |] During that lifetime, did some of the other nuns place a curse on roses to be used as contact points for attracting witchcraft energies to me? [| Y |]

Curses that haven't been cleared carry forward into a person's later lifetimes. *I was being directed to remove all rose items from my place because they attract witchcraft energies!*

(!!!) Should I remove all photos of Mollie taken after I was born, especially those with her and me together? [| Y |]

I put the "rose items" in my garage until I could give away or discard them. My apartment felt lighter, indicating that negative energies were attached to those items.

After removing the "Mollie items," I did a clearing for my apartment for negative energies:

1. Directed negative energies to leave.
2. Carried a lit candle into each room with the intention for the light to clear dark energies,
3. Opened windows so the breeze could blow through, representing the Holy Spirit clearing negativity out and flowing in peace and joy. My apartment felt lighter!

Does my apartment still need clearing? [| Yes, there is a lingering effect. |]

What did I still need to clear? The answer is coming up shortly. Look for the answers to Questions 1 and 2.

(!!!) Was the pimple I had that didn't heal for such a long time a sign that things need to be cleared and healed in my family line? [| Y |] Did it take that long to heal so I would eventually ask Fern to come to my apartment to check for negative vortexes, learn that Mollie's Soul was here and that I needed to remove all the "Mollie" and rose items? [| Y |] Wow!

Why would the presence of Mollie's Soul or things connected with her affect me negatively? It took a while before I learned the answer.

(Jun 4, '07)   Affected by Mollie's Distress

My head is bothering me a lot. Do I have karma to clear with somebody, a need for forgiveness? [| Y |]

Maybe karma between Aunt Mollie and me from previous lifetimes prevents me from becoming free of her attempts to contact me by making sounds in my car. Perhaps she is trying to tell me she disapproves of telling my story and the family story and making plans to publish it, even though I am not using people's real names.

Did Mollie cause the pressure and discomfort in my head that I have had frequently for over three years? [| Y |] Is the anger I sometimes feel from her also? [| Y |] Are my high systolic BP readings caused by or related to her? [| Y |]

Mollie had sinus drainage for many years. Is the sudden onset of sinus drainage I have experienced lately a sign that she is around and affecting me? [| Y |] My eyes have been itchy the last two years, also something that I didn't have earlier. Is that allergic reaction related to Mollie? [| Y |]

End of 1-A: MYSTIFYING EXPERIENCES

1-B: SOUL INCORPORATION

(Jun 4, '07)   INCORPORATED IN MY BODY?

When people hear the word reincarnation, they usually think of the dictionary definition:

> reincarnation *n.* 1 rebirth of the soul in another body, as in Hindu religious belief (Web p. 1208)

That word has also had another meaning for me since Nov 25, '85. That day, *"reincarnation"* came to mind, and I felt prompted to go to the library to find a book that would show how my mother's Spirit had somehow been "reincarnated" in me. None of the books on reincarnation seemed to apply, so I looked at the books next to them about the mind. In a book written by Maria Montessori, I found:

> "It may be said that we acquire knowledge by using our minds, but the child absorbs knowledge directly in his psychic life. Simply by continuing to live, the child learns to speak his native tongue. A kind of mental chemistry goes on within him.

We, by contrast, are recipients. Impressions pour into us and we store them in our minds; but we ourselves remain apart from them, just as a vase keeps separate from the water it contains. Instead, the child undergoes a transformation. Impressions do not merely enter his mind; they form it. They incarnate themselves in him." (Montessori p. 25)

Holy Spirit, did a portion of Aunt Mollie's Soul become "incarnated," *incorporated*, within me as a child in the sense Maria Montessori described, that her Soul is within cells in my body? Did I "absorb" her Soul as a child? [| Y |]

Did the incorporation of Mollie's Soul within cells in my body occur early in my life? [| Yes, at age five or earlier. She wished you were her little girl. |]

I told Fern what the Holy Spirit said several years ago: *"You will be grateful for everything you have gone through after you come to the place I am bringing you."*

[| (Fern/Holy Spirit) That time has come. The thirty years before this laid the necessary groundwork for you to free the Souls of relatives incorporated in cells in your body. |]

Is a portion of Mollie's Soul still incorporated within some of the cells in my body? [| Y |] Is a portion of Mom's Soul incorporated within cells in my body? [| Y |]

A portion of Grandma Leigh's Soul? [| Yes, because your grandma's and mother's Souls are enmeshed. |]

Is Grandma's Soul enmeshed with Mollie's Soul, also? [| N |]

Can I clear the incorporation and enmeshment of Mom's, Mollie's, and Grandma Leigh's Souls from cells in my body at the same time?

[| Yes, but pray daily for each of them while you do the clearing. |] I will also need to clear the enmeshment between my Soul and each of their Souls, our Souls being "mixed together."

After I clear the incorporation and enmeshment of their Souls, should I release them from me as a unit? [| Y |]

After their Souls leave, will it be my task to clear the enmeshment between Mom's and Grandma's Souls? [| Y |]

15

This is funny! Will my apartment still need clearing after Mollie's Soul is no longer with me? [| N |]

QUESTION 1: What else did I need to clear for my apartment to be fully clear of negative energies from Mollie and from items with roses on them?

ANSWER: *I needed clearing!*

QUESTION 2: Why does the presence of Mollie's Soul or things connected with her affect me negatively?

ANSWER: *Because her energy level is lower than mine.*

My inner self told me about having volunteered to be hypnotized as a child and that somebody implanted sexual suggestions. Was that a real happening? [| N |] Was hypnotism, in that case, a symbol of family tendencies being incorporated within cells in my body? [| Y |] Did those tendencies trigger my actions with Joel and others of my brothers and sisters? [| Y |]

(Jun 9, '07)   SOUL INCORPORATION EXPLAINED

A person's Soul being "incorporated" within another person's body means that part of that person's Soul is within some of the cells in the host person's body. With portions of Mom's, Mollie's, and Grandma Leigh's Souls being incorporated within cells in my body, it stands to reason that I am being affected by their energy and emotions! It will affect me if they feel angry, anxious, guilty, or whatever.

(!!!) Did some of my judgmental thoughts about various people come at least partly from Mom's, Mollie's, or Grandma Leigh's incorporated Souls? [| Yes, from all three. |]

Does the distress they feel about secrets needing to come out affect me? [| Y |] Did the presence of Mom's Soul hinder me from hearing as well from the Holy Spirit these last ten years? [| Y |] Did the presence of Mollie's Soul also hinder me from hearing as well from the Holy Spirit? [| Y |]

(Jun 10, '07)   Clearing the Incorporation

I received understanding from the Holy Spirit what steps to take that should gradually free the incorporated portions of Mom's, Mollie's, Grandma's, and any other Souls from cells in my body. Cells are constantly being replaced, so preventing the incorporated Souls from entering new cells will ease those Souls out of one's body. I began taking these steps each morning:

1. I blessed my food for the day,
2. I declared that only my Soul may enter new cells as they form in my body,
3. I asked the Holy Spirit to place a protective shield around every cell in my body.

(Jun 20, '07) I did those steps daily for the last two weeks. Has the incorporation of Mom's, Mollie's, and Grandma Leigh's Souls within cells in my body lessened during that time?
[| Yes. You no longer need to make that intention. |] Wonderful!

I first cleared enmeshment between my Soul and Mom's, Mollie's and Grandma's Souls, and then between their Souls. I intended for those clearings to take place in their recent lifetimes and all previous lifetimes. Thank You, Holy Spirit!

Is Mollie's Soul free to leave now? [| N |] Do I need to become freer and more healed *so I release her?* [| Y |]

Is a portion of Mollie's Soul still with me because I need to clear karma between her and me? [| Y |] Do I need to clear karma between Mom and me? [| Y |]

The next day, I went through a process of forgiveness between Aunt Mollie and me, and Mom and me, to clear karma.

(Jul 7, '07) Is Mom's Soul cleared from me? [| Y |] Are Grandma's and Mollie's Souls cleared? [| Y |] Will they all be ready to go to the light soon? [| Y |] Thank You, Holy Spirit!

(Oct 28, '12)   RETROACTIVE CLEARING

The top of my head is very uncomfortable. Is there a portion of an unloving Soul in my brain (see 1-D)? [| Y |] Is it incorporated within cells in my brain? [| Y |]

(Nov 15, '12) I did the steps for clearing Soul incorporation for the last six weeks. Is the incorporation of that portion of an unloving Soul cleared from within cells in my brain? [| N |] Does it take longer to clear incorporation from brain cells because those cells don't get replaced as often? [| Y |]

(!!!) **Should I ask that the clearing be retroactive**, making it so I had been doing it much longer? [| Y |] I mentioned several time frames that were not long enough. Should I ask for it to be retroactive for three years? [| Y |]

I said aloud: "I choose and declare that I stated in my spirit every day for the last three years that only my Soul is allowed to enter new cells as they form in my body."

As soon as I finished stating that, I asked: Holy Spirit, is the incorporation of that portion of an unloving Soul cleared from cells in my brain? [| Y |] Is that Soul portion loving now? [| Y |] To me, that was a miracle!

Should I ask it to go to the place for visiting Souls surrounding my aura? [| Y |]

"I ask that Soul portion and any other Soul portions that are in my brain to go to the place for visiting Souls. Thank you!"

Did they go to the place for visiting Souls? [| Y |] Great!

End of 1-B: SOUL INCORPORATION

1-C: FAMILY DISTRESS

(Jun 20, '07)   AFFECTED BY OTHERS

Fern and I saw clearly by that time that people can experience physical and emotional symptoms because of family members and friends, living or are on the other side, being in distress, and reaching out for help. We decided to call that happening **family distress**. I believe what happens is that people are affected by negative energy that they pick up from other people and Souls.

(Jul 19, '07) (!!!) Does family distress have a stickiness to it that one needs to clear from the Souls who asked for help even after those Souls have gone to the light?
[| Yes. Do a clearing for the lingering effects (residue). |]

Would it help to say prayers for clearing? [| Y |] Would asking for a Holy Spirit demagnetizing shower to flow through oneself and one's surroundings clear that sticky residue? [| Y |]

I began to ask daily for a Holy Spirit demagnetizing shower to flow through me, my home, car, and apartment building.

(Sept 1, '07) Is the sinus drainage I have been having for the last several months caused by family distress? [| Y |]

Was the recent increase in sinus drainage I am having brought on by a Soul of Mollie's from a previous lifetime that wants to go to the light? [| Yes. Several Souls from past lifetimes of hers want help to go to the light. |]

Family distress has been affecting me mainly as discomfort at the top of my head, a light-to-medium stinging and burning. I also feel pressure in my head, like something is stretching my scalp. The discomfort lessens somewhat after I learn which relatives are asking for assistance and pray for them for a few days. That happened often enough that it shows the head discomfort I have been experiencing is related to family distress.

Holy Spirit, do I easily pick up emotional distress from family members and other people?
[| Yes. Pray for clearing and protection daily and stand in the large copper ring for a while. |] I began doing that.

(Apr 23, '20) (!!!) Fern and I learned that energies of distress that people are experiencing can pass to others through soul ties and spiritual umbilical cord connections!

Holy Spirit, please place a protective valve that allows only love to pass in each direction in all soul ties and umbilical cord connections between me and others. I cut all detrimental soul ties between me and others. Please thin out the umbilical cord connections and dissolve them when You see fit. Thank You!

(May 29, '08) Are people affected by everyone in their family relationship who needs healing even if those people and Souls don't reach out to family members? [| Y |] Is it the energy of those people and Souls that affects family members? [| Y |]

End of 1-C: FAMILY DISTRESS

1-D: UNLOVING SOULS

(Jan 11, '08)   WHAT'S THE CAUSE?

Holy Spirit, I have been having much head discomfort for the last few months, and my systolic blood pressure has been quite high in the afternoons. Are those things connected with my afternoon work? [| Y |] Does Mamie, who works in that office in the morning, have a lower energy level than I do? [| Y |]

I began asking for protection for myself and did a clearing for the office every day. During the next three months, I often cleared the enmeshment between Mamie's Soul and mine, cleared negative energies from me, and rested more.

Doing those things didn't help with my head discomfort or high blood pressure readings. I have to figure this out!

(Apr 4, '08) My BP at noon was 139/70. At 5:00 P.M., it was 172/74. This is getting ridiculous! Holy Spirit, is Mamie's energy so strong that it gets past all the protection I have in place? [| N |]

(!!!) *Have unloving Souls been with Mamie?* [| Y |] That's why my blood pressure has been going so high! Unloving Souls have a very low energy level. I cleared unloving Souls from Mamie and that office and felt much better afterward. Thank You, Holy Spirit!

(Nov 8, '08) [| Lorrie, things will get worked out more rapidly for you now that you have learned what energies are affecting you. At the level your Soul is at, it is very disruptive to have unloving Souls anywhere near. Even with asking for protection, the low energy level of unloving Souls can still affect you and cause your blood pressure to rise.

All loving Souls have the right to direct that unloving Souls may not be near where you live, work, visit, shop, etc. Planet Earth was created and prepared for habitation by loving Souls. You have every right to set rigid boundaries beyond which unloving Souls may not go.

State that all Souls and energies detrimental to you, family members, and coworkers must stay away from your home, workplace, surrounding areas, your children, and their homes.

People who came in with loving Souls who then became unloving because of painful circumstances have a chance to return to being loving Souls. Hopefully, that will happen for all or most of them. As more people understand the concept of keeping their spiritual environment clean, those born with unloving Souls will be drawn to move near other people born with unloving Souls to finish living out their lives together. They will feel at home there.

You are not to judge the unloving Souls of people living on Earth, those in the astral plane, or elsewhere as bad, less-than, or some such. Accept them as "neutral." Please choose the path of non-judgment and love. []

Thank You, Father God!

(Dec 5, '08)   Throbbing Was The Worst Ever

My systolic BP has been very high several times recently, including today. I felt jittery at work this morning, and the top of my head was throbbing, the worst it had ever been. When I got home at noon, my BP was 207/91!

I called Fern to ask about it. (!!!) The owner's wife made copies on the printer in the office this morning, right next to me! Does she have an unloving Soul? [| N |] Were unloving Souls hanging around her? [| Y |] No wonder my blood pressure went so high! (It returned to normal after I did a clearing for negative energies.)

(Mar 28, '10) (!!!) Holy Spirit, did portions of unloving Souls attach themselves to my Soul as I came into this life?
[| Yes. Your Soul was wide open to invasion at the time of your conception. Father God has protected you by keeping a shield of spiritual lead around those Soul portions. |]

Are portions of some unloving Souls in the upper part of my head now? [| Yes. It is not surprising you are experiencing discomfort in that area. |] Do they react strongly to negative energies? [| Y |] (I assume they are attracted to negative energies.)

If a lot of dark energy has entered a Soul, would that Soul be called "unloving" even if it came forth as a loving Soul? [| Y |] Do some Souls that came forth as loving Souls become unloving because of their choices, what they learned, or as a reaction to difficult circumstances? [| Y |]

Father God says in *Right Use of Will* that there are Spirits of Loving Essence that thrive on love and Spirits that are not of Loving Essence that seek "reduction in consciousness, compression, and death." He says every Spirit has the right to be in the place that feels right for them. Loving Spirits and unloving Spirits are not meant to be together. Unloving Spirits were allowed to enter the Earth by people having sex without love. (Right pp. 42, 50)

For an unloving Spirit, "going to the light" means going to the "right place for unloving Souls."

End of 1-D: UNLOVING SOULS

1-E: DARK ENERGIES, ENERGY CENTERS

(Jan 16, '08)   NOT TO FEAR

Holy Spirit, I have a feeling of pressure in my head. The top feels like it wants to "lift off." What would help release it?
[| Take deep breaths to release tension, anxiety, and fear. When you wish to clear non-beneficial energies from an area of your body,

bless those energies first. Then, ask them kindly to transmute to neutral energies or go to another dimension.

After you have directed maverick energies (those unsuitable for you) to clear out, it would be good to ask for a Holy Spirit demagnetizing shower to clear negative residue.

Go forward with blessing into this new day, Lorrie. Do not be afraid. Fear attracts negative energies. Bless you! []

(Dec 6, '10) [| <FERN> Lorrie, thank you for the time and effort you are putting in to bring the lessons together that the Father-Mother God and the Holy Spirit want to give to the world as a "breakthrough" present. The project is on schedule!

The topic of dark energies will open up soon: energies that have a very low vibration level. That is one reason Father God asked you to spend additional time with Him. Good night, and God bless you! []

Good night, Fern! God bless you!

(Dec 11, '10) My head bothered a lot the last four days, indicating that Souls or beings that are with me or nearby have negative energy. The Holy Spirit may have allowed my head to get very uncomfortable, so I will finally ask about dark energies.

[| Lorrie, completely relax. (Pause) OK. First, there is nothing to be afraid of, including dark energies. They are not out to hurt or overpower anyone. Like everything else in creation, they will flow into nearby areas if a passageway opens, just as water flows into available openings.

Everything that "is" has its place to be. Loving Souls, unloving Souls, and dark energies: Each has its right place to be.

You are making headway in lessening the effects of negative energies on you. It would help to ask the Holy Spirit for a protective valve in all soul ties between you and other people and Souls and between those people and other people and Souls.

Stay open to whatever you can do that would help bring release and protection from negative energies. (Being filled with love would take care of the problem.) Any negativity within you prevents you from being filled with love. Anxiety is a significant factor, but the trick is to release anxiety without being anxious about it! Bless you! []

Thank You, Father God!

(Dec 21, '10) My systolic BP reading has been high lately, even when I have been home all day. Is the negative energy attached to Mollie's First Communion Certificate in my garage affecting me?
[| Yes, Lorrie. Water will come in through every crack it finds, and so will dark energies. Dark forces look for every avenue by which energies with a lower vibration energy level than yours can reach you so dark energies can ride in with them.

Some dark energy has managed to infiltrate your apartment and car, and small amounts are here and there within your body and aura. It is good that you have begun putting the large copper ring on your bed during the day. []

I did a clearing for myself and my home. Holy Spirit, are the dark energies cleared from me and my home?
[| Some have been cleared. It would be good to do clearing again. []
I did another clearing.

(Apr 19, '11) [| Good afternoon, Lorrie! I will say something about dark energies from a different perspective than you would expect. Rest assured that you are not generating this message yourself.

> dark adj. 1 a) entirely or partly without light b) neither giving nor receiving light... 5 hidden; secret 7 gloomy; hopeless; dismal 8 angry or sullen 9 evil; sinister 10 ignorant; unenlightened (Web p. 367)

Most of those definitions apply only somewhat to dark energies, even "entirely or partly without light." In the spiritual world, there is more than one kind of light: loving light and unloving light. Lucifer's light is very bright, but it is unloving, cold, and calculating. He thinks his way of thinking is right and does not doubt it one bit.

I said earlier that darkness is the absence of light. The fuller understanding is that *darkness is the absence of loving light.* []

If a person would truly love and accept all dark energies that are with them, even in cancerous areas, would or could those dark energies be transformed into loving energies?

[| Yes. It might take quite a bit of loving, though, because dark energies are like kids who feel stubborn and angry about being shamed. |]

Could loving and accepting all energies within oneself and loving every part of one's body prevent much of the damage caused by cancer and other diseases? [| Y |] Then it would be good to say often and mean it: "I love and accept myself as I am." [| Y |]

(Mar 28, '12)   Putting Evil in Perspective

I understood from books that I read that evil energies are very powerful, but Jesus gives a different picture in *Love Without End: Jesus Speaks*:

"Is evil the opposite of goodness?

"No more than illness is the opposite of health... Like illness, evil has been misconceived to have power of its own. Far too much attention and regard have been given to the concept of evil tempters, disrupters, and fallen angels under the misguided consideration that they have any power of their own... Good and evil were not established as equal and opposite forces... Evil is simply disconnection from God and denial of the love that you are! ...

"In the beginning... There was only good! ...[T]he source of all evil is the denial of love which results in the ill-fated chaos of life unsupervised by love... No one...can initiate evil without a long term progression toward it, for there is no evil at the core of any child of God.

"The greatest protection you have is to simply be the love that you are. ...God is greater than any rejection that can be made of Him, and He will not allow assaults of evil to disturb the oneness of spirit. ...Once you have made the decision to love, evil has no more hold over you." (Greene, pp. 145-147)

"Evil is only ignorance of Divine Law. None would resist God's will if they were aware that it consists of their own joy, bliss and eternal happiness.

"Although the negative energies may seem not to flow with God's natural Laws, they are indeed present in your physical world doing God's Work. Without them, you would not be offered a choice between darkness and Light and your growth process would be much hindered. So, you see, they are a necessary ingredient. These energies are not masters, they are servants of God's Will, although they would be the last to admit that." (Emmanuel's Book p. 85)

(Mar 30, '12)   Ministry Team Appointed For Me

Holy Spirit, are one or more negative spirits attached to or with me? [| Y |] Are portions of unloving Souls with me? [| Y |] Please set up a Spiritual Ministry Team to do healing and clearing for me and join me when I do clearing and healing for others. Thank You!

I learned from the Holy Spirit that the Ministry Team that has been set up for me consists of Lord Melchizedek, Mighty Astrea, Archangel Michael, Archangel Haniel, Jesus, and a few members of my family lines who were not named.

Evening: I asked the Ministry Team to do clearing for me.

(May 31, '12)   ENERGY-SEEKING CENTERS

When I prayed for clearing for three of my nieces yesterday, I asked the Holy Spirit about each of them: Is a dark energy center attached to her? The answer was "Yes" for all three.

I named several family members and asked about each of them: Is a dark energy center attached to them? The answer was "Yes" for all of them. [| Y |] Is a dark energy center attached to me? [| Y |] I was becoming alarmed.

Father God, do You have any comment?

[| Good morning, Lorrie! I realize it somewhat "threw you for a loop" when you learned that many dark energy centers are attached to people and Souls In your family lines. Many energy centers are attached to everybody.

Not all Soul portions in energy centers have dark energy. Some

26

centers have Soul portions with medium-to-high energy levels. Please begin calling them *energy-seeking centers.* You can say "energy centers" but have "seeking" in mind.

It occurred to you, and it is correct, that the small Soul portions sent out by Souls seeking healing are like spiritual runners with tiny sponges at the tips to soak up love and blessings! All is well. Peace! |]

Is it natural for a Soul to send small portions of its Soul to energy centers attached to other Souls to receive healing for those Soul portions and the rest of its Soul? [| Y |] Has that process been taking place throughout time? [| Y |] Is it being made known so people can help heal the Souls in energy centers that are attached to their Souls and bring healing to those Souls and themselves? [| Y |]

Thank You very much, Father God! I feel better.

(Jul 29, '12) I learned more about energy centers from the Holy Spirit: A portion of a Soul that needs love attaches itself to another person's Soul to receive healing from them. The energy of that attached Soul portion attracts other Soul portions that need the same type of healing, so there are many Soul portions in energy centers.

How does an energy center become a dark energy center? The low-vibration energy level of some of the Souls in the energy center attracts dark forces that put a casing around the Souls (auras), turning the energy center into a dark energy center, a contact point for dark energies.

(Sept 6, '12) [| Lorrie, you are wondering if "a contact point" for witchcraft and other dark energies is another term for a dark energy center. A dark energy center is one type of contact point for dark energies. Those contact points can be put in place by someone making a firm intention for that to happen or by someone using witchcraft energies to create and place them in a chosen location.

Dark forces try to lessen the strength of those Souls who are sending out a great deal of love and light and are drawing in many unloving Souls and energies that receive the love and light and choose to become loving. They label such Souls as "dangerous" and put them on their prime target list. But do not worry! The means for protecting oneself are available for all, and, to remind you, the greatest protection is love. []

Thank You, Father God!

(Oct 20, '12)   Two Main Types

I learned from the Holy Spirit that there are two main types of energy centers: *Dark energy centers* and *right-order energy centers*. Both types have Soul portions within them, but for different purposes.

Dark energy centers use the energy of the compressed Soul portions to continue attacking loving Souls and portions of Lost Will of Mother God that are in the centers.

Soul portions in *right-order energy centers* seek love and healing from the Souls they are attached to. They have no intention to harm, although the host person may experience discomfort caused by negative energies attached to some of those Soul portions and from picking up some of the pain that Souls in the energy center are feeling.

The goal regarding dark energy centers is to clear dark energies from and free the compressed Soul portions held prisoner by dark energies and transform the centers into loving energy centers.

The goal regarding right-order energy centers is to extend love to the Soul portions that make up that energy center, help clear negative energies from them, and extend love and blessings to them so they can return to their Home Soul when they are ready.

Right-order energy centers can get taken over by dark energies from the person they are attached to or from Souls from previous lifetimes of the Soul portions that are in the energy center. Once dark energies enter an energy center, they attract other dark energies and portions of unloving Souls.

Holy Spirit, do all dark energy centers have witchcraft energies as the primary operating force?

[| No. Some operate on the energies of anger, lust, etc. []

Do dark energy centers draw on the energy of the people and Souls targeted by witchcraft and other dark energies? [| Y |]

Is the energy of the Lost Will of Mother God mixed in with witchcraft energies? [| Y |]

End of 1-E: DARK ENERGIES, ENERGY CENTERS

1-F: NEGATIVE THOUGHTFORMS, DEMONS

Mar20, '23   THEIR ORIGIN

A synthesis of definitions offered by several schools of thought: A thoughtform is an energetic construct, a floating vibration of energy, created every time words are spoken, or thoughts are thought. They attach to or hang over people who have similar energies.

Father God, is negative energy created by people's thoughts? [| Y |] Is all negative energy composed of fear? [| Y |] Are all negative thoughtforms composed of fear? [| Y |]

"Are there conscious dark or evil forces at work in opposition to God?

"No. No. No. There is only ignorance, which breeds fear. Fear creates what seems to be darkness. When you consider that all things are God, how could there be evil?" (Emmanuel's Book II p. 205)

Father, instead of commanding negative energies to leave, should we dissolve the energy of fear they are composed of and ask for that energy to be transmuted to beneficial energy? [| Y |] *Did You create the original thoughtform of fear?* [| Y |]

(FATHER GOD) "There were no words at first, only a feeling that I had existence. I had desire to know more. Already, although I did not know it, I had Lost Will that did not believe I could know more. I had given birth to fear and did not know it because I had no understanding." (Original p. 1)

Father God, is "demon" another name for a negative thought form? [| Y |]

"A demon is an energized thoughtform creation, not a discarnate entity. Some people are highly developed in thoughtform creation and can empower these forms with subtle energy so they materialize... Since demons are creations of human thought, they have no soul or eternal spark...it is possible to have them dissolved...and their energy transmuted [transformed to another form]." (Starr pp. 87, 98)

End of 1-F: NEGATIVE THOUGHTFORMS, DEMONS

1-G: SIAMESE TWIN AND INTERGRAFTED SOULS

(Oct 15, '11)   SIAMESE TWIN SOULS: TWO TYPES

Twin Soul came to mind twice recently. I sensed it referred to me in some way. Then, last evening, I watched a TV movie, "A Gifted Man," about a doctor stressed out by a loud voice he heard in his head. A friend told him about a shaman who could help him. The shaman ascertained that the Soul of the man's vanished twin was with him. He cleared the Soul of the doctor's twin, and the doctor was OK.

Father God, would You like to comment on that?

[| You are wondering about the words "twin Soul" that came to mind, followed by your happening to see a TV movie about that topic a short time later. With identical twins, it sometimes happens that the original embryo, the baby's body, divides completely, but the Soul does not. I will call those connected Souls **Siamese identical twin Souls**.

Also, the Souls of non-identical twins sometimes mesh together before birth, resulting in what I will call **Siamese fraternal twin Souls**. What can happen In both cases when one of the babies does not survive is that the Soul of the deceased baby remains with the surviving twin.

What you are surmising is correct: A Siamese identical twin Soul being within a person would likely cause more problems and inner

30

turmoil than the Soul of a fraternal Siamese twin would. That's all for today. Bless you! []

Thank You, Father! Thank you, Fern, for helping me.

(Oct 19, '11) Father God, is my Soul a Siamese identical twin Soul? Did I have an identical twin who died early in the pregnancy whose body was resorbed by my mother's body, but that twin's Soul is still with me? [| Y |]

That evening, I cleared the enmeshment between my Soul and the Soul of my identical twin and asked angels to guide her to where she was meant to be. Thank you, angels!

(Oct 30, '11)   INTERGRAFTED SOULS

Years ago, while a friend was praying with me, I "saw" a partly divided cell and understood that it represented my mother and me, that our Souls weren't fully separated as I came into this life. I received the understanding that a mother's Soul sometimes enmeshes with her child's Soul in a manner that connects the mother with the child. I am calling Souls in that situation **intergrafted Souls.**

Holy Spirit, do You have a comment?

[| Intergrafting of a mother's Soul with her baby's Soul does take place. What happens is that a baby's Soul often enters its body gradually. If its mother is very protective of her person out of fear, that protectiveness extends to and into the baby and somewhat "glues" the portion of the baby's Soul that is present at that point to the mother's Soul.

People whose Souls are intergrafted feel the pain of the other person and will likely develop the same health problems the other person has. The child may feel like something is missing or not quite right within themselves.

A person whose Soul is intergrafted with their mother's will be in harm's way if their mother (even after crossing over) enters the world of dark energies. In such a case, the person should ask for strong protection and clear the Soul connection between their Soul and their mother's Soul or have somebody do it for them.]]

Was my mother's Soul intergrafted with my Soul when I was born? [| Y |] Are they separate now? [| Y |] Wonderful!

End of 1-G: SIAMESE TWIN AND INTERGRAFTED SOULS

CHAPTER 2

ONE SURPRISE AFTER THE OTHER

Healing for Prior Lifetimes: Lee and Me 3

2-A: RON, LEE, AND ME

Note: Ron and Lee are my former husband and brother-in-law.

(Aug 2, '07)   ISSUES IN JAHNER FAMILY

I asked the Holy Spirit questions about my children, and Fern received the answers. Is Patty's Soul asking for prayer?
[| Yes, regarding Ron's anger when she was younger. His anger was about outside issues, but she was still afraid. |]

Is Lori's Soul asking for prayer? [| Yes, also in connection with Ron. |] Was she terrified of his anger as a child? [| Yes, and she still hasn't gotten over your divorce. |] (Ron and I divorced in 1986.)

Is Nita's Soul asking for prayer? [| Yes. You are picking up on her repressed anger. |]

Is Pat's Soul asking for prayer, too? [| Yes. He also has issues with his dad connected with Ron's anger. |]

Were issues that Pat has related to his Dad's anger allowed to take place to bring healing between Pat and Father God?
[| Yes. One more thing: Some of your children are also afraid of their Dad directing his anger at their children. |]

(Aug 14, '07) (!!!) Is Bill Jahner Ron's birth father? [| N |] Is his birth father one of Bill's brothers? [| N |] One of his mother's brothers? [| Y |] Is Bill Jahner Lee's birth father? [| Y |]

Fern and I learned that two other maternal uncles fathered

some of Ron's and Lee's siblings, so incest was rampant on Ron's side of the family. What a mess!

Did Ron's mother ever sexually abuse him? [| N |] Did his dad? [| Y |] Poor guy! That's so sad!

Is distress that Ron's dad's Soul is experiencing one cause of Ron's health problems? [| Y |] Is Ron affected by distress from other deceased relatives? [| No, from living relatives. |]

Is Ron being affected by a spirit of lust? [| Y |]

Is Lee being affected by a spirit of lust? [| Y |] Did he pick it up from me? [| N |] Can I do a clearing for him for it? [| Y |] A few days later, I cleared the spirit of lust from Lee.

Did Ron's mother go to the light? [| Y |] Did his dad? [| N |] I will invite him to go to the light this Sunday at church.

I needed to get things off my chest, so two weeks later, I met with my pastor, Pastor Eric, and I told him about having become pregnant by Lee four times (with no memories about those encounters) and about the Jahner family being affected by the spirit of lust. Sharing those things was difficult.

(Aug 18, '07)   Ministering to Ron

Father God, please place protection around Ron. If his Soul is willing, I ask for clearing to take place as I pray for him.

In the name of Jesus, I command the spirit of anger, the spirit of lust, and all other negative energies that are with Ron to leave! (I coughed to assist those energies in leaving.)

I direct that all outside Souls with Ron that are not meant to be with him must leave now! (Coughed)

Father God, please seal Ron's aura. Thank You!

Holy Spirit, did much of Ron's anger get cleared? [| Y |] Other negative energies, also? [| Y |] Did many outside Souls leave that were not meant to be with him? [| Y |] Thank You!

(Aug 28, '07)   PRIOR LIFE: LEE, ME, BABY BRYCE

Does karma need to be cleared between Lee and me?

[| Yes. You were married in another lifetime and expecting a child, which Lee was very happy about. You had a miscarriage you could not have prevented, but Lee still blamed you. Those hard feelings have not been cleared. |]

Was it a boy? [| Y |] I will name him **Bryce**. Has Bryce gone to the light? [| Not yet. Put his name in the copper ring, and you and Lee should celebrate his life. |]

I did that a week later, with Lee present only in spirit. I also cleared karma by doing a process of forgiveness between Lee's and my Souls in that earlier lifetime. I explained to Lee that I couldn't have prevented the miscarriage and felt bad about losing our baby. I closed with a blessing for him.

(Sept 21, '07) With quiet music playing, I asked the 24 archangels, Jesus, and my guardian angels to be present. I asked Lee to be present in spirit. I held Bryce's picture (a picture of a young boy) as I stood with Lee in spirit In the copper ring and spoke love and blessing to Bryce. Then, I created a positive vortex at the side of the room for Bryce's Soul to go to the light. I left it open for half an hour.

The next day: Has Bryce gone to the light? [| Yes. But he will still be at your place with the other Young Souls. He will just be in a happier place within himself! |] Thank You, Father God!

(Feb 18, '08)   Lee and Me: Pondering

With me, it couldn't have been a separate personality made up entirely of the spirit of lust that had sex with Lee. Maybe Grandma Leigh's or Mom's Soul mostly took over my body at those times, but when the details of my encounter with Lee when I got pregnant with Nita surfaced, it felt like it was happening to me.

Should I process that incident some more? Well, I was raped, so hell, yes, I should! Just because I was raped several times earlier, at ages 3, 5, and 16, doesn't mean it is old hat.

I don't consciously remember doing it, but I know I willingly opened myself to Lee. I considered him worthy of my intimate trust. Can any man be completely trusted?

Father-Mother God, I place all my experiences, emotions, and hopes in Your care. I do desire to love and be loved. I need a lot of healing to become less uptight within myself and when I am with others. Please fill and encircle me and those around me with Your peace and love. Thank You, and good night!

[| Good night, dear one! We are glad you are feeling better. |]

(Jul 3, '08)   A Curious Situation

Two months ago, the stopper in my bathroom sink suddenly stuck in the closed position. The maintenance man freed up the sink stopper, but it stuck in the open position after he left. Instead of bothering him again, I set a container in the sink and emptied the water into the bathtub. Out of habit, I pulled up on the stopper this morning, and it worked!

Was the stopper being stuck a signal from a Soul?

[| Yes. Lee's Soul caused it. He wants to tell you something. |]

Does he want to say he is sorry about having raped me when Nita came along? [| He didn't think of it as rape. |]

I don't suppose he would have. Getting that much insight helped settle things for me regarding that incident.

(!!!) **Did Lee live a previous life as Grandpa Leigh's brother Mike, who lived with Grandpa and Grandma for many years?** [| Y |] **Were Uncle Mike and Grandma Leigh lovers?** [| Y |]

Is a part of Uncle Mike's Soul incorporated within cells in Lee's body? [| Y |] A portion of Grandma Leigh's Soul was incorporated within cells in my body for many years.

(!!!) Did Uncle Mike and Grandma Leigh continue their relationship in some way through Lee and me? [| Y |] Wow! That helps explain why Lee doesn't remember when he and I were together and why I don't remember.

End of 2-A: RON, LEE, AND ME

2-B: NICHOLAS AND ROZ^{MP}

Note: ^{MP} (Me Prior life) is omitted after Roz in this section.

(Nov 8, '07)   AN ABANDONED BOYFRIEND

My head is feeling very miserable today. Are some relatives asking for help? [| Y |] One of my children? [| Y |] Kate? [| Y |] For their son Scott? [| N |] For their son, Nick? [| Y |]

Should I pray for Nick? [| No. Pray for Kate and David. |] I began praying daily for Kate, David, and their son Nick.

Do I have inflammation in my brain? [| Yes. Kate's and David's concern for Nick brought it on. |]

(!!!) Is the situation with Kate, David, and Nick a re-creation of a situation in another lifetime in which they were in the same family? [| N |] Was there a similar situation in an earlier lifetime of Nick's? [| Y |] I will call him **Nicholas** in that lifetime. Was Kate Nicholas' mother? [| Y |] Was David his father? [| N |] Did they solve Nicholas' behavior problem? [| N |]

Was I Nicholas' grandmother? [| N |] Aunt? [| No. You were his girlfriend. |] I will call myself **Roz**.

Do I need to clear karma related to that lifetime? [| Yes. You were very angry with Nicholas and haven't forgiven him. |]

For the next 9-10 days, I breathed deeply several times daily to help lessen the discomfort in my head. I put the names Kate, David, and Nick in the large copper ring and prayed the Blessing Prayer several times daily for them.

To help bring about a clearing between Nicholas and Roz in that earlier lifetime, I said aloud to Nicholas' Soul several times, "Nicholas, I am sorry for everything that I said or did that hurt you. Please forgive me." I asked God to bless him in that lifetime and prayed that his Soul could come to peace.

(Nov 11, '07)   Nicholas' Emotions Surface

(On the phone with Fern) Is the discomfort at the top of my head related to my grandson Nick's previous lifetime as Nicholas? She didn't reply for several minutes.

Fern said her head began throbbing as I asked that question, and she heard Nicholas screaming, "Why didn't you wait for me? I loved you! I still love you!" She said she felt like screaming but didn't because she lives in an apartment. She sensed Nicholas fell to his knees, curled into a ball, and cried. He was shivering and felt like he was in a bottomless pit.

> I was the girl Nicholas loved who wasn't there for him when he came home after the war. That's pretty heavy!

Did that take place during World War II? [| Y |] Was Nicholas imprisoned in Germany? [| Y |] Tortured? [| No, but there was a heavy psychological effect on him from being away from home and imprisoned for a long time. He wasn't American. |]

Was he French? [| Yes, in the Navy. At that time, you couldn't get in touch with prisoners. By the time he was freed, Roz had married and moved to the United States. |]

Did Nicholas eventually find someone else to love? [| Y |] Did they have children? [| Y |]

Did Nicholas ever get over Roz? [| No. He needs alone time with you. You didn't wait for him. |]

The top of my head throbbed most of the next day, possibly from the emotions in Nicholas' Soul, so I spoke to his Soul as Roz in the evening. It felt impassable, so I closed the conversation. Suddenly, I felt uneasy and asked for angels to protect me. By speaking to Nicholas, I had invited his Soul into my apartment! I didn't know what energies might be within or with his Soul. I asked Archangel Michael to escort him out.

I told Fern about the situation and asked: Did Nicholas leave my apartment when I told him to?

[| Yes. But I suggest that if you speak to Nicholas again, you do it at a park or church, but not in Mercy Church, so his Soul won't start showing up there uninvited. |]

I blessed Nicholas every day for a long while. I trust that his Soul came to a place of peace.

End of 2-B: NICHOLAS AND ROZ^{MP}

2-C: DARIN^{LP} AND DARLA^{MP}, NATE^P

Note: ^{LP} (Lee Prior life) is omitted after Darin and Darin[2], ^{MP} (Me Prior life) after Darla, and ^P (Part of me) after Nate in this section.

(Aug 26, '07)   I LEARN ABOUT NATE

(At Fern's) For many years, I have felt like dragging my feet about visiting people other than Fern, even my children. That feeling becomes more pronounced when I am away from home for a few days. Is a part of me afraid when I am away from home? [| Yes, a child part. |] A girl? [| N |]

By naming letters of the alphabet, Fern and I learned that the name of that boy part of me starts with "I." Finally, is his name *Ignatius*? [| Y |] That's a big name! I will call him **Nate**.

Did the Nate part of me split off during the trauma of sexual abuse at age 3? [| N |] During the trauma at age 5? [| No, he was an observer. A portion of his Soul is in the house you lived in at age 3, and a portion is in the house you lived in at age 5. |]

Does Nate's fear cause my blood pressure to rise? [| Y |] Is he at my apartment now? [| Yes. He is staying with you because you opened your heart to him. |] Would playing music help him feel better? [| Yes, especially symphonies. |]

(Sept 3, '07, at Fern's) Three distinct sounds are coming from the dashboard of my car. Is the medium sound from Lee's energy in this lifetime? [| Yes. His thinking about you causes it. |] Is the somewhat louder sound also from Lee?

[| Yes, but it is caused by his energy from a previous lifetime in which you and Lee were a young married couple, Darla and Darin. Nate was your only child. All three of you died in an automobile accident while on your way to pick up a puppy. |]

Was it the trauma of that accident that scared Nate so much? [| Yes. The lighter sound in your car is from him. |]

Fern asked questions silently and told me: [| Nate is 6, has green eyes, and curly, blonde hair. |]

(Back home) I told Nate about the other "children" and that he could sleep with Robert[P] 7 and Peter[P] 5.

(Sept 6, '07, at Fern's) [| Nate said he wants a puppy. |]

ME: "Father God, I ask that the spirit of the puppy that Darin and Darla were going to buy for Nate can be with him now in the astral plane. I have a name: Waggums!" Fern laughed.

Did Nate come with me tonight for us to learn about him? [| Yes. His parents are here, too. Darla is on your right, Darin is on your left, and Nate is trying to climb on your lap! |]

Would they like to come to church with me sometime? [| Yes, but you would have to invite them. |]

ME: Darin, Darla, and Nate, I invite you to attend church with me this Sunday. Nate, would you like to go to the front with the other kids when Pastor Eric teaches them? [| Yes! |]

FERN: (To Nate) I wonder what Pastor Eric would say if you told him you were there!

ME: OK, Nate, you'll have to behave yourself!

FERN: Nate might be a mischief-maker!

(Sept 9, '07)   Getting Closer

I sat down for a quiet time.

DARLA: What is Nate doing right now?

DARIN: He's out back playing with some stones. He's quite the kid! We are some lucky ducks to have him as our child! I wouldn't trade him for all the gold in the world. A chip off the old block, that's what he is! You couldn't find a nicer kid.

(He moves close to Darla.) And a guy couldn't find a nicer girl to be with, either! Boy, I'm one lucky guy!

O God in Heaven! Blessings to You for watching out for us so good! We ain't got nothing to worry about. My job's going good, we are healthy, and that spat with your Dad is cleared.

Darla is quiet but thinks deeply. What a wonderful future she foresees! All of us are in good health. Nate is starting school and doing exceptionally well.

DARLA: Nate, you said yesterday you would like to get a puppy. I think you are big enough now that we can get one, and we have a big yard with a fence. Of course, you'll have to ask your Daddy first. (She smiles at Nate and tousles his hair.)

NATE: (Smiles and jumps up and down.) Oh good! It will be great to have a puppy! All my own! But you and Daddy can help take care of him, OK?

DARLA: Yes, son, we'll help care for the puppy.

CAME TO MIND: Seniority. Mediocrity. Remonstrate. Vacillate. Participate. END.

[| Getting closer. Don't observe. Just receive. Just be a pen. |]

CAME TO MIND: A trip into the wild blue yonder. END.

[| The memories and emotions you are trying to reach are not "up yonder and far away." Some of the physical hurt that came with those memories and emotions is within you, as real as those you retrieved from your present lifetime.

Darla and Nate are parts of your Full Soul, so there is a direct spiritual connection between your Soul and their Souls. Darin's Soul and Darla's Soul are open to each other, so you also have a spiritual connection with Darin's Soul. Write how you feel, and then write what comes to mind. |]

Nothing more important came to mind.

(Sept 11, '07)   THE ACCIDENT

(Recorded, typed later.) Holy Spirit, please guide me as I see if I can get in touch with Darin's, Darla's, and Nate's emotions.

CAME TO MIND: Time to go. Turn left. Turn right. Turn the right way. END.

[| How do you feel, Lorrie? |]

I feel angry and stubborn, maybe because I have a headache. I feel that way every so often and don't know why. Could it be related to how Darin and Darla feel about their lives having been cut short? And that their son Nate died so young?

Darin and Darla in the astral plane after they died:

DARIN: God, that's not fair! What are You thinking? We had such big plans, and everything was going so good!

DARLA: He was our precious child, born perfect, and look at what happened. It's so sad!!! (Pause) Lorrie, you are wondering if Souls shed tears in the astral plane. Yes, spiritual tears, tears of the heart. If only I could have tears of joy again.

DARIN: Darla, I know exactly how you feel, but neither of us said it until now. Thank you, Lorrie, for helping us do this! You see, our emotions are within you. It is part of what pulls you this way and that. The more important that a part of you is that you connect with, the more you get pulled in.

People who have crossed over who were important to you are the ones who will be the most likely to affect your physical health because you would like to help them. They are trying to let you know they want help. So there go the aches and pains, the headaches, arthritis, or whatever. That's how things work.

ME: Thank you, Darin. Father God said your memories and emotions are within me because they are a part of the cellular memories passed on to me. I will say whatever comes to mind now. (I took some deep breaths.)

[| Lorrie, what do you say from your deep self that is still hurting and feels cut off? You experienced the accident on a Soul level along with Darin, Darla, and Nate. Your mind could describe what happened, but getting in touch with the emotions, the scare, that sudden traumatic jolt when the car hit the light post is more important. Think, how would that feel? []

DARIN: You're trying like crazy to get a good hold, to turn the right way, but no. Smash!!! And you're blacked out. Often, when somebody gets blacked out, they have no thoughts in their mind, but if in that instant the Soul leaves the body – gets blasted out – so to speak, there are instant thoughts: No! God, what's happening? Darla! I can't see you!

Nate! Nate!! NATE!!! (Each time he cries, "Nate!" his voice rises higher.) Where are you? Oh no! Is that me down there? Are my leg and head bleeding? I'm all slumped over in the car. Nate must be in the back seat. But the car is all twisted up! There would be no room for him there! He had just been playing and talking so nice.

Oh God! No! No! NO! NO! (His voice is getting so squeaky from being uptight that he can barely talk.) Darla! Darla! (Crying) Darla-a-a! Na-a-ate! No! (He goes into a wail.) No! No!

Darla is in the front seat, but she's slumped down. Her head is against the door, her feet are sideways, and her leg is turned backward! (Squeaky voice) God in Heaven, help her!

(Darin stops crying and has a determined sound to his voice) God, I thought that You are a good God. I know that You are. Please help Darla! Help her stay alive for Nate! I think that's what happened: I just died instantly because my body is all beat up. (He pauses between sounds.) No! No!

NATE: (In his mind) What was that? What was that? I can't see! (Crying.) My head hurts so bad. What? I can't move my arm! I can hardly even lift my head. Oh, no! (Crying) Daddy! Mamma! Where are you? I can't talk very loud, but can you hear me?

Jesus! God! (His voice quivers.) I'm so-o scared! (He cries, sounding like fear has almost taken his voice away. His voice rises higher but is still muffled.) I-I-I'm so sca-ared! (His breathing becomes shallow.) Oh! My head hurts!

There, my left eye opened. But everything is black. Is it night? No! We were going to get a puppy! It was right after supper! It's supposed to be light out! Oh no! Maybe we can't get a puppy now! Oh no-o-o! (He takes a quick breath in.)

(Crying) Mamma! Daddy! Mamma! Mamma! (He stands up in the back seat. He can't see, but he reaches around to feel. He feels something wet when he touches his dad's head.) What's that? (It doesn't smell like anything he recognizes.)

Is this what it's like to be blind? (Pause) Daddy! Daddy! (He pushes on Darin's head, but his Daddy doesn't move. He can't figure that out. He hasn't experienced death or even heard it described. Crying) Mamma! Mamma! (His cry turns into a wail. He reaches to the side and finds Darla's shoulder. He crawls between the front seats and manages to get onto her lap, crying very hard.) Mamma! Mamma! (He pushes her arm, but she doesn't respond. He cries uncontrollably.)

(He feels something running down the side of his head.) What's that? Oh no! We need a doctor, but I can hardly talk. I can't tell anybody we need a doctor! (Continues crying.)

If I press the horn, maybe somebody should hear it! (He pushes on it. It toots, but he can't push very hard because he's in such an awkward position. He soon gets too weak and quits pushing.)

(Nate starts crying again. On and on, the tears flow, but he is getting weaker. His head feels funny.) What's happening? (His voice rises higher.) What's ha-a-ppening? Mamma and Daddy aren't moving, and there is nobody else here! It's just me! (He cries with quick breaths, rising fear.)

(As he leans against his mom, his hand happens to take hold of the heart necklace she is wearing, and he remembers that his picture is in it. He knows his Mamma loves him! She carries his picture near her heart all the time.) Mamma and Daddy come in at bedtime, hug and kiss me, and pray with me. I wish they could pray with me now.

(His voice shaking) I'm so scared, and I'm sh-h-a-king. (He takes several breaths to try to calm down.) I can't breathe good. I don't feel good. Uh, uh, uh. (His sounds slow down, and then there are no more. His hands fall limp.)

(I typed this far and had to stop and cry very hard.)

(Nate's legs are across his dad's knees, and he is lying against his mother's dead body as he enters the next life. He had no idea what it means to die – which of us do? ...but a six-year-old! He is still shaking when he finally can see with his spiritual eyes. He is ice cold and feels numb.)

(Whispering, halfway crying) Daddy! Here I am! (Almost in a whisper, his voice shaking) Here I am. Can you hear me?

Something makes Darin turn in that direction, and he sees Nate! Nate isn't hurting or bloody, but Darin can tell he is very scared. He is as white as a sheet and shaking.

DARIN: Come, Nate! Let me hold you! (He holds Nate until his sobs quiet down, then he looks down at the car again and sees Nate lying between his body and Darla's.) I have to find Darla! Where is she?

Just then, Darla's Soul leaves her body. Darin sees her as she rises and is suddenly near where he is. She looks great, but he can tell she is an emotional wreck. When a person's body is badly hurt, it also affects their astral body.

DARIN: (Softly) Darla! Darla! Darling, come! I found Nate! Here we are. Look this way!

(Darla doesn't notice or hear Darin immediately because this is all new. She doesn't know where she is. Darin had already gotten a little accustomed to it. He read about the astral plane one time and figured out that's where he is now, that he is dead. But Darla doesn't know yet that she is dead.)

DARIN: (Calls softly) Darla! (He walks over and embraces her. She cries in his arms, shaking. Darin holds Nate with one arm and Darla with the other. They stay that way long, trying to figure out what happened.)

DARIN: I guess we'll never figure it out, but God decided our time was up. I'm angry about that! I'm angry!!! We were such good people, worked hard, never stole or lied, and loved each other. We had the start of this beautiful family! And, oh no! Now Nate won't get a puppy! Nate, we'll have to do something to make it up to you!

Nate is so glad he can see again! He tells his dad that he pushed the car horn to get somebody's attention. As they look down, a car stops, and some people get out. They can't believe what they see. They check Darin's, Darla's, and Nate's pulses, then leave. They call the police and ambulance, and the earthly situation gets taken care of, but Darin's, Darla's, and Nate's Souls are just beginning a new experience in the continuing life of their Souls.

(Evening) Thank You, Holy Spirit, for helping me get somewhat in touch with Darin's, Darla's, and Nate's emotions. Jesus, please give Darin, Darla, and Nate a big hug! Thank you!

I called Fern and told her about having gotten in touch with Darin's, Darla's, and Nate's emotions at the time of the accident and shortly afterward. I asked: Does Darin need to release more emotionally? [| N |] Does Darla? [| N |] Nate? [| N |] Good!

Based on those answers, I thought I was finished dealing with the emotional effects of Darin's, Darla's, and Nate's painful cellular memories that I have been carrying in my body, but that was not the case.

(Nov 10, '07)   GRIEF CRASHES IN

As I washed my face in the morning, my right ear was getting hot. Nate has been causing that sometimes to be playful, but this time, I felt like cupping my hand over my ear. As I did so, it occurred to me that Nate's ear might have gotten injured in the accident. With my right hand still over my ear, I put my left hand on my forehead and asked God to bring healing and comfort to Nate in the car after the accident.

I broke down and cried extremely hard as I connected with Darla's anguish as Nate lay against her while dying, and she couldn't hold him. Using a pillow to represent Nate, I tried to comfort him as he lay dying. I felt such utter anguish that I could only describe it as deep devastation.

I haven't lost a living child in this lifetime, but now I know, at

46

least somewhat, what parents experience when they lose a child. It felt like I wouldn't ever be able to stop crying and agonizing, but I knew I shouldn't let myself cry for hours.

I was finally able to quiet down after about 30 minutes. I asked Father God to hold Darla/me, and Nate.

[| Lorrie, as a human being, experiencing loss seems to present a bottomless void that one cannot cross. You feel like you almost can't endure the loss, with it feeling like it could annihilate you at any moment. Know that the seemingly bottomless void that opens before you in your sorrow does have a bottom, for you always rest securely in and on Me.

You are now living a life and have lived many lives before this with the same purpose: to expand your horizon, deepen your compassion, and broaden your understanding and Mine. Your Soul wants you to learn how to get in touch and stay in touch with your Higher Self (Full Soul) even while experiencing the pathos and pain of body and Soul.

With each experience you allow yourself to feel to the depths or the heights, your being expands and deepens. I am a feeling God; consequently, you are a feeling being. Count yourself lucky if you can experience gut-wrenching sorrow and supreme bliss!

Thank you for opening yourself up to feel the depths of pathos that a parent goes through upon the death of a child. Thank you for allowing Me to hold you as anguish poured out of your Soul. Since you are one with all, your grief is tied in with the grief of everyone who has experienced the loss of a child. You brought every bereaved parent with you when you allowed Me to hold you and your dying child.

You bridged the time gap between this lifetime of yours and your previous lifetime as Darla. You were unconscious after the accident, but your Soul was aware that Nate had been badly hurt, and you felt very afraid and alone. You held him in your arms just now and grieved over his death, which Darla couldn't do at the time of the accident but was able to do now. |]

(I am crying very hard, my stomach wrenched with sorrow.)

47

[| Darla was grieving for Nate in her mind and Soul as she lay dying. She grieved that she wasn't able to hold and comfort him. You have just now made that possible for her. Through you, Darla could hold him and express her anguish. By letting those emotions come out through you, you brought further healing to Darla, Nate, and yourself in this lifetime. Bless you, Lorrie! Remember, I am only a thought away. |]

God, what a wonderful Father-Mother You are! Thank You!

(Dec 30, '07)   DARIN^2: OVERHANGING SHADOW

Note: ^{P} (Part of me) is omitted after Sarah and ^{MP} (Me Prior life) after Clara in this section.

[| You have been thinking about becoming pregnant with Nita by Lee, that the situation was akin to being raped, but you hesitated to call it that. Honor your feelings and intuition. |]

(!!!) Darin may have done the same thing to Darla (raped her)! A few days ago, I learned that parts of me named **Clara**^{MP} and **Sarah**^{P} split off while Lee was sexually abusing me. I hope both of you are feeling better now.

Can I get in touch with you, Clara?

CLARA: You can get in touch with me easily, Lorrie, because, in a way, I am you, and you are me. I am a part of you that isn't a "real" part, but your body feels like mine.

I am a portion of Darla's Soul that split off out of fear and tremendous hurt when Darin sexually abused her. By splitting off, I allowed her to go forward in life. She did fairly well emotionally because she did not remember what happened, but it damaged her confidence and self-esteem.

A low-energy portion of Darin's Soul, **Darin**^{2}, attacked Darla. Darin felt confused about what he had done and desperately wished he hadn't done it and that he could be united with Darla in love again. The Darin^2 portion of Darin's Soul split off after the attack

48

and was in the astral plane until it could "come back home" by immersing itself in Lee's Soul.

Darla and I would be grateful if you would separate your Soul from Darin's Soul and from Lee's Soul since Lee is another lifetime of Darin's. The way things are, I can't reconnect with Darla because of the shade of Darin^2's Soul that is oppressing me. Also, Darin's Soul has clung tenaciously to me since he died, like a stranded child looking for its mother. This situation needs to get cleared up for your sake and the sake of Darin, Darla, me, and Lee.

A portion of Darin^2 is with you, Lorrie, and you have a soul tie with Lee. Please clear Soul enmeshment between your Soul and mine and between your Soul and Darin's, Darin^2's, Darla's, and Lee's Souls as soon as possible. I sense that you will feel great release afterward.

Lee told you that he has often wondered why he has "hurt so many women" (possibly meaning that he would love and leave them). I am guessing that when he veered over into being out of the bounds of propriety sexual-wise with you, a big part of what caused him to act that way was the low-vibration energy level of Darin^2's Soul that was riding on his shoulders.

Since Lee is the birth father of your children, Lori, Nita, Teri (miscarried), and Elaine (stillborn), It would be good for you to continue blessing him and his family line, but please do not worry about him because worry creates a type of soul tie.

It feels good to get this out! Bless you, Lorrie! Thank you!!

ME: You're welcome, Clara! I will do the separating of Souls that you asked me to do. Thank you for explaining things.

(Dec 31, '07) I cleared the incorporation of Clara's, Darin's, Darin^2's, Darla's, and Lee's Souls from cells in my body and cleared enmeshment between my Soul and each of those Souls. Afterward, I opened a positive vortex for Clara's Soul to go to the light. I sensed that she did. Thank You, God!

The next day: Did Clara's Soul go to the light? [| Y |] Great!

(Jan 5, '08) (!!!) Was Darin^2 a portion of Darin's Soul from another lifetime in which he had chosen negative energies?

[| Yes. Darin didn't know what to do with those energies. |]

Is Lee's Soul separated from the portion of Darin[2]'s Soul that joined with him earlier in this lifetime? [| N |]

Lee might not remember attacking me. Am I meant to confront him about it in person?

[| No. If you feel you need to confront Lee, do it in spirit. |]

Holy Spirit, was it a portion of Darin[2]'s Soul that is with Lee that took advantage of me? [| Y |] Are you asking me to minister to the part of Darin[2]'s Soul that recently separated from Clara and to the part still connected to Lee?

[| Ask for soul ties between Lee's Soul and those two parts of Darin[2]'s Soul to be severed. |]

Holy Spirit, please cut soul ties between Lee's Soul and those two portions of Darin[2]'s Soul. Thank You!

Father God said a while back that my Soul was split when I came into this lifetime. What does that refer to?

[| Your Soul was split because of not being healed from your lifetime as Darla. |]

Clara split off from Darla. Are Darla and Clara united now?

[| Yes, and their healing brought healing to you, also. |]

Did that prayer for healing change things in Darla's past life?

[| No, but it changes things for the future for Darla and you. |]

End of 2-C: DARIN[LP] AND DARLA[MP], NATE

2-D: YOUNG SOULS WITH ME

Note: [YS] (Young Soul) is omitted after names of the Young Souls in this section: My miscarried and deceased children from this lifetime (Perry, Patrick, Teri, Diane), and my children from prior lifetimes (Nate, Paulie, Jacinta, Bryce, Fannie Mae).

(Sept 10, '07)   MORE ABOUT NATE

ME: Hi, Nate! I am Lorrie. I learned from the Holy Spirit that you and your Mom and Dad died in a bad accident on the way to get a puppy. That's sad. I asked the Holy Spirit to send you a spirit puppy. Do you have one to play with now?

NATE: Geeows, yes! I have a puppy, and it's the nicest puppy ever! I am teaching him tricks, and my Daddy is helping me. Isn't that great!?

ME: Geeows, yes, that's great, Nate! Wonderful!

NATE: I like the name "Waggums" for my puppy. I heard you say that. And that's a cute stuffed cat that Fern has! I'll let you in on a secret. I saw you sew it for her! That was fun! Can I play with Waggums now?

ME: Yes, Nate. We'll talk again, maybe soon!

(Sept 18, '07) I was by my computer at work with my boss standing beside me. With nobody touching the mouse, the cursor began slowly across the screen from left to right.

I said, "Look!" My boss said, "You have a ghost in your machine! Maybe the mouse got bumped." (It didn't). The cursor moved a little more. It stopped when I touched the mouse.

(At Fern's) Did Nate make the cursor move at work? [| Y |] Does he cause my right ear to get hot sometimes? [| Y |] Has he been doing that for several years? [| Y |]

Does Nate's anxiety cause my blood pressure to rise when I am not at home? [| Yes. He wants to be with you wherever you go but feels anxious when you are away from home. |]

Has Nate met my stillborn daughter **Elaine?** [| Y |] (!!!) Is she staying at my place? [| Y |] Is **Bryce,** Lee's, and my son from an earlier lifetime with the Young Souls, too? [| Y |]

(Oct 26, '07) (At Fern's, my right ear became warm.) Did Nate cause my ear to become warm just now?

[| Yes. he wants to tell you he was with you when you were in an accident with Aunt Mollie in a previous lifetime (Corrie^AP and Corella^MP). He has been with you several lifetimes. |]

Did Nate cause the faint sound I heard in my car today?

[| He is concerned about **Teri** (miscarriage), that she hasn't gone to the light yet. Also, taking care of Bryce, Elaine, and Teri is a lot for him. He needs you to verbalize your support. |]

Using my doll to represent her, I held Teri and loved her.

(Nov 5, '07) Has Teri gone to the light yet? [| No. She needs more love and attention before she will be ready. |]

During the next week, I often held Teri (my doll) In a blanket and had her sleep with me. I talked to her the way I would have if she were alive. I prayed that she would feel loved.

I invited the Young Souls to go to the light during the Sunday service. Did Teri go to the light? [| Y |] Wonderful!

Are Nate, Bryce, Teri, and **Elaine** (stillborn) all at my apartment? [| Y |]

(Nov 30, '07) Does Nate want to tell me something? [| Yes. Souls of some other children have come to your place, and it's more than he can handle. |]

Have some adult Souls come to my place, too? [| Yes. Word travels from one Soul to another about a place to stay. Besides asking for protection each day, you should also set spiritual boundaries. Say: "At all times, only those beings of love and light may be with me or in my home or car who have permission from the Holy Spirit, my Higher Self." |]

Are the Young Souls with me because I am holding onto them? [| No. They are with you to help guide and protect you. |] Even though they are young? [| Y |] Neat!

Will they leave when the time is right for them or me? [| Y |] Are they somewhat bound together as a group? [| Y |] Then they might leave as a group when they are ready to go. Will that be at the end of my life? [| Y |] That's fine with me!
[| Nate is worried about Elaine. |] Does she need more love? [| Much more. |] I'll minister to her some more using my doll.

(Dec 5, '07) I "held" Elaine a lot the last few days. I asked for my love for her to multiply and go out to other Souls who didn't receive enough love, especially Souls of stillborn, miscarried, and aborted babies and children who died young.

(Dec 8, '07) Is Elaine more healed now? [| Y |] Does she need more ministry? [| N |] Is her Soul my Soul from a previous lifetime in which I didn't receive enough love? [| Y |] Was I a stillborn child?

[| N |] A child who died young? [| Yes. It was a lifetime in which you and Lee were a couple. |]

So, I lived concurrent lives: I was Elaine and Elaine's mother! I understood I could not be there for my baby because my Soul was malnourished. That means Lee wasn't there for me.

(Dec 10, '07)   PAULIE, PERRY, and PATRICK

FERN: Didn't we learn that Darla[MP] was pregnant at the time of the accident in which she, Darin[LP], and Nate died?

ME: Let's ask. Holy Spirit, was Darla[MP] pregnant at the time of the accident? [| Y |] Has that young Soul gone to the light? [| No. It was a boy. |] I will call him **Paulie**.

FERN: Paulie will be with you now, too. Tell Nate, Darin[LP], Darla[MP], and the other Young Souls that he is Nate's brother.

ME: Is Paulie at my place already?
[| He wasn't at your place before this but is now because we talked about him, and your Soul welcomed him. |]

After I returned home, I ministered to Paulie, holding a little wooden boy doll to represent him.

[| Lorrie, please try to relax more. Ask angels to help you with your work or whatever you are doing. I am looking forward to you putting another puzzle together, and, of course, so are the young Souls Nate, Paulie, Bryce, Teri, and Elaine! |]

Thank You, Father God!

(Feb 7, '08) Uncle Art, who raped me at age 16, died three days ago. I wrote on a sheet of paper: "Uncle Art, blessed son of God. May you rest in peace." While holding that paper, I said, "Uncle Art, I forgive you for the sexual attack on me as a teenager. I learned that the spirit of lust plays a strong part in your actions. That makes a big difference. Father God, please forgive Uncle Art. He did not know what he was doing."

I put the paper in the copper ring for a few days.

(At Fern's) Was the baby I miscarried during high school a girl? [| It was a boy. |] I will name him **Perry**.

Has Perry gone to the light? [| Y |] Would he also like to be at my place? [| He is already there! |]

I had invited him by thinking about that baby earlier today, wishing he could be at my place with the other Young Souls.

Did Nate come along this evening? [| Y |] Did another young Soul come with him? [| Y |] I named the others, but none were there. (!!!) Is Nate's dog, Waggums, here? [| Y |] Does his spirit want to go to the light? [| Y |] I'll have him in mind on Sunday.

(Feb 12, '08, at Fern's) Did Nate bring somebody along this evening? [| Y |] It wasn't any of the other Young Souls staying at my place. Is Darla^MP here, Nate's mother? [| Y |] Is she in need of prayer? [| Y |] I'll pray for you, Darla^MP.

This last month, sounds have come from my left car door while I drive. Is a Soul trapped in it? [| Y |] I asked about people I knew who had died, but none of those Souls were there.
[| Nate knows. |]

(!!!) Is a baby's Soul in the car door that wants to go to the light? [| Y |] Four months into my pregnancy with Patty, I felt movements high up in my abdomen and down low, making me wonder if I might be going to have twins. I read that when a baby dies early in the pregnancy, its body sometimes gets resorbed by the mother's body. Did Patty have a twin who died in utero? [| Yes. It was a boy. |] Is that the baby's Soul that is in my car door? [| Y |] I am happy to learn about him! I will name him **Patrick**. I invited Patrick to join the Young Souls.

Did Patty's Soul sense that she had a twin? [| Y |] Should I tell her about it sometime? [| Yes, whenever it works out. |]

(Jul 21, '08)   To the Dog Park

(At Fern's) Does Nate's puppy, Waggums, stay at my place? [| No, but Nate sometimes takes him to the dog park in town. |] Some of this stuff is almost enough to blow a person's mind!

Is there a dog park in Heaven? [| Heaven has separate places for tame, wild, and aquatic animals, plants, trees, etc. []] What about bugs, ants, and spiders? [| Yes, for them, too. []

My right ear suddenly became warm. Nate, do you want to say something?

[| (Nate) Yes, I do, Lorrie. You are a great sort of a Mom to us. Thank you for your love and blessing. []

I have no idea what your life is like on the other side.

NATE: Everything is hunky-dory, and it's always getting hunky-dorier! Please don't worry, Lorrie. We can see the effects on you when you are anxious. Father God said that things are working out, so you don't have anything to worry about!

If something needs to be worried about, I would be glad to do the worrying for you if I could arrange it (I know I can't). Worry affects your energy so much that I almost feel like worrying about it, but I don't know how to worry, so that puts me in a pickle!

As I understand it, when you realize you are worrying, that's the time to say, "I don't allow negative energies like you to be with me or in my home! Leave now!" Anxiety has to leave when you tell it to. You might still feel somewhat worried after dismissing the anxiety, but most of it would come from a habit of worrying you have gotten into. Remember, you can unmake anything that you made by deciding to.

We kid Souls will be snickering when you are worried, wondering how soon you will catch yourself and dump that old worry into the trash! By the way, Hi! from the rest of the Young Souls! We love you! []

What a blessing you and the other Young Souls are, Nate! Fern is grateful, too, for the upliftment you give her. I'll keep in mind what you said about not worrying. 'Bye!

[| 'Bye to you, too! []

(Jan 25, '09)   JACINTA AND FANNIE MAE

(At Fern's) I told Fern about having learned that Bryce has an older sister, **Jacinta**, who is with the Young Souls. Lately, while I am driving my car, a clicking sound comes from the right side of the dashboard. Is that sound being caused by a baby's Soul that I miscarried in a prior lifetime? [| Y |]

A sibling of Jacinta's and Bryce's? [| Y |] Younger than them? [| Y |] A girl? [| Y |] **Fannie Mae** came to mind.

I said, "Fannie Mae, I invite you to be with your sister Jacinta and your brother Bryce at my place."

OK, Fern, let's see how fast this works. Holy Spirit, is Fannie Mae at my apartment now? [| Y |] Wow!

I ministered to and talked to Fannie Mae for a week using my doll. She would "take a long nap" while I was at work.

(Jan 28, 09) My right ear became very warm.) Hi, Nate! I suppose you are aware that Fannie Mae is with us now.

[| (Nate) Yes, I am. All of us are happy to have her with us! The part of your Full Soul that is her mother (you) Is also very happy that Fannie Mae is lovingly taken care of.

It benefits you spiritually to reunite with parts of your family from previous lifetimes. Think how much more whole you are after learning about Paulie, me, Jacinta, Bryce, and Fannie Mae from earlier lifetimes of yours and about Perry (miscarriage at age 16) and Patrick (my daughter Patty's deceased twin) from this lifetime. It is a blessing for you and all of us!

Lorrie, I suggest you take time off from accomplishing things to have fun, OK? |]

OK. Thank you, Nate!

(Jan 30, '09)   Back to Nate

I couldn't open the driver's door of my car for the last two days. Before church this morning, it wouldn't open, but after church, it opened right up! Holy Spirit, did Nate prevent the car door from opening to bring it to my attention that Fannie Mae is at my place? [| Y |]

(Mar 4, '09) A few days ago, my iron wouldn't heat up. I reasoned that the connections might be loose because the iron had fallen to the floor twice. (!!!) Is Nate maybe playing a trick? I said aloud, "Nate, if you are preventing the iron from working, quit it right now!" That didn't help.

I checked the iron the next two days, and it still wouldn't heat up, so I bought a used iron at a thrift store. When I got home with the used iron, on a hunch, I rechecked my iron, and it worked! I figured Nate had prevented it from heating up to play a trick on me, but I didn't have time to ask him about it just then. The iron kept working fine, so I returned the used one to the thrift store.

(Jan 8, '10) My right ear became warm. Do you want to say something, Nate?

[| (Nate) Yes, Lorrie. You are not wasting time as you work on the writing. It helps you work through issues and learn new things, and since you are doing it in love, it helps those who will be reading or hearing about those lessons in time to come.

Healing across time is happening in more ways than you can imagine. For example, when a mother or father thinks ahead to when their daughter or son will be grown up, and they feel loving towards them, that love has been given to them in that future time!

You still feel anxiously eager quite often. Please get out of the habit of calling up anxiety. When you realize you are feeling anxious, focus on breathing peace in and anxiety out. []

Thank you, Nate! I hope you Young Souls are doing OK.

[| Yes, we are, thank you! []

End of 2-D: YOUNG SOULS WITH ME

2-E: GOODBYE, FERN

(Jan 30, '09)   A BLOW FOR FERN

Fern has been having a lot of pain in her back. She had scans taken yesterday that showed a mass (cancer) between two ribs on her right side. The doctor said it was too large to remove. They will have to use radiation to shrink it. Fern feels devastated, of course. She has had a lot of pain over the last 10-15 years, including surgeries to remove a small cancerous growth from her back and a larger one from her lung. She will be having more tests.

Bless you, Fern! I prayed to clear the spirit of cancer and its roots from Fern's Soul and the Souls of her relatives in every lifetime. I prayed for healing for every part of Fern's body.

Father God, is the spirit of cancer cleared from Fern's Souls in past lifetimes? [| Y |] In this lifetime? [| Y |] Has it been cleared from Souls from previous lifetimes of Fern's family lines? [| No. They need more clearing. |]

Fern's mother was adopted, so clearing would also be needed for the family lines of her birth mother and father and her adoptive mother and father. [| Y |]

With the spirit of cancer having been cleared from Fern, will prayer for shrinking the cancerous tissue be more effective now than it would have been before this? [| Y |]

Did Fern's Soul agree before coming into this lifetime to have these various situations become part of the lessons we are learning on healing family lines? [| Y |]

(Feb 1, '09)   Prayer for Fern's Family Lines

Is there a connection between unhealed areas of Fern's family line and cancer showing up in her body? [| Y |] Are some of the Souls in her family line in great distress? [| Y |] Is their distress showing up physically within Fern's body? [| N |] Is it affecting her body negatively? [| Y |]

I read that when a person's emotional struggles are too much for them to deal with, the emotions will sometimes collect in areas of their body and become cancerous. When the cancer is removed, the person is free of the negative effects of those strong emotions, but if they don't deal with the emotions that are causing them so much pain, their body will develop more cancerous areas.

Has distress from Fern's family lines been collecting in Fern's body, specifically within the mass on her right side, so that it can be removed and thus bring some freeing for the family? [| Y |] Is anger collected there? [| Y |] Besides anger, are there roots of other negative spirits in members of Fern's family line that should be dissolved for the sake of healing? [| Y |] Is karma between people and Souls in Fern's family lines also playing a part? [| Y |]

I invited the Ministry Team to join me as I did a clearing for Fern's father's family lines, her mother's birth and adoptive family lines, and Fern's family lines from all other lifetimes.

Recent tests showed several cancerous growths in Fern's brain, two in her lower body and one the size of a small lime in her back. No wonder she is having so much pain!

Father God, I offer everything I do today as a prayer for healing for Fern. I ask for clearing of cancer and other health problems she has. May she be enabled to hold onto faith and hope. Thank You, Father!

(Feb 8, '09)   Cause for Great Joy!

Father, thank You for the healing and clearing that has taken place for Fern, her family, and me! I sense that my family lines aren't fully cleared, though, and that major clearing may still be needed regarding Aunt Mollie.

[| Dear one, the Young Souls are happy, I am happy, and all of Heaven and the whole universe are happy about the tremendous breakthrough that is coming about in clearing for Fern's and your family lines!

You have been wondering about something. Yes, as with Fern's Soul, your Soul agreed to have your family lines cleared through you. Every family line has a Soul that has volunteered to do that for their family lines. You realize, of course, that families are so interconnected that each person has tie-ins with many family lines, particularly since previous lifetimes are also involved; so the clearing that one person does for their family also benefits many other families.

As this family-line healing process gains ground, a great change will occur in the world and the universe. Each family has many Souls in Heaven that are already rooting for it and will continue to do so in the months and years ahead.

Bless you and Fern and everybody for your faith-filled patient waiting and for your impatient waiting! We go forward together to victory. Hooray! And Halleluiah! []

Thank You, Father God!

(Feb 23, '09)   I AM DOING THIS FOR YOU

Father God, I am very concerned about Fern. She moved to a nursing home recently and will have three weeks of radiation treatments to shrink cancerous growth.

Please heal her and shore up her faith and hope! I ask that the radiation only affect cancerous growth and leave good tissue untouched. Thank You!

[| Lorrie, all is going well from the Divine perspective. I choose not to give you a prognosis regarding the treatment Fern is receiving. Not knowing the future makes you more inclined to turn to Me for assistance, healing, and guidance. People's request for help changes what the future would have been like had they not asked for help.

All of Heaven is cheering for and uplifting Fern. The light from her Spirit is drawing Souls in her family lines to come to it to be cleared and cleansed. Her Spirit is saying to her family:

"I am doing this for you, accepting what comes in my life because I love you! I want all of us to be healed and come together as a family in the light and love of God. I love you!"

Bless you, Fern, and everyone in your family in every lifetime! Please let Me and Mother God hold you while you rest, sleep, and any other times you wish. Know that your dear mother is ministering to you constantly and has rounded up many other ministering Souls to join with her. Shalom! []

Thank You very much, Father God!

(Mar 2, '09)   Nearing Completion

[| Lorrie, you do not need to worry about Fern. Mother God and I are with her, and angels, her mother, and nurse helpers are ministering to her. Whichever way things work out for Fern, her Spirit has chosen it. Please continue to bless her and all the people and Souls ministering to her.

Much freeing and healing has been and is taking place in Fern's family lines in this lifetime and previous lifetimes. The circle of healing in her family and Soul connections is nearing completion. Please assist her in releasing all of the refuse cleared from her family lines from the present and years past.

Fern's Spirit is saying:

"Family refuse, I release you to the ethers to return to where you came from! I declare that my family lines are healed and cleared of negativity!

"Father-Mother God, I speak for myself and my family in saying 'Yes' to life, to what love desires to bring forth. I place my hand in Yours, trusting that all is well.

"Shalom to everyone in my family and my friends and neighbors! Shalom to the world and the universe! And blessings to You, our great loving God!"

Shalom to you, dear Fern, to everyone in your family, the world, and the universe! My heart swells in gratitude for your generous ministering love. I will continue to be with you for whatever comes next. I wish that you and the many others in difficult circumstances can come to the point where, with My Help, you and they can face the future with joy no matter what comes next! So may it be.

Thank you, Lorrie, for taking the time to listen and write! |]

You are welcome, Father God! Thank You from both of us!

(Apr 14, '09) Fern was in the hospital for three days with shingles. She is on a morphine drip for pain from cancer. I sensed there was another prayer step I should take for her healing. A way of doing full-body prayer came to mind, and I prayed for her that way, using pillows on my couch to represent her. These are the steps I took:

1. I asked angels to be on hand for protection and asked Jesus and Reiki Masters to minister to Fern along with me. I pictured Fern in a cocoon formed of peace.
2. I spoke to each area of cancer in Fern's body for the low-vibration energy level of cancer to choose to transmute to neutral energy, return to their original form, and go back to where they came from
3. I asked Father God that even if Fern were to leave this world soon, she would no longer have much pain
4. I asked for healing to flow into Fern so she would feel much better by morning. I put on a music CD and asked angels to minister to Fern until the music finished playing.

Thank You, Father God! I know You heard my prayers and those of other Souls who joined in praying for Fern.

[| Thank you, Lorrie! I have been drawing you to pray in a special way for Fern. This type of full-body prayer is part of the process I am teaching you to bring about the transformation and healing of a family line and individuals in those families.

You can intend to apply the prayers you just said for Fern to every person in her family lines in every past lifetime and future lifetime! |]

I ask that my prayers for Fern be applied to her and everyone in her family lines in every past, present, and future lifetime. Good night, Father!

[| Good night, Lorrie! May you sleep well, knowing that I have heard your prayers and those of others. |]

(Apr 17, '09) I stopped by to see Fern and give her a "Praying for You" card. She told me that recent tests showed that the radiation treatments were not shrinking the cancerous growths. She won't have any more treatments. After praying so often for healing for Fern, it didn't seem real that she would be dying in the not-too-distant future. I was still holding onto the hope of instantaneous healing for her.

I visited Fern at the nursing home the following week and prayed with her. I told her that the card I gave her a few days earlier was a goodbye card and asked her if she realized that. She said she did. I asked her if she had been able to accept how things were going for her. She said, "Mostly."

Bless you, dear Fern!

(Apr 26, '09)   Magnified a Thousandfold

Bless you, Fern! That's all I can do for you.

[| Lorrie, the time for Fern's crossing over is imminent. You and Fern are spiritually connected, and that connection will not be affected by one or the other of you releasing your physical body. The increased restlessness and achiness you have been having are related to Fern's deteriorating physical condition. Know that all is well at all times for both of you.

Continue to wish Fern peace and blessings. Love from you and other people is sustaining her. She will have her wish granted of having somebody with her when she crosses over. One can be present in spirit as well as in person. Peace! |]

(May 14, '09) [| Fern will be all right. Do not worry about her feeling disgruntled or shortchanged in having such a short time left in this life. It is good that she is feeling and acknowledging her emotions. That will lighten her Spirit for going forward.

Your thought is correct: As you ask for angels of protection to be constantly around Fern, you can assist innumerable other Souls by intending protective angels to be around whoever else is in that type of situation. That, too, is part of the process of praying I am teaching you:

By making a simple intention, you can magnify the benefits and blessings of your love and prayers by a thousandfold, or a millionfold, in some cases. |]

Thank You so much, Father God!

I read the April 14, '09, and May 14, '09 messages from Father God aloud to Fern's Spirit. Bless you, Fern!

(May 23, '09)   RESISTANCE HELD AT BAY

[| Thank you, Lorrie, for being willing to hang in there in working on the writing project! Fern's hanging in there benefits you more than you will ever know. |]

(!!!) Father God, has Fern's physical and emotional discomfort these last eight months been labor pains for bringing forth the completed work, *Healing Across Time I* and *Healing Across Time II*? Are resistant energies coming into play?

[| Yes, how things have been going for Fern is a part of the overall process of completing the writing project. Her Spirit deflects much of the energetic resistance to the project you would otherwise have to deal with. You have also experienced the effects of that resistance.

There is resistance whenever a change is made to the status quo. You have learned that when one person changes their attitude, activities, and such, it forces everyone else in their family to make changes, too.

You can help soften that resistance by blessing everyone who has already been or will soon be affected by the changes coming about. Please say the Prayer of Blessing often for every person (Soul) at every moment of every lifetime. Thank you!

Bless you, Lorrie, Fern, and everyone! Bless All That Is! |]

(Jul 25, '09) [| Lorrie, please continue to bless Fern profusely. She is being prepared for a glorious entrance into eternal life. |]

(Aug 18, '09) Fern crossed to the other side this afternoon. One of her friends was with her at the time.

"Eternal rest grant unto her, O Lord, and let perpetual light shine upon her. May she rest in peace."

End of 2-E: GOODBYE, FERN

CHAPTER 3

DIVES INTO THE PAST

Healing for Prior Lifetimes: Me 4

3-A: CORRIE[AP], CORELLA[MP], LASSIE

Note: [AP] (Aunt Mollie Prior life) is omitted after Corrie, and [MP] (Me Prior life) after Corella in this section.

(Sept 2, '07)   HEALING PAINFUL MEMORIES

Is my head discomfort caused by painful cellular memories trying to surface? [| Somewhat. |] From previous lifetimes? [| Y |] Are some of those cellular memories from a lifetime in which Mollie and I were related to each other? [| Y |]

Was Mollie my mother in another lifetime? [| Y |] Did she mistreat me? [| No, but other people did. |] Do I have painful cellular memories from that lifetime? [| Y |]

(Nov 19, '07) [| Write what comes to mind. |]

(I inserted names after I learned who was speaking.)

CORRIE: Stand up straight! How can I be proud of you when you look like that? Pull your tummy in. Don't hold your head up like you are better than others. God knows, there may not be anything you are better at doing than anybody else.

Do you look better than others? For sure not. "Look what the dog dragged in!" Hah! Hah! Your smile? It's as crooked as all get out. Well, at least it matches how you stand. You should be able to stand straighter, even though your right leg is shorter. One of Pam's legs is shorter, too, and she stands straight.

Who knows what you are being punished for in being born with a crooked smile and one leg shorter than the other? It sure isn't anything I did. In my opinion, the best bet is that God knew ahead of time what you would do during your life. So don't go feeling sorry for yourself about being a little crippled. You brought it on yourself somehow. For sure, I won't feel sorry for you!

I have gone through enough tough stuff that I know it makes you tougher. It isn't "tough shit." Don't ever think of it that way. Remember, "When the going gets tough, the tough get going."

Corella, 10, shrinks into herself a little more with each insult. She tries not to let the insults bite her self-esteem, but they still do. Her self-esteem wouldn't cover the head of a pin. Her emotions are raw. She thinks: Woe is me! What can I do?

CORELLA: (To herself) Nothing, girl. You can't stop fate. It's your fate to suffer, and you can't escape it. The only thing that might help a little is if you could dream that you are normal and pretty like other girls are. But even in the middle of a dream, you know it isn't real and never can be.

CORRIE: Alack and Alas! I think that's what we should name you, Corella. One part of you can be "Alack" and the other part "Alas." That way, you'll have company! (Corrie is obviously amused, but her face looks somewhat like the Wicked Witch of the West in The Wizard of Oz, showing more derision than innocent amusement.)

Corella often gets muscle twitches as she tries to get through the day without falling apart. She doesn't have many friends. In fact, she doesn't have any. The kids at school are just kids she knows, like knowing your neighbors' names.

She doesn't have human friends, but she does have a dear animal friend, the neighbor's dog, Lassie. Corella coaxes Lassie to come over to the doghouse in her yard every chance she gets. She had a puppy when she was little, but it got run over.

Corella always waits inside the doghouse for Lassie. She isn't very big, so there is plenty of room for both her and Lassie. It's the only place she can be with Lassie and not be seen. So far, she has managed to keep their meeting place a secret. Here comes Lassie now!

CORELLA: Hi, Lassie! Come here, girl!

Lassie reacts affectionately by licking Corella's hands. Corella had eaten a cookie earlier and rubbed it on her hands so that Lassie could taste it. She hugs Lassie and curls up beside her. Corella can't control her emotions anymore. She buries her face in Lassie's fur and cries uncontrollably.

I stopped writing because I realized this was another painful cellular memory opening up. I was planning to go to Fern's place shortly. The Holy Spirit said it would be better for me to be with Fern or another loving person when a painful memory opens up. Please be with me, Father God!

(At Fern's) I told Fern that painful memories were in the process of opening up. To get myself back into Corella's emotions, I read aloud to Fern what I had just written. I turned on my tape recorder. Fern sat in a rocking chair. I lay on the floor in front of her with a pillow beside me to represent Lassie.

CORELLA: (Crying) Lassie, I've got nobody except you. You're the only friend I've got. I am so glad you love me! Nobody else does. I don't think Mom loves me even one little bit.

(Still crying) Lassie, do you ever have to cry? Did you ever cry so hard that it feels like your insides are coming out? Or that your eyes will fall out? That's how I feel a lot of times. Sometimes, I wake up at night and can't go back to sleep. I keep thinking about all the things Mamma says all the time.

I wish Daddy would still be with us. I don't know what he did that was so bad that Mamma said he had to leave! (Breaks down crying in a somewhat muffled way.)

LASSIE (Fern): You always have me.

CORELLA: (Lifts her head) Who are you? Are you Lassie?

Lassie: Yes.

CORELLA: I can hear you talking, but your mouth isn't moving, and you look at me tenderly. I think you do care! (Cries)

LASSIE: Yes, I do, more than you can imagine.

CORELLA: I wish you could come to school with me and then return home, but it's too far. I'm gonna call you my doggie!

LASSIE: That's fine.

CORELLA: I want to tell you something, Lassie. Sometimes, my leg starts shaking, and I can't stop it. I think they call it spasms. I take medicine for it, but it doesn't do any good. And then sometimes I kind of shake and jerk.

LASSIE: And the medicine doesn't help?

CORELLA: Only a little.

LASSIE: Does it help to spend time with me?

CORELLA: Yes. I try not to shake when I'm around Mamma because I think she would get even madder, which would be terrible! She always thinks of something worse to say. I am a nobody.

LASSIE: No! No! No! No! No!

CORELLA: That's what I feel like.

LASSIE: You are very special to God. Very, very special.

CORELLA: Really? I thought God was just somebody who punishes you when you're bad.

LASSIE: No, you're special to God. You wouldn't be here otherwise.

CORELLA: Really? I never heard that before. Lassie, you are wise!

LASSIE: Maybe your Mom blames herself, thinking she wasn't good enough that you didn't come out how she felt you should.

CORELLA: But there are a lot of little kids who are crippled, and they are cute and nice! What's so terrible about me?

LASSIE: There is nothing terrible about you.

CORELLA: It will be ten years until I'm grown up. Can you imagine, Lassie, listening to that stuff for ten more years?

LASSIE: We'll have to think of a different way for you to hear it.

CORELLA: What d'ya mean?

LASSIE: When your Mom says those things, to hear how much she is hurting, how much she may blame herself.

CORELLA: Hmmm. Maybe your Mom misses your Daddy.

LASSIE: I think she does. And I think she sometimes feels that everything is more than she can handle alone.

CORELLA: We don't have much money. I wish I could earn some.

LASSIE: Well, maybe if you asked about walking, brushing, or feeding me. You could earn money that way. I would like that!

CORELLA: I will ask the Smiths. No, I better ask Mom first.

LASSIE: Maybe the Smiths could ask your Mom, saying it would be great if you could do that for them, that they would be willing to pay you as people pay for babysitting.

CORELLA: I'm big enough to walk you! And do you know what, Lassie? It is so good that you don't criticize me! That's why I like to be with you, 'cause you are so happy to see me!

LASSIE: I'm always happy to see you.

CORELLA: That's so good, Lassie! (She hugs Lassie.) I'm glad you live next door to me! I don't have many kids to talk to and play with.

LASSIE: Well, you can walk and play with me anytime.

CORELLA: It would be nice if some other kids would walk along!

LASSIE: Yes, as long as they know I am your dog.

CORELLA: "My dog" to take for a walk. That's such a good idea! Well, I better get going because Mom will wonder where I am and what I'm doing. You go out first. Go back home, OK? Go, Lassie! (Whispers) Good girl!

LASSIE: Will I see you again?

CORELLA: (Still whispering) Yes! I'll see you, Lassie!

(I shut off the tape recorder and sat quietly.) That was quite a session! Thank you, Fern, for being Lassie for me!

FERN: You are welcome. I am always happy to help.

(Nov 19, '07)   INJURED IN AN ACCIDENT

In my lifetime as Corella, was my mom from this lifetime my aunt? [| N |] My sister? [| Y |] Was she 9 or 10 years older than me? [| Y |] Was Grandma Leigh my sister? [| No, your cousin, the same age as your sister. They were good friends, but they spent time with you, too. |]

Were my experiences with having a sarcastic mother in that lifetime a part of the plan for my Soul to develop compassion for others? [| Y |] Did Mollie's Soul agree to play the part of being a critical, unfeeling Mom for me? [| Y |] Wow!

Corrie came across as without feeling, but did she feel that life had skipped over her? [| Y |] Was she affected by family distress from an earlier lifetime when she was subjected to verbal abuse? [| Y |] I sensed that she put on a tough exterior to keep from breaking down in front of people.

(Nov 19, '07) An area on the back of my head to the upper right has bothered me for years. Does a painful cellular memory I am carrying have to do with an injury to that area? [| Y |] From a car accident? [| Y |] Did that accident happen during my lifetime as Corella when Aunt Mollie was my mother, Corrie? [| Y |] I also have steady soreness in my left shoulder. Even with massage, the muscles stay sore and tight. Did I injure my left shoulder near my neck in that accident? [| Y |]

(Dec 2, '07) Did Corrie die because of the accident? [| Y |] Soon after? [| No, a couple of years later. |] So, she wasn't well. That's too bad. [| She needed constant care. |] Did Corella give her that continuous care? [| She helped with it. |]

Did Corella get somewhat crippled from the accident, also? [| Y |] Was her right arm hurt? [| Y |]

(Jan 3, '08) Is a portion of Corrie's Soul with me? [| N |] A portion of Corella's Soul? [| N |] Is part of Corella's Soul enmeshed with Corrie's Soul? [| Y |] Is the sinus drainage and chest congestion that I continue having related to Aunt Mollie's lifetime as Corrie? [| Y |] I felt brief pains here and there recently. Are those pains from cellular memories from my lifetime as Corella? [| Y |] (!!!) Are they cellular memories of Corrie's that Corella carried that need healing? [| Y |]

How old was Corella when she died? [| Sixteen. |] Has Corrie gone to the light? [| Y |] Has Corella? [| No, but she is ready to. |]

Should I assist her in going to the light at home? [| No. She wants to go to the light in a church. |] She can go to the light this Sunday!

(Dec 5, '10) [| Lorrie, Corella is concerned about her mother, Corrie, and would like you to pray for her. I know you don't want to pick up lower-level energies by saying Corrie's name so you could ask for blessing and clearing for "Corella and her mother." []

Good idea, Father God! Thank You!

I began blessing Corella and her mother quite often.

(Dec 23, '10)   To the Light

I have a hunch that energies from Aunt Mollie from her recent lifetime and earlier lifetimes are the principal cause of the head discomfort I have been having. Do I have ties with her?

[| Yes, the main tie is that you were Mollie's daughter, Corella, in her lifetime as Corrie. []

Would it help lessen the effects of family distress on me if I would minister to Corella? I have been saying lately, "Bless you, Corella, and bless your Mom and Dad!"

[| Blessing them is helping lessen the amount of discomfort you would otherwise be experiencing. []

Is a portion, or all, of Corella's Soul with me?

[| Part of her Soul is with you for being affirmed and healed. []

Can I do something else to lessen the head discomfort and help keep my blood pressure at a more normal level?

[| Yes, having music playing would benefit you a great deal. Also, the more relaxed you can be about everything, the better you will feel. When you tense up, parts of your Souls from other lifetimes that are with you also tense up. Corella, for one, reacts strongly to situations of discord. Bless you, Lorrie! []

Thank You, Father God!

(May 1, '11) This morning at church, I invited the portion of Corella's Soul that is with me to go to the light.

Holy Spirit, did that portion of Corella's Soul go to the light?

[| She went to the light and had a joyous reunion with her Full Soul! That will benefit you, too. []

(Jan 23, '12)   Canceling Prior-Life Vows

It feels like a tight band is around my head. The sisters at Mary Convent, where I attended high school, wore headbands.

(!!!) My cousin Marcie, three years younger than me, also wanted to become a nun, but she died in a car accident when she was nine. Does she need to be released from private vows of poverty, chastity, or obedience that she made? [| Y |]

I sensed that Marcie's Soul is with a Soul of mine from a previous lifetime who also wants to be released from private vows that she made. Is Marcie with Corella? [| Y |]

(Jan 27, '12) I invited Corella and Marcie to join me as I canceled the private vows of poverty, chastity, and obedience they had taken as children. Thank You, Holy Spirit!

(Feb 5, '12) Marcie is released from all of the vows. Corella is released from the vows of poverty and chastity but not obedience. She imagined taking the vows when she was older and became a sister, so her vow of obedience connected with the nun who was Mother Superior. That Mother Superior's Soul isn't yet willing to release Corella from the vow.

Two weeks later, I spoke kindly to the Mother Superior from that lifetime about releasing Corella from the vow of obedience, explaining that religious vows only apply while the person is living. I told her that she had died and Corella did, too.

(May 29, '12) Did the Mother Superior release Corella from the vow of obedience? [| Y |] Wonderful! Thank You, Holy Spirit!

End of 3-A: CORRIE[AP], CORELLA[MP], LASSIE

3-B: ERIK[MP] > KIM AND TOM

Note: [MP] (Me Prior life) is omitted after Erik in this section.

(Sept 18, '07)   PARTS OF ME ARE AFRAID

(At Fern's) I asked the Holy Spirit about parts of me still being afraid. Kim 10, Peter 5, Robert 7, Tom 15, Aaron and Harry are. Are they afraid because there aren't as many boys as girls?
[| No. The male parts of you are afraid and ashamed because they could not protect you when you were young and afraid about what might happen to them.

(!!!) Are they afraid when a man is around, even my sons? [| Y |] Are the girls afraid, too, when a man is around? [| Yes, but there is safety in numbers. |] I began speaking to the parts of me, telling them we are safe wherever we go.

(Instead of narrating all the questions that Fern and I asked the Holy Spirit and the answers we received, I will tell this in a narrative style.) Male parts of me are afraid that a man might sexually abuse them. Kim is the most afraid, but even so, he stood guard over Dora and me during and after I was sexually abused at age 5, to the point of thinking he had shot an intruder. Kim and Tom were parts of my Soul in a prior lifetime.

Was I a male in that lifetime?

[| Yes, your name was **Erik**^MP. As a teenager, as you were about to be sexually abused, Kim, age 10, split off into a separate personality and took your place.

Tom, age 15, wanted to help Kim and split off, also. He saw the abuse taking place and was petrified. He felt guilty that he wasn't able to help Kim. He didn't tell anybody. He was afraid the same thing might happen to him. The rest of you (Erik) closed off and didn't get affected much by the abuse. Kim's right arm was twisted behind his back during the abuse. |]

That ties in with the soreness in my right arm while I am learning about this incident! Is the numbness I am experiencing lately in my rectal area coming from cellular memories of that sexual abuse? Is Kim trying to tell me what happened through that symptom? [| Y |]

Did the sexual abuse happen to Kim more than once? [| Yes, but Tom didn't know about the other times. |] Was it the same man? [| Y |]

How did Kim and Tom come to be with me in this lifetime?

[| They came into this lifetime with you to protect you. Also, they wanted to experience what it was like to be a female. |]

What about Erik? [| Erik became a counselor who worked with both males and females who were sexually abused. He wants you to know his wife's name: *Gabby*, short for Gabriella. They had 16 children, with five sets of twins in the mix. |] Wow!

Holy Spirit, do I have other painful cellular memories that need to be released?

[| Yes, you are carrying painful cellular memories in your body, mind, and Soul that are meant to be healed during this lifetime, but you should be with Fern when you do the processing to receive direct comfort. |]

(Oct 27, '07)   HEALING FOR KIM AND TOM

I went to Fern's place to have her help bring about healing for Kim, 10, and Tom, 15, split-off portions of Erik's^MP Soul who are with me. Fern sat in a rocking chair, and I sat on the floor in front. Fern spoke for Kim's and Tom's Mom and Dad. I spoke for Kim and Tom. (Recorded and typed later.)

ME: Kim, I think one reason you and Tom are with me is to clear fear from you and every part of me. Thank you for taking care of little Lorrie-me and my little sister Dora. You were very brave! (Emotions were rising from Kim, making it difficult for me to keep talking. I pulled into a fetal position and stayed that way much of the time as Fern was ministering to me). Are you here, Kim?

KIM: (Crying) Yeah, I'm here. I don't know why I feel like crying. You'd think boys shouldn't cry, but (he sobs for quite a while). I haven't been feeling very good lately, and I don't know why, but I'm starting to remember something. (Sniffling) I'm not sure where Tom was. He wouldn't want me to be alone. (He tries to get control of his emotions.)

MOM: You are not alone.

TOM: (Crying) I am here, Kim, your big brother Tom, and you know what? You weren't alone, but I couldn't come to where you were because I didn't know what that guy was doing! He was a big guy. You were so scared and were crying and trying to get away. And I couldn't help! (His voice keeps rising higher as he cries harder.) I wish we could have told Mom or Dad, but Dad is a man, so I didn't know what to think.

ME: Kim and Tom, this is Lorrie. I want to tell you something your mom and dad didn't get around to telling you. There is what is called "sexual attraction." It makes boys want to have girlfriends, and men and women want to get married.

Some men are attracted to boys or other men, and some women are attracted to girls or other women. They want to be close to the person they are attracted to and want to make love to them.

Kim, I don't know if the guy who abused you felt like he loved you or if he was angry. But no matter what, he shouldn't have done what he did!! You shouldn't have had to go through that, and I'm so sorry you did. (I was crying, too.) You can stay curled up as long as you need to. That's what Father God said to me one time when I felt like I needed to stay curled up, that He wouldn't force me to straighten up.

Tom, it would be good if you would hug Kim.

(Tom hugged Kim, using a pillow. Kim continued crying, very uptight, trying to stifle his tears. Then a determination set in, and he spoke up to the man who was molesting him.)

KIM: (Talking to the man who molested him) Get away from me! (Through his tears) Get away from me! Whatcha doing? (He catches his breath, and fresh tears burst forth.) Uh! Uh! (He tries to catch his breath.) That hurts!! What are you DOING? Mister, I'm gonna GETCH YOU! I'm gonna getcha GOOD! (Short breaths, emphasizing each word) You've got no damn business doing that! (His voice has a very high pitch caused by pain.) What! NO!

(His crying goes to an extremely high pitch as he grimly endures what is happening to him. It's like he can't believe what is happening, but the pain that he feels confirms that it is happening, whatever it is. He continues crying, going into a wail, almost getting hoarse. Finally, he catches his breath and says through his tears)

KIM: The guy is leaving now. (Another release of tears washes through him. He cries for quite a while like a frightened young child who is alone, badly hurt, and extremely afraid, almost too afraid to even make a sound while he cries. Finally, he says unsteadily:)

Mamma, where are you? (He continues crying and sniffling.) No! No! No! (There is agony in his voice.)

Mom: (Tenderly) If only I had known, I could have helped.

(Kim lifts to half-kneeling. He turns towards his mom, who embraces him. He is too uptight to lift his head. He cries with short breaths and then can finally speak again.)

Kim: Something terrible happened! (He continues crying, ending with a wail as he says,) Something ter-rr-ible! (He finally gets his voice back and says through his tears,) Do you kinda know what happened, Mom?

Mom: No,

Kim: That's good that you don't know (catching his breath), but it wasn't good. (Short, quick breaths.)

Mom: I would have protected you if I had known.

Kim: I bet you could have because you're strong. (He takes more quick breaths.) When I get big, I will help anybody who needs help! (He catches his breath.)

Mom: That's good.

Kim: Tom told me that he was there. Did you know that?

Mom: No. Did he help you?

Kim: Well, maybe by holding his breath. He said he didn't know what to do. He was so scared! You better take care of him, too. OK, Mom?

Mom: OK.

Kim: Because he's my brother, and I love him. He is a good kid. (He is still almost out of breath.)

Mom: Yes, he is. And brothers stick together.

Kim: And mothers and sons stick together, too.

Mom: Yes, and you should feel you can tell me anything.

Kim: (Catching his breath.) What about dads and sons?

Mom: Dads and sons, too. That's what we are here for.

Kim: Lorrie said Jesus made men big and strong to protect and care for kids! Is that what Daddy is like?

Mom: Yes, he is.

KIM: I don't want to grow up and be like that guy. (He catches his breath.) I want to grow up and be like Daddy.

MOM: Daddy would have helped you.

KIM: If Dad had been there, he would have felt like shooting that guy! I felt like shooting him, but I didn't have a gun and couldn't get hold of anything to hit him with.

MOM: Daddy would do anything to protect you. (Kim cries harder.) And that's what Moms do, too.

KIM: I'll have to love myself a lot to feel better. (Unsteadily) It isn't good to stay mad at somebody.

MOM: If you stay mad at him, you let him still have control.

KIM: I didn't think of that! Should I wish him good things?

MOM: You could wish that God forgives him and loves him. And that God can show him a better way. If you hold on to being mad, that guy still has control. I know it's hard.

KIM: I'll work on it. (He talks with his Mom and tells her he feels almost numb.) Mom, Tom is probably feeling pretty awful, too. I'll let him be here.

Tom, did you hear what Mom said? She said that, for sure, guys aren't supposed to do what that guy did; they are supposed to be good, and that dad is good! I told her what happened. I hope you heard Lorrie saying that some guys are attracted to boys or men.

MOM: Yes. Guys are like that sometimes but are not supposed to touch children. That's not right!

TOM: (Sitting with his back to the rocker. His Mom rubs his shoulders as they talk.) Mom, I felt bad for Kim but was scared from the top of my head down to the ground! (Deep breaths.)

MOM: But you wanted to help Kim, didn't you?

TOM: Yes, I did!

MOM: You couldn't stop what the guy was doing, but you being there helped him. Like I said to Kim, try to let go of being mad at that man because otherwise, he still has control.

TOM: But it feels like I'm going to stay scared.

MOM: Remember that God is always with you, and so is your guardian angel. Ask your guardian angel to protect you.

TOM: That will help! Did you hear that, Kim? We've got an angel with us! A real one! You're such a good kid, Kim! (He hugs Kim using a pillow.) You held up, and you were mad at that guy. That way, it didn't affect you as much. I'm glad you could cry because holding the hurt inside is too hard. I cried just now, too, and it felt good! Let's remember as we get older that it's good to cry if something bad happens.

KIM: (To Fern) Could you be Dad for a bit?

FERN: Yes.

KIM: Dad, I told Mom a little about this. I felt terrible! This guy did something to me, and maybe you would understand better than Mom. He somehow put his big thing up into my seat, which hurt something terrible, but he wouldn't stop! I tried to get away and I couldn't! (Crying.) I couldn't tell anybody! At the time, I couldn't. But that's what happened, Dad!

DAD: I wish you would have come to me (Kim takes deep breaths, trying to relax and clear his voice.) You couldn't scream? Wouldn't he let you scream?

KIM: I was feeling so mad! I just wanted to hit and kick him, but I couldn't! Or shake him off, but I couldn't! (He takes a deep breath.) I was trapped! It felt terrible!

DAD: I'm sure it did. I wish I could have been there!

KIM: You would have pulled him off and scooted him out the door, wouldn't you? And bawl him out!

DAD: Yes!

KIM: You would have even used some swear words, which would have been OK! He deserved it!

DAD: You bet I would have used some swear words!

KIM: Like "damn"?

DAD: But don't repeat them to your mother.

KIM: OK! (A little laugh) That can be our secret, huh?

DAD: Kim, even though Tom was there, it wasn't his fault. He couldn't have done anything to stop it.

KIM: Yeah, I know.

DAD: Does he know that?

KIM: I think so, but he feels bad that he couldn't stop it.

DAD: Things happen we can't control. That man was big!

KIM: I forgot to tell Mom about this. That guy hurt my arm. He twisted it back, and it's sore! (His dad massages Kim's arm.)

KIM: (After a bit) My arm feels pretty good now. Tom could use a shoulder rub, too. He's pretty uptight.

DAD: OK, Tom, let's see about this. (He rubs Tom's shoulders.) Were you afraid it might happen to you, too?

TOM: Sure, if I had gone in there. I just couldn't!

DAD: Did you or Kim know this man?

TOM: Yes. That's what makes it so bad. I almost shouldn't tell you, but you asked. (Whispering) It was your brother, Uncle Fred. That dumb guy! (He breaks down crying.)

DAD: My brother and I will be having words later!!!

TOM: That dumb guy! (Crying harder) He's a dumb ass!

DAD: Yes, he is! (Tom cries uncontrollably.) My brother and I will have words, and he will never touch you or Kim again! You let me know If he touches you in some way.

TOM: I'm feeling numb, just like Kim said he did. (Takes some deep breaths.) I think that's from being scared. I have to relax. Hey, Dad, please give us a blessing! (They kneel.)

DAD: Father, Son, and Holy Spirit, we want the best for Tom and Kim. May they always be there for one another. May their guardian angels protect them. Bless you, Tom and Kim!

TOM: I'm going to grow up and be good like you are, Dad!

KIM: I am, too!

DAD: I believe that!

TOM: I feel a lot better, but I think Kim and I should do something to relax. Kim, let's shoot some baskets!

KIM: OK!

ME: Thank you very much, Fern! I feel much better.

(The next day) Holy Spirit, are Kim and Tom healed now?

[| Yes, and they are no longer within you. They are now guardians for you. |]

That is overwhelmingly wonderful! Thank You, Father God, Mother God, Holy Spirit, and Jesus! Thank you, Fern!
[| So you know, Kim has been with you. for several lifetimes. |]

Did he decide to be with me during earlier lifetimes and in this lifetime in hopes of being healed so he could go to the light? [| Yes, and to learn from your Soul. |]

Did he know I would become aware of him at some point and let the tension surface of his having been sexually abused in that earlier lifetime? [| Y |] Could he have gone to the light if that trauma hadn't surfaced? [| No. The rape was allowed to happen to clear stuff from way back for him and for you. |]

What an experience! Thank You, Father God, for the clearing and healing that took place! Bless you, Kim and Tom!

End of 3-B: ERIK^{MP} > KIM AND TOM

3- C: MARY^{MP} AND LAURA^{MP}

Note: ^{MP} (Me Prior life) is omitted after Mary and Laura in this section.

(Jan 13, '08)   MARY, OBEDIENT DAUGHTER

[| Allow yourself to get sleepy. |] (I wrote what came to mind.)

CAME TO MIND: For love or money. For the love of money. What if someone, my Dad in another lifetime, figured the family might as well get easy money the down-to-earth way? I've got a pretty daughter. END.

DAD: Hey, Mary, come here!

MARY: What do you want, Dad?

DAD: Do you remember when I showed you what men like to do? We need more money, and it would be great if you could help us. You're ten now and will soon be a young lady. Letting some young guys practice on you a few times a week would bring a pretty penny. You wouldn't even have to leave home. We'll take good care of you.

What d'ya say? Could you do that for your dear old Dad even if I'm not old yet? I'd be a heap obliged to you. You know you are my special, favorite daughter! Even if I had more girls, you would be my favorite! You can have a dime from every dollar to spend however you want!

MARY: I don't think other girls do that.

DAD: Honey, we need the money to buy groceries! Your younger brother Bruce is doing what he can to help out, cleaning at the hardware store. (He pulls her close and whispers in her ear.) Your Mamma, bless her Soul, used to help us out by doing that sometimes when we were short of money. Now that she's gone, you're the woman of the family. Please, won't you do it for her? You would make her happy.

MARY: (She twists the toe of her shoe in the dirt, then looks up shyly.) I could try it so we'll have enough money, and seeing how you can't work all the time like some other guys. It's too bad you hurt your back. Sure, Daddy, I'll do it for you. I'll make you and Mamma proud of me.

(Her dad looks very happy. He hugs her and squeezes her butt a little. It felt kind of good to her.)

(The present) I tried to go back to sleep but had to cry and pull myself together. My crying had a deeper sound, not like a young child. It felt like I was looking at the situation from the outside but feeling it inside, too. I (Mary) loved my Dad but was also angry at him. Such conflict could make a person go crazy. Maybe I did.

(Morning) I sense that in that lifetime as Mary, I vowed to take care of everybody that type of thing had happened to and that I wanted to help everyone who was suffering.

That would help explain the magnetic connection between me in this lifetime and relatives, friends, and me in previous lifetimes. It's like I vowed to reach back in time later on and make things right. But it isn't my place to be there to help everybody! I decided to cancel that vow. Speaking aloud, I said:

"I cancel the vow I made to take care of everybody who is suffering. And, if I made vows similar to that in other lifetimes, I cancel those vows also."

(At Fern's) Did the Holy Spirit help open up that memory so I would become aware of my vow to help everybody who had suffered abuse and cancel it? [| Y |]

Does my desire to help people who were victims of sexual abuse create a magnetic connection between those people and me? [| Y |] Does placing everyone in God's care clear those connections? [| Y |]

Father-Mother God, I place everybody in Your care!

(Feb 5, '14) Holy Spirit, lately, I feel like steering clear of Pastor Joyce, the pastor at Mercy Church, where I attend. Am I afraid of her? [| Y |]

(!!!) Was Pastor Joyce my Dad in my lifetime as Mary, in which he made me work as a prostitute to earn money? [| Y |] Did he use me sexually, too? [| Y |]

Holy Spirit, if a Soul needs help, does it sometimes need to be placed in a "spiritual helicopter" or "healing ball" to be lifted from where it is? [| Y |] Would you suggest I ask for that help for Mary's Soul? [| Y |]

Mary's guardian angel and helpers, please go to where her Soul is and take her to Heaven Hospital. Thank You!

I saw angels place Mary's Soul in a healing ball of light and carry her to Heaven Hospital. Thank You, God!

(Feb 14, '08)   LAURA, IN BONDAGE

I told Fern that the prayer service at a funeral home that I attended for *Lonnie,* a member of Mercy Church who died unexpectedly three months ago, felt "heavy." Holy Spirit, are a lot of Souls hanging around that funeral home and other funeral homes that haven't gone to the light? [| Y |]

The following Sunday, I created a positive vortex during the church service for Souls to go to the light, particularly Lonnie and

Souls hanging around local funeral homes. I felt strong upliftment several times, especially while we were singing.

(I called Fern.) Did Lonnie's Soul go to the light this morning? [| Y |] Did other Souls go to the light that had been hanging around funeral homes? [| Yes, a great many. |]

Is Lonnie's Soul still in need of ministry? [| N |] Does he understand that Father God has forgiven him? [| Y |] Even though he is on the other side, is he trying to have me think of him as special? [| Y |] Is his Soul with me now? [| Y |]

I was uncomfortable with that, so I said, "Lonnie, I don't want you near me. Leave now!"

Did Lonnie leave? [| Y |] Is there a reason from another lifetime why I feel almost an aversion towards him? [| Y |] Were we partners in that lifetime? [| No, but he wanted to be. He raped you. He wants forgiveness and acceptance. |] Is he staying out of my apartment and car? [| Yes, but he is at church. |]

The next day I said aloud, "I forgive you, Lonnie. Bless you!"

(Feb 3, '13)   Connection: Lonnie's and My Souls

I asked the Holy Spirit questions about Lonnie and learned more about him. He was Louie, and I was Laura[MP] in the lifetime that he raped me. Louie died before Larua did

When Louie died, his Soul entered Laura and stayed with her for the rest of her life. She didn't feel entirely free in whatever she was doing. Most of Laura's Soul went to the light when she died, but part of it was enmeshed with Louie's Soul in the astral plane.

Lonnie's Soul and the portion of Laura's Soul that is enmeshed with it are asking for help to clear the enmeshment between their Souls and between their Souls and Louie's Soul.

(Feb 6, '13) I went through a process of forgiveness between Laura and Louie, then cleared Soul enmeshment between Laura and Lonnie, Laura and Louie, and Lonnie and Louie. Guardian angel of each of those Souls, please guide them to the healing ring surrounding their Full Soul. Thank you!

Holy Spirit, is Lonnie's Soul in the healing ring that is around his Full Soul? [| Y |] Is Laura's Soul in the healing ring that is around her Full Soul? [| Y |]

Is Louie's Soul in the healing ring that is around his Full Soul? [| No. It is in the astral plane for him to learn what he needs to learn. |] Thank You, Holy Spirit!

End of 3-C: MARY^{MP} AND LAURA^{MP}

CHAPTER 4

CONNECTED ACROSS LIFETIMES
Healing for Prior Lifetimes: Lee & Me 2, Ron & Me 1

Mar 24, '10   LOVE CONTACT POINTS

Are portions of Mom's Soul with me?

[| <FERN> Small portions of your Mom's Soul are with you from her recent lifetime as your mother, but it isn't a problem. Small portions of Souls are with their loved ones as a contact point between them. Contact points get established between the Souls of parents and children, husbands and wives, lovers and friends. Those contact points give both persons (Souls) a sense of belonging and being loved. Through them, people sometimes sense that their loved one is in trouble or has died.

Everyone has a love contact point with God, but that connection is such that every portion of one's spirit, body, and Soul is connected with God. That connection cannot be broken or dissolved because each of you is one with God. |]

Do portions of Mom's Soul feel vituperative towards me?

[| <FERN> No, and that is a great blessing! She and you have shared many lifetimes. When things work out that two Souls benefit greatly from relating with each other in one lifetime, they often choose to share more lifetimes. |]

While you were alive, were portions of your Soul with me?

[| <FERN> Not within your Soul, but our Souls meshed while we spent time together. That brought much healing for our Souls, including some of our Souls from prior lifetimes. |]

Thank you for telling me that, Fern! That's special.

Apr 2, '10. Father, do parts of me feel vituperative towards me? [| Y |] Are those parts partially split from my Soul?

[| Yes. You learned that you have partial personalities within your system. Some of them have chosen to be vindictive. |]

> vituperate vi. to speak abusively to or about; berate, revile (Web p. 1599)

(!!!) Are some of those parts that feel vituperative towards me portions of my Soul from previous lifetimes of mine?

[| Yes. Sometimes, a portion of a Soul that strongly disagrees with its Parent Soul will split off. Since that portion is from the same Parent Soul that all the person's other Souls come from, it has no problem attaching itself to or joining with a later Soul of the same person. |]

Father God speaks about the parental parts of Souls (the Parent Soul) being with Him:

> "All the spirits that emerged have subsequently fragmented because they were unable to hold themselves together without the Will presence which they rejected, denied or lost. I have the parental parts of these Spirits with Me now, and they are still a great presence even without their missing parts" (Original p. 69).

Apr 8, '10. Fern, is the itchiness in my eyes the last 2-3 days a sign of Souls asking for prayer? [| Y |] Is it triggered by the Soul of my brother-in-law Jared who died two days ago?

[| <FERN> A fair amount of it is. Some of it is related to Mollie and Grandma Leigh. They are anxious about getting freer soon. Tell them they may not be here at this time. |]

Thank you, Fern. I'll do that.

A new topic: Fairly often, I have had a pulling sensation in my abdomen when my son Chad is hurting. Do I have an umbilical cord connection with him of the same type my mother had with me and my brothers and sisters? [| Y |]

Does that umbilical cord draw energy only from him?

[| <FERN> No, it goes both ways, but the giving of energy is the main pattern. That does not mean that the connection is beneficial, however. An umbilical cord is a spiritual pathway, a type of soul tie not part of the original design of how God fashioned people's bodies and spirits to interrelate. It is a part of the learning process for human beings. []

Does that spiritual umbilical cord contribute to the muscle spasms that Chad is having as he heals from surgery?

[| <FERN> That can't help but be the case because it is a pathway that energies can follow. Being anxious about how he is doing also affects him somewhat. []

Should I ask the Holy Spirit to thin out that umbilical cord connection slowly?

[| <FERN> Yes. It is wise to spread it over several days. The easiest thing for you to do would be to tell Chad in spirit what you plan to do and why and ask his Soul for permission. Then, give the Holy Spirit permission to thin out and eventually dissolve the spiritual umbilical cord. That way, you will not need to worry about it anymore.

To save yourself from trying to figure out which of your other children you have that type of detrimental soul tie with, do the same process for each of them individually, not as a group. []

Thank you, Fern! Bless you!

Holy Spirit, please place a protective valve in the spiritual umbilical cord between Chad and me to prevent anxiety from affecting either of us. Please thin it out and dissolve it when the time is right. Thank You, Holy Spirit!

May 10, '10   MAJOR AREA TO FREE UP

Father God, would You like to say something?

[| Lorrie, you were thinking about how you are doing overall. You would say you are "caught up on what you need to do." You relax between times so you can return to accomplishing things. It is not so much a "spirit of accomplishment" that is pushing you to do and do, but a "need to accomplish." That need is based on what you believe about yourself, life, and doing things that are "worthwhile."

Anything that a being does, whether that being has positive or negative energy, is worthwhile. Breathing, sleeping, eating, and playing games are all worthwhile.

You think you have not been affected much by the earlier teaching you received that "God will judge everyone as to what they did and did not do." Up to middle age, your mind stayed at the level of accepting everything the priests and sisters said was God's truth. Even after you learned and accepted as truth the freeing concepts taught in *A Course in Miracles*, a big part of you remained caught in cemented beliefs from your formative years.

For the most part, the completely-split and partially-split parts of you believe the old religious teachings. However, the main part of you does not fully trust the teachings in *A Course in Miracles*, either.

Your holding onto confining beliefs is a major area in which you need to be freed up, and, as with other inner healing processes, as you get freed up, many others will be freed along with you. I will guide your thoughts as you think about this message over the coming days. Bless you. []

Thank You, Father-Mother God! Bless You!

Jun 12, '10. Hello, Father God! Bless You!

[] Thank you for that blessing! When you bless somebody, it triggers a blessing for you from them in response!

To quite an extent, you still feel like you need to protect yourself, even in the safety of your home. That is a learned response, so you can "unlearn" it. When you notice you are tensing up, relax your muscles and say, "There is nothing to fear."

You have decided on your sister Ann as the person to share with about what has been going on with you, memories that have opened up, and so on. That is who the Holy Spirit wants you to share with. Good night now from Fern and Me! []

Good night, dear Father God! Good night, Fern, dear one!

Jul 5, '10   Pent-Up Anger

Holy Spirit, years ago, I received the understanding that I had rage within me. Is there a ball of anger within me?

[| You do not have a "ball" of anger, but you do have bottled-up anger within you that you are dealing with in the same way that you dealt with early childhood trauma and with having a secretive relationship with Lee while yet married to Ron: You blocked it out of your mind. It is as though the anger does not exist to you, but deep down, you are almost deathly afraid that it might break loose and take over your person. |]

The topic of anger has come up many times. I have somewhat believed there is anger within me, but that's as far as things went. I hope some of it dissipated when I expressed anger toward my Dad and Ron in writing.

Holy Spirit, do You have a suggestion for what to do about the blocked-up anger and when? If it were up to me, I would leave things as they are, at least for now.

[| Lorrie, leaving the anger pent up is not safe. It could explode unexpectedly. Each day, a shield is placed around it as you ask for a shield around all nonbeneficial energies.

I suggest picturing a release valve at the top of the "iron room" where the anger is stored. Bless that energy of anger in being what it is and inform it that it can begin escaping through that spiritual release valve, a small amount with each exhale of your breath. Ask for flexible bronze tubing from the release valve extending into a suitable area of the astral plane.

I join you now in creating that. Also, we place a bronze spray head on the end of the tubing that transmutes the energy of anger back to neutral energy. (I pictured doing that.) There, it is in place!

While that blocked anger is leaving your body, you may feel out of sorts towards someone at times, possibly even God. That would be resonance from anger that is leaving. Bless that energy again at those times, and love and bless yourself as you are. This process is a spiritual version of draining fluid from the physical body. |]

What should I do about the "iron room" the anger is in?

[| A portion of your Soul became like steel in response to you wanting strong protection around the anger. Once the anger has dissipated, you can ask that part of your Soul to soften up and return to normal.

As the anger is released, you may recall hurtful situations and feel yourself responding with anger. It will be wonderful if that happens, for you will have the chance to release the ties that the anger has to those situations! Take deep breaths and thank God for removing some of the fetters from your Soul.

Your Soul is rejoicing so much right now, Lorrie, that you would not believe it, both your current Soul and your Full Soul! I am rejoicing, and Father God is saying, "Let us rejoice! For this child of Mine has returned home!" Go in peace. []

Aug 15, '10   HEALING AFTER SURGERY

Today is the first time since having major surgery two weeks ago that I have the energy to sit and listen. Thank You, Father-Mother God, for being with me during and after the surgery and that I am healing nicely. Thank you for your help, Fern!

[| <FERN> You are welcome, Lorrie! So that you know, I was with you during surgery, while you were in the hospital, and while you were at your sister Ann's place for four days afterward. Your mother was with you that whole time, too. The time you spent with Ann benefited both of you spiritually. []

[| (Father God) Ask for healing for the areas of your body that need healing and believe it will happen. Also, tonight, ask the Medical Assistance Team to minister to you while you sleep.

The top of your head has felt somewhat hot lately, causing discomfort. Ask often for a Holy Spirit shower to flow through you to clear residue and to flow through everyone who needs assistance. Continue saying *The Lord's Prayer* and extending blessings often to your family and friends who need assistance. Those prayers will help both them and you.

I realize it will be difficult for you to begin sharing your past and present struggles and some of the more intimate details of your life with your sister Ann because, except for counselors, you haven't shared much with anybody. Begin by sharing a few things with her and see how it goes. Sharing with her will be of great benefit to both of you. Peace! []

Thank You, Father-Mother God!

Oct 29, '10   Picking Up Vibes from Parts

I have had pressure in my head lately. Is someone I visited with recently asking for prayer?

[| No. The stronger vibrations of neediness you are feeling come from young Lorrie and young Sylvia[P]. You have lowered some of the barriers of protection you have had in place since grade school to protect yourself from the "badness" of those parts. You are picking up vibes of yearning and desperation from them that they have lived with for years. You now know that neither of them will hurt you. Accepting their actions and reactions as being your actions and reactions will not hurt you.

That is the next step the Holy Spirit wants you to take, Lorrie: To fully accept these two younger parts of yourself and all other parts that are real parts of your person.

As you love and bless every part of yourself and receive them without judgment, you also receive and love everyone else without judgment, thereby helping free them from shame and guilt. Have a nice evening, Lorrie. []

Dec 9, '10   A REAL BREAKTHROUGH!

(!!!) I thought *Marcie* was a part of me, but she showed up in a dream wearing a white First Communion dress. The next thing, she was in bed with my daughters. She might be:

1. A portion of Grandma Leigh's Soul,
2. A portion of my cousin Marcie's Soul, who wanted to be a sister but died in a car crash at age 10,

3. Part of my Soul from a previous lifetime in which Mollie was my mother. I have a connection with Mollie because she is my godmother.

Father God, should I ask Marcie to leave?

[| Lorrie, this is a real breakthrough for you to pinpoint that this Soul portion that is with you is not part of your real person! She has been hoping you will not put two and two together. She is a young portion of Mollie's Soul who wanted to enjoy wearing the First Communion dress Mollie sewed for you. With part of her Soul being with you, Mollie had a basis for thinking of you as her daughter.

Please destroy the pictures of you taken at your First Communion. Bless that Soul portion that you call Marcie and tell her she is a part of Mollie's Soul, not yours, and that she has to leave. Ask her guardian angel to guide her where she is meant to be. Also, tell Marcie she may not return. |]

I tore up my First Communion pictures, blessed Marcie, and explained to her that she isn't a part of my Soul and has to leave and may not return. I asked her guardian angel to guide her to where she was meant to be and told her to leave.

4-A: LEE, DARIN^LP, DARLA^MP, DARIN^2

Note: ^LP (Lee Prior life) is omitted after Darin, ^MP (Me Prior life) after Darla, and ^YS (Young Soul) after Nate and Paulie in this section.

(Mar 24, '10)   DARIN^2 WAS WITH LEE

Was the Darin^2 portion of Darin's Soul with Lee since birth?

[| No, it first hung around him during puberty to get a thrill from his sexual activity. Then, at a time when Lee was feeling very passionate and on the verge of forcing himself on a young woman, it entered him, and the added impetus of, "I don't care how you are feeling, I'm going to take what I can get," resulted in Lee raping the woman.

The spirit of lust also entered Lee at that time. It was attached to Darin[2], a split-off of Darin's Soul. Lee's choosing to act under its influence allowed it to enter his Soul. |]

Was Lee under the influence of lust when he didn't think I was serious in saying, "No!" and I became pregnant with Nita? [| Y |] Was he also under the influence of the unloving energy of Darin[2] at that time? [| Somewhat. |]

(Jul 18, '10)   Darin and Darla Are Grateful

[| <FERN> I constantly pray for you, Lorrie. I have seen dark forces trying to encroach on you several times since I crossed over. The Young Souls are doing tremendously well in protecting you. They are grateful each time you think of them and wish them well.

Darin and Darla are very grateful for your ministry and love for their boys, Nate and Paulie, and for being willing to let the horror, shock, and sadness associated with their death in a car accident surface and get expressed through you. They credit your empathy for them with helping them heal their relationship. They say, "Thank you, Lorrie! God bless you in who you are and in who you are coming to be!" |]

You are welcome, Darin and Darla! Thank you, Fern!

(Oct 2, '10)   MINISTERING TO DARLA AND ME

Am I being affected by Darin[2]'s negative energy?
[| Darla still has a soul tie with Darin[2]. You and Darla are from the same Full Soul, so yes, you are affected by his energy.
1. Ask Darla to join you in clearing detrimental soul ties and enmeshments between Darin's and Darin[2]'s Souls from every lifetime and her Souls.
2. Clear the detrimental soul ties and enmeshments between your Souls and Darla's, Darin's, and Darin[2]'s Souls from every lifetime.

3. Clear the residue from Souls and negative energies from your Soul in this lifetime and all other lifetimes.

4. Ask for healing for your aura and every part of you that needs healing in this lifetime and all other lifetimes, which includes your lifetime as Darla. []

I asked the Ministry Team to join me as I did that clearing and healing. Thank you, Ministry Team!

(Afterward) Father God, are there still detrimental soul ties between Darla's and Darin[2]'s Souls?

[| No. They are all cleared. Darla is very grateful. |]

Are there any remaining detrimental soul ties between Darla and Darin? [| No. They have a good relationship now. |]

Do I still have a detrimental soul tie with Darin? [| N |] Good.

(Jan 2, '11)   Clearing for Our Family Lines

DREAM: My daughter Lori, 6, was by the pantry. Half-grown daddy long-leg spiders began showing up on the shelves and pantry door. Lori calmly picked them up and squashed them between her fingers. (My alarm woke me.) END.

Do Lori's and Nita's family lines need clearing? That would be Lee's and my family lines.

[| Yes. Lori's and Nita's family lines need clearing. You have learned about Lee having shady connections with negative energies. That is the next step for you to take, to clear the *Lee and Lorrie family lines*. In particular, clear negative spirits that are overhanging your family lines.

Also, clear the *Ron and Lorrie family lines*. Much of it will overlap, but Lee's and Ron's previous lifetimes play a part in the spiritual condition of the family condition at present. Include Lori's and Nita's current and past lifetimes and the lifetimes of the young Souls that are with you.

Roots of negative energies may have to be cleared in the present and past lifetimes of each of them and in your present and past lifetimes. You do not have to figure out where such roots originated. Just cover all the bases. []

For Lee and me, the young Souls that clearing would apply

to: Nate and Paulie from our lifetimes as Darin and Darla; Jacinta, Bryce, and Fannie Mae from an earlier lifetime; and Teri (miscarried) and Elaine (stillborn) from this lifetime.

For Ron and me, the young Soul that clearing would apply to is Patrick (Patty's twin who died in utero).

(Jan 4, '11) For Lee's and my family lines and our children, and Ron's and my family lines and our children: I cleared unloving Souls and negative energies, returned Soul portions to others, dissolved detrimental soul ties, placed protective valves in remaining soul ties, and asked that each person (Soul) be healed and filled with the light of Christ.

A week later: Are family lines cleared for Lee, me, and our children? [| Y |] Are they cleared for Ron, me, and our children? [| N |] I will do more clearing.

(Sept 20, '11)   Clearing Curses from Our Families

Are any curses hanging over Lee? [| Y |] Over Lee's and my children in this lifetime: Lori, Nita, Teri^{YS}, and Elaine^{YS}? [| Y |]

I did a clearing for curses that were hanging over Lee and our children. Are all curses cleared from Lee? [| Y |] From Lori, Nita, Teri, and Elaine? [| Y |] Thank You, Holy Spirit!

Are any curses hanging over Ron? [| Y |] Over Ron's and my children? [| Y |] Over the families of some of our children? [| Y |] Will clearing the curses hanging over Ron also clear whatever curses are hanging over our children and their families? [| Y |] Will it also clear any curses hanging over our grandchildren? [| Y |] Wonderful!

(Sept 30, '11) I did a clearing for curses hanging over Ron, me, and our children in this lifetime and all other lifetimes. I asked God to forgive us for any thoughts, words, or actions that would draw a curse down on us.

Are all curses cleared from Ron connected with previous lifetimes? [| Y |] Connected with current lifetimes? [| Y |] Are all curses cleared from Ron's and my family? [| N |]

(Oct 28, '11) I did a clearing again for curses that were hanging over Ron and our family. Are all curses cleared from our family? [| Y |] That's wonderful!

Are any *karmic curses* hanging over Ron in this lifetime or previous ones? [| Y |] The energy of those curses would affect Ron, my children, and me. Should I do a clearing for those karmic curses at some point? [| Y |] I will also do a clearing for karmic curses hanging over Lee because those curses would also affect our children and me.

(Dec 15, '11) I cleared karmic curses from Ron and Lee connected with this lifetime and previous ones. Are all of them cleared from Ron? [| N |] From Lee? [| Y |]

Holy Spirit, I have had stomach discomfort again for the last two weeks. Is that discomfort caused by one or more portions of unloving Souls being in my abdomen, as has happened in the past? [| Y |]

Do those Soul portions want help to become loving?
[| Yes. The way to help Souls become loving is to extend much love and blessings to them for quite some time. It would also help to clear erroneous early imprinting for them. |]

Are the unloving Soul portions in my stomach and the portions of unloving Souls in my head from the same Soul? [| Y |] Are they portions of Lee's Soul from this lifetime? [| N |] Are they portions of his Soul from a previous lifetime? [| Y |] (!!!) Portions of Darin[2]'s Soul? [| Y |]

I said, "Bless you, Lee!" quite often lately. Did saying Lee's name permit the unloving portions of his Soul from his previous lifetime as Darin to enter me? [| Y |] Did You allow them to enter because they were asking for love? [| Y |] Is Lee still in great need of prayer? [| Y |]

(Mar 26, '12)   I Cancel Unwise Promises

Are portions of Lee's Soul with me, whose energy is detrimental to me?
[| Yes, within adult you and within parts of you. |]
Am I hanging onto one or more of those Soul portions?
[| Parts of you are. |]

Did I promise Lee in this lifetime or in a previous one that I would never let go of him? [| Y |] I will cancel that.

Aloud: "I cancel the promise that I made to Lee in this life or a previous lifetime that I would never let go of him."

Bless you, Lee! I ask kindly and command that you leave!

(Feb 8, '15) I learned from the Holy Spirit that in a previous lifetime, I promised to be available to help Lee's Soul in every lifetime of his. Because of that promise, Souls from some of Lee's lifetimes have asked me for help in various ways.

Aloud: "I cancel the promise I made to Lee that I would be available to help him in every lifetime."

(Dec 10, '15) Did I promise Lee that I would never love anyone else? [| Y |] I need to cancel that promise!

Aloud: "I cancel the promise I made to love only Lee. I declare that I am free to love whomever I choose."

Is that promise canceled now? [| N |] Oh! I need to choose that for every lifetime!

Aloud: "Speaking for every lifetime, I declare that I will always love Lee but that I am free to love others, as well."

Is my promise to love only Lee canceled? [| Y |] I am glad about that. It feels good to have those ties cleared.

End of 4-A: LEE, DARIN[LP], DARLA[MP], DARIN[2]

4-B: MARIE[GM], TONY[RP], HAROLD[LP], KATHERINE

Note: [RP] (Ron Prior life) is omitted after Tony, [GM] (Grandma/Me Prior life) after Marie, [LP] (Lee Prior life) after Harold, [MP] (Me Prior life) after Marie[1], and [GP] (Grandma Prior life) after Marie[2] in this section.

(Jul 5, '08)   GRANDMA LEIGH: MY SOUL MATE

Are a Soul and their soul mate portions of a Soul that split? [| Y |] Does it refer to the most recent split of the Soul? [| Y |]

Do I have a soul mate? [| Y |] Is it female? [| Yes, and she is directly related. |] Is she on the other side? [| Y |] After asking about others: Is Grandma Leigh my soul mate? [| Y |]

I will call the Soul that split into Grandma Leigh's Soul and my Soul **Marie**. Grandma and I were the "same Marie." It wasn't just that individual Soul that split, though. The Full Soul split that Marie's Soul was a part of. I will call the new Souls "Grandma Leigh's Full Soul" and "my Full Soul."

Did the split occur before a portion of Grandma Leigh's Full Soul came to Earth as Mavis Leigh? [| Yes. That was the first lifetime of Grandma Leigh's Full Soul after the split. |]

Was part of my Soul with Mavis Leigh (who became my grandmother) during her lifetime? [| Y |] Were our Souls somewhat connected both then and now? [| Y |]

(Jul 13, '08)   Prayer for Grandma at Death

I feel jittery. Is Grandma Leigh affecting me?
[| <FERN> Yes. Grandma Leigh suffered from jittery spells like you are experiencing this evening, but something more needs clearing that is affecting your Soul and your mother's. |]

Evening: I put Grandma Leigh's picture in the large copper ring. Then, as I pictured her sitting in a chair with family members from her recent lifetime and earlier lifetimes present with her in spirit, I prayed for healing for her family lines.

I felt led to pray for Grandma Leigh at the time of her death, using pillows on the couch to represent her. (She died relatively young from a ruptured appendix). I blessed her love relationship with Uncle Mike, told her she could still be with her family and help them after she died, and that great healing for families would come from her family line.

I spoke for Grandpa Leigh, Uncle Mike, and each of her children, blessing her, asking her for forgiveness if needed, and saying goodbye with many tears. Then the Angel of Peace came to take her Soul with him. I saw her spiritual body rise out of her physical body as she left with the angel. Very powerful! Thank You, Father God, for further healing for the family!

(Mar 28, '10)   Grandma Leigh in My Apartment

(Fern relayed the Holy Spirit's answers to me.) Was Grandma Leigh in my apartment yesterday? [| Yes. She feels she has the right to be with you, which benefits you. |]

Did her presence cause or add to my headache? [| Her energy level is quite different than yours, which added tension. |]

Does the Holy Spirit say Grandma Leigh shouldn't be near me now and for some time? [| Y |]

Does a person have the right to command their lower-energy-level soul mate to stay away from them?
[| Yes. Making that command will place a solid protective shield around that Soul. |]

Grandma Leigh, I ask and command in the name of Jesus that you stay away from me until your energy level is compatible with mine. Leave now! (I coughed to assist her Soul in leaving.) Thank You, Holy Spirit!

Grandma Leigh's low energy level indicates that she needs clearing. Did the needed clearing related to Grandma's and my lifetime as Marie take place?
[| Most of it is. You can't prevent being affected by family pressure from that lifetime since what needs clearing is both hers and yours. Being open to your emotions and what is trying to surface through your dreams is the best thing you can do about it. The prayers you are saying for Grandma Leigh will help clear what needs to be cleared and help heal what needs to be healed. |]

(Apr 3, '10)   MARIE AND TONY, KATHERINE

I hesitated to face the issues I sensed were about to open up regarding Grandma Leigh's/my lifetime as Marie.

Fern said in my thoughts, "You know what you need to do." I broke down crying, touched by her loving concern. My emotions have been blocked lately, so release and healing for Grandma and me would be wonderful.

(Fern relayed the Holy Spirit's answers to me.) Is the presence of unloving Souls in my head related to Grandma's lifetime just before her lifetime as Marie? [| Y |]

I asked the Holy Spirit questions and learned that Marie was married to **Tony**. She had an affair with a neighbor, **Harold** (married to Wilma.) Marie and Harold had a child, **Katherine**.

Holy Spirit, to help with clearing and healing for my Soul as Marie, do You suggest that I ask Katherine for forgiveness? [| Yes. Even if Katherine only sensed it in her spirit, being an illegitimate child in that day and age was very difficult. |]

Tony and Marie's Relationship

Was Ron (my former husband in this lifetime) my husband Tony in that lifetime? [| Y |] Did Tony suspect that Marie was having an affair? [| Y |] Was Marie deathly afraid of him? [| Y |]

Did Tony abuse Marie physically? [| Y |] Sexually? [| Yes, but we won't get into details. |] Did he have an unloving Soul? [| Yes, he was pretty much caught up with that type of energy because of his experiences as a young child and growing up, but he came into that life as a loving Soul. |]

(!!!) Did Tony kill Marie? [| No, but he came close to doing so. Father God sent angels to protect her. |]

Did Marie end up killing Tony? [| No, but in her mind, Marie had strong inclinations to do it. Only the grace of God held her back. The stronger thoughts about killing him did not come from her, though.

She was influenced by the spirit of murder, which is related to the spirit of death. So, when you pray for healing for that lifetime, pray specifically for clearing those negative spirits from you and your family in that lifetime and other previous lifetimes. |]

Before coming into this lifetime, did Ron's Full Soul and my Full Soul choose that we would get married so I could make up for my ill will towards him in our lifetime as Tony and Marie? [| That is one reason why you married Ron. I will gently suggest something, though: It may be tempting to want to learn details about many situations. Please stay attuned to the Holy Spirit so when questions come to mind, you will sense if you are meant to ask them. []

That's a good suggestion, Fern. Thank you!

Harold's and Marie's Relationship

(Fern relayed the Holy Spirit's answers to me.) Was Harold a previous lifetime of Lee's? [| Yes. The purpose of coming to Earth to live as humans is for continued growth and healing. Souls closely connected spiritually often choose to share lifetimes in one relationship or another. []

Was Marie somewhat split, with part of her trying to stay proper and the other part wanting to be with Harold?
[| Yes. It is natural for people who were taught to live a godly life to feel conflicted over making such a choice. Tony's abuse played a big part in pushing Marie over the line. []

Was Marie's relationship with Harold a love union?
[| Yes, but it being out of the bounds of propriety spoiled it somewhat for both of them. Although rather unrefined, Harold was a kind, loving man. He was very happy to have a daughter with Marie. []

I'm glad! Was Harold affected by the spirit of lust?
[| Yes, and for some time Marie was, also. The spirit of lust was cleared before she died, but much residue remained. []

Did Harold have an unloving Soul?
[| Yes. Harold did not know that while he was alive, but after he passed on, things worked out for his Soul to go to its rightful place. He is no longer "around somewhere" where he can negatively affect Marie's Soul, Katherine's Soul, or the Souls of any of Katherine's descendants. However, Katherine's Soul and several Souls of her descendants are still dealing with unloving energies permeating their family line. []

Did Marie pick up unloving Souls that had been with Harold?
[| She picked up portions of unloving Souls from him. []

When Marie's Soul split during (after?) that lifetime, did some of those portions of unloving Souls remain with Grandma Leigh's Soul and some with my Soul? [| Y |] Did some of the lust residue remain with each of us? [| Y |]

Are portions of those unloving Souls still with Grandma Leigh's Soul? [| Y |] Are they sealed with spiritual lead? [| N |]

Does Father God want me to ask for that?

[| No. Father God wants you to allow your emotions related to Grandma Leigh's/your life as Marie to surface and for you to express them, freeing you and Grandma Leigh. |]

Were Harold and Uncle Mike prior lifetimes of Lee's? [| Y |] Wow! (!!!) I received understanding from the Holy Spirit:

Marie: While Marie (Grandma Leigh/I) was married to Tony, she had a love affair with a neighbor, Harold, who, as I just stated, was a previous lifetime of Lee's.

Grandma Leigh: While Mavis (Grandma Leigh) was married to Maury Leigh, she had a love affair with Maury's brother Mike, a previous lifetime of Lee's.

Me: While married to Ron, I had a love affair with Ron's brother Lee, a later lifetime of Harold's and Uncle Mike's.

The situation in Marie's (Grandma Leigh's/my) lifetime showed up in another lifetime for each of us because neither of us had gotten the guilt and anxiety worked through in "our" lifetime as Marie.

I also understood from the Holy Spirit that *Marie felt alienated from herself and from God when she died.*

Thank you, Holy Spirit, for telling me that.

(Apr 6, '10)   I Need to Ask for Forgiveness

(Fern relayed the Holy Spirit's answers to me.) I need to ask Tony for forgiveness for being unfaithful to him. I need to ask Harold's wife, Wilma, for forgiveness for having an affair with Harold. I sense that the Holy Spirit is prompting me to wash her feet in spirit and allow her to wash mine. That won't be easy, but I need to do it.

I could wash Nora's feet (Lee's wife) In spirit at the same time. That will be hard to do, but it's what I need to do.

[| That is what the Holy Spirit suggests for you to do. |]

I also should do clearing for Katherine, Marie's (Grandma Leigh's/my) daughter, and her family lines.

[| Yes. As you choose with your will to repent, you will be set free, and so will your daughter Katherine from that lifetime. |]

I'll close off, Fern. This has been wonderful. Thank you!

[| You are welcome, dear. Thank you for being open to the Holy Spirit's guidance. The coming release will help everyone. |]

Speaking as Marie, I asked Tony to forgive me for being unfaithful to him and asked Wilma to forgive me for having an affair with her husband, Harold. (I didn't do foot washing yet.)

(Apr 4, '10)   Clearing for Carnal Ties

(Fern relayed the Holy Spirit's answers to me.) (!!!) Is there a soul tie between Harold's Soul and Marie's/my Soul that I need to clear before I can clear the portions of unloving Souls that are with me?

[| Yes. There is a beneficial tie of spirit-to-spirit love between Marie's/your Soul and Harold's Soul, but also a carnal tie that is an aspect of the spirit of lust.

You have a strong emotional tie with Lee related to the love relationship you had (have) with him in this lifetime. You also have a carnal tie with Lee, like the one between Marie's/your Soul and Harold's Soul.

You are meant to learn about carnal ties and how to clear them so you can clear them for Marie (Grandma Leigh/you) and yourself. Other people will learn about that type of soul tie and how to clear them by sharing your story.

To clear the carnal ties between you and Lee and between Marie/you and Harold, you first need to fully disavow receiving any more carnal satisfaction from or through the spirit of lust. Choose with your will that you want it fully cleared from every part of your body, mind, and spirit.

Intend for Marie and you: While taking a shower, ask for a Holy Spirit shower to flow through your body, mind, and spirit to wash the spirit of lust out of your system. After the shower, thank God fervently for having cleared the spirit of lust, then ask for a Holy

Spirit shower to continue a few minutes longer to fill you with the holiness of God. []

Thank you, Fern, for helping me hear from the Holy Spirit!

(Apr 5, '10) I did a "shower clearing" to clear the spirit of lust from Marie's (Grandma's/my) Soul and Lee's and my Souls. Then I cut all detrimental soul ties between Marie's/my Soul and Harold's Soul and between Lee's Soul and my Soul.

Thank You, Holy Spirit, for the clearing that took place!

(The next day) Were detrimental soul ties between Marie's and Harold's Souls cleared yesterday? [| One was. |]

Are there other detrimental ties between Marie and Harold that need to be cleared?

[| Yes. The carnal tie isn't cleared, and the residue of the spirit of lust is attached to both of their Souls. |]

Is the carnal tie cleared between Lee and me?

[| Not completely, because, as you just realized, *you did not ask that Lee be cleared of the carnal tie.* That could taint the beneficial love connection between you and him. It is the same regarding clearing the carnal tie between Marie's and Harold's Souls. Please do not lose heart, though, Lorrie. Learning new things involves trial and error. You will get there.

The Holy Spirit wants you to wait until you feel well before praying for clearing, OK? |]

Yes, I'm happy to go along with that!

(May 20, '10) I did a clearing again for Marie's and Harold's Souls. Is the carnal tie cleared between them?

[| Not completely. Continue to bless their Souls. |]

Is the carnal tie between Lee and me fully dissolved?

[| Yes, it is. Father God is very happy that you are trying to stay open to loving Lee and receiving love from him on the Soul level. Please stay open. Your Soul needs nourishment. |]

(Apr 1, '10)   UNLOVING SOULS WITH KRISTEN

(Fern relayed the Holy Spirit's answers to me.) I felt good this morning, but the top of my head began hurting after I arrived at work. Were energies present that stirred up the portions of unloving Souls in my head?

[| Yes. Also, a portion of an unloving Soul in your abdomen reacted to low-level energies at your workplace. []

Are they attached to someone at work? [| Yes, to **Kristen**. []

I sense that a close relative of Kristen's has, or had, an unloving Soul, and Kristen is affected by that.

[| Yes. Also, portions of unloving Souls have been attached to her aura since birth, claiming her as one of their own. []

I sense I should pray directly with Kristen at some point for clearing for her and her family lines, but I should first pray for her for a while for spiritual and emotional healing, perhaps primarily for her inner child. [| You understood correctly. []

(!!!) I should first clear all portions of unloving Souls and negative and unloving energies from myself.

[| Yes, that is the first step when praying for healing for yourself or others. If a person is holding onto negative energies, those energies have the right to be with them. So, if someone has prayed for clearing negative energies or unloving Souls from other people and realizes that he (she) needs clearing for negative energies or unloving Souls, it would be wise to repeat the clearing they did for the other people. []

Thank you, Fern!

(Apr 4, '10)   Ties Between Katherine and Me

Note: Katherine was Marie and Harold's daughter.

(Fern relayed the Holy Spirit's answers to me.) Are unloving Souls waiting in the astral plane for the portions of their Souls in my head to be returned to them? [| Y []

Does an unloving Soul hang around Kristen at work?

[| Yes. That occurred to you because it is the case. []

Is the more pronounced sinus headache I have been having related to the presence of those portions of unloving Souls, signaling that they want to "get out"? [| Y |]

Were unloving Souls with Katherine during her lifetime? [| Yes. Katherine did her best not to be affected by them, bless her heart, thus protecting the Souls of her descendants who would otherwise have had much lower energy. |]

(!!!) Is Kristen a great- or great-great-granddaughter of Katherine's? [| Y |] That is why the Holy Spirit wants me to pray for Kristen and her family lines sometime. She is family! Has my Soul been holding onto the portions of unloving Souls that are with me until I learned that Katherine, my daughter in my lifetime as Marie, needs to be freed? [| Y |] Wow!

(Apr 09, '10)   Witchcraft Energies

(Fern relayed the Holy Spirit's answers to me.) Was Marie affected by witchcraft energies? [| Yes. When Grandma Leigh's/your Soul split after that lifetime, you both carried witchcraft energies. Those energies got cleared from you when you did clearing for yourself and the Leigh and Goerger family lines. Grandma Leigh needs more clearing. |]

Does Katherine need clearing for witchcraft energies? [| Yes. Witchcraft energies plagued that family line for several generations before she was born, and some attached themselves to her Soul. |]

Did witchcraft energies pass down to Katherine's grandchildren and great-grandchildren? [| Yes, to most of them. Your fellow worker, Kristen, a descendant of Katherine's, has witchcraft energies attached to her aura. The Holy Spirit has already said you are to pray with Kristen when the time is right. Please bless her and pray for her every day to help prepare the way. |]

I will do that. When I pray for clearing for Kristen and her family lines, will some of the witchcraft and other negative energies get cleared from Grandma Leigh, too? [| Y |] Wonderful!

(Apr 10, '10)   Clearing for Katherine and Myself

(Fern relayed the Holy Spirit's answers to me.) My stomach has been extremely unsettled the last few days. Does the larger portion of the unloving Soul in my abdomen want to leave? [| Y |] Did small portions of it leave with the burping I've been doing? [| Yes, small portions did. |]

Does the main portion of that unloving Soul plan to wait until the portion within Katherine's Soul is set free? [| Y |]

Would it be OK to do clearing soon for Katherine's family lines? [| Yes. Incorporation of the unloving Soul within cells in your abdomen is almost cleared. |]

Will that unloving Soul portion connect on its own with the portions of itself that are with Katherine?

[| Yes, but it would be good to say out loud, "Portions of unloving Souls that are in my abdomen and my head, I release you and command every portion of you to leave, including all portions that are with Katherine." Stay neutral about the portions of the unloving Soul, with no judgment.

After they leave, create a negative vortex outside and send negative residue into it from within and around you. Ask for a Holy Spirit shower to flow through your home, car, and you. |]

Thank you, Fern, Holy Spirit!

That afternoon, I cleared unloving Souls, the spirits of witchcraft and lust, and all other negative spirits from Marie's Soul and from Tony's and Marie's family lines.

I commanded the portions of unloving Souls in my abdomen and head to leave and take along the portions of their Souls that are with Katherine. I also commanded all portions of any other unloving Souls that were with Katherine to leave. Thank You, Holy Spirit!

(Apr 11, '10) Did some of the portions of the unloving Souls that were with Katherine leave? [| Y |] Did all of the portions of unloving Souls that were in my head leave?

[| One unloving Soul left, but portions of other unloving Souls didn't. |]

Did that clearing help Grandma Leigh? [| Yes. She can now join in praying for the full clearing of her family line. |]

(Apr 14, '10) My head feels much better than yesterday. Is that because I placed a protective shield around all portions of unloving Souls and lower-level energies that are present?
[| Yes. That helped a great deal. |] Did blessing the unloving Souls help? [| Blessing always helps. |]

Is the Holy Spirit directing me to clear the portions of unloving Souls from my head despite not feeling the best?
[| No. Never do clearing when you do not feel up to par. |]

Thank you, Fern!

(Apr 29, '10)   For Katherine's Family and Me

I did a clearing for Katherine and her family lines

1. I commanded all unloving Souls and negative energies to leave Katherine and everybody in her family lines.
2. I sent negative residue from Katherine and her family lines into a negative vortex to be transmuted to neutral or loving energy.
3. I cleared detrimental soul ties between Marie and Harold and Katherine and her Dad Harold.

Then, I did a clearing for myself for the portions of unloving Souls that were still within my head. By the time I finished, I felt so tired that I slept for an hour!

(Apr 30, '10) (Fern relayed the Holy Spirit's answers to me.) Did all unloving Souls leave Katherine?
[| Sizable portions of the unloving Souls left, but Katherine's Soul was unwilling to release them fully. The remaining portions are portions of some that are with her father Harold's Soul. She and Harold need prayer to heal their relationship. The detrimental soul ties between Katherine and Harold must be dissolved before the unloving Souls can be cleared. |]

Does Katherine need further clearing for negative energies?
[| She needs clearing for residue from the unloving Souls and negative energies. Praying for Kristen will help her. |]

Are all unloving Souls cleared from Marie?

[| Yes. Since Marie is you in that previous life, her Soul having been cleared of unloving Souls will help you feel better. |]

Is the spirit of lust cleared from Marie? [| It was mostly cleared through your prayers for clearing your family lines. It would be good, though, to clear negative residue again. |]

Are all unloving Souls cleared from Harold?

[| Not completely, but you do not need to worry about it because when you prayed for clearing for Katherine's family lines, you asked that all portions of unloving Souls and negative energies remain with those Souls be encased with a protective shield until those Souls become willing to release them. |]

Does the Holy Spirit want me to pray for Harold again?

[| Yes. Harold is family. What helps him helps you and your whole family. Blessing him now and then would help a lot. |]

Did more portions of the unloving Souls leave my head?

[| Yes, but they think they had the right to return. You still have a connection with Harold's Soul that permits them to stay. Like it is with Katherine, the portions of unloving Souls in your head are portions of the unloving Souls within Harold. |]

Did the portions of unloving Souls that left my head join the unloving Souls that left Katherine?

[| Yes, but you need to make it clear that they may not return, or your head will become even more uncomfortable than it is now. Ask to have three strong gatekeepers, protectors, at the base of your skull, which is the entryway to one's Soul. |]

Father God, please assign three powerful gatekeepers to the base of my skull. Thank You!

Holy Spirit, do You have other recommendations?

[| Get enough rest and do not let yourself get caught up with things that cause you to feel anxious. Do not watch violent TV programs or those likely to have very low vibration energy levels. Having classical music playing would help. Bless yourself often, and occasionally, ask for a Holy Spirit shower.

I will close off now. God bless you, Lorrie, dear one! |]

Bless You, Holy Spirit! Bless you, Fern, dear one!

Is Katherine ready to go to the light?

[| No. Katherine has a very loving Soul and yearns for her dad to go to the light at the same time she does. |]

That would be neat!

(Apr 17, '10)   HEALING FOR MARIE AT DEATH

Holy Spirit, is the bothersome headache I have had for over two weeks from unshed tears?

[| No. This pain is more throughout your muscles. |]

Is it mainly related to Grandma's/my lifetime as Marie?

[| Yes. That is the big thing that is surfacing now. It is reaching a peak as to the importance of what is on its way up and out and the eagerness of Marie's (Grandma's/your) Soul and your Soul in this lifetime to become free and happy finally. |]

I feel angry about "having to" have a headache so much of the time. I haven't done much about the anger because I feel trapped and helpless regarding having headaches. Does bottled-up anger play a role in causing me to have headaches?

[| Bottled-up anger is one of the causes of your headaches, but it is not currently a major cause. |]

I read in my notes from two weeks ago: "Marie felt alienated from herself and from God when she died." When Marie's Full Soul split into Grandma Leigh's and my Full Souls, did about half of those emotions go with Grandma Leigh's Soul and half with my Soul?

[| Yes, because neither half of Marie's Soul was free. |]

I broke down crying as I thought about Marie/me feeling alienated from herself/myself and from God as she/I was dying. She/I must have felt so lost!

With Marie feeling guilty about having an affair with Harold while married to Tony, she couldn't have been a fully accepting and loving mother to her daughter Katherine.

Katherine's inner child needs a lot of healing, and I sense that

Grandma Leigh's inner child and mine do, too. As I minister to *Katherine's* inner child, *Kristen's* inner child will also get ministered to.

Holy Spirit, please join me as I minister to the inner child of Marie and Katherine in that earlier lifetime. And Fern, please help me in whatever way you can.

[| I'll do that, Lorrie. You can count on it! |] Thank you!

(Apr 18, '10)   Deathbed Confession

As I thought about Marie/me feeling "alienated from herself (myself) and from God when she/I was dying," I suddenly wanted to have Pastor Eric minister to her/me In spirit back in that lifetime. I lay on the couch, covered with a sheet, and asked Pastor Eric to minister to Marie/me In spirit. Speaking as Marie, I told him how hopeless I felt and thought God could never forgive me. I confessed to committing adultery with a neighbor, Harold, and felt like killing my husband, Tony.

Through the Holy Spirit, I understood what Pastor Eric said in spirit: God forgives sin when a person acknowledges it, is sorry, and asks for forgiveness. He anointed Marie's/my forehead with blessed oil for when she/I would pass into eternity.

He also anointed my daughter Katherine. He asked God to put a protective shield around all unloving Souls that are with Katherine or around her.

It was a powerful, moving experience to go through that deathbed confession, to confess my sin aloud to God and a loving pastor. (I cried for a while.)

Father God, thank You for Your forgiveness and healing!

Holy Spirit, did that confession help Grandma/me a lot?

[| <FERN> Very much! I am happy for you and Grandma Leigh. God is true to His word. Healing is coming about! |]

Did the spirit of alienation get lifted from Marie's/my Soul back at the time of her/my death?

[| Yes. As soon as a Soul separates from its body, it is in the now of eternity. Your Soul confessed your wrongdoing and expressed sorrow to God about it, so you can depend on it that your Soul was freed from feeling alienated from God. More clearing is needed, but this is a major victory! |]

When Marie/I made a deathbed confession asking God for forgiveness for being unfaithful to Tony, did Grandma Leigh also ask Grandpa for forgiveness for being unfaithful to him?
[| She was aware of you making a deathbed confession as Marie and joined you fully in that action for that lifetime. That is as much of an answer as the Holy Spirit is giving, for you do not have responsibility for or need to be concerned about situations regarding Grandma Leigh's other Souls. |]

Thank you, Fern, Holy Spirit!

(May 10, '10) Did my repenting for having sinned in my lifetime as Marie clear karma for me related to that wrongdoing?
[| The karma has been cleared well enough that your Soul will not draw the same circumstances to you again. |]

Since Grandma Leigh and I were one Soul in that lifetime, has karma been cleared for her, also related to that lifetime?
[| You are separate Souls now. Your processing of the circumstances of that previous lifetime in which the two of you were one Soul helped her greatly. However, in this lifetime, you experienced with Lee a repeat of the situation that occurred in that previous lifetime and have worked through repentance and forgiveness concerning it that had nothing to do with Grandma Leigh. Where she is at regarding karma is for her to deal with.

If you still feel responsible for helping make things work out for Grandma Leigh, please let that go. Your relationship with her now is like with any other relative: to wish her well and bless her. |]

Thank you, Fern, Holy Spirit! That's a wise answer.

(May 1, '10)   An Encouraging Word

The times I felt like crying over the last few days (including a bit ago) might be emotions beginning to surface from my lifetime as Marie. Father God, do you want to say something?
[| Lorrie, you have a question in mind to ask Me:

"With so much clearing needed for the past and present, and

new incidents continuing to happen, how will I or anyone ever become clear of repressed emotions, guilt, etc.?"

Your next thought was, **"Is going through the process the purpose of it?"** The answer to that is yes. Going through the process is the purpose of the challenge. Life is about evolving, similar to the growing stage of plants, but you, human beings, and I do not stop growing. We grow and bloom, then grow and bloom some more.

I am experiencing all of this with each of you. I feel the pathos, rejection, and hurt, but those are just obstacles to be overcome that result in a more vibrant life. I repeat from earlier, "The living and the loving will make life worthwhile."

This saying fits here, too: "Anything worth achieving is worth striving for." We are in this challenging life together. We can sink or swim. Hope and courage say to swim. Life says to live. Bless you! []

Thank You very much, Father God! That helps a lot.

(Jul 4, '10) [| Please arrange to pray soon to clear Kristen and her family lines. She is Marie's descendant, so what needs to be cleared within her must also be cleared within the Leigh family lines. []

(Sept 23, '10)   RON: EVERY BIT AS IMPORTANT

I had a dream about Ron in which he was still trying to be with me sexually. I thought it might indicate that a portion of his Soul from an earlier lifetime was with me, so I commanded every part of his Soul from other lifetimes to leave.

Father God, was a portion of *Tony's* Soul with me?

[| Yes, in fact, quite a large portion. []

Did it leave?

[| Only part of it left because Marie's (Grandma's/your Soul) has unfinished business with Tony relating to that lifetime. []

Do I need to repent more fully for having had an affair with Harold? [| That is part of it. |] I also need to repent for looking down on Tony, for considering that I was better than he was. [| That is correct. [] And I need to repent for feeling that way about Ron in this lifetime. [| Yes. The Holy Spirit will help you. []

Did Ron's Soul choose to live that lifetime as Tony and his lifetime as Ron, with his Full Soul knowing ahead of time that Marie/I would be unfaithful to him during both of those lifetimes, with the express purpose of playing a vital role in bringing healing to our family lines and to the many other family lines that will be healed as people learn how to "heal across time"?

[| Yes, Lorrie. **And you had better believe that Ron's role in this undertaking is every bit as important and necessary as yours is or will be.** I say again, this process is the work of the whole Sonship. []

Thank You, Father! Please help me change my attitude.

(Sept 25, '10) While out walking, I apologized sincerely to Tony for being unfaithful to him and asked him to forgive me. I again apologized to Ron for being unfaithful to him and asked him to forgive me, and again asked Father God to forgive me. Thank you, Tony, Ron, and Father God, for forgiving me!

(Sept 29, '10)   Prayer for Kristen's Family Lines

Father God, my head has been very uncomfortable the last few days. Are people and Souls asking for prayer?

[| You are affected by distress from Grandma Leigh, Mollie, and Kristin at work. []

I mentioned to Kristen the idea of praying with her to heal her family lines. She said she was overwhelmed with her son's pending divorce but would like me to pray for her sometime. Father God, would it be OK for me to pray for clearing Kristen's family line without her being present?

[| Yes. Kristen gave permission and wants healing to take place in every necessary way. []

(Sept 30, '10) I prayed for clearing unloving Souls and negative energies from Kristen and members of her family lines. I asked that a protective shield be placed around those who have an unloving Soul and around all unloving Souls and portions of unloving Souls that are with any of them.

Thank You, Holy Spirit, for the healing that took place!

(Oct 2, '10) Are unloving Souls hanging around Kristen? [| N |] Are unloving Souls or portions of them within her?

[| There is a residue of unloving Souls within her. That will get cleared as you continue to bless her and ask for a Holy Spirit shower to flow through her. Ask that each day for Kristen and your other coworkers. |]

(!!!) Holy Spirit, does Kristen's mother have an unloving Soul? [| Y |] Should I ask for extra protection for Kristen?

[| No. Daily filling with the crystalline white light of Christ, the *Bless You Prayer*, and a *Holy Spirit shower* will be enough.

The effects of family (Soul) distress on you will soon lessen, Lorrie, enough that it will be very noticeable.

Father-Mother God and the whole universe thank you for your ministry to Kristen and her family lines, as do those Souls. It has helped Marie's and Grandma Leigh's Souls very much. If they could cry tears of happiness, they would be doing it! |]

Thank You, Holy Spirit! Thank you, Fern! Bless you!

(Dec 25, '10)   How Things Are with Me

Father God, is a portion of my Soul with Ron?

[| Yes. Through the years, Ron related with you the way a child does with their mother. A portion of your Soul is with him to nurture his Soul. Ron is not angry with that part of you, so there is no problem in that way, but a portion of Tony's[RP] Soul is with him, so I recommend you call that portion of your Soul back to you. |]

The portion of my Soul that is with Ron, please come back to me. I embraced myself and said, "Welcome back!"

Is a portion of Tony's Soul with me?

[| You have a connection with Tony's Soul, but no portion of his Soul is with you. You carry deep guilt for being unfaithful to him as Marie, his wife, during that lifetime. You felt then, and still feel, that you had to make up for your wrongdoing while thinking that it was too horrendous to be made up for.

I hope you are learning through My teaching and the teachings of *A Course in Miracles* that nothing is so horrendous as to cut you off from love. You remain a holy child of God through all experiences brought about by you or by others.

Please apply that teaching to yourself in this lifetime and every lifetime, Lorrie. Receive forgiveness, the undoing of all mistakes, from the Holy Spirit. Let Jesus see you as the holy child of God that you are and receive that as real.

You can make many mistakes while here on Earth, but all the while, you are (can be) growing in love and compassion. No condition is so set within you that I cannot heal you and bring good out of it. []

Thank You, Father God! Thank you, Fern!

[| <FERN> You are welcome, Lorrie! |]

(May 29, '10)   Portion of Marie²'s Soul With Me

(Fern relayed the Holy Spirit's answers to me.) Fern, it feels like parts of me are objecting to writing. Are all "parts of me" at this time portions of my current Soul? [| N |]

That might be tied in with Marie's Soul splitting into two Full Souls. Was one portion larger?

[| The question is not whether one portion was larger but "On what basis did it divide?" You have learned that a Full Soul sometimes divides when parts have too much disparity in their energy levels. That was the basis for the split of the Full Soul that was Marie's/your Soul: One portion was of a somewhat higher energy level, which your current Soul is a part of, and the other portion was of a more average energy level that Grandma Leigh's Soul is a part of. |]

Did that split take place while Marie was still living?

[| No, but the energy differences in your Full Soul at that time resulted in a regrouping of the individual Souls that were part of it. Marie's (Grandma Leigh's/your) Soul picked up on the regrouping and became a partially divided personality. That added to the stress that Marie/you felt. |]

I will call my portion of Marie's Soul **Marie**¹ and Grandma Leigh's portion **Marie**². Is a portion of Marie²'s Soul with me? [| Y |] Does she feel like she is a part of me? [| Y |]

Is the Marie^2 Soul portion incorporated within cells in my body? [| To some extent. |]

Does Marie^2 invite portions of her Full Soul to "visit" me? [| Yes, and while those portions are with you, they "eat at your table" and bask in your energy, causing ill effects for you. |]

Is more than one portion of Marie's Soul with me? [| Yes, a few portions of Marie's Soul are with you to benefit your Soul and hers. You can think of Marie's Soul as fully your Soul because, from your perspective, it was. From Grandma Leigh's perspective, it was fully her Soul. |]

Marie's husband, Tony, was abusive towards her. Ron is another lifetime of Tony's. Are the portions of Marie's Soul that are with me angry that I married Ron? [| Yes. Even though your Full Soul and Ron's Full Soul chose to get married in this lifetime, the portions of Marie's Soul that are with you still objected to it. |]

Are those portions of her Soul also angry that I didn't let Lee move in with me back in November '07? [| She was very angry about it, but you do not have to worry about her feelings. You have your feelings and emotions to sort through, and Marie's Soul has her feelings and emotions to work through. When your Soul or Marie's Soul releases negativity, expresses emotions, and chooses to be loving, it helps the other Soul tremendously. Still, neither of you is responsible for caring for the other one. I hope you get the idea. |]

Yes. We are not responsible for taking care of other people's problems, no matter the situation.

(Jun 1, '10)   INFESTATION BY MARIE^2'S SOUL

Holy Spirit, did Marie's Soul fully divide when she died? [| Y |] Is it correct that Marie^1's/my Soul had a somewhat higher energy level than Marie^2's/Grandma Leigh's Soul? [| Y |]

Did all of Marie[1]'s Soul return to the higher-energy Full Soul where it was supposed to go?

[| Not all of it. Some portions were restless and had karma that needed clearing. Those portions were in the astral plane for a while and then with you for several years. They returned to your Full Soul a couple of years ago after you had worked through the adultery situation. Marie[1] is praying for you and offering encouragement! |]

Thank you, Marie[1]!

Is it correct that the Marie[2] portion didn't all return to its Full Soul, either? [| Y |]

(!!!) I understood without words that portions of Marie[2]'s Soul were in the astral plane for a while. When the time came for my conception in this lifetime, they "got an idea." They moved close to the new Soul that was a part of my Full Soul as it awaited the time to inspirit the fertilized egg that was to become me. As the Holy Spirit breathed that new Soul into my body, those lower energy portions of Marie[2]'s Soul flowed in with it, intermingling with my Soul. Is that an acceptable way to describe what took place?

[| Yes, that's a general idea of what took place. Don't try to figure out more details. |]

I received the understanding years ago that I have "inner rage" and "war in my members." Is that rage within the portions of Marie[2]'s Soul that are with me?

[| Most of it is. You do have some rage within you that you have not uncovered and released as yet. |]

Does "war in my members" refer to the turmoil caused by "squatter" portions of Marie[2]'s Soul being with me?

[| Most of that phrase does. You do have skirmishes between some of the actual parts of you, though. Those will get settled as time goes on. It will help to have the "squatter" Soul portions cleared. |]

Two days ago, I began the Nine-Day Process of clearing the incorporation of the squatter portions of Marie[2]'s Soul from cells in my body, so in a week, those portions should no longer be incorporated.

Is there something else the Holy Spirit suggests to do?

[| Yes. Bless Marie[2]'s Soul and the "squatter portions" of her Soul that are with you. Ask the Holy Spirit to thin out and dissolve soul ties between your Soul and those squatter Soul portions. Ask that clearing and healing can begin even now for your Soul and those portions of Marie[2]'s Soul. Thank you for that, Lorrie! Bless you! |]

Holy Spirit, please take charge of thinning out and dissolving detrimental soul ties between my Soul and the squatter portions of Marie[2]'s Soul that are with me. Please begin clearing and healing my Soul and Marie[2]'s Soul. Thank You, Holy Spirit!

I spent several minutes talking to and blessing the portions of Marie[2]'s Soul that were with me.

(Jun 2, '10)   Squatter Souls Trigger Discomfort

Fern, about a week ago, I began having pain in my lower back that occasionally extends down my right leg to my ankle. A chiropractic treatment didn't help. I suspect that squatter portions of Marie[2]'s Soul are causing the pain.

[| <FERN> Yes, angry energy in the squatter Soul portions causes tightness and inflammation in your body tissues. A fair measure of that inflammation is related to portions of Marie[2]'s being incorporated within cells in your body.

The soreness set in when you learned about the infestation by Marie[2]'s Soul. Her Soul responded with fear because of not knowing what would be happening to "her," and also with anger, for that Soul fully believes it is a part of your Soul.

The best way to deal with this is to be kind and understanding toward those Soul portions. Explain things at least two more times. The Holy Spirit says to please be patient a while longer. You becoming free and clear along with many family members, and being able to pass the "how-to" along to everyone else is worth being patient! |]

I told those Soul portions to leave my back and right leg. Might that help with the soreness?

[| It is not likely that any command will bring about a change by the squatter Souls. The only effective action would be to address them with love and respect. They have begun to realize it doesn't make for comfortable living for them to be with you. Tell them you are taking steps to release the incorporation of their Souls from cells in your body and that in a week or less, they will be able to leave freely.

You are learning and applying this important lesson, Lorrie: Every being has the right to be itself, and you are to hold no judgment against anyone or any being. You are doing well in following that direction. |]

The course of action is to apply the remedy of love to all situations. Thank you, Holy Spirit!

(Jun 9, '10) Is Marie^2's Soul like a personality within me?

[| Yes, Marie^2's Soul is a separate personality that is making itself at home within you. That portion of her Soul has its own will and ideas, separate from your mind and will. I join you in blessing all of Grandma Leigh's Souls in every lifetime, including Marie^2. The separation of her Soul from yours is taking place. Just continue the process I gave you of "applying the remedy of love." |]

Thank You, Holy Spirit! Thank you, Fern!

(Jun 13, '10)   A Joyous Reunion

I have been extending steady love and blessing to the portions of Marie^2's Soul that are with me. During the church service this morning, I asked family members to be on hand to welcome those portions of Marie^2's Soul to the light to join her Full Soul.

As we began singing the second hymn, I sensed Marie^2's Soul was ready to leave. Prompted by the Holy Spirit, I whispered to her, *"Father God says you are forgiven."* I felt a strong upliftment, letting me know those Soul portions left! Bless you, Marie^2!

Did the portions of Marie^2's Soul that were with me leave during the church service this morning?

[| <FERN> Yes, they did. You were correct that the strong upliftment of spirit that you felt meant a release was taking place. |]

Did they join Grandma Leigh's Full Soul?

[| <FERN> Yes, and it was a very joyous reunion for them, for that Full Soul. They all say, *"Thank you and bless you, Lorrie!"*

Blessings and thanks to you, Lorrie, for achieving the clearing of the infestation of a portion of your Soul from an earlier lifetime. The whole universe is grateful to you, for this clearing is the prototype and example for an explosion of clearing of Soul infestation and incorporation that will be taking place amongst people!

Years ago, you received an impression that you would be like a battering ram to open the door for many women (people) to receive emotional healing. There is, will be, more to it than that. The Holy Spirit is flowing the message through you that clearing and healing are possible *and that ordinary people can do it.*

You are, of course, only one in a multitude of people and Souls working together to bring forth this healing message. Rejoice! Much has been cleared and accomplished, and much more will be! Father God says:

"It is all worth it, My people! When your energy is flagging, it does not mean the reservoir of spiritual energy has run dry. It means you need to seek refreshment for your Spirit. If you do not have one, keep your eyes open for somebody who can be your spiritual partner, somebody to pray with and support each other. You can have more than one.

"When you are hurting and running out of energy, please rest with and within Me. I am touched when you ask to sleep in My arms, for you are then more open to being refreshed as you sleep. Good night!"

I, too, say goodnight, Lorrie, and good night, good day, or good afternoon to whoever is reading this. Peace! []

Thank You, Fern! Thank you, Father God! ·

(Dec 9, '10)   Negative Forces at Work

[| Lorrie, your head is often uncomfortable because you have become more sensitive to lower-level energies. I mentioned this before: You might become aware that you are exposed to more negative energies at your morning workplace than your system can handle.

I know it would be a sacrifice for you to give up that part-time job, but your Soul is willing to do it in the interest of getting your primary task of the writing project completed. I will provide the finances, so do not worry about that.

Unloving Souls have been at your morning workplace that came in with customers, and a couple of times, one or two of them have been hanging around your fellow worker, Kristen. That energy still affects you even with protection in place. Please add each day, "Holy Spirit, I ask for a shield of glass gold around me for protection. Thank You!" I love you! []

(Dec 23, '10)   MY BOSS: A LIFETIME OF RON'S

Father God, my boss Warren's attitude reminded me of Ron this morning. (!!!) Is he another lifetime of Ron's?
[| Yes, he is. You learned recently about Tony, another lifetime of Ron's. Ron's Soul is very sympathetic to Tony's Soul. |]

Is a portion of Tony's Soul with Warren? [| Y |]

That's a recipe for disaster! If I continue working there, staying fully protected from Tony's animosity towards Marie would be almost impossible because she and I are from the same Full Soul.
[| It is up to you, but I recommend completing the procedure handbook and taking steps to close off working there. |]

Did that portion of Tony's Soul join Warren recently?
[| No, it has been with Warren since you began sharing your writings with Fern (four years ago). At that time, dark forces were already sizing up the situation to see how to prevent the distribution of the writings. |]

(Jan 8, '11) [| You wondered what I meant when I said a month ago that your Soul is willing to close off working at your morning job to complete your primary task of the writing project. By saying that, I inferred that you would have a difficult time with the energies there, enough so that it would be detrimental to your health, spiritual strength, and motivation. You will not be giving up something desirable in exchange for drabness.

Things will go well for you. Look forward to what Spirit will be doing in your life. []

Thank You, Father God!

(Jan 22, '11) I gave my 4-week notice for closing off my morning job. It turns out that my boss knows of a qualified person looking for part-time bookkeeping work!

[| Thank you, Lorrie, for being willing to follow the leading of the Holy Spirit. |]

You are welcome, Father God!

(May 26, '18) I suddenly felt very chilly. (!!!) Holy Spirit, is a part of me allowing any Soul to enter that wants to? [| Y |] Is a portion of Marie[2]'s Soul still with me and allowing Souls to enter? [| Y |] Is that portion of her Soul still connected with my Soul like we are Siamese twin Souls? [| Y |]

Do I have the right to tell Marie[2] that she may not allow Souls to enter without permission from my Full Soul? [| Y |] Would she have to agree? [| N |] Will she have the right to invite Souls as long as her Soul is enmeshed with mine? [| Y |]

Is Marie[2]'s Soul meant to get separated from mine? [| Y |] Are there some parts of me that would allow her to return? [| Y |] Would those parts like to leave with her? [| Yes. They are portions of her Soul masquerading as parts of you. |] Wow!

I asked the Ministry Team to join as I did a process of forgiveness between every part of Marie[2]'s Soul and my Soul, retroactive clearing of incorporation of her Soul from within cells of my body and clearing of enmeshment between her Soul and mine. I directed every part of her Soul to leave (coughed).

Thank you, Ministry Team!

End of 4-B: MARIE[MP], TONY[RP], HAROLD[LP], KATHERINE

4-C: SOUL INFESTATION

(Apr 7, '10)   INFESTATION UNCLOAKED

DREAM: My daughter Nita was the only person in the dream. There were little bugs here and there in the room and some small dead fish in a pail of water. END.
(Fern relayed the Holy Spirit's answers to me.)
Does Nita's Soul have an infestation of some kind?
[| Yes, but we won't get into that topic just now. |]

I dreamt about wormy cabbage. Does that dream signify infestation? [| Y |] Does having a Soul within one's self that doesn't belong there called being "infested" by it?
[| Yes. The Holy Spirit led you to ask these questions to bring up the topic of Soul infestation. |]

Are portions of Grandma Leigh's Soul with me without permission from the Holy Spirit?
[| Yes and no. Some portions of her Soul are within you without permission, but Father God is allowing it to serve as an example of Soul infestation and how to clear it. |]

Does the unauthorized presence of Soul portions within a person cause a spiritual boil to develop that needs to be cleared for their spiritual health? [| Y |] And their physical health? [| Yes, more than you would realize. |]

Would the core of such a boil be the outside Soul portion that is not meant to be with that person? [| Y |]

Do I have a Soul infestation within me?
[| Yes. I will not explain just now what to do about it, but I will say this: A person's having outside Soul portions with a much lower energy level within their body is akin to having radical cancer cells in their body, but those outside Soul portions do not stay in one place. They "flit" or "crawl" throughout your body, Soul, and aura. Hence the term "infestation."

Bless you, dear one! The Holy Spirit is happy that this material is finally coming forth! |]

Thank you very much, Fern. Holy Spirit!

(May 31, '10) (Fern relayed the Holy Spirit's answers to me.) When somebody's Soul is infested with portions of a squatter Soul, can it cause some of the same symptoms as a virus?

[| Yes. A virus is somewhat of a spiritual entity. The physical component of a virus causes physical problems, and an energetic component (energy) exudes from it that penetrates body tissues and causes the person to feel miserable.

The issue is the same with viruses and squatter Souls. Neither of them is meant to be within a person. One could eliminate most or many of the problems with viruses by blessing every being and energy "in who and what it is" and "in who and what it is coming to be" and by asking them to stay where they are meant to be and thanking them for doing so. []

Are there other effects that could result from having portions of a squatter Soul within oneself?

[| All of the family distress symptoms of the squatter Soul and their family members could conceivably show up. []

Would a protective shield around those Souls help?

[| No, because squatter Souls are enmeshed with the host person's Soul, but it would help a lot to ask daily for a protective shield around all negative energies and portions of unloving Souls that are within or around you. []

When a squatter Soul is within someone, could that person be affected by cellular memories of the squatter Soul?

[| There could be a sense of sadness or other emotion that the person feels coming from cellular memories of the squatter Soul. It is also possible that a painful memory coming from the squatter Soul or its family line could break through into the consciousness of the host Soul. Should that occur, it would have been allowed by the Holy Spirit as part of the plan of the Soul of the host person and the squatter Soul. []

Might the host person (Soul) be affected by the negative energies of, and tendencies towards, alcoholism, lying, lust, and such that affect the squatter Soul's family line?

[| Yes, but again, there is nothing to worry about. It would be no different than for the person to encounter similar negative energies in another manner or place. |]

Thank you, Fern, Holy Spirit, for your answers. Bless you!

(Jun 18, '10)   INFESTATION: THREE TYPES

Holy Spirit, is there more than one type of Soul infestation?
[| Yes. You had the first type of Soul infestation: a portion of a loving Soul – Marie[2]'s[GM] Soul – intermingling with your loving Soul sometime between conception and when your Soul entered your body. [See 4-B (Jul 1, '10)]

The second type of Soul infestation, a more serious form, is a portion of an unloving Soul intermingling with a loving Soul sometime between conception and the moment that loving Soul enters the baby's body.

The third type of Soul infestation is one or more negative energies intermingling with a loving Soul between conception and the moment that loving Soul enters the baby's body. |]

Thank you, Holy Spirit!

(Nov 8, '10)   Type Two: How to Clear
[| Good morning, Lorrie! You just recalled that your daughter Nita needs to have an infestation cleared from her Soul. We do not want it to manifest physically. It is time for you to learn about the other types of Soul infestation and how to clear them. |]

Does my daughter Nita have the second type of infestation?
[| Yes. It is not easy for a person who has a loving Soul to encounter unloving Soul energies within them. Nita feels "who she is" is a person who often "doesn't give a shit" about other people or, at times, even about right living. She has a fair amount of unloving Soul energies within her: a larger portion of one unloving Soul and two smaller portions of unloving Souls from the same unloving Soul group.

Nita first needs to get established in who she is. Who a person

126

fundamentally is is meant to get established while in their mother's womb and throughout the first year of life. You becoming pregnant with Nita was not a happy time for you (being coerced by Lee to have sex with him), so you did not have a welcoming attitude toward the infant that was on the way.

After Nita was born, your heart softened quite a bit, but she had a rather scowling disposition that did not make for good bonding between you and her or between Ron and her.

The first thing to do is to help Nita get established in knowing that she is a good, loving person, a child of God, of love, from the first moment of her conception. Begin speaking that truth to her back in the womb. Even now, you can ask for a protective shield to be placed around her person and her loving Soul back at that time, preventing the energies of the portions of unloving Souls that are with her from affecting her.

Healing can and does take place across time. Protection can be put in place for someone at an earlier point in time that can and will change present circumstances to be what they would be if that protection had been put in place at that earlier time. Begin ministering to Nita from the beginning of her life and as a baby. That will begin to bring about heartwarming changes.

Also, tell Nita's Soul that unloving energy intermingled with her loving Soul as it entered her body at conception and that Father God is teaching you how to clear them. Give her tremendous love: barrels-full, baths, rain showers of love! Her Soul has softened enough that she will soak in love gratefully. She may still come off exactly how she used to be for a while, but much of that might come from habit.

I have been showering Nita with love all along. She is my beloved child, as are all of you. []

Thank You very much, Father God, for helping!!

1. Over the next three weeks, I spoke lovingly to Nita while in my womb, telling her she was a dear, loving child of God and my dear, loving child.

2. At the end of that time, I told her that unloving energies had intermingled with her Soul at conception, but Father God taught me how to clear them.
3. I prayed for protection and clearing for her Soul at conception.
4. I did the Nine-Day Clearing of Incorporation to clear the incorporation of unloving Souls from cells in Nita's body.
5. I commanded all portions of unloving Souls to leave her.

(Dec 10, '10) Are all portions of unloving Souls cleared from Nita? [| Y |] Thank You, Holy Spirit! That is wonderful!

(Nov 11, '10)   Type Three: How to Clear

My grandson Chris has problems with his eyes. Holy Spirit, does Chris have an infestation affecting his eyes? [| Y |]

Is it the third type of infestation: negative energy intermingling with his Soul at the time it entered his body? [| Y |]

Did Chris's Soul allow that so the method of clearing that third type of infestation could be presented to the world? [| Y |]

Do I need to know what type of negative energy it was?
[| No, because the clearing would be the same for whatever negative energies. |]

Does an infestation of negative energies in someone's Soul have ongoing negative physical effects on the person?
[| Yes, but they are not all noticed by the affected person or family members. If the effects get more pronounced, it is a sign that the negative energies want very badly to get free because the person's energy level is too high for them to tolerate. |]

I asked Chris's Soul to join me in asking for a protective shield around all negative energies within or around him and stating that only his Soul may enter new cells as they are formed in his body. I will do that for ten days.

(!!!) I could pray for Chris at the moment of his conception, asking for the egg and sperm to be washed clean and a protective bubble placed around them like LeAnn did when she prayed for me. Holy Spirit, do You suggest that I do that?

[| Yes, that will help a lot to loosen the connections between Chris's Soul and the negative energies intermingled with it. |]

Are those negative energies present as irritants rather than spirit entities energizing the tissue?

[| Yes. There is no life force in negative energies. |]

Do You recommend that I do clearing for Chris and his wife's family lines? [| Y |]

Should I do a clearing for Chris's family lines from previous lifetimes? [| Yes, and in both cases, include clearing curses. |]

Thank You, Father!

(Nov 21, '10) I commanded all negative energies to leave Chris and prayed for protection and clearing for his Soul at conception and for clearing for his and his wife's family lines.

Holy Spirit, is the infestation of negative energies cleared from Chris's Soul? [| Y |] Thank You! I am overjoyed!

(Dec 2, '10)   CLEAR INFESTATION FROM FAMILY

DREAM: In a kitchen. There were many flies and bugs that I was swatting. A worm was on the curtain. END.

That dream might signify Soul infestation.

Father God, can a person clear Soul infestation from many members of one's family, whose Soul agrees to it, by making the intention each day for nine days that only each person's Soul may enter new cells as they are formed in their body?

[| Yes. Doing that would clear much Soul infestation from within those people. Also, ask for a protective shield around all incorporated Soul portions to remain in place until no longer needed. At the end of the nine days, ask for a Holy Spirit shower to flow through each person to clear residue. |]

Would it benefit Souls on the other side to do a process of clearing Soul infestation for them and ask that it be applied while they were still living?

[| It would benefit many of them. It would not clear outside Soul portions from their Soul back when they were still living, but it would loosen up their Soul so they can eventually become free of them. Also, ask for a protective shield around each of them to remain in place until no longer needed. |]

Thank You very much, Father God!

End of 4-C: SOUL INFESTATION

CHAPTER 5

ONWARD WE GO

Healing for Prior Lifetimes: Me 1

5-A: WHY IS MY SOUL A MAGNET?

(Mar 23, '10)   SOME MEANT TO BE

I have had a protective wall around my Soul for only two years. Have unhealed portions of Souls been attracted to me?
[| Yes. You have been like a magnet, but in a good way, because of the healing that has come about. Your Soul is like a miniature hospital. Angels and healing Spirits have been at work. After a Soul portion has been healed, it returns to its original Soul. Not many Soul portions have come since you put a wall around your Soul. |]

Of the Soul portions who were with me for a while, were many of them parts of Souls who were working through abuse? [| Y |] As I expressed fear, consternation (anger), and such, were those Souls expressing their emotions along with me and thus got more freed up? [| Y |] So that's one way that Souls on the other side can express their emotions! [| Y |]

Did portions of unloving Souls attach themselves to my Soul as I came into this life? [| Yes. Your Soul was wide open to invasion, so a couple of portions of unloving Souls managed to attach themselves. Father God has kept a shield of spiritual lead around them for your protection. |]

It occurred to me last evening that I am holding unloving Souls bound to me by judging them as worth less than loving Souls. I need to allow them to be who they are.

[| That is right. It is wonderful you realize that and are willing to change your viewpoint. |]

Is residue within me from Souls that had been with me?

[| Yes, from the portions of Mollie's Soul that left yesterday and from Souls that were with you earlier. Ask for a Holy Spirit demagnetizing shower to flow through you to clear that residue. Any Soul residue at all can cause problems. |]

(Apr 15, '10) At work, I developed a headache across my forehead and the back of my head, different than the usual pattern. Did the presence of an unloving Soul cause that?

[| <FERN> No. The residue of an unloving Soul that is with Mamie caused it. |] (Mamie works there in the morning.)

Thank you, Fern! I'll do a clearing for Mamie and the office.

(May 5, '10)   Anxiety and a Curse in the Picture

Holy Spirit, I have been feeling anxious about every little thing lately. (!!!) Are the spirit of anxiety and the portions of unloving Souls that are with me enmeshed so one can't leave without the other? [| Y |]

I understand that anxiety has a very low vibration energy level and that unloving Souls do, too. "Like is attracted to like." Do I need to separate the two before I direct them to leave?

[| No, but if they were separated, it would be easier to get them to leave. |]

Is anxiety somewhat incorporated within cells in my body?

[| Yes. That is one reason why you feel it in your muscles. |]

(May 16, '10) Over the last ten days, I did the process of clearing the incorporation of portions of unloving Souls and the spirit of anxiety from within cells in my body. The incorporation is most likely cleared by now.

I cleared enmeshment between:

1. My Soul and parts of me, and the unloving Souls that are with me
2. My Soul and parts of me, and the spirit of anxiety
3. Unloving Souls that are with me and the spirit of anxiety

I commanded the portions of unloving Souls and the spirit of anxiety to leave every part of me. (I coughed a couple of times.) Thank You, Holy Spirit!

(May 25, '10) Was a curse placed against me that caused me to soak up negative energies like a sponge?

[| Yes, and it is not fully cleared yet. It is a type of curse that could be called a hypnotic suggestion. You just saw an image of doors around the edge of your aura that automatically open when negative energies get near it.

The protective shield you ask for each day protects you, but you should still do clearing for that "Open Sesame!" curse. |]

Thank you, Holy Spirit! I cleared it a few days later.

(Oct 26, '11)   Lack of Boundaries

I still feel like I should include everybody when I pray for protection and clearing. Doing that might create an opening for Souls to visit me. (I suddenly felt very chilly.)

Is a Soul present that is asking very strongly for prayer?

[| Good morning, Lorrie! There are always people and Souls reaching out to others for help. There will be many extra Souls pressing for those people to pray for them whom they have seen praying for others and getting results.

Up to now, you have not specified boundaries for whom all you lift in prayer. You have been praying for protection and blessing for "everyone in your family and extended family" and asking for that prayer to be applied "to every individual, both living and on the other side."

Saying that gives the impression that whoever wants to ask for prayers for protection and healing may do so. It is OK to include everyone once in a while, but We recommend that you set boundaries. Specify:

"Only those Souls may approach me for help or prayer or be with me who have permission from the Holy Spirit, and then only when they have permission to do so."

Ordinarily, that would include your spouse (if applicable),

children and their immediate families, grandchildren, parents, grandparents, and siblings. Bless you, dear one! []

(Jan 8, '12)   Holes In My Soul Wall

Does a Soul have a wall? [| Y |] Are there holes in my Soul wall that allow outside Souls and negative energies to enter? [| Y |] (!!!) Would asking for *a golden mesh of love* around my Soul seal up those holes? [| Y |] That golden mesh can act as a framework to be filled in as the Soul wall is restored.

> "Holy Spirit, please seal holes in my Soul wall and the Soul wall of all of my Souls from other lifetimes with a golden mesh of love. Thank You!"

Holy Spirit, are the holes in my Soul wall sealed with a golden mesh of love? [| Y |] Thank You!

(May 9, '13)   FAMILY DISTRESS, PICKING UP PAIN

I continue feeling a lot of pressure in the upper part of my head. I asked the Holy Spirit about several possible causes, for which the answer was "No."

Am I carrying the trauma that Ron experienced when he fell from a truckload of hay and landed on his head? [| Y |] Does he have a supraphysical shell (see Glossary) in his head brought about by the trauma of that fall? [| Y |] Am I experiencing the pain physically that Ron's Soul is experiencing spiritually? [| Y |]

I also have areas of pain from sinus congestion. Mollie had a sinus problem for many years. Does her Soul have a supraphysical shell in her sinus areas caused by having sinus infections earlier in her life? [| Y |] (!!!) Am I experiencing the pain spiritually that Mollie experienced physically? [| Y |]

(!!!) Am I picking up the energy of pain from my sister Alice? [| Y |] Am I picking up pain, fear, and so on from women and girls who have been or are being abused? [| Y |] Is there a connection between my picking up pain from others and my muscles being sore all over my body? [| Y |]

I often feel like I want to help everyone. I think, "Who will help them if I don't?" I need to leave things in God's hands.

Father God, speaking for all of me, I place every person and situation in Your hands. I will do what the Holy Spirit asks me to do and leave the rest for You to take care of. Thank You!

(Mar 4, '14) Hello, Father God! I met with Pastor Joyce this morning to tell her about how easily I pick up negative energies. While I was speaking, she said she saw herself holding a large ball representing my burdens.

I said, "Father God, I place everyone and everything in Your hands." Pastor Grace said the spiritual ball disintegrated as I placed my burdens into God's hands. Wow!

Later: Father, I think You are telling me that I am to hold people and problems outside of myself, the way You directed me years back to hold concern for Ron outside of myself and not within me, that otherwise my heart would tear and bleed.

[| You summarized that nicely, Lorrie. Yes, When you minister to people, We want you to hold the person (Soul) who needs healing In love in your spiritual arms and let the Divine Love within you wrap around them. You have been feeling *sympathy* for others rather than *empathy*, which is the wiser road. |]

> sympathy *n.* 4 a) pity or compassion felt for another's trouble, suffering, etc. (Web p. 1450)
>
> empathy *n.* 1 ...; ability to share in another's emotions, thoughts or feelings (Web p. 466)

[| There is no reason to be sorrowful about people's problems. Where each person is at is a result of their actions, thoughts, wishes, etc., in their current lifetime combined with the actions, thoughts, wishes, etc. that they had in previous lifetimes.

Everything that takes place in everyone's life is cause for joy because each situation is another step in that person's coming to be who and what they are meant to be!

To quite an extent, what you have been doing regarding people's problems is to feel sorry for them that they have to suffer and to take some of their sufferings onto or into yourself to lighten their load. Keep in mind: *People going through difficult situations is their way of being healed and coming into wholeness.* []

Wow again! Thank You, Father!

(Mar 18, '14)   KARMA AND RESIDUE

Holy Spirit, does karma need to be cleared for this lifetime or an earlier one between me and each outside Soul that is with me? [| Y |] Is karma between people and Souls often cleared by them being together? [| Y |] Would extending love and blessings to everyone go far in clearing karma? [| Y |]

(!!!) When a person sends a Soul (Soul portion) away, is there usually Soul residue left behind that attracts other portions of that Soul to the person? [| Y |] When a person clears negative energy from themselves, is residue usually left behind that attracts more of the same energy? [| Y |] Has that been happening to me? [| Y |]

Is it my task to clear negative energy from a Soul that is with me before I command the Soul to leave? [| Y |]

Almost every time I ask about it, portions of other people's Souls or my Souls from other lifetimes are with me. Are some of those outside Souls meant to be with me? [| Y |]

I learned several years ago that portions of several Souls from earlier lifetimes of mine latched onto my Soul to receive help as I came to Earth to live this life. Did my Full Soul help those Soul portions join with me? [| Y |] Is helping Souls that are with me go to the light one of my Soul's purposes? [| Y |]

Am I meant to remain *a composite Soul* with portions of separate Souls functioning together as a system? [| Y |]

I am happy to learn that because I thought I hadn't been protecting myself well enough! Do many people have a composite Soul? [| Y |]

(!!!) Are some parts of me allowing Soul portions with negative energies to visit them? [| Y |] Should I direct those parts to leave that have been doing that? [| Y |]

I asked Jesus and the Holy Spirit to help as I blessed and sent away portions of my Soul not meant to be with me. Thank You, Jesus and Holy Spirit!

(Jun 25, '14)   Centuries-Old Karma

I received the understanding several times that when I came to Earth for the first time, I turned my back on God and said I didn't need Him, that I would take care of myself and figure out how to help everybody be saved and healed, and that I wouldn't turn anyone away who asked for help.

Holy Spirit, did I take that stance before my first lifetime? [| Yes. You took that stance before your first lifetime and many other lifetimes. |] Lord, have mercy!

Did my Full Soul see to it that that situation of turning my back on God was repeated in other lifetimes until karma related to doing that would get cleared, that I would repent of closing myself off to God and fully choose to allow Him to be in charge, to be God? [| Y |]

"Father God, I am sorry for holding a grudge against You. Please forgive me. Choosing with my will, I cancel the egotistical idea I had that I don't need You. Please forgive me. Thank You!"

(!!!) Are portions of some of my Souls from the lifetimes when I turned my back on God coming to me for help, thinking they couldn't ask God for help after what they had done? [| Y |]

(Nov 30, '14)   A Clearing Place for Souls

(!!!) When I came into this life, did I, my Soul, agree to be a clearing place for Souls? [| Y |] Would the Ministry Team love, bless, and do clearing for outside Souls that are with me if I asked them to? [| Y |]

Have many Soul portions that were enmeshed with each other come to me to get the enmeshment cleared? [| Y |] Are some of the Soul portions that are with me ready to leave? [| Y |] Would it be OK to release them as a group? [| Y |]

I ask for a Holy Spirit demagnetizing shower and spiritual conditioner to flow through me to make it easier for outside Souls to leave. Guardian angels, please guide those Souls to where they are meant to be. Thank you!

In the name of Jesus, I command all outside Souls to leave that are not meant to be with me. (Cough)

Holy Spirit, did several Soul portions leave? [| Y |] Did every Soul portion leave that was meant to leave? [| Y |] Wonderful!

(Aug 20, '16)   Black Hole

(!!!) Holy Spirit, is a part of my Soul closed off?
[| Yes, to protect the rest of your Soul from negative energies that are with that portion. You could compare that part of your Soul to a black hole. Portions of some of your Souls from previous lifetimes that are holding judgment, fear, guilt, and so on are caught in that black hole. |]

Did my Soul agree to have those Soul portions from earlier lifetimes with me so the gunk could get cleared from them? [| Y |] Have some of the negative energies been cleared? [| About three-fourths of what those Souls came in with has been. |]

Are the negative energies within that closed-off part of me one of the reasons why negative energies and Souls with negative energies get attracted to me? [| Y |]

Do the Soul portions in that black hole want help to get cleared and become loving? [| Many do. |] Are some of them unloving because they did not receive enough love during their lifetime? [| Y |] Should I send those Soul portions away that do not want help to become loving? [| Y |]

Ministry Team, please join as I pray for the Soul portions in that closed-off part of me. I send blessings and love to all the portions of my Soul that are in that black hole. In the name of Jesus, I ask kindly and command all those Soul portions who do not want help to become loving to leave now! (Cough)

Thank you, Ministry Team, for assisting me!

Over the next several days, I asked many times for all loving Souls in my Soul line and family lines to join me in flowing blessings and love to the Souls in that closed-off part of my Soul. Thank you, everybody!

(Aug 29, '16) Is a part of my Soul still closed off? [| N |] Wow!

End of 5-A: WHY IS MY SOUL A MAGNET?

5-B: MY BROTHER JOEL AND ME

(May 13, '10)   YOUNG JOEL IS WITH ME

Is a young portion of Joel's Soul, about 5, with me?
[| Yes, a young portion of Joel's Soul got attached to you as a mother figure at that age. He still feels the hurt he felt at age 5 when you walked too fast for him to keep up with you going from the chicken coop to the house. Please think of young Joel with love and apologize for that.

A young child's hurts can be very deep. Those hurts continue to affect the adult person until they are relieved somehow. Tears on Joel's part would help heal his inner child, but those often do not come easily, especially for a man. Speaking for Joel, I say, "Thank you!" |]

Do I have a carnal tie with that young portion of Joel's Soul related to lust, connected with me molesting him at age 5?
[| Yes. As you have learned, a carnal tie is one type of soul tie. To clear it, express sorrow to Joel in spirit for any advantage you took over him, and ask him to forgive you. Ask God for forgiveness and for all residue of the spirit of lust to be cleared from you and Joel back when your egregious actions towards him were taking place and in the present.

Then, ask the Holy Spirit to begin thinning out that carnal soul tie and dissolve it when it is OK. Thank Father God for His forgiveness, and thank the Holy Spirit for seeing about clearing the carnal tie. God is so good! |]

Yes, God, You are wonderful! Thank You!

Joel, I am truly sorry. Please forgive me for taking advantage of you when you were young. Thank you!

Holy Spirit, please flow a demagnetizing shower through Joel and me to clear the residue of lust. Please thin out the carnal soul tie between my Soul and that young portion of Joel's Soul and dissolve it when the time is right. Thank You!

(May 25, '10)   Affected by Fear

Joel's strong belief in the teachings of the Catholic Church could be described as *religiosity* and *denominationalism.* Was a curse placed against him that caused him to have "tunnel vision," stuck where he is in his beliefs?

[| <FERN> Whatever "tunnel vision" Joel has is not a result of a curse. He clings very tightly to Catholic teachings out of fear. He is not only afraid of punishment by God if he were to discontinue believing the teachings, but he would lose the only source of affirmation he has of being a worthwhile person (being an ordained deacon in the Catholic Church).

The Holy Spirit says not to worry about Joel's beliefs. Grace will work within him if and when he is meant to change. Continue blessing him and all other family members and ask for protection for yourself as needed. []

Thank you, Fern, Holy Spirit!

(Feb 26, '14) Holy Spirit, is a 5-year-old portion of Joel's Soul with me from when he became very upset when I walked too fast from the chicken coop back to the house? [| Y |]_Is the presence of that portion of Joel's Soul contributing to my having higher systolic blood pressure readings? [| Y |]

Does the energy of the portion of Joel's Soul that is with me cause me stomach discomfort? [| Y |] Is it bewildered and doesn't know where to go? [| Y |] Should I meet with Joel to have that 5-year-old portion of his Soul returned to him? [| Y |]

(!!!) *Is a supraphysical shell of fear* attached to that young portion of Joel's Soul? [| Y |] Should I clear that shell before I have that Soul portion return to Joel? [| N |] Does adult Joel's Soul also have a shell of fear attached to it? [| Y |]

(Mar 30, '14) I learned from the Holy Spirit that a spiritual umbilical cord formed recently between 5-year-old Joel and 10-year-old me. Those parts of our Souls are connected by the animosity that 5-year-old Joel feels towards me for leaving him behind while walking from the chicken coop to the house.

I learned that the Holy Spirit prompted 5-year-old Joel to reach out to 10-year-old me with neediness so that earlier situation from his childhood would come to light. Ten-year-old me responded and cared for him, creating a spiritual umbilical cord connection between us.

(Sept 12, '14)   PRESSURE FROM JOEL

Is the energy of denominationalism coming from Joel causing the circular pressure around my head? [| Y |]

Years ago, I asked Joel not to pray for me to return to the Catholic Church, but has he been praying for that subconsciously? [| Y |] Is he obsessed with getting me to return? [| Y |]

Holy Spirit, I ask an angel to be with Joel to deflect from me any subconscious praying he is doing for me to change.

In the name of Jesus, I break the stranglehold that Joel's Soul has on my Soul, on me! I speak for the spiritual vise around my head to be dissolved and for whoever is involved with it to be sealed with spiritual lead!

Holy Spirit, is that spiritual vise dissolved? [| Y |] Are the Souls that were involved with it sealed off? [| Y |] Thank You!

(Jan 10, '15) I had great discomfort in the upper part of my head that I sensed was caused at least partly by Joel's wanting me to return to the Catholic Church.

Holy Spirit, has that strong wish of Joel's bruised the brain area of my astral body? [| Y |] Is the 3/4" diameter bald spot on my head related to Joel's strong wish for me to return to the Catholic Church? [| Y |]

I asked the Holy Spirit for protection and healing. My hair grew back in the bald spot within a few weeks. Thank You, Holy Spirit!

(Mar 6, '19)   HEALING FOR PAST AND PRESENT

My digestive system "emptied" every Sunday morning for the last few years (only on Sundays). I suspect that the negative energy from Joel related to his wanting so strongly for me to return to the Catholic Church is affecting me.

I asked Joel to come for a visit so I could tell him about the situation and ask him to "leave me in Father God's hands."

Joel and his wife Sara came over this afternoon. I asked Joel to join in role-playing him and me going to the chicken coop to gather the eggs when he was five, and I was ten, and he became upset when I walked back to the house too fast.

I used dresser drawers for chicken nests and put eggs in them. I let Joel carry the eggs and walked slower so he could keep up as we returned to the "house" (kitchen). Speaking for Mom, I said, "Thank you, Joel, for getting the eggs!"

Then I asked Joel to forgive me for going too fast for him. He forgave me. I also asked him again not to pray for me to return to the Catholic Church, that "the negative energy from his wanting so strongly for me to return was affecting me."

He asked, "Why do you call it negative energy?" I replied, "Because it goes contrary to what I choose, using my free will, and to what I believe the Holy Spirit is guiding me to do." He said he would leave me in God's hands. Thank you, Joel!

By the next day, my stomach felt better than it had in a long while! And it didn't "act up" on Sunday mornings anymore! Thank You, God!

(Jul 11, '19) Holy Spirit, do I still have a carnal tie with young Joel? [| Y |] I did another clearing for it.

A week later: Is it cleared? [| Y |] Did the young portion of Joel's Soul return to him? [| Y |] That's good. Thank You, Holy Spirit!

(!!!) Was my acting out with Joel when he was young "karma" for Joel, that my actions squared something away for Joel from earlier lifetimes? [| Y |] Thank You, Holy Spirit! That helps me feel a little better about the situation.

End of 5-B: MY BROTHER JOEL AND ME

5-C: CORRINE^{MP}

Note: ^{MP} (Me Prior life) is omitted after Corrine in this section.

(Nov 2, '10)   AN OUTSIDE SOUL TOOK OVER

(3:00 A.M.) I was hospitalized for four days following major surgery at the end of July. In early September, I realized I didn't remember most of what happened while I was in the hospital.

Father, did a part of my person, a split personality, take over much of the time during those four days? [| No. A low-vibration energy portion of your Soul from a previous lifetime that was with you took over. |] Is that Soul portion still with me? [| A major portion of it is. |]

Is it detrimental for me to have that Soul with me?
[| Your energy gets drained when that Soul does not have protection around it. It would be good to ask daily for a protective shield around all parts of you and all outside Souls that are with you, that feel vituperative towards you, and whose energy level is incompatible with yours.

Also, make this request with the intention for it to remain in effect until no longer needed: *"Holy Spirit, I give you permission to direct Soul portions that are with me to leave if their presence is detrimental to me."* |] I made that request.

There seems to be a "shadow" with me lately, a judgmental attitude that prevents me from receiving understanding from

Spirit and causes me to always think ahead about what is "OK" or "worthwhile" to write. Please guide me!

[| The overhanging "shadow" that you sense is related to the low-vibration energy portion of your Soul from a previous lifetime that took control of your mind and body much of the time following your surgery at the end of July.

When an outside Soul takes over a person physically and mentally, it leaves a magnetic resonance throughout that person's body and mind and a tinge of resonance within their Soul. That magnetic resonance causes attraction between the "take-over spirit" and the "sponged-upon" Soul. You can clear that attraction by asking for a Holy Spirit demagnetizing shower to flow through your whole person to clear (seal up) the magnetic quality of negative energies.

Follow that up with an infilling of the crystalline white light of Christ throughout your body, mind, and Soul, and a Holy Spirit shower of love to clear any remaining residue. []

Did my Soul permit that takeover by another Soul to serve as the basis for another lesson? [| Y |]

Were dark forces trying to take over during that time? [| Y |] Did they take over that low-vibration energy Soul from a previous lifetime of mine and use it to set up contact points for dark energies within me?

[| Yes. Do clearing for dark energies and contact points for dark energies that may have gotten positioned within your person or Soul. Look back as to how you cleared contact points related to witchcraft. []

Thank You, Father! Thank you, Fern, for helping me hear clearly! Thank you, angels and Young Souls, for protecting me!

(Dec 11, '10)   Permission to Be With You

Father God, the top of my head is stinging, and my scalp is sore. It feels like a large hand is grasping the top of my head. Is the low-vibration energy portion of my Soul from a previous lifetime that took over while I was in the hospital still with me?

[| I will call that part **Corrine**. She is part of your Full Soul that you and parts of your Souls from other lifetimes have shunned and are shunning because "she is not good enough." In the world of the Soul, she is like a woman who lives on the street.

Yes, a portion of Corrine's Soul is with you with permission from the Holy Spirit and your Soul. Also, portions of your Souls from other lifetimes are with you to be healed and bring further healing for you.

You might think, "Oh no! Something else I need to remember to pray about!" You do not need to do something more, Lorrie. As you pray for protection and clearing for yourself, intend to apply your prayers equally as much to parts of your Soul in this lifetime and to portions of your Soul from other lifetimes that are with you.

Full healing is coming about for you! Extending love and compassion to all parts of your Soul and everyone without exception will help speed up that healing. Be tender with yourself. Do not place recrimination on your shoulders. Thank you!

I will close off now with a blessing for you and everyone! |]

Thank You, Father, for being patient with me. I realize I look down on women "who live in the gutter." By judging them, I have been judging myself in my lifetime as Corrine. I am sorry for judging you, Corrine. Please forgive me.

(Feb 27, '11)   TIES WITH CORRINE

Father, I have been thinking about and praying for the portion of Corrine's Soul that took over my person for a few days following my surgery last July. I invited her to go to the light this morning during the church service.

Is that portion or another portion of her Soul still with me?

[| Yes, Lorrie, a portion of Corrine's Soul has been with you, somewhat mixed in with your Soul these past seven months. The Holy Spirit allowed that to bring about further healing for both of you and to add a deeper understanding of human relationships with the spirit world. []

Does Corrine's presence add to the level of my anxiety?

[| Yes, quite a bit. Corrine spent her whole life wondering how to become even halfway OK, how to get away from the guilt she was carrying connected with her search for love, and how to find a way to be saved so she could spend eternity in a better place than hell had to offer.

You have searched and struggled with those same issues. Anxiety about them has carried forward in your Soul through several lifetimes. In this lifetime, you have reached the point where your energy level is high enough to hear clearly from Spirit. The Holy Spirit is guiding you in being healed!

You wonder if the portion of Corrine's Soul that was with you went to the light this morning. Most of it did. A couple of portions are still with you that need more affirmation and love and need to become free of anxiety.

Please bind and dissolve the roots of anxiety related to your previous lifetimes, including your lifetime as Corrine. Then, clear the spirit of anxiety so it can return to its rightful place. []

Thank You, Father God! I'll do that.

(Apr 15, '11) I asked the Ministry Team to join me as I did a clearing for the spirit of anxiety and dissolved the roots.

Holy Spirit, did some of the roots of my anxiety in previous lifetimes get cleared? [| Y |] Thank You!

(May 1, '11) During the church service, I invited the portions of Corrine's Soul that were still with me to go to the light.

Fern, did Corrine go to the light this morning?

[| <FERN> Yes, Lorrie. She went to the light and reunited joyfully with her Full Soul! That will help you greatly, too, because you have a direct spiritual connection with her Soul. |]

(Jul 5, '12)   Clearing Infestation, Incorporation

My sister Dora called to wish me a belated happy birthday. She said I appeared somewhat fidgety or nervous at a relative's memorial service a week ago. I assured her I was OK.

For several months, I have noticed that I constantly move my arms, fingers, or body position when on the phone. I have been attributing it to parts of me being bored or maybe being afraid to talk with the person on the phone.

(!!!) Might a Soul be with me that is so mixed in with my Soul that it can make movements with my body? Holy Spirit, is an outside Soul with me? [| Y |] Corrine? [| Y |] Does her Soul trigger muscle movements in my body? [| Y |] Does she taste, see and hear with my body? [| Y |] In her experience, is she living this life? [| Y |]

Is a portion of Corrine's Soul incorporated within cells in my body? [| Y |] Incorporation usually happens early in a child's life. Has a portion of her Soul been with me as a Soul infestation since my conception? [| Y |]

Are portions of other Souls incorporated within cells in my body? [| Y |] Is that incorporation detrimental to me? [| Y |] Is it always detrimental to have Souls incorporated within cells in one's body? [| Y |]

I began the 9-day process of clearing the incorporation of Corrine's Soul and other Souls from cells in my body.

(Jul 14, '12) Is the incorporation of Corrine's Soul cleared? [| Y |] Is all other incorporation cleared, too? [| Y |] Wonderful!

I cleared the enmeshment between my Soul, Corrine's Soul, and the other Souls that had been incorporated. Then I opened a large positive vortex on a heavenly plane for Corrine's Soul and those other Souls to go to the light, with Father-Mother God, the Holy Spirit, and Heart overshadowing it, the 24 archangels around it, and angels with music a great distance away. I invited those Souls to go to the light. (I left the vortex open for an hour.)

Did Corrine's Soul go to the light? [| Y |] Did many other Souls, also? [| Y |] Thank You, God! That is so great!

(Feb 6, '13)   Corrine: Another Part With Me

My head has been bothering me a lot even though I ask for clearing and protection daily and seal up dark energies.

Holy Spirit, are one or more Soul portions in my brain that have dark energies attached to them? [| Y |] Is my Soul allowing those Soul portions to be there? [| Y |]

Is a portion of Corrine's Soul with me? [| Y |] Are the dark energies that are with her Soul Lost Will, denied emotions, of her Soul? [| Y |] Are some of the other dark energies that are in my brain portions of the Lost Will of some of my Souls from other lifetimes? [| Y |]

Is a portion of Corrine's Soul incorporated within cells in my body? [| Y |] I learned earlier that her Soul joined my Soul as an infestation at my conception.

(Sept 27, '13) I learned that portions of Corrine's Soul have been with me as an infestation for many lifetimes. During those lifetimes, I was judgmental of alcoholics, prostitutes, etc. Those judgments prevented those portions of Corrine's Soul from going to the light. This lifetime is the first in which I am at least somewhat nonjudgmental.

I am sorry for judging you, Corrine. Please forgive me.

(Dec 28, '13) My stomach felt irritated. I learned from the Holy Spirit that a low-energy portion of Corrine's Soul was in my aura that wanted help to become loving. I prayed for her, and that portion of her Soul went to the place for visiting Souls where she can receive further healing.

(Jul 18, '14)   More Healing-Clearing Needed

I felt dizzy all day. I looked at the clock at 12:30 P.M. A short time later, I looked at it again and was shocked to see that it was already 2:30 P.M.

Holy Spirit, did a part of me take over for those two hours? [| Y |] Was it Corrine? [| Y |] Was the dizziness I had connected with the presence of her Soul? [| Y |] It feels like something is grabbing my head. Is a part of Corrine's Soul wrapped around my brain? [| Y |] Is there a supraphysical shell attached to parts of her astral body? [| Y |]

(!!!) Before that portion of Corrine's Soul joined me, was she with Mollie? [| Yes. She was with Mollie for much of Mollie's life. |] Did her Soul transfer from Mollie to me in the fall of 2003? [| Y |] That's when I began having elevated blood pressure and increased discomfort (pressure) in the upper part of my head!

I suddenly "knew" that Corrine is a holy Soul but is affected by erroneous imprinting that makes her believe she is not worthy of being loved. Holy Spirit, is that correct? [| Y |]

Thank You, Holy Spirit! I will clear erroneous imprinting for her and other Souls who choose to have it cleared. I did that clearing immediately and asked for clearing and healing for Corrine in every way needed. Bless you, Corrine!

I emailed Beth, told her about my dizzy spells earlier in the week, that my head was still bothering me, and asked if she could minister to me by phone soon.

(Jul 20, '14) Beth called. I told her that a portion of Corrine's Soul has been hanging onto my brain and that several portions of it have a supraphysical shell attached, that after I ministered to Corrine two days ago, a portion of her Soul went to the place for visiting Souls, but since then I have been experiencing much discomfort and a feeling of pressure in the top of my head.

I could feel the discomfort and pressure in my head receding as Beth ministered to me in silence. By the time she finished, I felt discomfort only at the top of my head. Beth told me afterward that she saw chunks fly out of my head at one point and disappear. They were very likely pieces of the supraphysical shell that was disintegrated.

Thank You, Holy Spirit! Thank you, Beth!

(Jul 28, '14)   Help from Angels

When I woke up, it felt like something was on top of my brain that was too big for the space.

Holy Spirit, did Corrine take over somewhat during the night? [| Y |] Did an unloving portion of her Soul enter my brain? [| Y |] Did my Soul permit it to be there? [| Y |]

Is a portion of another unloving Soul enmeshed with the unloving portion of Corrine's Soul that is in my brain? [| Y |]

(!!!) Is it a portion of one of Lucifer's angels? [| Y |]

Early in the "history of Souls," did unloving Souls get mixed in with loving Souls? [| Y |] Was the unloving Soul that is enmeshed with Corrine's Soul a part of the cluster of Souls that joined with my Soul as I came to Earth for the first time? [| Y |] Is Lost Will of Mother God enmeshed with that unloving Soul? [| Y |]

Holy Spirit, please seal all unloving Souls and negative energies that are with me with spiritual lead. Thank You!

(!!!) A new method of clearing and healing came to mind. I asked immediately:

"Holy Spirit, I ask for my head and whole body to be immersed all day and night in a Love Bath of Golden Saffron to bring clearing and healing. Thank You!"

Will that love bath help Lost Will separate from unloving Souls? [| Y |] Will the Lost Will then be loving? [| Y |]

(Aug 6, '14) My head was bothering me a lot again.

(!!!) Holy Spirit, has Corrine's Soul somewhat taken over within me again? [| Y |] Is a split-off portion of Corrine's Soul that feels vituperative towards me out to get me? [| Y |] Should I ask In-God-We-Trust Angels to come with their nets (Starr, Preface p. 4) and carry that portion of her Soul to another plane? [| Y |]

I thought about giving that portion of Corrine's Soul another chance, but the Holy Spirit said not to. She is being mischievous and trying to control parts of me.

In-God-We-Trust Angels, please come and carry the portion of Corrine's Soul away that is causing problems. (Pause) Did that portion leave? [| Y |] Thank You, Holy Spirit!

(May 21 '18)   Coming To The Rescue

My head was bothering me a lot. A portion of Corrine's Soul is in my aura above my head. She wants to leave, but my lack of forgiveness toward her is holding her back. Speaking for every

Soul of mine from every lifetime, I asked Corrine to forgive me for judging her, for looking down on "her kind."

I understood that Corrine was likely a prostitute. I thanked her for living well to the best of her ability, which was part of my Full Soul's learning and growth process. I blessed her, and she left.

Holy Spirit, is a dark energy center above my head? [| Y |] (!!!) Is a portion of Joel's Soul from this lifetime helping operate it? [| Y |] Is an outside Soul with a low-vibration energy level with that portion of his Soul? [| Y |] A portion of my Soul from a previous lifetime? [| Y |] A portion of Corrine's Soul? [| Y |]

I asked daily for loving Souls from my Soul line and Joel's and my family lines to join in sending a deluge of love and blessings to every portion of Corrine's and Joel's Souls from every lifetime.

(May 23, '18) The portion of Corrine's Soul that had been with Joel's Soul left and went to a healing ring. Thank You, Holy Spirit!

End of 5-C: CORRINE[MP]

CHAPTER 6

OPENING UP CONTINUES

Healing for Prior Lifetimes: Lee and Me 2

Mar 4, '11   CARRY ON

My systolic blood pressure readings are continuing to be quite high, even though it has been two weeks since I quit working at the morning job that I had. I have been quite anxious most of the time, too.

[| Lorrie, I am glad you are trying to relax. You and some parts of you need clearing for the spirit of anxiety. Ask your sister Ann to pray for clearing negative energies using the healing touch method and the usual prayers for clearing anxiety and other negative energies from you and all parts of you in this lifetime and previous lifetimes.

It would help you to feel less anxious about various tasks if you would say, "I place this in Your hands, Father God." As to feeling anxious, know that "This, too, shall pass." Have a wonderful rest of the day! Peace and blessings to you! |]

Thank You, Father God!

Ann prayed with me the next day to clear anxiety and ministered "healing touch" to clear negative energies.

Apr 26, '11. [| Lorrie, as each minute passes, you are finished with it. The discomfort in your head and joints is with you a second at a time and then is gone.

The increased discomfort you have been having is related to your sister Alice's deteriorating health, stress buildup within Mother Earth, and your habit of feeling anxious about various things. Also, you are still being affected by your connection with your Aunt

Mollie. Thank you for blessing family members, including her, every day. Carry on! Bless you! []

Thank You, Father God! Thank you, Fern! Bless You!

May 25, '11. [| Good morning, Lorrie! You are making progress with not allowing anxiety to have so much "sway and say" over you. Love the anxiety. Fully accept it as a part of your emotional being that you have been unwilling to accept up to this point. (If you were filled with unconditional love, the aching and other problems would disappear.)

You are getting there, Lorrie, and Oh! How We rejoice with and for you and with and for everyone! You have heard the expression, *"It is better to light a candle than to curse the darkness."* That is what your life and experiences are, Lorrie, a light for the world. Just as another candle can be lit from the first one, more lit from that one, and so on, so is it coming to be through you and the many others who are allowing love to come fully into them. Light is being passed on. Peace! []

Thank You, Father-Mother God!

Jun 6, '11   CLEARING ERRONEOUS IMPRINTING

Bless you, Fern. Thank you for loving me! I (again) broke down crying at the thought of being loved.

[| Lorrie, you are greatly loved by Spirit. Mother God and I love you deeply, and Heart (Jesus) loves you deeply. Your guardian angels love you deeply. The Young Souls love you deeply. Your Full Soul loves you deeply. Everyone in your family in this lifetime and all other lifetimes loves you deeply. In short, everyone in the universe, and the universe itself, loves you. Have we left anyone out?

The missing link for you to be and feel fully loved is yourself. You felt the same way in most of your other lifetimes.

Not feeling worthy of being fully loved stems from your original creation. It is not your fault that you find it hard to believe that God or anyone else loves you. Early on, when large groups of Souls were coming forth, I, Spirit, was not fully present to them, to you, with My love and acceptance (Original pp. 49-64, 83-93, 102-107). All of those Souls, all of you, were imprinted in varying degrees with the erroneous belief that you are not worthy of being loved.

The remedy for that is to spiritually remove the imprinting of *"I am not worthy of being loved"* and replace it with the freeing message, *"I am worthy of being loved because I come from love. I am love, just as Father God, Mother God, the Holy Spirit, and Heart are love!"*

You can make that change by using your imagination and choosing with your will to have it take place. All of Us will join you in making that choice. I, Spirit, will be present when you come forth into life, this time with the fullness of love. The onus you have been carrying of not feeling worthy of being loved will be dissolved and replaced with a banner that proclaims, *"I am a beloved child of God!"*

We will join you now, Lorrie, as you make that replacement. It is time for that freeing to take place! []

I said aloud, "I am worthy of being loved because I come from love. I am love, just as Father God, Mother God, the Holy Spirit, and Heart are love. Father God loves me! Mother God loves me! The Holy Spirit loves me! Heart, Jesus, loves me! The universe loves me!

"And I love me and receive that love. Father God says I am a beloved child of God! Mother God says I am a beloved child of God! The Holy Spirit says I am a beloved child of God! Heart, Jesus, says I am a beloved child of God! The universe says I am a beloved child of God!

"I join them in saying and proclaiming that I am a beloved child of God! Thank You, God and everyone, for your love!"

Holy Spirit, I ask for erroneous imprinting to be cleared for every Spirit as it came forth back in time. Thank You!

6-A: LOST WILL OF MOTHER GOD, SOULS

(Apr 11, '11)   SIZING UP THE SITUATION

[| Good morning, Lorrie! Thank you for taking time lately to review the set of books, *Right Use of Will*. As you learned from reading them, powerful, unloving energies try to hinder efforts to understand the Will and to help restore Lost Will. |]

The origin of the set of books, *Right Use of Will:*

"The insights presented in this book have been channeled from the highest source...received from God in the first person." (Right, Introduction, p. ii)

Definition of *"Right Use of Will"* from their website:

"Right Use of Will is a path...freeing our Will, and helping it come into Heart balance with our masculine mind/Spirit side ...about finding the freedom of full self–acceptance within our self that is necessary to bring true Heart balance between our Spirit and Will and manifest it in our Body as unconditional love." (rightuseofwill.com)

"I have Four Parts and none are meant to be separated from the others. Spirit, Will, Heart and Body must all be together in a state of balance and alignment for life to last." (Original, Introduction p. xi)

Spirit is the Holy Spirit. Will is Mother God, the emotional body of God. Heart is Love, the Son. Body is Father God. Everyone's Soul consists of portions of each of those parts. Lost Will of Mother God is emotions that She did not accept (because, at the time, Father God was not accepting of them). Lost Will of our Soul is emotions we repressed and denied feeling.

Father God, I have had a lot of dreams lately. Is my awareness of what is in my subconscious expanding?

[| Your subconscious is a little more open than previously. You are less afraid of what might be in it and more accepting of your emotions. When one's emotions are not accepted, that emotional energy shrinks up and hides. Some of it leaves the person and is in a place of darkness, although it still has magnetic connections with that person.

All emotions must be accepted, loved, and welcomed into one's life for optimal physical, mental, emotional, and spiritual health. You can think of emotions as little children who need to be allowed to speak, cry, laugh, and express affection and be cared for in a safe place so they can grow up with healthy emotions.

You are wondering if Beth Stein is another lifetime of Fern's. Yes, she is, but let her find that out when she reads this.

Bless you, Fern, Beth, and Lorrie! Bless everyone! |]

Thank You, Father God! Bless You!

(Jun 21, '11) The top of my head is bothering me a lot. That can be a sign that Spirit wants to speak. Good morning, Holy Spirit!

[| Good morning, Lorrie! When your head bothers, I suggest you pray for the people (Souls) who are crying out in their Spirit for help. It just occurred to you that some of the anguish Mother God experienced way early on might be affecting you the way stress experienced by family members does. Just in case, please include Mother God when you pray for those in distress. Thank you! |]

Thank You, Holy Spirit!

{Jun 26, '11) Father God, the top of my head is hot.

[| Some of the discomfort you are experiencing at the top of your head is related to family distress and world distress. You are also picking up some of the distress not yet cleared for Mother God. The distress She feels includes the distress felt by the many people who have large portions of Her Lost Will within them so It can be nurtured and healed.

Thank you for your prayers for your friend Nette, who you learned has portions of the Lost Will of Mother God within her. As you minister to her, please ask that the prayers be applied to everyone who is carrying portions of Lost Will of Mother God at this time, those who carried portions in previous lifetimes, and those who will do so in the future. Healing occurs across time, even back to the beginning of time.

The Holy Spirit, Heart, Mother God, and I say thank you! Her happiness over the upcoming release is brimming over in tears of joy, and so is Mine!

Please add to your spiritual understanding that Mother God has been and is always with you and with everyone, just as I have been and am. We are one God: Father, Mother, Spirit, and Heart. Bless you, Lorrie! []

My heart is welling up in gratitude, Father! Thank You!

(Sept 27, '12)   MOTHER GOD IS TARGETED

Holy Spirit, from the beginning of time, have all curses using witchcraft energies included Mother God as a target? [| Y |]

Are the people who have sizable portions of Lost Will within them selected as primary targets by dark forces? [| Yes. Dark forces are attempting to destroy Mother God. |] Do dark forces see those people as good places to place dark energy centers so the dark forces can beam witchcraft energies, curses, and such into their families and communities?

[| Yes. Dark forces target all lightworkers, so We recommend that they protect themselves (that you protect yourself) regularly. Bless you, Lorrie! Bless you, Fern! Bless All That Is! |]

Thank You, Father God!

(Jul 29, '13)   Lost Will of My Soul

Father God, I have been having a lot of mixed emotions lately. I think some of them are Lost Will portions of my Soul that hope to reunite with me: feelings of depression, self-hate, anger, anxiety, fear, and guilt.

Parts of me still get on my back pretty badly. I felt like I was watching myself several times lately, and the skin on my legs felt somewhat numb. Those are symptoms of dissociation.

[| Lorrie, keep doing what you are doing regarding how you feel: accepting the way you are feeling and fully loving yourself at every moment. Ease up on the expectations you have for yourself. If a part of you finds fault with you about something, extend love and blessing to that part and teach it to be more compassionate of you and the other parts.

This time of feeling somewhat unsettled is a good time in the life of your Soul. You will see that later on as you look back. Bless you, Lorrie! Good night! []

Thank You, Father God! Good night!

(Sept 30, '13) Is adult me mostly just a shell, that I only feel emotion when I allow parts of me to come to the fore? Am I, as I know myself, the part of my personality that is frozen and "holding rancor towards the rest of my Soul?" Do I automatically shut emotions down because I don't want to let "the people who hurt me" win (get the satisfaction of seeing me cry), or because I believe that when somebody who has received many blessings (which I have) does hurtful things, it is much worse than when others who haven't been as blessed, do hurtful things?

(!!!) Holy Spirit, are Lost Will portions of some of my Souls from early lifetimes with me, including my first lifetime? [| Y |]

Does my Full Soul hope that those repressed emotions will all be accepted so the Lost Will portions of those Souls can go to the light during this lifetime?

[| Yes, Lorrie. Bringing that about is one of your Soul's purposes for this lifetime. You have been wondering why you feel led to focus primarily on healing yourself and parts of you. You are a microcosm of the One Spirit with Its many parts.

`This is not a time to ask "Why me?" or "Why this way?" "This Way" has evolved from Spirit and is still evolving. Others played a part in bringing healing to the One in the past. You and others are cooperating with Spirit in bringing healing in the present, and many others will do so as time goes on.

Quite often, when your head has been (is) uncomfortable, it has been (is) caused by the Lost Will of some of your Souls from previous lifetimes that are with you. Many portions of Lost Will of your Souls from previous lifetimes are with you, so it cannot be helped that some are often in your head.

Peace to your Soul! Have a good night's sleep, and "carry nary a worry" about anything. Shalom! []

Thank You, God! I am overwhelmed!

"Will polarity...cannot lift out of the Body the way the Spirit has been able to do. Will has felt abandoned when Spirit has left it at death." (Original, Introduction p. viii)

I learned from the Holy Spirit earlier: Most of the Soul portions in the healing ring surrounding my Soul are Lost Will portions of my Souls from other lifetimes that haven't yet gone to the light. One purpose of the healing ring is to gather together and bring healing to Lost Will portions of one's Soul.

Many Lost Will portions of my Souls from other lifetimes are with me to help me express my feelings. A few of them plan to stay with me and go to the light when I do. Some have already gone to the light and returned to help. How loving!

(Sept 9, '14) Are portions of Lost Will of Mother God attached to my aura, trying to receive love? [| Y |] Do they want help to get free? [| Y |]

I asked for a demagnetizing shower, spiritual silicon, and spiritual conditioner to flow through me and around me to clear any stickiness holding the Lost Will portions of my Soul bound. I asked Archangel Michael and Mighty Astrea to help them get released and asked angels to guide them to the healing ring surrounding Mother God, the healing ring surrounding my Soul, or wherever they are meant to be.

Holy Spirit, are the portions of the Lost Will of Mother God that had been attached to my aura all cleared?

[| Yes. Some went to the healing ring surrounding Mother God, and some to the healing ring surrounding your Soul. []

That's wonderful! Thank You, Holy Spirit!

End of 6-A: LOST WILL OF MOTHER GOD, SOULS

6-B: DARIN^LP, DARLA^MP, DARIN^2, LEE

Note: ^LP (Lee Prior life) is omitted after Darin and Darin^2, and ^MP (Me Prior life) after Darla in this section.

(Mar 1, '12)   ACROSS LIFETIMES

I learned from the Holy Spirit that a portion of Darla's Soul and a portion of Darin's Soul are with Nate^YS. Do Darla and Darin want Nate to go with them to where they are? [| Y |]

Is that portion of Darla's Soul unloving? [| Y |] Because she is bitter that they had to die? [| Y |]

Is that portion of Darin's Soul unloving? [| It is on the border between loving and unloving. Dark forces are forcing those Soul portions to follow their bidding. |] Are the larger portions of Darin's and Darla's Souls in Heaven? [| Y |]

Nate, what would you suggest that I do for your parents?
[| (Nate) Do a process of forgiveness again between them, between you and Lee, and between Lee's and your Souls in all previous lifetimes when he and you were a couple. |]

I told Darin's and Darla's Souls I would be doing that. I blessed them and asked those portions to leave. They left.

Holy Spirit, when I do a process of forgiveness in spirit with Lee, should I ask him to speak for all men in the Jahner family line? [| Y |] Should I speak for all of the women? [| Y |]

Later that day, I went through a process of forgiveness between Darin and Darla, between Lee and me in this lifetime (speaking for ourselves and all of the men and women in the Jahner family line), and between Lee and me in all other lifetimes when we were a couple.

Thank You, God, for the clearing that took place!

(Jan 31, '13) I often have pain and discomfort on the left side of my neck, extending into my shoulder. It felt better after a chiropractic adjustment yesterday but is again very sore. Holy Spirit, Is a contact point for dark energies located in that area? [| Y |]

(!!!) Is that contact point attached to a Soul that is in my neck? [| Y |] A portion of Ron's Soul? [| N |] Lee's Soul? [| N |] Darin²'s Soul? [| Y |] Is his Soul enmeshed with my Soul? [| Y |]

Do I need to forgive Lee more fully for pressing himself on me when I became pregnant with Nita, and do Darla and Clara need to forgive Darin/ Darin² more fully for his assault on them before Darin²'s Soul and the contact point can be cleared from my neck and shoulder? [| Y |]

I immediately did a process of forgiveness between Lee and me and between Darla/Clara and Darin/ Darin². I did a clearing for Darin²'s Soul and the contact point that is attached to it.

Is that portion of Darin²'s Soul cleared from my neck and shoulder? [| Yes, but a residue of dark energy remains. |]

I ask for a continuous Holy Spirit demagnetizing shower to flow through me to clear that residue. Thank You, Holy Spirit!

The left side of my neck and shoulder felt much better after that clearing. Thank You, Father God!

(May 22, '13)   My Astral Body Needs Healing

Holy Spirit, do I have inflammation in my brain or some other problem I should see a doctor about?

[| No, but you have inflammation in the brain of your astral body. Darla has much more grief to release. |]

Holy Spirit, would You like for me to release emotions for Darla? [| Y |] I spoke to Darla and Darin that evening and released some emotions. I didn't feel well enough to cry much.

Is a portion of Darla's astral body within the brain of my astral body (Starr p. 4)? [| Y |] "Festering emotions" came to mind. Are Darla's emotions festering from Darin having belittled her? [| Y |] And from his having raped her while under the influence of Darin²? [| Y |]

Emotions originate in the heart. Is Darla's heart inflamed? [| Y |] Is it caused partly by Darla's contempt for herself? [| Y |]

If someone doesn't deal with having contempt for themselves, does that carry over to their next life? [| Y |] Darla's contempt for herself might be rooted in another lifetime.

"...there are hospitals in the etheric realm where the etheric and astral bodies can be healed and revitalized in cases of a long illness... [or] when a person has been burned to death." (Starr p. 9)

After a person dies, is their astral body repaired, and is it the astral body for their next lifetime? [| Y |] Is my astral body the same astral body that Darla had? [| Y |]

(Oct 24, '13) My right hip has been very sore again lately. Chiropractic treatments haven't helped. I asked the Holy Spirit about it. Portions of Lost Will of Mother God and lost Will of my Soul from this lifetime are in that area, but the pain comes primarily from my etheric body.

The right hip area of Darla's etheric body got severely damaged in the crash that killed her, Darin, and Nate. In this lifetime, my etheric body was weak in that area. Then it got damaged when my feet slipped out from under me at age 21 as I walked down wet stairs and landed on my right hip.

That day and for the next 30 days, I prayed: "Holy Spirit, please restore the perfect original blueprint for every cell in my etheric body and my physical body, especially in my neck, back, right hip, and leg. Thank You!"

(Aug 22, '14) Is the brain area of my astral body damaged because of the car accident that killed me in my lifetime as Darla? [| Y |] Is a supraphysical shell related to that accident attached to the brain of my astral body? [| Y |] Is a portion of Darla's Soul with me? [| Y |]

Twice a day for the next four days, I asked Angels of the Violet Flame to do a clearing for that supraphysical shell.

(Aug 26, '14) Has the supraphysical shell from the time of Darla's accident been cleared from me? [| Y |] Thank You, God!

(Apr 24, '15)   RESCUED BY SPIRIT

Note: This is a portion of a Reading Mandy did for me.

MANDY: We are delighted that you have invited us again. We are here to assist you in remembering that you have done nothing wrong, that you are OK, that you are perfectly divine, and that you are here to live your life in a state of acceptance. It is time to release any expectations that there must be something more you can do. And so, we ask you, what is your most important question?

ME: For over 11 years, I have had a problem with having a lot of pain and discomfort at the top of my head. I learned that in an earlier lifetime as Darla, my husband Darin and I, and our 5-year-old son Nate, died in a car accident.

MANDY: It is quite true that the part of you that is Darla suffered the trauma that you are speaking of. You must be aware that that past lifetime is happening now. There is no time. Everything is happening at one time. You are focused within the body of Lorrie here, yet this one that is you of Darla is in a post-traumatic stress type of situation.

In her life in the world she is living in, Darla keeps reliving the trauma of the car accident. And since she has passed over, she is reliving it within her being. It's like she captured herself in a web of fear and pain, like her mind wants to track it and jumps onto the web, this highway of fear, and cannot get off. She is in this state of posttraumatic stress, and anything can trigger that thought within her that brings her back to the trauma of the accident.

Darla had trauma to the top of her head, where her crown chakra is located, where one allows in the life force energy from the Divine, called a vortex. The more Darla focuses on the trauma, the tighter the vortex becomes. It is much out of alignment. It moves clockwise like a tornado so that the energy comes in and feeds the whole form. Her vortex was knocked out of place by the trauma. It is not straight upright and is not swirling in a complete circle.

Darla relives this trauma on many different levels, from when the accident happened, from before when she was creating the accident, from the trauma afterward, and her death. Even in death, she struggles. She is not allowing herself to heal and release and relieve.

Darla is a part of you, and you are a part of her. It is all happening at the same time. You are connected with her through a dimensional trigger that bleeds through for you. That "bleeding through" happens the most when you suffer trauma, stress, or anxiety in the present, or emotional aftereffects from earlier trauma that you experienced. That triggers Darla's ability to bleed into your life. She, her energy, comes through the top of your head. Are you following this?

ME: Yes.

MANDY: The webbing she is in becomes your webbing, so you begin to feed her fears, which keep her vortex closed. "Her vortex" refers to the clockwise-spinning spiritual connection between her Soul and God located at the top of every person's head, sometimes called a "silver cord."

Darla is not doing this on purpose. She is not even aware of you, as you are not aware of her, but the dimensional fields now are so small that the parallel worlds exist close together and are merging and blending. For you to release the pain from within your head becomes a journey for you to help Darla get released from the post-traumatic stress that she is in.

You will need to make a conscious effort to help Darla. You may want to begin speaking to her. When the effects of her post-traumatic stress come through, note where you start to hurt and what the emotion was before the pain began.

Darla's emotion jumps onto that web that bleeds through to you, and, as it does, your emotion connects with the webbing that she experiences as post-traumatic stress. The more she struggles, the more the pain connects with you.

You have helped people who died see or go to the light. It is almost as if that is what Darla needs. Only she is in this world of hers in which she is reliving this over and over. The accident and all the trauma that went with it are over and done with, but it is being recreated repeatedly by Darla's thought system. Are you following this?

ME: Would it be wise for me not to pay much attention when my head is uncomfortable, not to think, "What's wrong?" "What should I do?" "What could be causing it?"

MANDY: Yes, because what you focus on will increase, which causes the webbing to get even more intertwined with yours, causing Darla to feel more and more of her trauma because that webbing is holding you together somehow.

Pain is not an easy thing. The biggest thing you must learn to do is say "No" to the pain and focus on something else. You no longer need to carry the emotional trauma of Darla's accident and the death of her child along with Darla. That is a past event. In some way, you would be helping her not to focus on her pain. If you focus on your pain, it is like you are saying, "Oh, that was so horrible for you! Tell me more."

Darla feeds on whatever sympathy you extend to her, so she can hardly move from her web. But you can unweave that web by blessing it. Oh, Darla, I bless you! All is well. This will take care of things, Lorrie.

ME: Wonderful! Thank you very much, Mandy!

MANDY: You are welcome, Lorrie! Blessed be! (She left.)

Evening: I felt uneasy all day about something Mandy said. I told her I had learned that in a past lifetime, roses were set up as a contact point for a curse hanging over me and my family lines to attract witchcraft energies. Mandy pooh-poohed that idea and said I should "fill my home with roses." That made me feel somewhat wary of her.

I felt comfortable with the rest of what Mandy said. I began paying as little attention to pain as possible, especially in the upper part of my head. I was dealing with another situation during the same time frame that was also causing pain and discomfort in the upper part of my head, but the pain in that area had substantially lessened in the weeks ahead.

(Jul 17, '15) [| Darla is doing much better since you began blessing her and not commiserating with her. |]

Thank You for telling me that, Father God! That's great.

(Aug 26, '15)   Portions of Lee's Souls with Me

I became aware of a presence behind my left shoulder and asked the Holy Spirit about it. Portions of Lee's Soul and Darin[2]'s Soul that are enmeshed with my Soul were there.

Ministry Team, please assist me as I clear enmeshment between my Soul, Lee's Soul, and Darin[2]'s Soul during every lifetime that we shared, and between Lee's Soul and Darin[2]'s Soul, if Lee chooses that. I cleared the enmeshment between my Soul and those portions of Lee's and Darin[2]'s Souls, then commanded them to leave. (Cough)

Did those portions of Lee's and Darin[2]'s Souls leave? [| N |] Is part of me hanging onto Lee's Soul? [| Y |] Is a portion of Lee's Soul from a different lifetime with me? [| Y |] Is that Soul portion enmeshed with my Soul? [| Y |] After I cleared that enmeshment, those Soul portions left. Thank You, Holy Spirit!

(Aug 29, '15) Are portions of Lee's Soul with me? [| Y |] Did parts of me allow them to enter? [| Y |] Is getting those Soul portions cleared out important? [| Y |]

After clearing the incorporation of portions of Lee's Soul from cells in my body and clearing the enmeshment between his Soul and mine, I commanded all of those portions to leave that didn't have permission to be with me.

Holy Spirit, did all of the portions of Lee's Soul leave that were with me without permission? [| Some of them did. |]

Archangel Michael and Mighty Astrea, please see that all portions of Lee's Soul that are with me without permission leave. Thank you! (Pause) Have all of them left now? [| Y |]

(Sept 27, '15) I sensed a Soul was present. Holy Spirit, is part of Lee's Soul present? [| Y |] With permission? [| N |] Did a part of me that made love to him permit him to be with me? [| Y |] That could be Georgette[PM].

(!!!) Is a Soul (Soul portion) with me that is leeching energy from me? Is it a portion of Lee's Soul from the lifetime when he was angry with me for having had a miscarriage? [| Y |]

I commanded that portion of Lee's Soul to leave and asked Archangel Michael to see to it that it does. It left. Thank You, Archangel Michael!

(Apr 25, '16)   UMBILICAL CORD CONNECTIONS

Is Darla's astral body somewhat enmeshed with mine? [| Y |] Is her vortex enmeshed with mine? [| Y |] Is a portion of Darla's Soul with me? [| Not directly. |] Is a portion of her Soul in the healing ring? [| Y |] Does she have permission to be there? [| Y |] Is it correct that I cannot help but be affected by her energy because she is a part of my Full Soul? [| Y |]

(Sept 4, '16) The top of my head is bothering me a lot. Holy Spirit, are the vortexes of some of my Souls from previous lifetimes caught in, enmeshed with, my vortex? [| Y |]

(!!!) Does an umbilical cord connection between people and Souls cause their vortexes to be enmeshed? [| Y |] Do I have an umbilical cord connection with Lee? [| N |] Does Georgette[P] have one? [| Y |]

Am I being affected by the umbilical cord connection between Georgette and Lee and by Lee's connections with other people? [| Y |] Is the vibration energy level of Lee's Soul compatible with mine? [| N |] Is Georgette willing to have the umbilical cord connection between her and Lee cleared? [| Y |]

Holy Spirit, please place a protective valve in every soul tie and umbilical cord connection between my Souls and parts of them and Lee's Souls and parts of them in every lifetime that we were together so that only love can travel in each direction. Thank You!

6-B: DARIN[LP], DARLA[MP], DARIN[2], LEE

6-C: MARIE[GM], HAROLD,[LP] KATHERINE

Note: [GM] (Grandma/Me Prior life) is omitted after Marie, [RP] (Ron Prior life) after Tony, and [LP] (Lee Prior life) after Harold in this section.

(Mar 2, '11)   ISSUES TO CLEAR UP

Is everything settled between Grandma Leigh and me regarding our lifetime as Marie when we were one Soul?
[| No, things are not fully settled regarding that lifetime. |]
(Aug 3, '12) Holy Spirit, is negative energy emitted from Ron's and my family's picture? [| Y |] By asking more questions, I learned that negative energy is coming

1. From Ron's image: related to his prior lifetime as Tony[RP], during which Tony's wife Marie was unfaithful.
2. From my image: related to a curse Tony placed against Marie (a wish for her to go to hell). Negative energy from that curse is hanging over Ron, also.

(Aug 17, '12) I have been perplexed for several years about why I feel ill at ease with my younger son, Pat. Holy Spirit, is there something that I need to clear up? [| Y |]
At the time of Marie's death, her Full Soul split into the Marie[1] Full Soul and the Marie[2] Full Soul. Did Marie[2] feel abandoned after the split? [| Y |] Was she very angry with Marie[1]? [| Y |] Did she utter a curse against Marie[1]? [| Yes, for Marie[1] to never find love in future lifetimes. |]
(!!!) Is Pat's Soul a portion of Marie[2]'s Full Soul? [| Y |] Does he feel abandoned? [| Yes, even by God. |]
I understand without words that I should ask the Young Souls to minister to Pat in his earlier years. His dad, Ron, began having emotional problems shortly after Pat was born. Young Souls, please minister love, blessing, and healing to Pat as a baby and young child. Thank you!

(Feb 21, '13) I learned from the Holy Spirit that Marie had Parkinson's disease. A portion of her Soul was within Mom's Soul as an infestation. That's where she got Parkinson's from.

Portions of Marie[2]'s Soul and Mom's Soul are incorporated within cells in my body. It causes me to feel afraid when they feel afraid. The enmeshed spirits of Parkinson's disease and fibromyalgia are hanging over me and others in the family.

(Feb 22, '13) I cleared enmeshment between the Souls of Marie[2] and Mom, Marie[2] and me, and Mom and me; cleared incorporation of Marie[2]'s and Mom's Souls from within cells in my body, and commanded those Soul portions to leave. That Sunday, I invited them to go to the light.

I did a clearing for myself for the spirits of Parkinson's disease, fibromyalgia, and all other negative energies.

(Feb 24, '13) Holy Spirit, are the Incorporation and enmeshment of Mom's Soul cleared from me? [| Y |] Did that portion of her Soul go to the light last Sunday? [| Y |] Great!

Are the incorporation and enmeshment of Marie[2]'s Soul cleared from me? [| No |] Are the spirits of Parkinson's disease and fibromyalgia cleared from me? [| Residue remains. |]

During the next six weeks, I did further clearing for Soul incorporation, Soul enmeshment, and dark energies.

(Jun 14, '13)   AN ONUS GETS CLEARED

Holy Spirit, is an onus hanging over me that I placed on myself? [| Y |] Is it a result of karma (something I did)? [| Y |]

I saw an image of several contact points for dark energy surrounding the top of my head. I learned from the Holy Spirit that those contact points are a network of dark energy centers, connecting points for witchcraft and other dark energies. Lost Will of Mother God and Lost Will from my lifetime as Darla and other lifetimes are stuck to those contact points.

Holy Spirit, did those contact points get placed there because of an onus I placed on myself? Is that onus a karmic curse? [| Y |]

I received an understanding of the situation: In my lifetime as Marie, I placed a curse against Tony for him to get sick. He died fairly young. Is that curse resting on Ron now (another lifetime of Tony's)? [| Y |]

To double-check that answer, I asked again: Is that curse resting on Ron now? [| N |] Did it get cleared just now because I wanted it to be? [| Y |] Did the curse against Tony get cleared just now, too? [| Y |] So the onus I placed on myself is cleared? [| Y |] Wonderful! (I could hardly believe it!)

Does karma need to be cleared between Marie and Tony? [| N |] Unforgiveness? [| N |]

Thank You over and over again, Holy Spirit!

(Feb 25, '14) An unloving portion of Tony's Soul is in my abdomen. He wants to bring me to damnation if he can. A portion of Marie²'s Soul is enmeshed with that portion of Tony's Soul. I did a clearing to remove their Souls.

(Mar 2, '14) Holy Spirit, are the portions of Tony's and Marie²'s Souls cleared from my abdomen? [| Y |] Thank You!

(Aug 21, '14)   To Where They Belong

I had trouble falling asleep the last several nights because of feeling antsy and anxious. I asked the Holy Spirit about it. With permission from the Holy Spirit, portions of Marie²'s Soul are still with me, including in my brain. She feels anxious when I am about to go to sleep and is afraid all the while I am sleeping. The discomfort in my head is caused partly by the presence of Marie²'s Soul. Also, there is karma between my Soul and Grandma Leigh's Soul regarding the split of our Full Souls after our lifetime as Marie.

Holy Spirit, are You suggesting for my Full Soul and Grandma Leigh's Full Soul to be reunited? [| N |] For me to allow some portions of Grandma's Soul to join my Full Soul? [| Y |] And to allow some portions of my Soul to join Grandma's Full Soul? [| Y |] Should I leave it up to You which parts are meant to rejoin the other Soul? [| Y |]

(!!!) Have portions of my Soul been hanging onto portions of Marie²'s Soul and not allowing them to leave? [| Y |] Are the portions of my Soul that latched onto the portions of Marie²'s Soul meant to leave with Marie² and join her Soul? [| Y |] Will the portions of Marie²'s Soul that latched onto portions of my Soul remain with me and join my Soul? [| Y |] Holy Spirit, I am so glad that you are in charge!

Do Soul portions latch on to other Soul portions because of a magnetic connection? [| Y |] When that happens, is it often a reconnecting of an Original Soul? [| Y |] Wow!

When I give permission, will the portions of my Soul that are attached to Marie²'s Soul leave and join her Soul? [| Y |]

I asked for retroactive clearing of any Soul incorporation and clearing for enmeshment that was needed and then said:

"Portions of my Soul that are attached to Marie²'s Soul, I give you permission to leave with her and join her Full Soul. Portions of Marie²'s Soul that are attached to my Soul, I give you permission to join with my Soul."

Holy Spirit, did those portions of Marie²'s Soul leave? [| Y |]

I asked Marie to forgive me for judging her during that lifetime of hers/mine when our personality was split, and she asked me for forgiveness (each half of Marie's mind and Soul asked the other half for forgiveness).

Holy Spirit, is the karma cleared between Marie² and me? [| Y |] Thank You, Holy Spirit!

(May 6, '18)   Resistance to Leaving

Even though the temperature in the room was 78 degrees, I felt cold, a sign that a Soul was present. I learned that several Souls were with me and directed them to leave.

(!!!) Holy Spirit, is a part of me allowing any Soul to enter that wants to? [| Y |] Is a portion of Marie²'s Soul still with me that is allowing Souls to enter? [| Y |]

(!!!) Is that portion of her Soul connected with my Soul like we are Siamese twins? [| Y |] As long as her Soul is enmeshed with mine, will she have the right to invite Souls in? [| Y |]

Is that portion of Marie[2]'s Soul meant to be separated from mine? [| Y |] Would some parts of me allow her to return? [| Y |] Would some parts choose to leave with her? [| Yes, the portions of her Soul that are masquerading as parts of you. |]

Heavenly helpers, please join me as I separate Marie[2]'s Soul from mine. Thank you!

I did a process of forgiveness between every part of me and every part of Marie[2]'s Soul, did a retroactive clearing of incorporation of her Soul from cells in my body, and cleared enmeshment between my Soul and the portions of her Soul that are with me. I directed every part of her Soul to leave.

(May 10, '18) Holy Spirit, did all portions of Marie[2]'s Soul leave when I directed them to leave? [| No, because parts of your Soul weren't willing to release her. |]

Are the parts of me that are unwilling to release outside Soul portions whose energy is incompatible with my energy meant to be dismissed until my Soul permits them to return? [| Y |] Is it normal for parts of a Soul to leave for a while and then return when the person's Soul gives the OK? [| Y |]

I cleared the incorporation of Marie[2]'s Soul from cells in my body and the enmeshment between every part of her Soul and every part of my Soul. I blessed the portions of her Soul and my Soul that have been unwilling to release her Soul and commanded all of them to leave. They left happily! They have been wanting to leave!

Holy Spirit, just now is my Soul as Lorrie, the only Soul with me? [| Y |] (I had to cry.) Thank You, Holy Spirit and heavenly helpers! Please flow healing love through me.

(May 14, '18) My neck and lower back were hurting a lot. I learned there were spiritual umbilical cord connections between me and two men from church.

Holy Spirit, is my Soul so open that it allows hurting people to form umbilical cord connections with me? [| Y |]

End of 6-C: MARIE[MP], HAROLD[LP], KATHERINE

6-D: PENNY AND PETER

(Feb 5, '12)   PENNY, MY TWIN SISTER

Is my Soul a Siamese identical twin Soul? Did my embryo divide to become identical twins, but my Soul divided only partially? Did my twin die, my mother's body re-absorb her body, and her Soul is still with me? [| Y |]

Penny came to mind. Is Penny's Soul experiencing this life as if she is living it? [| Y |] Does her Soul sometimes take over my body while I sleep? [| Y |] As a child, did she sometimes take over while I was awake? [| Yes, quite often before age 5. |]

Did Penny's Soul take over my body during the rape by Dad at age 3? [| Y |] Is trauma from that trauma still buried in her Soul? [| Y |] Did her Soul also take over my body during the rape by my Dad's brother, Uncle Art, at age 16? [| Y |] Does Penny need clearing for negative energies? [| Y |] Is her Soul incorporated within cells in my body? [| Y |] I began clearing the incorporation of her Soul from within cells in my body.

(Feb 11, '12) Is the incorporation of Penny's Soul cleared from cells in my body? [| Y |] I cleared the enmeshment between her Soul and mine. During church service the next day, I invited Penny to go to the light. Holy Spirit, did she do so? [| Y |]

(Feb 21, '12)   Infestation In Penny's Soul

Before going to work, I prayed for clearing for the office and asked for all portions of unloving Souls and dark energies that were in or near the office to be encased with spiritual lead. When I returned home, my blood pressure was 186/77. Holy Spirit, are there dark energies in the computer at work or attached to it? [| N|] Somewhere else in the office? [| N |]

Is an "actual" unloving Soul or a portion of one attached to or within the computer? [| Y |] Does that unloving Soul want help to become loving? (No answer.) Is it being controlled by dark forces at this time? [| Y |]

(!!!) Has a portion of that unloving Soul been following me around, getting as close to me as possible? [| Y |] Does the presence of that unloving Soul trigger a great deal of anxiety within my Soul and parts of me, causing me to have elevated systolic blood pressure readings? [| Y |] Wow!

Is the unloving Soul following me around a part of my Soul in this lifetime or from a previous one? (No answer.) Is it part of Penny's Soul, my twin? [| (Slow answer) Yes. |]

Is that unloving Soul part of Penny's Soul because it entered her Soul as an infestation at the time of conception? [| Y |] Penny and I were identical twins, so do I have an infestation of a portion of that unloving Soul in my Soul, too? [| Y |]

Is that infestation a portion of the Soul of a relative? [| Y |] Has the rest of that relative's Soul gone to the light? [| Y |] That could mean Heaven or "the right place for unloving Souls." Did that Soul go to the right place for unloving Souls? [| Y |] Do You want me to know whose unloving Soul it is? [| Y |]

(!!!) Is it Mom's younger brother Hal? [| Y |] Is the portion of Hal's Soul that is in the right place for unloving Souls crying out for help to become loving? [| Y |]

I immediately began clearing the infestation of Uncle Hal's Soul from Penny's and my Souls and sending a steady flow of love and blessings to Hal to help his Soul choose to become loving.

What a breakthrough! Thank You, Holy Spirit, for giving me the questions to ask and the answers to them. Please guide me as I clear the infestation and assist those separated portions of Uncle Hal's Soul in choosing to become loving and going to the light if and when he chooses. Thank You!

(Feb 22, '12)   Uncle Hal and Me: Connection

Is much of the discomfort in my head coming from Mom, Aunt Mollie, and Grandma and Grandpa Leigh being concerned about their brother (son) Hal? [| Y |]

(!!!) Holy Spirit, was Uncle Hal my child in a previous lifetime? [| Y |] Before I came into this life, did my Soul agree to allow my Soul and Penny's Soul to become infested with Uncle Hal's Soul so I (we) could help him become loving? [| Y |] Wow!

Is Uncle Hal's Soul part of my Full Soul? [| It is part of a split-off portion of your Full Soul. |] From before it split into two Full Souls? [| Y |] That explains why his Soul could become infested within mine. Thank You, Holy Spirit!

Are some portions of my Full Soul unloving that lived lifetimes during which they didn't receive enough love? [| Y |] Father God, I ask for all unloving portions of my Full Soul to be ministered to in a spiritual copper ring. Thank You!

(!!!) Holy Spirit, will I continue to experience discomfort in one way or another until all portions of my Full Soul that want to become loving have received help to become loving? [| Y |]

I continued extending love and blessings to portions of Uncle Hal's Soul and expanded it to include all portions of my Full Soul that want help to become loving.

(Feb 23, '12)   PETER, MY TRIPLET BROTHER

Beth was here for a visit. I told her about Penny and asked questions that came to mind. We learned from the Holy Spirit that I was a triplet: Penny and me, identical twins, and Peter. I talked with Peter several times through the years, thinking he was a part of my personality.

(Apr 25, '12) I learned that a portion of Penny's Soul is in my aura. It hasn't joined the rest of Penny's Soul yet because a small part of her Soul is still incorporated within cells in my body. I did the process of clearing incorporation for two weeks.

(May 18, '12) Is the incorporation of Penny's Soul cleared from cells in my body? [| Y |] Did it join the rest of her Soul? [| Y |] Did she go to the light?

[| Yes. Penny and Peter are both fully free. They went to the light and are now staying with you as part of the group of Young Souls. |]

Is the portion of Uncle Hal's Soul that had been incorporated within cells in my body and within Penny's "body" now loving? [| Y |] Did the portion of his Soul leave that had been with me? [| Y |] I am so happy!

(Feb 7, '13)   We Want To Be Baptized

My Feb 6 paycheck "disappeared" from the envelope after I put it in my purse. After looking for it for two days, I asked:

Holy Spirit, did one of the Young Souls take my check to get my attention so they could tell or ask me about something?
[| Yes. Peter took it. He wants to tell you that he and Penny want to be baptized. |]

(Feb 8, '13) I baptized Peter and Penny with holy water, using Fischer Price wooden dolls to represent them. After that, I reminded them several times over the weekend that I expected my paycheck to show up. I checked my purse twice, but the check wasn't there.

(Feb 11, '13) I asked my boss, Josh, for a replacement check and put it in my purse. After Josh left for the day, I took the envelope from my purse the original paycheck had been in to put it on Josh's desk so he could reuse it. Something was in it: My original paycheck! I put the duplicate check on his desk with a note that I had found the original. I am mystified!

End of 6-D: PENNY AND PETER

6-E: DUAL SOULS: MIA[MD] AND ME

Note: [MD] (Me Dual Soul) is omitted after Mia in this section.

(Mar 31, '13)   LIKE SIAMESE TWINS

During church this morning, I felt like part of me was objecting, differing from me, like I was watching myself. I learned from the Holy Spirit that the split of Marie's[GM] original Full Soul into two Full Souls wasn't quite complete when a portion of Marie[1]'s[MP] Full Soul went out to begin this life as Lorrie. *My Soul was connected to Marie[2]'s[GP] Full Soul by a narrow strip of Soul essence,* so when my

Soul entered my body, that connected Soul entered, also. I will call her **Mia**.

I also learned that Mia's Soul is incorporated within cells in my body and thinks of my body as hers. There are two Souls and two minds within my body: mine and Mia's. Are we somewhat like Siamese twins living in the same body? [| Y |] Does Mia think I should be the one to leave this body? [| Y |] When I say, "Only my Soul may enter new cells in my body," does Mia say that, too, for her Soul!? [| Y |]

Has Mia felt like she is competing with me for love? [| Y |] Has she caused some of the aversion and fear I have experienced regarding dating? [| Y |] Does she often take over my body while I sleep? [| Y |] Is much of the soreness in my muscles and tendons caused by the conflict between Mia's Soul and my Soul within the cells in those areas? [| Y |] Is that type of conflict one of the causes of fibromyalgia? [| Y |]

I haven't been able to get all of the incorporation and enmeshment of outside Souls cleared from me. (!!!) Holy Spirit, are the Soul portions that I haven't been able to clear in parts of my body where Mia's Soul is incorporated? [| Y |] Her Soul is also enmeshed with those outside Soul portions!

Are Mia's and my Souls enmeshed? [| Very much so. |] When a portion of Marie²'s^{GP} Soul entered as an infestation at the time of my conception, did she enter only Mia's Soul? [| Y |]

As I mentioned earlier, I remember very little about the three days following surgery at the end of July 2010. I learned later that a portion of Corrine's^{MP} Soul had taken over. Did Mia take over during that time, also, maybe even more than Corrine did? [| Y |]

In the middle of my junior year in high school, I realized that I couldn't remember anything about my classes for the first semester. Did Mia take over during that time? [| Y |]

Now, this is interesting! My Soul and Mia's have different energy levels. Since I ask for protection for myself every day, my energy doesn't get drained directly to Mia, but some of it gets drained to her at the base where my Soul and hers are connected.

Holy Spirit, please place a protective valve in the narrow strip of soul essence that connects Mia's and my Souls so that only love can go through. Thank You!

Did a protective valve get put in place? [| Y |] Great!

(Apr 3, '13)   EFFECTS OF MIA'S PRESENCE

I have been having increased discomfort within the top of my head for the last few weeks, so I checked my blood pressure regularly. One morning, my systolic BP reading was 167. It has been averaging 145. I think Mia is getting uncomfortable.

A feeling of being "antsy" and stressed was building up within me while I was shopping this morning. While driving home and for several hours after I was home, I felt slightly jittery and *like I wanted to get out of my body,* like a war going on within me.

Holy Spirit, is a portion of Grandma Leigh's Soul in my brain making me feel jittery? [| Y |] Is the overall feeling that "things aren't right" within me caused by Mia's personality (Soul) being more to the forefront than usual? [| Y |] Does Mia experience discomfort when I experience discomfort? [| Y |]

I will clear the incorporation and enmeshment of Mia's Soul, clear karma between her and me, and clear negative energies from myself. After that, I will ask my sister Ann to do spiritual laser surgery to separate Mia's Soul and my Soul, where a narrow band of Soul essence connects them.

(Apr 9, '13)   Message from Mia

Father God, thank You and the Ministry Team for helping with the clearings and blessings I have been doing!

[| You are welcome, Lorrie. I want you to know that things are going well with your work on the writings and ministering to the people and Souls the Holy Spirit has been asking you to. Maybe you can bundle up that encouragement and carry it with you!

Mia is happy that her Soul will soon be separated from yours. She understands that writing about the effects on you of having her

Soul almost connected with yours will help other people along the way. I will have her speak for herself. []

MIA: Hi, Lorrie! I feel much better now than compared to earlier when you didn't know I was here! Before this, I felt like I needed to protect myself from you and be ready to fight to keep my place within this body that, up to now, I firmly believed was my body. The Holy Spirit told me that your body is meant to be fully your body, and I am OK with that. It is freeing for me!

ME: Are you willing to have enmeshments cleared between your Soul and mine and between your Soul and other Souls?

MIA: Yes.

ME: That's great! Thank you!

(Apr 8, '13) I cleared the incorporation of Mia's Soul from within cells in my body by a 9-day process beginning March 29. Today, I cleared the enmeshment between her Soul, my Soul, and other Souls and did a process of forgiveness between Mia and me.

(Apr 10, '13) Results of those prayers: The incorporation of Mia's Soul is cleared from within cells in my body. Enmeshment is partly cleared between her Soul and mine and mostly cleared between her Soul and other Souls. Karma is cleared between Mia and me. The spirits of anger and pride have not been cleared from Mia or from me. Thank You, Holy Spirit!

(Apr 22, '13)   Direction and Encouragement

(My right ear became very warm. Father God sometimes uses that as a signal that He wants to say something.)

Good morning, Father God!

[| Good morning, Lorrie! You already picked up on this: For the sake of the integrity of the writings and your person, I ask you to quit playing any card games on the computer even though you feel strongly drawn to playing them. Aaron[MP] and Mia are playing a part in that strong attraction. When you accede to their wishes to do physical things, it makes it much more difficult for their Souls to separate from yours.

The clearing of enmeshment between outside Soul portions

and your Soul that you did last evening went well. The enmeshment between your Soul and Mia's Soul is mostly cleared. I will soon give further instructions regarding getting her Soul separated from yours. Thank you, Lorrie, for taking the time to listen. Thank you, Fern, for your assistance. Peace! |]

Thank You, Father God! Thank you, Fern, for your help!

In the evening, I baptized Mia.

(Apr 24, '13) Off and on for the last six months, the first four fingers of my left hand have become partially numb for a few minutes. Was that tied in with Mia in some way? [| Y |]

(!!!) Was her Soul, and not mine) almost fully incorporated within cells in the nerve line connected with that area? [| Y |] I felt only slight numbness this last month. That makes sense because the incorporation of Mia's Soul from within cells in my body is almost cleared!

Is Mia's emotional body enmeshed with mine? [| Y |] Would flowing spiritual conditioner through me make it easier for the strands of her emotional body to be separated from my emotional body? [| Y |]

Is the incorporation of Mia's Soul cleared from cells in my body, and the enmeshment between her Soul and mine cleared well enough that I can arrange a time for Ann to do spiritual laser surgery? [| Yes. Only the Will portions, the emotional bodies of your Souls, need to be separated. |]

(Apr 27, '13) A large portion of Mia's Soul went to the light last Sunday at church, but a portion of it is still with me.

Bless you, Mia! Thank You, Holy Spirit!

(Apr 30, '13)   More About Mia

I asked the Holy Spirit questions and learned that Mia's Soul is still somewhat connected with my Soul. The connection between our Souls would be that "narrow strip of Soul essence" mentioned at the beginning of this section. I should extend much love and blessing to the portions of Mia's Soul that are still with me. They do not feel worthy of love. I should also clear erroneous early imprinting from her.

Mia felt somewhat guilty all her life, thinking she didn't have the right to be in my body and be born because I was born out of wedlock. She experienced some of the early sexual abuse along with me. She thought of herself as Mollie's little girl and Joel as her brother. She created a place in her imagination where they lived as a family.

I suddenly broke down, crying in empathy for Mia and crying as Mia. *I received the understanding that she has had excruciatingly strong physical and emotional feelings of, "I can't get out!" She felt like she needed to be "born out of me"!* I cried for quite a while. That was good for both of us. Those emotions have been pent up within Mia and me since our conception. Mia doesn't want me to worry about her but to help release pent-up emotions. She is feeling quite happy right now.

(May 19, '13)   Clearing for Mia

1. Retroactive for the last three years, I cleared the incorporation of Mia's Soul from cells in my body.
2. I cleared the enmeshment between my Soul, Mia's Soul, and all outside Souls that are with me.
3. I cleared erroneous early imprinting for those Souls.
4. I commanded all outside Souls to leave who could leave and asked their guardian angels to guide them to where they were meant to be.

(Jun 9, '13) Ann asked the Ministry Team to do spiritual laser surgery to cut the strip of Soul essence connecting Mia's Soul with my Soul. Thank you, Ministry Team! Thank You, Holy Spirit, that Mia's Soul and my Soul are separated!

(Sept 5, '13)   PUTTING THINGS IN ORDER

My head is bothering me more than usual today. Is a portion of Mia's Soul in my brain? [| Yes. Several young parts of you that Mia cared for are hanging onto her. |]

I asked the Ministry Team to clear the enmeshment between Mia's Soul and parts of me while I sat quietly for 15 minutes, then asked them to minister for another 30 minutes while I played quiet music. Thank you, Ministry Team!

[| Good evening, Lorrie! You are wondering what to do about the young portions of your Soul that are hanging onto Mia. Develop a relationship with them and teach them about their real heavenly Father-Mother. Leave Mia's care in the hands of the Ministry Team. Bless you! Time for bed! |]

Thank You, Father God! Good night!

(Sept 9, '13) I learned from the Holy Spirit that the portion of Mia's Soul that had been in my brain is now in the astral plane. There are beneficial soul ties between Mia and the young parts of me that hadn't wanted her to leave, through which they can receive love. There is a non-beneficial soul tie between Mia and Georgette[P].

Holy Spirit, please place a protective valve in those beneficial soul ties so that only love can travel in each direction, and please dissolve the non-beneficial soul tie between Georgette and Mia. Thank You!

(Sept 10, '13) Holy Spirit, You told me earlier that Mia's and my Souls came into this lifetime as dual Souls. Was every part of me partly my Soul and partly Mia's Soul until recently? [| Y |] Did the abuse incidents occur to both of us? [| Y |] Should I have Mia in mind as I do healing and clearing work for myself?

[| Lorrie, you are on your healing journey, and Mia was "along for the ride," so to speak. Your Soul's purposes are yours, and her Soul's purposes are hers. The coming times of emotional release for parts of you and your whole person happen on your Soul journey.

The time has come for portions of Mia's Soul that are still with you to leave. Unhealed portions of her Soul can release emotions

182

at the same time you do wherever they are. Do not worry about her. She is being lovingly taken care of, as are all of My/Our spirit children.

Onward We go, Lorrie, with Mother God, Jesus, and Me holding your hand at every age and stage of your life. []

Thank You very much, Father God!

I cleared the enmeshment between Mia's Soul and every part of my Soul, then asked and commanded every part of her Soul to leave. Bless you, Mia!

(Oct 5, '13) Holy Spirit, did the portions of Mia's Soul leave that were with parts of me? [| Yes, but a large part of your emotional body went with her. |]

I cleared the enmeshment between Mia's Soul and the Will portion (emotional body) of my Soul that was with her. I asked those Will portions to return to me. Thank You, Holy Spirit!

End of 6-E: DUAL SOULS: MIA AND ME

CHAPTER 7

VERY EARLY ON

Healing for Prior Lifetimes: Me 3

Feb 12, '12   HEALING CIRCLES AND SQUARES

Since last evening, it has felt like something is around my head. Holy Spirit, are portions of Souls wrapped around my brain? [| Y |] Are they unloving? [| Y |] No wonder my head is throbbing!

Should I have them go to the healing ring surrounding my Soul? [| N |] Lately, I have been asking Soul portions when they leave me to go into the large copper ring that I have to receive clearing and healing, but I don't want to put unloving Souls with loving Souls.

(!!!) Would it be OK to form a square with some of the copper rods I have for unloving Souls to be in to receive clearing and healing? [| Y |] I formed a square with copper rods.

In the name of Jesus, I command all portions of unloving Souls that are with me or attached to my aura to go into that copper square. Thank you!

Evening: Father God, I cleared portions of unloving Souls and negative energies from me, but my head is continuing to throb from elevated blood pressure. Is there another reason for my blood pressure being elevated?

[| Lorrie, to quite an extent, you are trying to figure things out with your human mind. Please let the energies that are within you and around you settle down. Being less anxious about what is happening with you physically and spiritually will help settle your system, including your blood pressure.

The copper ring you have and the copper rods forming a square

184

are signs in the physical of what exists in the spiritual. There are large spiritual copper rings and spiritual copper squares in a higher plane in which many Souls are being ministered to and healed.

A word to the wise: Do not inadvertently *expect* that Soul portions will enter your Soul or latch onto your aura, for doing that causes magnetism that draws them to you!

Good evening! Thank you for your willingness and effort! []

Thank You, Father God! Bless You and All That Is!

Apr 10, '13   The Wide Scope of Judgment

I sensed an outside Soul was in the room. Internally, I saw an image of a person "melting down" and understood that a Soul was present that was suffering under the weight of great condemnation by other people and Souls, including me. It is my Soul from a previous lifetime when I was a prostitute named **Petricartha**MP. I understood that when a person judges somebody because of a particular trait, they also judge everybody else who fits in that category.

Holy Spirit, does the condemnation directed towards one person rest on every person and Soul who, for example, is or has been a prostitute? [| Y |] In the same measure? [| Y |] Wow!

I am sorry, PetricarthaMP, for looking down on prostitutes, for looking down on you. Please forgive me.

Holy Spirit, did Petricartha forgive me? [| Y |] Did the Souls of many others who were prostitutes forgive me, also? [| Y |] (Wow!) Please assist Petricartha's Soul and those other Souls to go to where they can receive healing. Thank You!

Aug 8, '13   Dealing with a Spirit of Death

I feel dread throughout my body. Is a spirit of death with me? [| Y |] My sister Alice is in the process of dying. Is a spirit of death hanging over her and our family? [| Y |] Is a spirit of fear mixed in with it? [| Y |]

Father-Mother God, what do You suggest I do about the spirit of death that is with me and hanging over our family?

[| Lorrie, while you are feeling dread, it is not good to dwell on death, funeral, cemetery, etc. Place the spirit of death and all other considerations into My hands. Ask the Ministry Team to clear it from you and your family (as much as can be cleared just now), and ask the Holy Spirit to keep all dark energies sealed. Please take it easy the rest of the day. Bless you! []

Thank You, Father-Mother God! That helps a lot!

I asked the Ministry Team to clear the spirit of death as I sat quietly for 15 minutes. I felt much better afterward. Later, I went to the hospital to see Alice. She is unresponsive.

Aug 9, '13. I again feel dread throughout my body. Holy Spirit, did a spirit of death that was with Alice come with me yesterday when I left the hospital? [| Y |] I asked the Ministry Team to join me as I did a clearing again for the spirit of death. I felt much better after that prayer. Thank you, Ministry Team!

The next day: Holy Spirit, is the spirit of death cleared from adult me? [| Y |] From every part of me? [| Some parts of you still have residue clinging to them. |]

I asked for a Holy Spirit demagnetizing shower to flow through me to clear negative residue.

Aug 11, '13. Alice died today. May you be at peace, Alice!

Apr 19, '14   UNHEALTHY CONNECTION

I saw an image of my sister Ann's Soul with extensions extending from her waistline in every direction, connecting with people she turns to for advice and affirmation. I learned from the Holy Spirit that a portion of the Soul of every person Ann asked advice from is with her. She is holding onto them in some way.

Did part of my Soul transfer to Ann each time she asked for my opinion about what she should do? [| Y |] Oh no!

Has the portion of my Soul that is with Ann reached the point that it is detrimental to me? [| Y |] Does more energy flow from me to Ann than from her to me when I am with her? [| Y |]

I won't give Ann advice anymore or even express my opinion about the choices she is considering making. Instead, I will encourage her to consider the pros and cons of the situation and decide things for herself.

Evening: I cleared the enmeshment between Ann's Soul and the portions of my Soul that are with her and asked all portions of my Soul to return to me. Holy Spirit, did all of the portions return to me that had been with Ann? [| Y |] Wonderful!

I cleared the enmeshment between my Soul and the portions of Ann's Soul that are with me and commanded all of them to leave.

Holy Spirit, did all portions of Ann's Soul leave that were with me? [| Not all. Some are hanging onto your Soul. |]

Holy Spirit, please flow spiritual conditioner and spiritual silicone through my Soul to make things slippery so those Soul portions can't hang on anymore. Thank You!

I again commanded all portions of Ann's Soul that are with me without permission from the Holy Spirit to leave.

Holy Spirit, did all of them leave now? [| One portion didn't leave yet. |] Oh! Is it enmeshed with other outside Souls that are with me? [| Y |]

I cleared enmeshment between that portion of Ann's Soul and all outside Soul portions that were with me. Then I said, "In the name of Jesus, I command that portion of Ann's Soul and all outside Souls that are with me without permission from the Holy Spirit to leave!" (I coughed.)

Holy Spirit, is Ann's Soul cleared from me now? [| Y |] Great!

Aug 20, '14   CAFFEINE CONNECTION

I am continuing to have discomfort and a feeling of pressure in the upper part of my head. (!!!) Holy Spirit, do some Souls crave caffeine? [| Y |] Are Souls that crave caffeine attracted to me because of the caffeine in my system (100 mg/day)? [| Y |]

Do some of them press against my aura to pick up caffeine energies? [| Y |] Do some enter my aura (body, brain) to pick it up?

[| Y |] Do some leave a small portion of their Soul with me to serve as a connecting link for picking it up? [| Y |] Wow!

I began sealing the caffeine energy within my body with spiritual lead so it wouldn't attract caffeine-craving Souls.

(!!!) Holy Spirit, can Souls release caffeine energy from themselves on their own? [| N |] What would help them? [| Ask for the light of the Holy Spirit to shine through those Souls day and night for three days. |] I asked for that.

If a person continues ingesting caffeine, those same Souls will return, and others will join them to pick up caffeine energies. Solution: Daily, seal caffeine energies within your body with spiritual lead or ask the Holy Spirit to shine continuously through the Souls around you.

Sept 8, '14   Clearing Supraphysical Shells

Holy Spirit, vinegar dissolves calcium deposits. Would spiritual vinegar dissolve the supraphysical shells, "calcified matter" (Starr p. 102) that is attached to the astral body of some Souls? [| Yes, but I suggest for you to take these steps:
   1. Ask for a compress of spiritual vinegar and Balm of Gilead on all calcified areas during the day
   2. Ask that your Soul and all Souls and Soul portions that are with you, including their astral bodies, be immersed in a love bath of golden saffron throughout the night. |]
Thank You for that information, Holy Spirit!
Sept 11, '14. I followed those steps for three days.

Holy Spirit, are all supraphysical shells cleared from the astral body of my Soul in this lifetime? [| Y |] Are they all cleared from the astral body of Souls from other lifetimes of mine that are with me? [| Many are cleared. |]

Thank You, Holy Spirit!

Sept 12, '14   Holy Spirit Vacuuming

Beth did a clearing for me today by a method that she calls "Holy Spirit Vacuuming." She stood behind me and placed her hands on my head with her thumbs outstretched, forming a circle. She asked the Holy Spirit to suction out negative debris, starting at the top of my head and working downward. She "saw" chunks fly out the top of my head.

After the gunk was cleared, Beth asked the Holy Spirit to fill all empty areas with white, sparkly, spiritual goo (love).

I felt much better following that clearing.

7-A: EARLY LIFETIME: PENELOPE^MP

Note: ^MP (Me Prior life) is omitted after Penelope in this section.

(Nov 12, '12)   ONE OF MY EARLIEST LIFETIMES

I felt dread as I thought about going to an upcoming Bible study. Then I thought about my coming visit with my daughter and family in Texas and felt even greater dread.

Holy Spirit, is that feeling of dread coming from an outside Soul that is with me? [| Y |] Has it been with me long? [| Y |]

I had a dream years ago in which a young woman I sensed was my "real self" was behind the bathroom door. She said, "Always be grateful to your God." We both knew we were supposed to join. We stepped toward each other, and I heard a light, clicking sound as her spirit body merged into mine. I felt thrilled when I woke up because I thought I had gotten in touch with my real self and would finally "be like I am supposed to be."

Holy Spirit, did the outside Soul that I just learned is with me enter during that dream? [| A portion of it did. |]

The name **Penelope** came to mind. Has a portion of Penelope's Soul been with me for quite a while? [| Y |] Was she with me at age 5? [| N |] At age 9, when I was abusing Joel? [| Y |] Did she play a part in that? [| Y |]

Is Penelope's Soul incorporated within cells in my body? [| Y |] In every cell? [| Y |] That means even in my brain! Do some cells have only her Soul in them? [| Y |] That's not good. Are parts of me afraid of her? [| No, but they are wary of her. |]

189

I immediately began the 9-day process of clearing the incorporation of Penelope's Soul from within cells in my body. My head continued to feel miserable, indicating that dark energies may be present.

(!!!) Is Penelope's Soul loving? (No answer.) Is a part of it loving? [| Y |] Is part of it on the border between being loving and unloving? [| Y |] Are witchcraft energies attached to the unloving portion? [| Y |] That's why my head has been bothering me so much! [| Y |]

I sealed the unloving portion of Penelope's Soul and the witchcraft energies with spiritual lead.

(!!!) By asking the Holy Spirit more questions, I learned that Penelope is a part of my Soul from very early on that was unwilling to go forward to live a life on Earth and got stuck in the astral plane. She is so afraid that God is very angry with her for not being willing to go to Earth to live a human life that it is deep dread. That is the dread that I am feeling.

(Nov 13, '12)   Sorting Things Out

(!!!) Does Penelope think of my body as being hers? [| Y |] When I speak, are both Penelope and I speaking? [| Y |] Does the unloving portion of Penelope's Soul attract witchcraft energies to her and me? [| Y |] Does food "filled with love" cause stomach upset for her? [| Y |] Wow!

Loving Souls in my Soul and family lines, please join me in sending love and blessings to Penelope. Thank you!

Holy Spirit, am I meant to clear the incorporation of Penelope's Soul from within cells in my body and the enmeshment between her Soul and mine and then assist her in going to the light? [| Y |]

Have all portions of Penelope's Soul that are with me chosen to become loving? [| Y |] I was overwhelmed with joy and relief and had to cry for a while.

I did a retroactive clearing of the incorporation of Penelope's Soul from cells in my body. Holy Spirit, is the incorporation of Penelope's Soul cleared from within all cells in my "adult" body?

[| Y |] From all parts of me? [| Not quite. |] Is her Soul still throughout my body? [| Y |]

I did a process of forgiveness between Penelope and me and retroactive clearing of incorporation of her Soul from every cell of my body.

(Nov 27, '12) Is the incorporation of Penelope's Soul cleared from all cells in my body? [| Y |] Is she ready to go to the light? [| Y |] I created a positive vortex and asked Jesus to welcome her Soul to the light. Thank you, Jesus!

Holy Spirit, did Penelope go to the light? [| Y |] Wonderful!

End of 7-A: EARLY LIFETIME: PENELOPE

7-B: INCIDENT IN HEAVEN

(Nov 17, '12)   A TRAUMATIC EVENT

I sensed several times during the last few years that a traumatic incident involving me occurred in Heaven before I left for Earth for the first time.

Holy Spirit, I ask this question carefully and with reverence. Did some kind of spiritual "joining" occur between Father God and me that part of me experienced as an assault? [| Y |] But another part experienced as an act of love? [| Y |]

Was my Soul divided before I came to Earth for the first time? [| Y |] *Is Penelope^MP the part of my Soul that experienced the spiritual joining as love?* [| Y |] Did she become very angry at Father God when He asked her to go to Earth to live a human life because she thought He was rejecting her? [| Y |]

And I, the portion of my Soul that went to Earth, am the part that felt Father God had abused me? [| Y |]

Father God spoke to me lovingly, saying He is sorry that that early experience in Heaven was so hard on me. He said He did not mean it to be hurtful but wanted to show me His love. Some of my reservations about the situation softened.

(Dec 27, '12)   Healing For That Incident

Mother God, do I need to recover some Lost Will of my Soul connected with that early incident with Father God? [| Y |]

Father God, I still feel a little tense when with people.

[| Good afternoon, Lorrie! I realize how nervous you feel in various situations involving people. That is a sign that you need more healing and clearing. Please start by doing a process of forgiveness between you and Me, especially before you went to Earth for the first time to live a human life. Also, parts of you in this lifetime still suffer greatly from fear related to the early sexual abuse you experienced as a child.

Minister to yourself and parts of you in the ways that you need. Know that I am, We are, with you at all times. Shalom! |]

(Dec 30, '12) Mother God, please help me get healed from the aftereffects of the early trauma I experienced as a spirit being in Heaven before I came to Earth. Thank You! (I cried.)

Did another part of my Soul experience the "joining" with Father God as traumatic? [| Y |] Did that portion of my Spirit live a lifetime as Erik?[MP] [| Y |]

Was Erik carrying a memory of that experience?

[| Not Erik himself but the part that split off as Kim did. |]

Did the healing of Kim's experience of being raped by his uncle help heal some of the aftereffects of the early traumatic experience we are talking about? [| Y |]

(Jan 2, '13.) Father God, I am almost scared to write lately because of the early traumatic experience I had with You in Heaven coming to the fore. I hesitate to do a process of forgiveness with You because of the emotional processing involved, but I need to face that issue.

[| I understand your hesitation, Lorrie. Do not denounce yourself for holding back. You have only gradually come to understand that I, God, have a full range of emotions similar to what human beings have, and that is true for every part of Me. It is the same for Me as for you that the incident you referred to is an unsettled part of My emotional experiences.

I have asked for your forgiveness in spirit, and in spirit, you have chosen to forgive Me. I am grateful for receiving that measure of forgiveness, but you and I know the clearing and healing are incomplete. Parts of you are still suffering negative effects from it.

You learned some time ago that your Dad's Soul volunteered to play the part of a sexual abuser to help you and your family lines receive the healing you need. And you understand that the traumatic incident in Heaven is related to the sexual abuse incidents with your Dad. When the early incident is healed, the others will be, as well.

All of your Souls carried memories of that early traumatic experience. Those memories colored your attitude toward love and sex and your gut-level concept of Me being a loving Father. Souls from all of your lifetimes will receive some healing when you and I go through a process of forgiveness. Other Souls that join with you in asking for and extending forgiveness in their relationship with Me will receive healing, also. []

Father God and Me: Process of Forgiveness

Father God, I am willing to go through a process of forgiveness with You but am afraid I might not do it well enough or be truly forgiving towards You and my Dad. Please help me. Thank You! And Mother God, I ask for Your help, too.

[| I am here with you, Lorrie. |]

Jesus, please be present, also.

JESUS: I am here.

Parts of me, please join me to whatever extent you choose. Other Souls who wish to join us as we go through this process of forgiveness may do so. I sense that forgiveness will take place on many different planes as many Souls from previous lifetimes take part. Ready, everyone?

Holy Spirit, I ask for a curtain of spiritual lead around this room so that unwelcome Souls can't come in. Thank You!

With many tears, I did a process of forgiveness with Father God and then with my Dad, mostly in my own words. I have spoken forgiveness to my Dad many times, but this time, I told him I understand the situation much better and am sorry it was so hard on him to follow his Soul's plan. Holy Spirit, please remove the erroneous imprinting regarding sexuality and love affecting me and others and replace it with correct, loving understanding.

Thank You, Holy Spirit! Thank You, Father God!

(Sept 28, '15)   PARTS OF ME ARE NOT OVER IT

Holy Spirit, are some parts of me still very angry with Father God about the incident I experienced in Heaven as an assault? [| Y |] That emotion of anger is part of the Will portion of my Soul. [| Y |] Did my Souls attract many such incidents over the years to try to get that original hurt cleared? [| Y |]

I did processing with Father God again but didn't record it.

(May 22, '16) I felt ornery. It seemed to be about "having to" go to church. Also, as has happened many Sunday mornings for a long while, my system emptied beforehand.

(!!!) The Church is "the Father's House." Are parts of me so afraid of Father God related to the trauma I experienced early on in Heaven that it affects my digestion? [| Y |]

Holy Spirit, did I place a curse against Father God in some of my lifetimes? [| Y |] Are some of those curses still in effect? [| Y |] (That's terrible!) Is that one reason I am afraid of Father God? [| Y |] Did I place a curse against Him in this lifetime? [| Y |] I knew what it was: An unspoken curse for His making men "the way they are."

The next day, I asked God for forgiveness for all curses I placed against Him, knowingly or unknowingly, in this lifetime and all other lifetimes. Thank You, Father God, for forgiving me. Thank you, Ministry Team, Fern, and Jesus, for being with me and helping me!

7-B: INCIDENT IN HEAVEN

194

7-C: CONNECTION WITH LUCIFER

(May 1 '13)   ORIGIN OF LUCIFER

Synthesis of Father God's description: Before Father God came to know the Will (Mother God) better, He was somewhat afraid of Her and felt He had to protect Himself against Her. At one point, without realizing it, He sent out a force of unloving light to get rid of that "thing" (the Will) that "kept pulling" on Him. Father God's light was unloving at that moment because it was driven by fear and a desire to destroy that "thing."

In a protective instinct, the Will repelled that force of unloving light from Father God so powerfully that it "caused this light to... break off and become Lucifer" (Heart, pp. 174-176). Lucifer's Spirit – that portion of Father God's Spirit – got locked into being unloving.

(May 20, '13)   Lucifer's Spirit Got Mixed In

BETH: Holy Spirit, is Lorrie an angel in human form? [| Y |]

ME: (!!!) Is my Soul a portion of one of the Angels of the Violet Flame that works with Archangel Zadkiel? [| Y |]

In the "early days" in Heaven, the angels enjoyed merging. As they merged, portions of their Spirit split off and remained with other angels (Original, Introduction pp. 73, 118). Holy Spirit, when Lucifer was still in Heaven, did other angels merge with him? [| Y |] Did portions of Lucifer's Spirit remain with some of the angels? [| Y |]

(!!!) Lucifer may have merged with the Angel of the Violet Flame that my Soul is a part of, and portions of his Spirit may have remained with it!

(!!!) Holy Spirit, are portions of Lucifer's Spirit enmeshed with my Soul from this or previous lifetimes? [| Y |] Are the Souls that have been showing up lately portions of my Souls from previous lifetimes that have portions of Lucifer's Spirit mixed in? [| Yes. They want help to get cleared. |]

Holy Spirit, please seal all portions of Lucifer's Spirit with spiritual lead that are with me and any of my Souls from previous lifetimes. Thank You! I began sending love and blessings to those portions of Lucifer's Spirit.

[| Lorrie, We know you are concerned about learning that a portion of one of Lucifer's angels is, or has been, with you. That is more common than you might think. Lucifer and the angels that later sided with him were in Heaven with all the other angels and archangels for quite some time. You learned that the angels did a lot of merging, and many portions did not get returned to their own Spirit. There is no reason to worry. Peace! |]

(May 21, '13)   Clearing Lucifer's Spirit From Me

It feels like a 2" diameter disk is within the top of my head. Is an implant for witchcraft energies in my brain? (No answer.) (!!!) Is a portion of Lucifer's Spirit in my brain? [| Y |] Are there some throughout my person? [| Y |]

Has a portion of Lucifer's Spirit been attached to or with me in every lifetime? [| Y |] Is his Spirit meant to get cleared from me and all of my Souls from other lifetimes? [| Y |]

(!!!) Does the portion of Lucifer's Spirit that is with me want help to become loving? [| Y |]

Should I ask Lord Melchizedek, Archangel Haniel, and the Ministry Team to join as I do a clearing this evening? [| Y |] Beth will come tomorrow. Should I ask her to pray for me for a full clearing of Lucifer's Spirit and healing? [| Y |]

I asked loving Souls in my family lines to join in pouring a deluge of love and blessings to all portions of Lucifer's Spirit that were with me, with Souls from other lifetimes of mine, and with other Souls. In the evening:

1. I cleared erroneous early imprinting from the portions of Lucifer's Spirit that were with me and with Souls from other lifetimes of mine.
2. I did a retroactive clearing of the incorporation of Lucifer's Spirit from within cells in my body.

3. I cleared the enmeshment between Lucifer's Spirit and my Soul in this lifetime and all other lifetimes.

4. I asked for those portions of Lucifer's Spirit to be ministered to in a healing ring.

(May 22, '13) I told Beth about the situation and asked her to pray with me. After she finished praying, she said the portions of Lucifer's Spirit that had been with me had left!

Thank You, Father-Mother God! Holy Spirit!

Later: Holy Spirit, are all portions of Lucifer's Spirit cleared from me? [| Y |] Are all portions cleared from all my Souls from other lifetimes? [| Y |]

(!!!) *Are all portions of Lucifer's Spirit that had been with my Soul and with Souls from other lifetimes of mine now loving?* [| Y |] *Are they reunited with Father God?* [| Y |]

That's wonderful!

(Mar 29, '14) I have a feeling of pressure in my head. Holy Spirit, is a portion of Lucifer's Spirit within my brain? [| Y |] I extended love and blessings to that Spirit portion and asked for a Holy Spirit demagnetizing shower to flow through to clear stickiness. I directed that Spirit portion and all other portions that do not have permission to be with me to leave.

Did the portion of Lucifer's Spirit leave? [| Y |] Did other Soul portions leave? [| Y |] Thank You, Holy Spirit!

(Jun 19, '14)   HOPE FOR LUCIFER

Holy Spirit, were portions of some of Lucifer's angels part of my original composite Soul? [| Y |] At some point, did my Soul agree to allow portions of Lucifer's Spirit and his angels to use me as a stop on their way back to Heaven? [| Y |] Wow!

A fair-sized portion of Lucifer's Spirit is back in Heaven. He and the angel my Soul is a part of were friends. That is why portions of his Spirit come to me for help. The Holy Spirit said that situation happened during many of my lifetimes.

Are portions of some of Lucifer's "fallen angels" choosing to be open to receive love? [| Y |] Are portions of Lucifer's Spirit that lived, or are living a human life choosing to be open to receive love? [| Y |] That's wonderful!

(!!!) Holy Spirit, since the fall of 2003, has one of the purposes for my having so much discomfort in my head and body been for other people and me to learn that even "damned" Souls have a chance to choose to become loving? [| Y |]

By that, I understand that a fair measure of the discomfort I experienced since then may have been caused by portions of Lucifer's Spirit and the Spirits of his angels, that they were with me to receive help to become loving. Does it often happen that only a portion of a Soul chooses evil? [| Y |]

(Sept 10, '15)   More Dealings with Lucifer

Before I left for my dental appointment this morning, I asked for protection from negative energies. Afterward, I stopped at the post office. When I got out of my car, my left hip suddenly hurt a lot. I almost fell and had difficulty walking.

The next day. Was an implant placed into my hip yesterday? [| Y |] Is a portion of Lucifer's Spirit embedded in my hip that had been with me earlier and then returned? [| Y |] Does it have unloving light? [| Y |] Does it want help to become loving? [| N |] Are parts of my Soul under Lucifer's control? [| Y |]

Holy Spirit, please seal that implant and portions of Lucifer's Spirit that are with me with triple-strength spiritual lead. Thank You!

(Apr 7, '16) Father God, I understand that Lucifer's Spirit is a portion of Your Spirit that got split off at a time of great fear*. Do You love him? [| Yes, I do. Do not judge him. Thank you! |]

I dealt with Lucifer's Spirit a few more times, but the situations I included give the picture.

End of 7-C: CONNECTION WITH LUCIFER

7-D: MANDY, MOLLIE AND ME

(Sept 14, '15)   UNSETTLED ISSUES

I have been having a lot of discomfort in the upper part of my head but almost don't have enough energy even to ask the Ministry Team to do a clearing. There always seems to be more clearing that I need to do. (My right ear became warm.)

Hello, Father God! Do You want to say something?

[| Yes, Lorrie, this is very important. You have been wondering whether Mandy's message for you last April may have had negative energies attached to it and whether some may have come from an untrustworthy source. That is the case.

That untrustworthy source placed a "web" over you to interfere with your connecting well with Spirit. They urged you to fill your home with roses so they could place contact points in them to control you with witchcraft energies. |]

I didn't trust Mandy's suggestion to fill my home with roses because the Holy Spirit had advised me to remove all rose items. Did I pick up negative energy from Mandy that day?

[| Yes. Your discomfort in the upper part of your head is related to that. When Beth asked for a Holy Spirit vacuuming for you two days ago, it didn't fully clear those energies from Mandy. They are connected to a curse placed on you in a previous lifetime for roses to be a contact point for witchcraft energies to be drawn to you.

Mandy was one of the nuns, along with Mollie, who placed that curse on you for that lifetime and future ones. Those energies were beginning to get vacuumed away but got stuck in your head because of being magnetically attracted to implants in a circle at the top of your head. |]

Is a portion of my Soul enmeshed with Mandy's Soul?

[| Yes, a portion of your Soul from this lifetime and several portions from other lifetimes are caught within Mandy. She has a powerful Soul, but no matter how powerful a Soul is, they are not to keep portions of other people's Souls bound.

Ask Beth to do another clearing for you for those implants and the negative energies attached to them and help the portions of your Souls that are with Mandy get set free. Then, follow the guidance of the Holy Spirit. Bless you, Lorrie! []

Thank You, Father-Mother God, Holy Spirit!

(Sept 18, '15) Holy Spirit, is Mandy's Soul present asking me to release portions of her Soul? [| Y |] Are some of my Souls from previous lifetimes also holding portions of her Soul captive? [| Y |] By judging her? [| Y |]

I am sorry for judging you, Mandy. Speaking for every lifetime, I release all portions of your Souls that I am holding captive by judging you. Please forgive me. Thank you.

(Sept 25, '15)   Cleared Umbilical Cords

I asked Beth to do further clearing for me over the phone. I told her about a curse having been placed against me by other nuns in a previous lifetime when I was a nun, using roses as contact points for attracting witchcraft energies, and that Mandy and Mollie were two of those who placed that curse.

Beth said she saw Mollie and Mandy with me, one on each side, with a cord extending from the one on my right side to my right shoulder and a cord extending from the one on my left side to my left hip. That hip has been very sore lately!

Beth said she would clear those cords and minister Reiki to me after we hung up the phone and that she would come to my place the following week for further clearing. I signed off on the phone and lay on the couch for 30 minutes while Beth ministered.

(Sept 26, '15)   My Soul Is Enmeshed With Theirs

This morning, Beth ministered to me in person. She said some of my chakras had been closed but were now open. Are the implants cleared from my head? [| Y |] That is good news!

Years ago, Mandy's eyes changed like she wasn't listening while I was telling her some of the symptoms of schizophrenia, referring to a friend. Does she have a split personality?

[| Yes, caused by a portion of Lucifer's Spirit that is with her. |]

Are one or more portions of Mandy's Soul with me? [| Y |] Is a portion of her Soul in my left hip? [| Y |] Did her Soul set it up to be with me so she could continue to affect me? [| Y |]

(!!!) Is Mandy still holding portions of my Soul from this lifetime captive? [| Y |] Portions from previous lifetimes? [| Y |] I ask for a protective shield around every part of me daily. Are the portions of my Soul that are with Mandy sealed? [| Y |] Am I still being affected by Mandy's and Lucifer's energy? [| Y |]

(!!!) Is a portion of Lucifer's Spirit enmeshed with the portions of Mandy's Soul that are with me? [| Y |] Should I leave that enmeshment in place when I clear the portions of Mandy's Souls from me? [| Y |]

Is there a spiritual umbilical cord connection between my Soul and Mandy's Soul in this lifetime? [| N |] Are there spiritual umbilical cords connecting her Souls from previous lifetimes with my Soul in this lifetime? [| Y |] Wow!

I need to do much clearing and healing and ask for protection for the relationship between Mandy's Soul and mine in this lifetime and earlier ones. Please guide me, Holy Spirit. Thank You!

(Sept 27, '15)   EARLY HISTORY OF OUR SOULS

By asking the Holy Spirit many questions, I learned that Mollie's Soul hated me early on in Heaven because we both wanted to be special friends with a certain angel. Out of anger, she placed a curse against me to never be able to give myself in love fully.

I learned that *Mandy's Soul is a split-off of Mollie's Soul,* so it was Mollie/Mandy who placed that curse against me. I, in turn, placed a curse against her (them) for things not to go well.

That curse of not being able to be fully open in love has been cleared from my Soul in this lifetime but not from several portions of my Souls from other lifetimes that are with me, so I am still being affected by it.

"Anger situation": Mollie and Mandy have held portions of my Soul bound by anger in every lifetime of theirs. Some of those Soul portions have never had a chance to return to the Soul they are a part of. In turn, during every lifetime of mine, I have held portions of Mollie's and Mandy's Souls captive by anger. Thankfully, most of those portions of my Souls are now willing to release that anger. (This is heavy stuff.)

1. That anger situation is the core of the boil, which has been working its way up through my spirit.
2. The word "stalemate" mentioned years ago refers to this anger situation.
3. The curse for roses to be used as contact points for witchcraft energies to affect me has anger at the root.
4. The implants at the top of my head are connected with anger, also. They are held in place by anger that I and parts of me are holding against Mollie and Mandy.

Holy Spirit, I need to own the parts of me in every lifetime that I consider "bad." Is that a big part of what needs to be done? [| Y |] Please help me and Mollie's and Mandy's Souls.

Mollie and Mandy, speaking for my Soul in every lifetime, I ask you to please forgive me for judging you, holding onto angry feelings toward you, and wishing ill against you. Thank you!

Can I choose with my will now to release the curse I placed on Mollie/Mandy early on for things not to go well for them? [| N |] So each portion of my Soul that placed that curse needs to choose that? [| Y |]

Portions of my Soul from early on who placed a curse on Mollie and Mandy for things to not go well for them, please choose with your will to join me in saying:

"Mollie and Mandy, I am sorry for placing a curse on you for things not to go well for you. I cancel that curse and wish the best for you. Please forgive me! Thank you."

Bless you, Mollie and Mandy!

(Sept 29, '15)   SETTING THINGS STRAIGHT

Father God, You said Lucifer had very bright light but that "he did not feel loving" (Original p. 50). Since Mandy has a portion of Lucifer's Spirit with her, does at least part of her Soul have unloving light? [| Y |] Do You suggest sealing up all unloving portions of her Soul(s) that are with me and in the astral plane? [| Y |]

Holy Spirit, please seal all unloving portions of Mandy's Souls from every lifetime of hers with triple-strength spiritual lead. I ask for that protection to remain in place until those Soul portions are willing to choose to become loving. Thank You!

(!!!) Do some of the portions of Mandy's Souls that are with me want help to become loving? [| Y |] Mandy, I flow a deluge of love and blessings to you. I pray that every part of you will be willing to receive the love and choose to become loving. Bless you!

Also, Mandy, speaking to your Soul in this lifetime and all other lifetimes, I direct you in Jesus' name to release all portions of my Soul from this lifetime and other lifetimes that are with you that are not meant to be. Thank you!

Speaking for every part of me, I release all portions of your Souls that are with me that are not meant to be.

Holy Spirit, please guide those portions of Mandy's Soul to where they are meant to be. Thank You!

Did all of them leave that had been with me?
[| Some left. The others will be released after you do a process of forgiveness between Mandy and you. You forgiving her will release the other Soul portions. |]

I did a process of forgiveness between Mandy and me for this lifetime and all other lifetimes. Mandy, I extend love and blessing to you. In the name of Jesus, I ask kindly and command all portions of your Souls from this lifetime and all other lifetimes to leave me that do not want help to become loving. (Coughed)

Holy Spirit, are all portions of Mandy's Souls that have unloving light cleared from me? [| Y |] Thank You!

(Sept 1, '16) I asked the Holy Spirit about Mandy. She needs prayer. A Lost Will portion of my Soul is with her that is unloving because of not having received enough love. It is enmeshed with Lost Will of Mother God and incorporated within cells in Mandy's body. Part of Mandy's Soul is holding that portion of my Soul prisoner.

Mandy has a lower vibration energy level than I do, so it is not beneficial for me to have contact with her. Dark forces are going through her to try to reach me.

Holy Spirit, please seal Mandy's Soul with Divine love every day. Thank You!

Ministry Team, please join as I do a clearing for Mandy. (I did the clearing.) Thank you, Ministry Team!

End of 7-D: MANDY, MOLLIE, AND ME

7-E: MISCONNECTION WITH MARY

(Apr 22, '15)   MY HEAD AND FEET AFFECTED

The top of my head was bothering me a lot. (!!!) Have statues and pictures of Mary (Jesus' mother) with a circle of stars around her head created implants in the head area of Mary's astral body? [| Y |] Is a portion of Mary's astral body incorporated within cells in my astral body? [| Y |] Has that portion of her Soul gone to the light? [| N |] Does it want to? [| Y |]

I asked the Ministry Team to minister to the portion of Mary's Soul that is with me, to clear the incorporation of her astral body from cells in my astral body and help her go to the light. Holy Spirit, are all portions of Mary's Soul cleared from me? [| N |] Have some been cleared? [| Y |]

(!!!) Is the almost burning sensation I have been having recently on the bottom of my feet related to statues and pictures of Mary standing on the head of the serpent? [| Y |] Are portions of Mary's Soul within my feet? [| Y |] Wow!

204

Ministry Team, please do a clearing for me. Thank you! Within two days, the bottoms of my feet were pretty much back to normal.

(Aug 21, '15)   IDOL-OF-MARY THOUGHTFORM

My feet feel almost hot lately, like last April. Back then, I learned that the sensation was related to statues and pictures of Mary depicting her standing on the head of the serpent.

(!!!) Somebody picturing Mary that way would create an idol in their mind! Holy Spirit, *Do I have idol-of-Mary energy within me?* [| Y |] Did I pick up some of that energy from a Catholic woman I played cards with recently? [| Y |] Is the stomach upset and the weird headaches I have been having related to the energy of that idol of Mary? [| Y |]

I received the understanding that people as a group have created a thoughtform of Mary as they picture her to be. I turned to Mary almost desperately during high school at the convent, talking to her "through" the statue.

Do I have an idol-of-Mary thoughtform within me?
[| Lorrie, you know the answer is "Yes." During those four years as a candidate, postulant, and novice, you turned to Mary often by saying the *Memorare Prayer:* "Remember, O most gracious Virgin Mary, that never was it known that anyone who turned to you was left unaided." You continued praying that prayer for many years after you left the convent. |]

Are parts of me still clinging to and energizing that idol-of-Mary thoughtform? [| Y |] Does that thoughtform have negative energy? [| Yes, because it is a phantom, a false figure of Mary. It has no connection whatsoever with Jesus' mother. |]

If I asked, would the Ministry Team clear that thoughtform from me and parts of me? [| Yes, but it will not get cleared from the parts of you unwilling to release it. |]

Do You suggest I direct those unwilling arts of me to leave?

[| After the thoughtform has been cleared, direct those parts to leave that are unwilling to release it, but with the stipulation, "If this is what my Full Soul chooses." Be at peace! |]

Thank You, Father God, Holy Spirit!

Ministry Team, please clear the idol-of-Mary thoughtform from me. (I sat quietly for 10 minutes.) Thank you!

If my Full Soul chooses, I direct those parts of me to leave that are unwilling to release that idol-of-Mary thoughtform.

(Aug 26, '15)   PRAYER TO FREE MARY'S SOUL

I again have an almost burning sensation in my feet. Holy Spirit, is a portion of Mary's Soul within my feet? [| Y |] Are portions of Mary's Soul trapped within statues of her? [| Y |] Does the astral body of those portions of Mary's Soul feel like their feet are burning? [| Y |] Am I picking up on her discomfort? [| Y |]

Do the prayers that people direct to statues of Mary keep portions of her Soul trapped in those statues? [| Y |] Do those prayers amount to idol worship? [| Y |] Could the prayers be separated from the false image of Mary people have? [| Y |]

Holy Spirit, please place a shield of spiritual lead around all statues of Mary so that prayers directed to Mary will bypass the statues and be directed to Mother God. I ask that the statues in front of which I asked Mary for help years ago be sealed with spiritual lead and that my prayers back then will even now be redirected to Mother God. Thank You!

Have those statues been sealed up? [| Y |] Have my prayers been redirected to Mother God? [| Y |] Have many portions of Mary's Soul been freed from statues of her? [| Y |] Thank You!

One would think that I would be used to having prayers answered almost instantly by this time, but I continue to be amazed when they are!

(Aug 26, '15) I cleared the incorporation of Mary's Soul from cells in my body and the enmeshment between her Soul and mine.

Mary's guardian angel, please guide those portions of her Soul to where they are meant to be. Thank you!

Are all portions of Mary's Soul cleared from me? [| Y |] Great!

(Sept 7, '15)   Cleared the Idol of Mary

Holy Spirit, do I still have an idol of Mary within me, with her standing on the serpent's head and stars around her head? [| Y |] Are portions of Mary's Soul trapped within that image in my mind? [| Y |] Is the discomfort in my feet and at the top of my head related to me holding onto that image? [| Y |]

I did a clearing for the idol of Mary that is within my mind.

Holy Spirit, are parts of me still hanging onto it? [| Y |]

I bound all negative energies and commanded them to leave and asked Jesus and Mother God to help every part of me be willing to release that idol image of Mary.

Is it cleared from every part of me now? [| Y |] Thank You!

                      End of 7-E: MISCONNECTION WITH MARY

7-F: ROSE OF LIMA[MP]

Note: [MP] (Me Prior life) is omitted after Rose in this section.

(Mar 8, '15)   SPIRITUAL CROWN OF THORNS

The top of my head has been hurting a lot lately. Is a portion of an outside Soul in my brain? [| Y |] (!!!) From my lifetime as Rose of Lima? [| Y |] Is part of her Soul in the aura above my head? [| Y |]

Rose, please leave and go to a healing ring. Thank you!

(!!!) Did Rose of Lima ask for a spiritual crown of thorns on her head? [| Y |] Did she vow always to wear a crown of thorns to make up for other people's sins? [| Y |]

(!!!) Is there a spiritual crown of thorns on the head of my astral body? [| Y |]

I cancel all vows I made in any lifetime connected with wearing a spiritual crown of thorns and remove the spiritual crown from my astral body. Is it cleared? [| Y |]

Holy Spirit, does my astral body have wounds from those thorns piercing it? [| Y |] Do the sore areas at the top of my bother more during Lent because people focus on Jesus' sufferings? [| Y |]

Holy Spirit, I ask for a Holy Spirit shower of love to help me feel better. Thank You!

(Apr 20, '15) The top of my head has been bothering me more again. Does Rose of Lima still have a spiritual crown of thorns on her head? [| Y |] Has her Soul gone to the light? [| A portion has. |] Does she think she is suffering in purgatory? [| Y |]

In the name of Jesus, I dissolve the spiritual crown of thorns from Rose of Lima's astral body. Mother God, please minister to her Soul and help her go to the light. Thank You!

Two days later. Has the spiritual crown of thorns been dissolved from Rose of Lima's astral body? [| Y |] Has her Soul gone to the light? [| Y |] Wonderful!

(Aug 26, '15) Is a portion of Rose's Soul with me? [| Y |]

(!!!) Has that portion of her Soul been with me ever since I portrayed her in a play I wrote in high school about her life as a nun? [| Y |] Is that Soul portion becoming uncomfortable, and I feel her discomfort? [| Y |]

I cleared the incorporation of Rose of Lima's Soul from cells in my body and the enmeshment between her Soul and every part of my Soul, then commanded her to leave.

(Nov 5, '15) Is Rose of Lima's Soul still wearing a crown of thorns? [| Y |] I learned from the Holy Spirit that she thinks she still has much to do penance for. When Rose became a nun, she took a vow of chastity. She considers that she broke that vow by allowing a man to kiss her, who then pressed himself upon her, fondled her, and attempted to have sex with her.

Father God, in Your eyes, does Rose of Lima have anything to do penance for? [| N |]

Is the curse using roses as a contact point for dark energies still being directed at her because of her name? [| Y |]

Since Rose's Soul is part of my Full Soul, would that crown of thorns dissolve if I chose for that to take place? [| Y |]

I choose for the crown of thorns on Rose's head to dissolve. Is it cleared now? [| Y |] Thank You!

(Mar 18, '16) I have been having much discomfort in the upper part of my head. I learned that a pious teenage portion of Rose's Soul is with me, wearing a spiritual crown of thorns *as penance for my actions.* (Wow!)

(Jul 27, '16) [| Lorrie, more clearing is needed related to roses used in the past and still being used as contact points for attracting witchcraft energies. You would be much worse off physically, spiritually, and emotionally than you are if you had not asked for protection daily. Peace! |]

Thank You, Father-Mother God, Holy Spirit!

(Aug 15, '16)   I Get the Message

My head has been bothering me extra much. Holy Spirit, is Rose of Lima still wearing a spiritual crown of thorns? [| Y |] Did a part of her Soul join me recently?

[| Yes, with permission from your Soul. |]

(!!!) *Is Rose wearing the crown of thorns as penance for me judging others, hoping the discomfort I am having will help me realize I am doing that?* [| Y |]

I asked the Holy Spirit about that and learned that I and parts of me are holding tiny portions of Souls prisoner by our judgments. Many of those Soul portions are in the upper part of my head. Lord, have mercy!

Every person and Soul I am judging now and have ever judged, please forgive me! Thank you!

Bless you, Rose of Lima. Please leave now. Thank you!

(Aug 29, '16) Is the spirit of judgment cleared from me?

[| Yes, it is cleared from you and your Souls from several other lifetimes. |] Thank You, Holy Spirit!

Did that portion of Rose of Lima's Soul leave? [| Y |] Is she still wearing a spiritual crown of thorns? [| Y |]

I will just have to leave her in God's care. Bless you, Rose!

End of 7-F: ROSE OF LIMA^{MP}

CHAPTER 8

GROWING AND LEARNING

Sept 13, '14   SOULS CAN CARRY PAIN

When a person experiencing pain dies, does some of it remain with their Soul? [| Y |] If their Soul were with another person, would the other person feel the pain that Soul is carrying? [| Y |] Would they feel it in the same parts of their body as the person who died experienced it? [| Y |]

Are small portions of Fern's Soul with me? [| Y |] Are they carrying some of the pain she experienced? [| Y |] Does the pain that portions of Fern's Soul carry trigger pain in my head? [| Y |] If I would ask for those portions of her Soul to be ministered to in Heaven Hospital, would that take place? [| Y |] While they are still with me? [| Y |]

Father, I ask that all portions of Fern's Soul that need healing because of experiencing pain be ministered to in Heaven Hospital with that applied retroactively so Fern will have been ministered to in Heaven Hospital every time she had pain. Thank You!

Sept 14, '14   My Body Speaks

The muscles in my neck became unusually tight and sore three days ago. (!!!) Did I subconsciously develop a sore neck to have an excuse not to attend our church's prayer time yesterday morning? [| Y |] And so I wouldn't feel guilty about not helping set up the church rummage sale? [| Y |]

Jan 10, '15. Holy Spirit, when parts of me were angry with me, did they sometimes move out into my astral body to purposely cause me discomfort?

[| Yes. Parts that were unsettled or wanted to leave have often been in your head, with their aura extending past the edge of your aura, causing spiritual pain in your astral body. |]

Did those parts have permission to do that so I would learn that that can be a source of discomfort?

[| Yes. It is one cause of the discomfort you experience at the top of your head. |] Now I know!

Jan 12, '15. My neck is very sore. Have Soul portions gathered there to cause pain and let me know they want to leave?

[| Yes. The ones doing that are Soul portions that joined your Soul early on and are now ready to leave. Also, several outside Soul portions that wish to leave are in the upper part of your head. They are hoping to receive blessings and love before they leave, though. |]

Thank You, Holy Spirit, for telling me that!

I extended love and blessing to those Soul portions, cleared enmeshment between them and between their Souls and my Soul, and directed them to leave. They left.

Thank You, Holy Spirit!

Nov 28, '15   Father God: Instructions

My right ear became warm. Good afternoon, Father God!

[| In case you don't realize it, Lorrie, there are still spiritual implants within your head and aura. Look in your notes to when you first learned about spiritual implants and what you did to clear them. Some implants were cleared two times when Beth prayed with you. *That shows they can be cleared.* For some reason, you are recreating them.

You have been extra achy the last several months. I suggest that you spend more time resting with Me and exercising. |]

I feel on edge. Are Souls or Soul portions with me whose energy is incompatible with my energy?

[| Yes, portions of relative's Souls are with you that are asking for help and, also, Souls that want to hinder your connection with Spirit and your work on the writings. This evening, ask the Ministry Team to do clearing and flow healing into you. |]

212

I feel almost jittery. Is Grandma Leigh with me?

[| Yes. Portions of Grandma Leigh's Souls from other lifetimes are with you. Since you and she used to be one Soul, it would be wise to include her when you ask for prayers for healing and clearing for yourself. By that, I mean to have her Soul in mind from earlier lifetimes when she and you were one Soul.

Also, this should help you feel better. Especially when you feel extra achy, have in mind to flow continuous blessings and love to all Souls and energies that are with you and that are in the healing ring surrounding your Soul at the moment and to those that were in the healing ring surrounding your Soul in other lifetimes. When asking for clearing for yourself, include every part of your Soul. Bless you, dear one! Take courage! |]

Thank you, Father-Mother God, Holy Spirit, Heart!

I asked the Ministry Team to do clearing and healing for me.

Dec 29, '15. Good morning, Father God!

[| Good morning, Lorrie! The head discomfort you have been having will eventually get cleared. It would help for you to ask for forgiveness from everyone in every lifetime that you injured, took advantage of, lied to, neglected, judged, abused, placed a curse against, took for granted, and whatever else. Then forgive everyone who mistreated, neglected, and judged you, and so on. Speak for every part of you as you do that process. Also, curses that were placed against you and members of your family still need to be cleared, some from far back.

Please don't get tired of doing clearing and asking for clearing and healing. *Some clearing occurs each time you pray and ask for it.* It takes time to clear some negative energies.

Bless you! Have a good day! |]

Thank You, Father God!

Jan 17, '16   Where Is Your Spirit?

Father-Mother God, I have been restless lately and having almost steady headaches. I ask that the headaches be cleared and for help to connect with You again.

[| Where is your Spirit, Lorrie? You would feel more connected with Spirit if you would spend 5 minutes now and then placing everything in My hands.

It occurred to you that when you pray, "God help me!" *you are asking Me to help you do things better, using Me as a crutch.* You received a lesson about that many years ago.

Of the things you spend time on, the only ones that have lasting importance for you are those that involve relationships with others. That is an element you need more of.

You are hindered by the straitjacket your ego ideal placed on it. You are much freer than you used to be, but some hindrance remains that would be best to remove.

Have a wonderful day, dear one! Please do not be hard on yourself because that "makes it hard" for all of Us. Bless you! |]

Thank You, Father-Mother God!

Sept 1, '16   TRANSFER ZONE

Good morning, Father God! My neck, head, and lower back have been extra achy lately. I have been praying for Shanna from Mercy Church for the clearing of arthritis that set in suddenly a few weeks ago. (!!!) Did a spirit of arthritis transfer to me from Shanna when I wished for healing for her?

[| Lorrie, I realize that you still feel that you cannot fully trust your intuition, questions that come to mind out of the blue, and a sense that the answer is "Yes." That is the case: The Holy Spirit allowed the spirit of arthritis to transfer from Shanna to you, so both the negative energy and the residue that is with her would be cleared.

I realize you do not feel well enough to do clearing for negative energies for yourself on your own, as though you are doing the clearing in your own strength. That is why a Ministry Team has been formed: *for you to work with them,* not for them to work with you. You could state each step in the process, then sit quietly as the Ministry Team does the clearing, assisted by your firm intention. Be aware that you are a part of the Team whenever they minister to you or others. Have a good day! []

Thank You, Father!

Holy Spirit, was the spirit of arthritis lifted from Shanna? [| Y |] Is there a place with or near a person for negative energies to transfer to that are meant to be lifted from them? [| Y |] Are those energies meant to leave immediately? [| Y |]

Is it OK to call that place a **transfer zone**? [| Y |]

By asking more questions, I learned that the transfer zone is around the edge of a person's astral body. When a person clears negative energies from someone, those energies go to an area of the transfer zone surrounding the prayer's astral body that corresponds with the area that they had been affecting the person you are praying for, such as the head.

Negative energies in the transfer zone get sealed up when a person asks for all negative energies within and around them to be sealed. Negative energies haven't been leaving me immediately as is meant to take place.

Has that been happening with me so I would learn about the transfer zone and teach others about it? [| Y |] Does a person's attitude determine whether the negative energies will leave the transfer zone immediately? [| Y |]

I can think of some reasons why someone might not release negative energies immediately:

1. The person wants others to see how much they are suffering to get attention.
2. Thinking they need to suffer to make up for wrongdoing.
3. Parts of the person not in favor of praying for other people may hold negative energies in the transfer zone, so the person won't feel well enough to pray for people. I am guessing that that fits my situation.

Ministry Team, please clear the spirit of arthritis and all other negative energies from the transfer zone that is located around my astral body. Thank you!

In the name of Jesus, I command all parts of me not willing

to release negative energies from the transfer zone to leave! Ministering Angels, please guide those parts of my Soul to where they are meant to be. Thank you!

Jan 23, '17   DRY DESERTS, DARK VALLEYS

Father God, "Something on my back" just came to mind. Am I under attack by dark forces?

[| Lorrie, everyone who walks in the light is a target for dark energies. If those energies consider someone a threat to their existence or territory, they will increase the attacks. The protection you are putting in place is adequate, but it weakens it whenever you allow energies of fear a foothold.

Ask Jesus, Love, to be within every part of you. Where Jesus is, there I, Mother God, and the Holy Spirit are also. Peace! |]

Thank You, Father God!

Feb 25, '17. Father God, I often wonder what You can say that will help with anything, such as to help me hear clearly, especially when I don't feel like listening. (I was feeling blue.)

[| Lorrie, let Mother God and Me take care of you. You just thought about maybe letting Us hold you during your quiet time. It would be OK if you would feel like crying the whole while. You still have much tension and anxiety to release.

You have become aware that you go through cycles, sometimes with a year or two between, of being pretty much closed off emotionally, and then your emotions surface again. Let them surface now that you are again beginning to open up emotion-wise. Do not lose heart.

The thought you just had is the case: Your Soul in this lifetime is a part of you that has wandered through deserts and dark valleys, thinking you were lost and alone. You are neither lost nor alone. All of Us are around you, flowing light into you and loving you. Your Spirit is bonded with us.

You are not alone in experiencing feeling lost and separated and then finding your way to light and love. Many others are experiencing that with you, and you are helping lead them to the light. It is always darkest, just before dawn. All is well. Believe and receive that. We love you! []

Thank You, Father-Mother God! Bless You!

May 8, '17. Holy Spirit, am I still trying to "go it alone" much of the time and just asking You (Father-Mother God) to help? [| Y |] Am I holding rebellion in my heart towards God? [| Y |]

Is my early traumatic experience with Father God at the root of why I want to do things myself and not let God be fully in charge? [| Y |] Early on, when I was a Spirit in Heaven, did I judge Father God and Mother God? [| Y |] Is it mainly the Spirit portion of my Soul that is angry at God? [| Y |]

> "I am not going to allow man to continue dissecting Me to try to find out what I am, because man can never know as long as his mind gives him theories and he denies the feeling body that can let him know what is true understanding and what is not. I have found that most of these men do not seek true understanding. They seek instead to take My power and use it for themselves." (Original, Introduction p. x)

Father God, am I trying to "take Your power" and use it for healing? [| Y |] Did I do that in other lifetimes? [| Y |]

Wow! I have a lot of stuff to work through!

May 26, '18   A Change in Course

Over the last several years, I have cleared many Souls and Soul portions from within me and then asked to be filled with love and light, but always more Souls show up.

(!!!) Holy Spirit, is attending Mercy Church hindering me from staying free of negative energies and having Soul portions latch onto me? [| Y |] Have I been picking up negative energies from people at church? [| Y |] Are many Souls of former church members and outsiders present in the church whose energy is incompatible with mine? [| Y |] Do You suggest I stop attending Mercy Church soon? [| Y |]

That evening, head and chest congestion began setting in. By 11:00 P.M., my head throbbed from elevated blood pressure, and I was experiencing dizziness. I asked my sister Joan to drive me to the ER, where the doctor gave me medication to lower my blood pressure, and I went home.

I slept most of the next three days with a fever reaching 102° Fahrenheit. I was somewhat dizzy and felt like anesthesia was in the process of getting cleared out.

Holy Spirit, was fever and congestion a way for my body and system to get cleared of negative energies? [| Y |] Wow!

[| Lorrie, don't base decisions on what you have done in the past. You are at a new starting point. You can be as you choose: healthy, happy, carefree, and affectionate. Be who you are, and those meant to come into your life will appear. Take a step toward those you feel inclined to get to know.

Just because you have a headache now doesn't mean you will have one tomorrow and the day after. *You are at a place where much of what you think comes to be, not necessarily immediately.* Pay attention to what you have just been idly thinking. Do you want that to come to be? If not, cancel the thought. Uncreate it.

Keep negative energies in their place by keeping yourself in your place. You are to be sovereign in your universe, meaning that nothing can touch you or harm you unless you have in some way allowed it. See everyone as harmless and existing in their sphere. You are safe in your sphere. |]

Thank you, Holy Spirit!

Jun 3, '18. I wrote a letter signing off as a member of Mercy Church for personal reasons and left it at the church office with my key. Nobody else was there. I felt very nervous.

Jan 14, '19   No Reason to Worry

Father, I haven't felt like sitting down with You for quite a while because of feeling apathetic and somewhat depressed.

[| Lorrie, I have seen how courageously you are dealing with the hard-to-understand emotions you have been experiencing the last several months. It has been a stretch of you "walking through the desert and dry places" to help you decide what is the most important for you.

Don't worry about the hodgepodge of dreams you have been having. All of it fits in with your Soul's purposes. Peace! []

Thank You, Father-Mother God! Good night.

Feb 14, '19. I have noticed that a part of me stands back and observes as I pray for protection. I have often become aware of being influenced and judged by some part of me. Is that coming from a strong ego ideal? From "Miss Perfect"? From one or more parts of me? What do I want deep down?

- To find and become part of a group that worships God but doesn't stress that one has to believe certain things.
- To come to feel and be free about choosing to do things while I am doing those things.

I feel tense while writing this. It feels like some parts of me are watching and judging me, not joining in.

[| Lorrie, whatever you are like, I fully accept you and every part of you at every moment, including parts that you may feel are judging you. You are one person, one Soul. You have one "spiritual mind." Your human mind may have some splits or partially separated portions, but that is of the earthly plane. []

Father God, are one or more portions of Grandma Leigh's and Marie[2]'s[GP] Souls still with me? Did my Soul agree to have portions of their Souls with me for them to work through unresolved issues? [| You may think you are manufacturing what I will say, but the answer is in that question. You have often seen that what you receive as a question is often a word from Me.

Yes, your Soul permits portions of Grandma Leigh's and Marie[2]'s[GP] Souls to be with you. They come and go. Portions of Souls are with you for a while, and then leave. Then, when your Soul and their Soul agree on it, another portion of their Soul will be with you for a while. They are connected to you through past lifetimes in which you and they were one Soul. Please choose to love them.

You don't need to know every aspect of how things are with

your Soul and mind. Love yourself as best you can. Love others as best you can. A big part of that is to allow others to have their own opinion about you, others, and the world.

Rest easy, Lorrie! Know that I love you and everyone and every aspect of each one. I am love. Blessings! []

Thank You, Mother-Father God!

May 8, '19   AM I A SECRET SCHIZOID?

I looked up "emotional detachment" online to see if I could figure out why I don't feel connected with people. This description of "secret schizoid" fits how I feel:

"Secret schizoids present themselves as...involved in interacting in the eyes of the observer, while at the same time, he or she is apart, emotionally withdrawn, and sequestered in a safe place in his or. her own internal world. ...detachment from the outer world...is sometimes overt and sometimes covert. Secret Schizoid individual is able to express quite a lot of feeling...but [is] in reality giving nothing and losing nothing, because since he is only playing a part his own personality is not involved." (Wikipedia)

Father God, I feel afraid of visiting with You, too. How I feel might be connected with my experiences as, and after, my Soul came forth in Heaven along with many other Souls. You said that when we spirit children came forth, we didn't receive full acceptance from You and Mother God because both of You had much healing to do. (Original p. 89)

[| Lorrie, your feeling emotionally distressed does have its roots early on in your existence.

We are happy that you are getting more in touch with your emotions, even if you cannot pinpoint what you are feeling. You don't need to know details as to what is going on with you regarding your emotions. You are being healed slowly but surely. Many other Souls are tied in with your healing and are being healed along with you. []

I plan to meet with my counselor soon.

[| Good. If your counselor concludes you have a schizoid personality, that's OK. "Schizoid" is just a human term describing somebody's emotional experiences.

Love yourself with every fiber of your being. Receive the eternal love that your mother and father in every lifetime of yours have for you now. Fully receive My love, the love of Mother God, the love of Spirit, and the love of Heart.

You are OK, Lorrie, as you always have been. You are a spirit being experiencing a human life in which you don't sense being connected with Us, but you are. []

Thank You, Father-Mother God! Bless You!

Jul 6, '19   Role of Beliefs and Expectations

Father God, I feel dissipated and unsettled.

[| Rest in Me for a while. (Long pause) People, Souls, you rest in Me, the true God, no matter what you believe or do not believe about God, about Me. Do not worry about you or other people being able to come to a place where you clearly understand what is true about the way things are.

Do not worry about whether you are attracting or allowing Souls to be with you whose energy is incompatible with your energy. You are in the process of coming to understand who you are and how to live with and cope with contrary energies in this dualistic world. Peace always! Choose peace. []

Thank You, Father-Mother God!

I have been thinking a lot lately about the concept that what a person believes and expects to happen will come about, that the universe (our Soul?) brings about what we focus on, what we believe will happen. I realized again that I have repeatedly said I am being affected by negative energies.

Holy Spirit, am I being affected by negative energies and by Souls that have negative energy because my beliefs and expectations have been drawing them to me? [| Y |]

I felt a sense of alarm. Many prayers in *Healing Across Time III*

221

are about protecting against and clearing negative energies. This just occurred to me, though: People are at various stages of growth and understanding. I believe that the people who need the type of prayers in *Healing Across Time III* will be drawn to it, and those at a different stage in their spiritual understanding and growth won't be.

Father-Mother God, Holy Spirit, I leave this in Your hands.

Sept 20, '19   PAIN LANGUAGE

I am continuing to have considerable pain in the back of my thighs and lower back. I asked the Holy Spirit questions that came to mind and learned that pain is an entity, low-vibration energy, that can be dissipated by loving it. (Wow!)

I also learned that pain can be a message from Souls. I understood that Soul portions from other lifetimes of mine that are with me are trying to tell me through pain in my back and legs that they want:

1. To receive love.
2. To be freed of judgment, mine and others.
3. Help to forgive others and to ask for forgiveness.
4. Clearing for negative energies.
5. Clearing for karmic curses.
6. Clearing for erroneous imprinting.

Over the next several days, I asked the Ministry Team to join as I prayed for those intentions. I am saying *The Lord's Prayer* for those portions of my Soul and blessing those Souls.

Jan 9, '20   Ever-Expanding Circles

Father God, this morning, I received this understanding:

1. A person can apply the prayers for retroactive clearing of Soul incorporation from within every cell in their body and the clearing of enmeshment between their Soul and other Souls *to every person (Soul) they have a Soul tie with.*

2. Those Souls can apply those clearings *to people and Souls they have a soul tie with,*

3. And those Souls can apply the clearings *to people and Souls they have a soul tie with in ever-expanding circles.*

If I apply that understanding, will it help prevent so many Souls from coming to me for help?

[| Yes, Lorrie, you understood that correctly. I do not want My ministering Souls to be burdened and hard-pressed. I realize you have felt that way a fair amount of the time for several years. It takes a while for a human being to discern the workings of the Holy Spirit, but you have done well in doing so.

Your efforts have brought about a breakthrough in understanding. All of Us are rejoicing with you and over you! |]

Thank You, Father!

Apr 14, '20   OK to Feel Aimless

Father God, I will try to describe my feelings. After signing off from Mercy Church in early June 2018, I attended several other churches to try to find one where I feel comfortable belief-wise. I feel like I am a stranger wandering around somewhat aimlessly. I sense that one or more parts of me have been resisting spending time with You because I feel restless.

[| Bravo to you, Lorrie, for recognizing the restlessness and searching in your spirit. Probably the strongest motivation that parts of you have for not sitting down for quiet time is that they (you) see it as a waste of time. Also, your ego ideal is constantly saying you "should" spend time in prayer and quiet time, and you resist having someone tell you what to do.

For you to come to where you feel truly free about how you spend your time, *you need to fully believe that you are free to do whatever you choose,* with no repercussions.

You are still controlled by the ingrained idea that to be good, you "should" or "should not" do this or that. It takes time for those life-restricting teachings to be recognized and challenged and replaced with full freedom of spirit.

If you do not feel inclined to attend or watch religious services, don't. If you feel freely inclined to attend or watch them, do so. Wherever you are, I am with you. Peace! []

Thank you, Father-Mother God!

This is the end of Part A. Next, we will return to April 2007 to learn what was happening "in the meantime."

B: FOR OUR FAMILY LINES

CHAPTER 1

FAMILY SECRETS UNCOVERED

Healing for Prior Lifetimes: Joel and Me 1

Apr 28, '07   PARENTAGE ISSUES

I learned the "family secrets" I tell about in this chapter shortly after learning that my mother's, Aunt Mollie's, and Grandma Leigh's Souls were incorporated within cells in my body (A: 1-B).

About My Birth Family, the Goergers

I told Fern the Holy Spirit prompted me a few months ago to give my sister Alice a printout of earlier lessons I received from Father-Mother God, the Holy Spirit, and Jesus.

[| Alice is your sister in more ways than one. |]

That could mean that Grandpa Leigh is Alice's birth father like he is mine. Is Grandpa Leigh Alice's birth father? [| Y |]

Did the belligerence and stubbornness Alice had while growing up come partly from her sensing that Dad wasn't her birth father? [| Y |] Did she feel like she didn't quite belong to the family because of that? [| Y |]

(!!!) Is Grandpa Leigh the father of other siblings of mine? [| Yes, two of them. |] Is Grandpa Leigh Joel's birth father? [| Y |] Do some of my siblings have a different father yet? [| Y |]

By asking the Holy Spirit more "Yes" or "No" questions, Fern and I learned that Great-Uncle Mike, Grandpa's brother who lived with Grandpa and Grandma for many years, is the father of my older brothers Dean and Jim and of my younger sister Flo. Mom's brother Will is the father of my sister Tess.

The Holy Spirit often prompted questions to ask so we would learn something Spirit wanted us (me) to know.

FERN: Do any of Lorrie's siblings have a different mother?

[| One of them does. |] By asking more questions, we learned that Aunt Mollie, Mom's sister who never married, is Joel's mother. Mom and Dad must have agreed to raise him as their child. Did Mom tell anybody about Mollie being Joel's birth mother? [| Y |] My brother, Father Ken? [| N |] The priest who married her and Dad? [| N |] The priest who baptized Joel?

[| Yes. Your Mom kept in touch with him through the years. |]

I am glad she had somebody to talk to about it.

I have no idea what I would have done with that surprising and unwelcome information about our family if I hadn't studied *A Course in Miracles* that says no matter what somebody does, they are a holy child of God, that God does not judge and we are not to judge anyone.

I often mention *A Course in Miracles.* The following are some of the passages that helped me deal with fear and guilt. (All of these quotes are also in *Healing Across Time I.)*

When you have accepted the Atonement for yourself, you will realize there is no guilt in God's Son (acim.org T-13.I.6:1).

There is no guilt in you, for God is blessed in His Son as the Son is blessed in Him (acim.org T-14.V.1:12).

Darkness is lack of light as sin is lack of love (acim.org T-1.IV.3:1).

Since love is all there is, sin in the sight of the Holy Spirit is a mistake to be corrected, rather than an evil to be punished (ACIM Preface Pg xi Par 3 Line 2).

What was regarded as injustices done to one by someone else now becomes a call for help and union. Sin, sickness, and attack are seen as misperceptions calling for remedy through gentleness and love (ACIM Preface Pg xii Par 1 Line 4).

No one is punished for sins, and the Sons of God are not sinners. Any concept of punishment involves the projection of blame, and reinforces the idea that blame is justified (acim.org T-6.I.16:4-5).

God does not forgive because He has never condemned. And there must be condemnation before forgiveness is necessary (acim.org W-46.1:1-2).

About Mom's Birth Family, the Leighs

What about the parentage in the Leigh family? We learned that Uncle Mike is Mom's birth father and the birth father of her brother Will and three of her sisters, including Mollie. Grandpa Leigh is the father of Hal, her younger brother.

That changes things for me. Grandpa Leigh, my birth father, is my uncle, not my grandfather. I prefer that.

Did Grandpa Leigh know about the relationship between his wife, Mavis, and his brother, Mike? [| Y |] Was Grandma Leigh a victim of incest? [| N |] Was she aware of her actions when she had sexual relations with her brother-in-law, Mike? [| Y |] Was she mesmerized by Mike? [| Yes, there was a powerful attraction between them. |] Was she affected by a spirit of lust? [| Y |]

(!!!) **Is the spirit of lust affecting the Leigh family line?** [| Y |]

About Mom

Was my mother's personality split, or somewhat split, like mine is? [| Y |] My siblings and I learned 20 years ago that Mom was sexually abused as a child *and* as an adult. Did (some) incidents of incest when Mom was younger, and the sexual activity between her and Grandpa Leigh, her Uncle Mike, and her brother Will as an adult happen with a separate part of her personality? [| Y |]

Did Mom's Uncle Mike and her brother Will pressure her to have sex with them? [| Y |] She was like a kidnap victim to a certain extent. [| Y |] Did she gradually repress memories of those incidents so it became as if they hadn't happened? [| Y |]

I received the understanding from Spirit a while back that I was a love child. Did Mom act freely with Grandpa Leigh when I came along? [| Y |] Did she act freely with Grandpa when my sister Alice came along? [| Y |] Did Aunt Mollie act freely with Grandpa Leigh when she became pregnant with Joel? [| N |]

I arranged eight weekly Masses for healing for the Goerger and Leigh families. I attended most of them.

A quote came to mind: *"Oh, what a tangled web we weave, when first we practice to deceive!"* (Sir Walter Scott, "Marmion: A Tale of Flodden Field")

An outside observer might think my mother and her family "deceived" family members by not telling them (us) the information Fern and I just learned about, but I don't think of it as their having deceived us. Hiding family secrets was (and is) "the thing to do" to protect the family.

About Ron's and My Family, the Jahners

Fern and I learned two weeks ago that there was incest and sexual abuse in Ron's birth family, the Jahners. Now Fern asked a question that surprised me: "Would you like to know if Ron ever did sexual things with any of your children?"

I thought about it and said, "OK."

Fern asked the Holy Spirit questions and received answers silently, then told me what she learned: Ron was the father of the baby that *Tara* miscarried at age 16 that she thought was her boyfriend's baby, and he was the father of the baby that *Nita* gave up for adoption during high school. (Oh, dear!) Nita's seventh-grade teacher was concerned about how sad she was. Did the incest begin before that? [| Y |]

Ron seldom drank too much, but I asked anyway, "Was alcohol involved?" [| Yes, in both cases. |]

FERN: "Would you like to know whether Ron touched any of your other kids inappropriately?" I said, "Yes." We learned that he had done so with two of our other girls.

I can't explain why, but I felt no emotional reaction to learning about Ron's egregious actions with our girls. The only response I could manage as I wrote about it was, "I'll need to do some processing about this."

May 15, '07   Secrets Need to Come Out

Holy Spirit, has my mother gone to the light? [| N |] My Dad? [| Y |] Aunt Mollie? [| N |] Grandma Leigh? [| No. It is time for the whole story about the parentage in the Leigh and Goerger families to come out to heal the families. |]

Do Mom's, Mollie's, and Grandma Leigh's Souls agree to that? [| Yes. They are ready to be healed. |] Can a family be fully healed only when family secrets are uncovered and shared with the family, at least in spirit? [| Y |]

"Making family secrets known" means telling the information to family members in person or in spirit, preferably aloud. It is like going to confession in the name of the family because when a person tells someone about a personal wrong in their life, they are confessing it to God at the same time.

Did my being willing to face the truth about Lori's paternity and other guilt issues in my life help others in the family, including those on the other side, become willing to have the truth come out about the family secrets Fern and I are learning about?
[| Yes, there is that, and Souls of family members were listening to the reading and discussions at the *Course in Miracles* meetings you held at your place for many years. By the way, your daughter *Lori's Soul* agreed to take part in bringing forth lessons about healing one's person and family lines. |]

Am I meant to share the parentage in the Leigh and Goerger families with my siblings? [| Y |]

I had already planned to share it with my brother, Father Ken, a trained counselor. Am I meant to share "my story," the parentage of my children, with Father Ken, too? [| Y |] Am I meant to share that information with my siblings and children at some point, perhaps in spirit? [| Y |]

Jun 10, '07   THE SPIRIT OF LUST

I learned recently that portions of Mom's, Aunt Mollie's, and Grandma Leigh's Souls are incorporated within cells in my body (Part A). Years ago, when LeAnn, the facilitator of an inner healing workshop I attended, sensed the spirit of lust within me, did she sense it related to Mom? [| Y |] Related to Aunt Mollie? [| N |] Related to Grandma? [| N |]

Did the portion of Grandma Leigh's Soul that is with me influence me to connect sexually with Lee? [| Y |] Is her Soul like a personality within me? [| Y |]

Was my being attracted to Lee and acting on that attraction influenced enough by Grandma Leigh that it almost wasn't me doing it but her Soul in charge of me? [| Y |] Did she particularly influence the Pandora part of me? [| Y |] Did the lust present in Mom's Soul also play a part?

[| Yes, because your mother's and Grandma Leigh's Souls are enmeshed. |]

Did my mother pick up the spirit of lust from Grandma Leigh? [| N |] Was it with her when she was young? [| No, she picked it up through incest. |]

Did Aunt Mollie see somebody sexually abuse me? [| Y |] Did Grandpa Leigh? [| Y |] Did Mom? [| N |] Did Mom's brothers Will and Hal see somebody abuse me? [| Yes, but they thought you had consented to it. |] How could they have thought that? I was only five!

(!!!) I should ask Mom, Mollie, and Grandma Leigh for permission to continue opening up about family secrets.

"Mom, Aunt Mollie, and Grandma, I ask permission to continue opening up family secrets as the Holy Spirit leads the way. I will assume that you give your permission because the will of one's Full Soul is the same as God's will."

I have had a lot of head discomfort lately. Is Mollie putting pressure on me to ask more questions and get answers? [| N |] Is the pressure coming from within me? [| N |] From outside? [| Y |] Is it a sign that not all the information is out yet? [| Y |]

Is Pastor Eric a key person in this process? [| Y |]

Jun 18, '07   Love Circle Connections

[| People do not know to what extent people in a family line are connected. For example, a mother's and father's love for their children doesn't go only to those children. Their love ministers to the people and Souls In the family line who need love while continuing to expand outward to the whole universe!

Multiply the thought of that mother's and father's love flowing outward by umptillion love circles, and add to that another umptillion love circles emanating from the loving hearts of all of My children. As those love circles ebb outward, they interact such that there is not a single spot in the whole universe, within All That Is, that is not transcendent in love!

It is time for that fact to become known. The most logical place to begin opening up that concept to the world is by demonstrating the spiritual nature of family ties that exist before and after the grave, between those two states of being. Your work and that of others is addressing that area.

You have done much already to bring healing to the Leigh, Goerger, and Jahner family lines. Rejoice with me that freedom is on its way! Everything will be accomplished as it is in the offing to be. Bless you! Sleep well! |]

Thank You, Father God! Bless You!

Jun 19, '07   Time to Tell the Family

Is it time to tell the family about parentage in the Goerger and Leigh families? [| Y |] Do I have enough background and material to set up a meeting with Father Ken? [| Y |] Should I ask Fern to be with me when I meet with him? [| Y |]

I called Fern to tell her my head was bothering me a lot. Is that discomfort being caused by distress from the family line? [| Y |] From Aunt Mollie's Soul? [| Y |] Mom's Soul? [| Y |] Dad's? [| Y |] Grandma Leigh's? [| Y |] Grandpa Leigh's? [| Y |]

I sense that the "boil" of unresolved issues of our ancestors is coming to a head, and pressure is building up in the family. Opening secrets could be compared to lancing a boil and applying pressure to get the core out.

Recently, I played a recording of the Preface of *A Course in Miracles* a few times and have been playing music much of the time. Is that helping lessen the effects of family distress on me? [| Y |] Did teachings from *A Course in Miracles* – that everyone is a holy Son of God (T-8, VI.8:8); that there is no real guilt (T-13, I.6:1) or hell other than what the ego has created; and that the final judgment will be that we are and always have been holy children of God (W-p2.10:5:1) – send enough hope to our ancestors that they are now willing to share their secrets because of no longer being afraid of being rejected and condemned? [| Y |]

Is uncovering and sharing family secrets regarding mixed parentage, abuse, or whatever else, along with unconditional love and acceptance for all involved, the most important factor in release and healing for our family? [| Y |]

Will the healing for current Leigh, Goerger, and Jahner family members help the whole family lines extend back to their ancestors? [| Y |] *Since we are all one in God, will healing for our families and family lines flow a measure of healing to all families of all time?* [| Y |] Wow!

Is Aunt Mollie getting frustrated with how long it is taking for healing to take place for the family? [| Y |] Does the whole Leigh family know about it? [| Y |] Do my great-grandparents know? [| Not yet, but they will be made aware. |]

Jun 19, '07. Mollie had a lot of problems with sinus drainage. Was that physical symptom a "message" from an earlier family member asking for assistance? [| Yes, her mother. |]

Would praying for the Leigh, Goerger, and Jahner families as a group help lessen the effects of family distress on family members? [| Y |]

Are many people in every family line affected by family distress so that family secrets can surface and there can be forgiveness and karmic release? [| Y |]

When something is amiss in one's body, symptoms often show up in the weakest areas. Is family distress the same?

[| Yes, it affects people in their most vulnerable areas. []

Does "distress coming from one's family line" include those on the other side and people who are still living? [| Y |]

Might Souls who have gone to the light bring on family distress by asking for help for hurting relatives or friends? [| Y |]

Jun 24, '07   A CURSE ON THE LEIGH FAMILY

Can a whole family or group of people be cursed? [| Y |] Would the opening up of secrets and extending forgiveness and blessing to all family members, living and departed, lessen the effect that curses would have on them? [| Y |] Would extending forgiveness and blessing to the family over a long while clear the curses? [| N |]

Does a curse placed on a family affect everyone in that family in some way? [| Y |] If one person or several people in a family have a curse laid on them, would that affect everyone in the family? [| Y |]

Would forgiving, blessing, and sending love to whoever placed the curse on the family or individuals in the family release the curse entirely? [| N |] Would the family need prayer for deliverance? [| Y |]

Can a curse be cleared from a family by holding a deliverance service for the family, preferably with some of the family members present? [| Y |] During such a service, should the group extend forgiveness and blessing to the person or persons who placed the curse on the family or individuals in the family? [| Y |]

(!!!) *Was a curse placed on the Leigh family?* [| Y |] On the whole family line? [| Y |] By a neighbor? [| N |] By a relative? [| N |] By somebody Grandpa Leigh did business with? [| N |] By someone from the other side? [| Y |] By the Soul of a man who had wanted to marry Grandma Leigh? [| Y |]

Does the whole Leigh family need a clearing for that curse, including Mom? [| Y |] Is the curse we are speaking of being passed down to everybody in the Leigh family? [| N |] Are the curse's effects passed down to everybody? [| Y |]

I understood without words that chickens were, and are, connected to that curse in some way and that family members suffer negative effects from eating chicken.

What the Curse Consists Of

Is the curse that was placed on the Leigh family for them to be poor? [| N |] For them to have poor health? [| N |]

(!!!) Is it a curse for members of the family to go to hell? [| Y |] Is the curse related to the spirit of lust that has shown up in the family? [| Y |] *Is the spirit of lust the curse?* [| Y |] Lust is one of the "deadly sins" related to going to hell.

When I meet with Father Ken, should I tell him about the spirit of lust in the family? [| Y |] Should all of our siblings be told about it eventually? [| Y |] When family secrets have come out, can the spirit of lust be cleared from the family? [| Y |]

Who Had (Has) the Spirit of Lust

Did Grandma Leigh have the spirit of lust? [| Y |] Grandpa Leigh? [| N |] Uncle Will? [| Y |] Aunt Mollie? [| Y |] Mom? [| Y |] Others in their family? [| N |]

Did Grandma Leigh pick up the spirit of lust from the man from the other side who placed the curse on the family? [| No. She picked it up from the curse the man placed. |]

Did Grandma Leigh pass the spirit of lust on to Mom? [| No. Your mother is affected by it because of incest in the family. |]

Did Mom pass the spirit of lust on to me? [| N |] Did I pick it up through incestuous sexual abuse that I experienced at an early age? [| Y |] Did I pass the spirit of lust on to Joel? [| No. It gets passed on when someone with the spirit of lust abuses another person. |]

Is the spirit of lust affecting people in my birth family, the Goergers? [| Y |] Do I need to know who is affected? [| N |]

Would prayer for clearing clear the curse? [| N |] Does the Goerger family need deliverance? [| Y |] By Pastor Eric? [| Y |]

I Need Clearing For the Spirit of Lust

Is the spirit of lust still attached to me? [| Y |] Is it within me? [| Y |] Is the spirit of lust within me only with *Pandora^P*, one of the parts that had sexual relations with Lee? [| No, it is also within another part of you. |]

Fern and I narrowed it down to a younger part of me named Kay[P]. (I didn't experience any effects from that spirit.) Do Pandora and Kay need prayer individually to clear the spirit of lust? [| Y |] Is Kay a teenager? [| Y |]

When I meet with Pastor Eric to clear the spirit of lust from the Leigh and Goerger families, I will also ask him to clear it from Pandora and Kay.

Did I pick up the spirit of lust from Uncle Art? [| No, it was from incest early in life. |]

Are some of my brothers and sisters affected by the spirit of lust? [| N |] Did the spirit of lust alight on me so it could finally get cleared from the family? [| Y |] Am I the only one in the Goerger family directly affected by the spirit of lust to make this method of clearing known to the world? [| Y |]

When the spirit of lust gets cleared from our family, will the process work backward in time to clear Dad's brothers and sisters, including Uncle Art? [| Y |] Wow!

After the spirit of lust has been cleared, will I and other family members be able to get in touch with Spirit more easily? [| Y |]

Should I have somebody with me when I ask Pastor Eric to pray to clear the spirit of lust? [| N |] Should I ask him to pray for me before I meet with Father Ken on July Fourth? [| Y |]

Jun 26, '07   Prayer for Our Families

I met with Pastor Eric for prayer to clear the curse of the spirit of lust from the Leigh, Goerger, and Jahner families and Pandora[P] and Kay[P]. I also asked for a clearing for the spirit of pride, if needed, and for the sense of shame and other negative effects on Ron and me from our "mixed-up" family backgrounds.

Pastor Eric prayed silently for a long while. Then he placed holy water on my hands and asked that I may come to be rooted totally in Jesus and that the roots of the spirit of lust would dry up in me and in our family lines.

Afterward, he said, he saw a large dangling spider before he began praying. I think of that dangling spider as a symbol of the spirit of lust waiting to ensnare its victims.

Thank you for the prayers, Pastor Eric! Bless you!

(Evening) Has the curse of the spirit of lust that was placed on the Leigh family years ago been cleared from me? [| Y |]

Has it been cleared from the Leigh family line? [| Not entirely, but the overshadowing of the spirit of lust on the family has been cleared. |]

Is the spirit of lust cleared from Pandora^P? [| Y |] From Kay^P? [| N |] Should I ask Pastor Eric to pray again for me to clear it from Kay? [| Y |]

(Aug 20, '07) I met with Pastor Eric for prayer to clear the spirit of lust from Kay^P. He blessed me with holy water and said prayers to renew my baptism. Thank you, Pastor Eric.

Is the spirit of lust cleared from Kay^P? [| Y |] Do I still have the personality named Kay? [| N |] Thank You, Father!

Jul 4, '07   Sharing with Father Ken

Father Ken will come to my place today for me to tell him about the Leigh and Goerger family issues that Fern and I recently learned about. Fern was here to give me support.

Father Ken arrived. After introducing Fern to him, I asked the Holy Spirit to guide our discussion. Ken said a prayer also. I took a deep breath and began sharing.

I gave Ken printouts that showed the parentage in the Leigh, Goerger, and Jahner families as the Holy Spirit made it known to Fern and me. I told him about the curse of the spirit of lust affecting the whole family, then sat tensely, waiting for his reaction.

I had just presented material that might have blown someone else away, but Ken said calmly, *"There are two ways I could respond to this. One would be my natural reaction (pause), and the other would be to look at this as being where you are at and to discuss it with you."*

I was truly amazed! Ken didn't make a single snide remark! There was not even a hint of criticism in what he said, in the tone of his voice, or his body language! He said he would read the printouts and pray about it.

Thank You, Father God, that the meeting went well!

Jul 7, '07   Mom Was Under Pressure

The amount of pressure Mom must have been under is unbelievable! Grandpa Leigh and Uncle Mike were "after her" sexually while she was growing up, and the two of them and Mom's brother Will were "after her" for the first ten years of her marriage to Dad! (Grandma Leigh died soon after Mom and Dad got married.)

Based on the ages of my siblings that they fathered, "pressure" on Mom by Great-Uncle Mike and Uncle Will continued for years until we moved further away from her home place. She couldn't say "No" to them for fear that:

1. They would tell her husband Herb what was happening in the present or what happened in earlier years.
2. They might use physical pressure like in the past.

Also, their approaching her to have sex would have caused her to revert to being a child or teenager again, pretty much helpless in the situation.

Bless you, Mom! I can't imagine how hard that was on you. I pray that you are healed of all aftereffects from those experiences or will be soon.

Jul 10, '07   A Welcome Change of Plan

When Fern and I met with Father Ken six days ago, we understood that, at some point, Father Ken or I would tell our other siblings about parentage in the Goerger and Leigh families.

Holy Spirit, is it still meant for Father Ken or me to tell Joel that Mollie is his birth mother? [| Y |] Should I tell Alice sometime that Grandpa Leigh is her birth father? [| Y |]

Do You still want me to tell the rest of my siblings about their parentage at some point?

[| No, that is no longer necessary. |] What a relief!

I called Father Ken to tell him we only need to tell Joel that Aunt Mollie and Grandpa Leigh are his birth parents and to tell Alice that

Grandpa Leigh is her birth father. He said he would have a chance to talk with Joel while they were out fishing.

Jul 14, '07   Clearing Karma

My head was very uncomfortable today, likely caused by the distress that family members are experiencing. I learned a few days ago I have karma to clear with my mother. I stood in the large copper ring and asked for archangels, angels, and helpers to be on hand for protection and assistance.

While holding a picture of my mother holding me as a baby, I said: "I intend that the forgiveness that will take place between Mom and me will include every lifetime that we shared.

ME: "Mom, I forgive you for whatever ways you hurt my feelings, neglected me, or whatever else I felt hurt by during this lifetime and all other lifetimes."

I invited Mom to join as I said: "Thank you for forgiving me."

ME: "You are welcome, Mom. Please forgive me for times that I hurt your feelings, judged you, or whatever else you felt hurt by during this lifetime and all other lifetimes."

MOM: "I forgive you, Lorrie. I love you!"

ME: "Thank you, Mom! I love you very much!"

Then, I did a brief process of forgiveness between:

1.   Mom and Grandma and Grandpa Leigh,
2.   Mom and Great-Uncle Mike,
3.   Mom and each of her siblings,
4.   Mom and each of us children.

Prayer for the Goerger and Leigh Family Lines

I went for a walk to help my head feel better. As I walked, I breathed peace in and negativity out for all of the Goerger ancestors and spoke blessings to them. After my walk, I prayed for clearing for the Goergers, Dad's family lines.

I planned to pray for Grandpa and Grandma Leigh's family lines next, but I broke down crying very hard when I looked at Grandma Leigh's picture. I held it to my heart, lay on the floor, and cried. It was as though some of the anguish she experienced was getting released through me.

After crying for a while, I prayed for clearing and healing for the Leigh family lines.

A few days later, I cleared karma using the process of forgiveness between myself and Dad, Grandma Leigh, Grandpa Leigh, Aunt Mollie, and Great Uncle Mike, asking for their forgiveness and extending forgiveness to each of them.

Thank You, Holy Spirit, for helping me with that!

Jul 19, '07   JOEL'S AND MY MISSION

Is Joel's having Grandpa Leigh and Aunt Mollie as his birth parents and growing up in the Goerger family a means of clearing karma for him and others?
[| Yes. In previous lifetimes, you and Joel were spirit guides for the family and learned what a mess it was in. You decided to find a way to help clear the family lines. |]

Who Placed the Spirit of Lust on the Leigh Family?

Was the man "on the other side" who laid the spirit of lust on the Leigh family because Mavis Leigh wouldn't marry him a prior lifetime of someone we know? [| Y |]

After naming several others, was it Joel!? [| Y |] Did Joel's Soul do that out of revenge? [| N |] Did he do it as part of the plan to present this example of healing for families to the world? [| Y |]

Are Joel and I connected in spirit?
[| Yes, by your Soul's purpose and to help each other. |]

Lesson From a Dream

DREAM: While Ron and I were out driving, we stopped at a restaurant to use the restroom. Several teenagers were waiting in line, so I used a nearby outhouse. While I was sitting in it, some teenagers also crowded in to use it. Some used the floor as a disposal place rather than waiting to use the toilet opening. They left without saying anything. END.

I see this dream as saying that people often need to clean up messes that others have left behind. It could also symbolize that we can help clear karma for our ancestors.

Clearing Karma in My Soul Line

I felt a lot of pressure within the top of my head, and it was hurting on the lower left side. I decided to speak aloud to clear karma between me and others in this lifetime and all other lifetimes. I asked for forgiveness for many possible situations that came to mind, ways that I may have hurt others. Then, I forgave each person in every lifetime for many situations that came to mind, ways in which they may have hurt me.

I affirmed aloud to the Souls that I had cleared karma with that each of us is a holy child of God and prayed the *Prayer to the Holy Spirit* for clearing for them. I turned on a fan and asked that all negative energies be blown away from me and everyone in this lifetime and all previous lifetimes.

Thank You, Holy Spirit, for that clearing!

Jul 26, '07   Unburdening Is Happening!

(!!!) I received the understanding, saw an image of it taking place, that many Souls in the Leigh and Goerger family lines who have not yet gone to the light are choosing to ask for forgiveness from living family members and those on the other side for hurtful things they did towards them.

Also, many Souls in the astral plane, inside and outside of our family lines, who hadn't confessed their wrongdoing to anybody before they died are now seeking out priests, ministers, and nonjudgmental people and Souls to unload their burdens onto and receive understanding and forgiveness.

The forgiving that is taking place is bringing more light to everyone in our family lines and the whole of humanity. Wonderful! [| Right on! These people and Souls need to hear the words:

"You are forgiven. You are a holy child of God. Heaven can be yours for the receiving. Bless you in who you are and in who you are coming

to be! If you let go of guilt, it will let go of you. You made the guilt, and you can unmake it."

All is well, Lorrie, even with you having discomfort in your head a good share of the time. More key things that are part of the picture and the process will be opening up.

Your Soul would have it no other way than to have things go just as they are. Without the physical symptoms coming into the picture, you would have no idea about the clearing needed for your family lines. Building a house or clearing a path through bramble and underbrush takes effort. In a way, you are in the process of doing both of those things.

The unburdening is a-happening and Oh! How happy your family lines are to see it coming about! Many prayers have been prayed and tears shed that also played a part in this clearing and healing process.

It may have seemed for many of those who prayed and shed tears that their prayers and pleading had gone unheard. I agonized with each of you as you begged for release, healing, and freedom for your loved ones. I hear every heart's cry! []

Thank You so much, Father God!

I add to that: "Bravo to everyone in each family line and in all of humanity who has not given up on your son, daughter, husband, wife, relative or friend, but have continued to believe in their basic goodness and that, in some way, grace would reach them and set them free! Together, we will reach our goal of total peace and harmony in our families and the world!"

All Three Went to the Light!

Fern called to tell me something exciting that took place during an evening meditation she attended. A "sensitive" (person who is sensitive to the working of the Spirit) said, "There are many Souls at a nearby baseball field waiting to go to the light, Souls of adults and children from various disasters, plus other Souls."

The meditation group (from where they were) created a positive vortex in the baseball field to help those Souls go to the light.

Fern said she asked the Holy Spirit later whether she knew any of the Souls that went to the light, then excitedly called to tell me wonderful news! My mother, Aunt Mollie, and Grandma Leigh went to the light! I had to cry for a while.

Aug 1, '07   Ministering While Sleeping

I read that the Soul of some people, while the person is sleeping, goes out to minister to people who are hurting, even halfway around the world at times. Their Soul leaves their body but stays attached by a silver cord.

Holy Spirit, should I make the intention for my Soul to go out in spirit while I am sleeping to minister to the Leigh family? [| No, another family member has been appointed to do that. |] Has that person already crossed over? [| Y |]

Has a living member of the Goerger family been appointed to minister at night to our family? [| Y |] More than one person? [| N |] After naming several others: Is it Father Ken? [| Y |]

Aug 2, '07. Is some of the discomfort in my head caused by concerns that Souls in the Goerger family have who have died but have not yet gone to the light? [| N |] Are living members of the family asking for help? [| Y |] Some of my siblings?
[| Yes. Joel's and Alice's Souls want prayer before someone tells them about their paternity. |]

I prayed for Joel and Alice often during the next few weeks.

Aug 10, '07   Resistance to Publication

Fern went to the emergency room four days ago with a bad migraine headache (the doctor treated it, and she went home). The next day, I suddenly developed a sore, stiff neck.

(!!!) Are some Souls trying to prevent me from getting my family story published? [| Y |] The Souls of some of my brothers and sisters? [| Y |] Some Souls who have gone to the light? [| N |]

Is *Aunt Mollie,* who died four years ago, trying to prevent the publication? [| Y |] If I didn't mention Mollie's name, would she still try to prevent it? [| N |]

(!!!) Is it Aunt Mollie's Soul from another lifetime in which she had a child out of wedlock that is trying to prevent the publication? [| Y |] Has that Soul gone to the light? [| N |]

Sept 2, '07. Did Mollie come into her recent lifetime loaded with painful memories of her own and from her family line so those situations could get cleared and healed? [| Y |] Is it correct that part of the needed clearing and healing took place through her having Joel? [| Y |]

Did some painful cellular memories that Mollie was carrying get passed on to Joel to get cleared? [| Y |] Were some passed on to me, her godchild? [| Yes, as her wishful daughter. |]

Sept 2, '07   Sharing with Family in Spirit

Fern suggested last week that I tell Joel in spirit that Grandpa Leigh and Aunt Mollie are his birth father and mother before telling him in person and to tell Alice in spirit that Grandpa Leigh is her birth father before telling her in person. That is a good idea! I told Joel and Alice in spirit the next day about their parentage.

Alice is south for the summer, so I can't meet with her. Is Joel's Soul ready for him to be told directly [| Y |]

(!!!) Should I tell my brothers Dean and Jim and my sisters Tess and Flo in spirit about their paternity? [| Y |]

After doing that, should I tell all of my siblings in spirit as a group about the parentage in the Leigh and Goerger families? [| Yes, but at a different time. |] Should I wait at least six months between times? [| Y |]

That evening, I told Dean, Jim, Tess, and Flo in spirit who their birth father was. Thank You, Holy Spirit, for Your help!

Nov 6, '07   Intentions Are Powerful

Through the years, I processed my emotions and received healing for abuse incidents shortly after they surfaced. (!!!) Could my processing of those sexual assaults also bring healing for Mom for similar experiences that she had? [| It will if you state that intention. |] Can I make that intention after having already processed the incidents? [| Y |]

Mom, I intend for my release and expression of emotions related to painful incidents that surfaced *to be applied to you* to help you heal from the aftereffects of painful experiences you had. I ask that my forgiveness for my perpetrators may, at the same time, be your forgiveness for your perpetrators.

Holy Spirit, if I would make the intention for my release and expression of emotions related to painful incidents that surfaced *to be applied to all of my relatives who need healing for such experiences*, would those people and Souls be healed, too? [| Y |] If one would intend for that healing *to be applied to everybody who needs healing*, would those people receive healing as well? [| Y |] Wow!

I intend for my release and expression of emotions related to painful incidents that surfaced for me to be applied to all my relatives who need healing related to such experiences. I ask that my forgiveness for my perpetrators may at the same time be their forgiveness for their perpetrators. And, Holy Spirit, please apply that clearing and healing to every person and Soul who needs healing and is willing for release and forgiveness to take place. Thank You!

Father God told me years ago that as I suffered sexual abuse, I became united in spirit with many others who had suffered sexual abuse. I think that means that I picked it up in spirit and became united with many who were sexually abused later than I was and that as I expressed anguish at having been abused, their anguish got released along with mine. I pray that is the case. Thank You, Father!

Do some people who experience sexual abuse have the ministry of clearing and healing others? [| Y |] If someone who has worked through experiences of sexual abuse would make the intention for healing to be extended to their perpetrator(s) as well, would that take place? [| Y |]

That opens a wonderful world of possibilities!

Nov 23, '07   ABUSE IN GOERGER FAMILY, TOO

By A Cousin and An Uncle

(At Fern's) My sister Amy was very shy growing up. Was Amy sexually abused as a young child? [| Y |] Is the person who did it still living? [| Y |] By asking the Holy Spirit the questions that came to mind, Fern and I narrowed it down to that person being one of our female cousins. Was it one of Uncle Leo's daughters, who lived near us for two years?

[| Yes. That woman remembers the abuse, and it still haunts her. She is sorry about it. Blessing her will help Amy. Some of Amy's health problems are related to sexual abuse. |]

My brother Joel told me about having had a recurring nightmare when he was younger, about wooly stuff getting closer and closer to his face, and when it reached him, he would have to vomit. Did Dad perform oral sex on Joel? [| N |] Did Dad's brother, Uncle Art? [| Y |] That's so sad! Did that incident create a split or partial personality within Joel? [| Y |]

By Mom

I mentioned in *Healing Across Time I* that Mom used the handle of a table knife on Ann when Ann was three years old and that Mom was somewhat of a trance at the time, reenacting something from her childhood. Did Mom sexually abuse some of us other kids, too? [| Yes, all of the girls, by licking. |] Did she abuse any of the boys? [| N |]

While growing up, did Mom and her sisters do sexual things to and with each other? [| Y |] That isn't surprising, considering that incest occurred in their home.

By Dad

Did Dad sexually abuse any of the other girls besides me? [| N |] Did he abuse any of the boys? [| Yes, all of them. |]

FERN: Your dad just said, "I had to make men of them."

We narrowed the age at which he abused the boys to 2-3 years old. Did Dad suck on their penises?

[| Yes, on all of them. He had the boys do it to each other, too. That took place a couple of times with each one. |]

Did Dad also abuse them manually? [| Yes, and again, he had them do it to each other. |] Did he abuse any of them at a later age? [| N |]

Did part of Joel's Soul split off when Dad sexually molested him? [| Y |] Is that split-off portion attached to, or within, Joel? [| No. It's in the astral plane. |]

Maybe Dad was taught that a father should do that type of "sexual training" for his sons "so they would grow up and be men." Did he do those actions out of love? [| Y |] Maybe it wasn't especially harmful to the boys then. Is that correct?
[| No. It was traumatic for them. |]

Nov 24, '07. I slept restlessly last night, and my temperature was slightly elevated this morning. Was that rise in my temperature related to Mom's and Dad's being willing to have this stuff come out? [| Y |]

Bless you, Mom and Dad! It must have been very difficult for you to acknowledge your abusive actions. Thank you for being willing to let some more secrets come out to help bring healing to our family.

It appears to be important, maybe even necessary, that our family secrets come out for healing to take place.

In some cases, it wouldn't be feasible or even beneficial to have people tell family secrets to family members physically. If people in that type of situation would tell their secrets to the Souls of the others who are involved, would that be sufficient to bring healing for the family as a whole and for individuals in the family?
[| Yes. The Souls of the others already knew about it, but those been holding the secrets are helped by getting them out. |]

Dec 6, '07   You Reached the Top
[| I am happy for you, Lorrie and Fern, that you "opened your Souls" to see the larger picture regarding healing family roots and relationships. You "reached the top of the hill" and can see the sunrise! With this new-to-humankind teaching coming forth and

248

other spiritual knowledge about to come on stage, people and Souls as a whole will be able to breathe a collective sigh of relief.

It would be good for you, Lorrie, to take deep breaths every chance you get to release tension, anxiety, and fear of every kind. You have much tension to release from the past, and because your Soul has become very sensitive, you easily pick up lower-vibration energy from people.

I want you to build up a protective layer around your aura composed of your belief that you are a beloved child of God and your trust that you, as a child of God, have built-in protection that exudes from your person as light energy. Peace! []

Thank You, Father God!

Dec 11, '07   Shore Up Your Gates!

I continue to have head discomfort, very likely caused by Souls in the family being in distress. What to do about it?
[| Verily, that is a puzzle, but puzzles have answers. Think back over the clues, Lorrie, and see if you alight on something that will shed light on the present situation:

"Smoke: fire somewhere. Growth: a plant. Plants have roots. ...The taproot is the most important." (HAT I p. 37)

Many people in every family line are in great need of prayer. There is no way to know who the neediness is coming from that you and others are picking up.

You need to shore up your gates and put a line of defense in place! You wonder what I am telling you to do. []

Yes, Father God. I would like You to give instructions on how to put blocks or gates in place to prevent undue family distress from overwhelming us. But, first, I want to ask, to what extent is it a person's responsibility to pray for people in our family relationships?
[| You asked a good question, Lorrie. I will answer that before telling about putting spiritual blocks and barriers in place.

The Holy Spirit and their Soul will let each person know their responsibility regarding praying for family members. []

I consider it my responsibility to pray for my grandparents,

parents, aunts, and uncles, but not their spouses or children; for my brothers and sisters, but not their spouses or children; for my children and their spouses, my grandchildren and great-grandchildren. "But not" doesn't mean I wouldn't pray for those people, but I don't consider that my physical or spiritual health should be open to being affected by their struggles and ills.

Dec 13, '07. Father God, please explain Your words, "Shore up your gates! Put a line of defense in place!"

[| Lorrie, first spend a while relaxing and breathing in love. Let fear and anxiety float up and away as though you were immersed in water, and fear and anxiety dissolve. Picturing things happening has more effect than you realize!

Line of defense: *Breathe in love and breathe out fear.*

Line of defense: *Stay your course. Follow the guidance of the Holy Spirit for you.*

Do not let fear of being criticized by others cause you to swerve from your course. Your course is set. The plan for your life is opening up and becoming a reality. You and the many other Souls working on this blessed project are bringing what was only a faint dream years ago to fruition. |]

Dec 14, '07   DOWN THE FAMILY LINE

> *"...I, the Lord your God, am a jealous God, punishing the children for the sin of the parents to the third and fourth generation of those who hate me"* (NIV Ex 20:5b).

Does that refer to how far back people can be affected by family distress? [| Y |] Is it important to get the roots of spiritual problems in the family line cleared?

[| It is very important that the roots of spiritual problems be cleared because what affects you affects your children, also. |]

My Dad, Herb Goerger, isn't my birth father and didn't adopt me. Does the connection to earlier generations hold for me with the Goerger family lines?

[| You are not affected directly by Souls in your dad's family line, but many of your siblings are, which affects you. |]

Does "my family line" include my former husband Ron's family back to the fourth generation? [| Y |] So, when a person gets married, they are connected to the family lines of their spouse just as much as to their birth family lines? [| Y |]

Are people still being affected by the family lines they were a part of in previous lifetimes?
[| Yes, they are affected by both living and deceased members of those family lines. |] Unbelievable!

Are the health problems I have a reflection of the spiritual health of our whole family? [| Y |] Is my body like a thermometer for the whole family? [| Yes, or like a boil. |]

Dec 17, '07. I have had mixed-up dreams that might indicate things are unsettled within me and my family lines.

Bless you, my mother and father, in this lifetime and every lifetime! Bless you, my grandparents and great-grandparents, in this lifetime and every lifetime!

CAME TO MIND: Tap the top. Taproot is the most important.
[| What is your taproot, Lorrie, the main root from which you originate? What was Grandma Leigh like? What was your birth father, Grandpa Leigh, like?

Encoded with. Bearer of. Are you a pallbearer or a joy-bearer? What is your natal strain? |]

The important thing is that I received life through them.
[| That's right. No matter what your Grandma and Grandpa Leigh were like, one thing is certain: I flowed My life through them to you. All that matters is the life coming from them. You do not need to know their strengths, weaknesses, likes, dislikes, health, or shortcomings.

Your grandparents and parents passed My life on to you, thus allowing you to live a human life within that family line. Bless your forbears for all you are worth! In a way, they deserve your reverence, for you received life through them, and life is sacred. By choosing to reverence your forbears, you help loosen the icy crust of self-loathing that is still present within many of them.

When dominoes are standing in a line, pushing against the first domino will make the next one tip, then the next one, and so on. Ladle self-abhorrence and lack of self-esteem into one ancestor and pair that man or woman with a partner with low self-esteem, and the dominoes are all set to fall down the generational line carrying that self-abhorrence and lack of self-esteem!

By viewing your forbears as sacred children of God, which they are, you cancel that falling domino effect in the family line! You make the present, present to your forbears. The resultant change in the earlier generations of your family line gets passed down the generational lines to the present, and now you have ancestors who felt good about themselves and taught their children to feel good about themselves!

Nothing is impossible with God! People say, "Taking one day at a time" is the way to get through difficult situations. I say that "Changing one thought at a time" is how to correct the erroneous beliefs of humankind. Be at peace, Lorrie! []

Jan 11, '08   Clearing Needed For Shades

Are shades, portions of the astral body, of some of my Souls from previous lifetimes with me? [| Y |] Will I feel lighter after those shades have been cleared? [| Y |]

Is my mother within me or casting a shadow over me, like "a shade of the past"? [| Y |] But the incorporation of her Soul from within cells in my body is cleared. [| This is different. It's a connection on the spiritual level. |]

Does "a shade of Mom's Soul being with me" signify a symbiotic connection between her and me in which our Souls draw energy from each other?

[| Yes. Your mother doesn't know how to relate in any other way. It is the only type of relationship she has known for many lifetimes. She lost her strength by being abused in her second-last lifetime. It created a weakened personality. Everything came to a head in her recent lifetime as your mother. []

I sense the "shade of Mom's Soul" needs to be cleared from me before non-beneficial energies can be cleared. [| Y |]

Did Mom's Soul from her second-last lifetime go to the light? [| Yes, but a shade from that lifetime that overshadowed your mother during her recent lifetime is still with your Mom's Soul. []

Do I have a shade of my mother's Soul from her recent lifetime and a shade from her second-last lifetime attached to me? [| Y |] Is a shade of my Dad's Soul attached to me? [| Y |] A shade of Grandpa Leigh's Soul? [| Y |]

Would clearing enmeshment between those Souls and my Soul and clearing enmeshment between the three of them clear the shade connections? [| Y |]

After clearing the enmeshments, I could ask them to leave.

[| Yes, Lorrie. You are learning just now that there are some "shadows of people," shades, that you need to shed. You cannot be very free if you are, so to speak, "shackled hand, foot, and whole body" to your Souls and the Souls of relatives and friends from other lifetimes. Magnetic attraction is causing your Soul in this lifetime and other lifetimes and other people's Souls from former lifetimes to cling together. Some of those magnetic bonds are very strong.

Please set as a priority today to clear shades from your Soul in this lifetime and all other lifetimes. Thank you! Peace! []

Thank You, Father God!

I first cleared shades from myself and from my Souls from other lifetimes. Then, after asking permission from the Full Soul of each of them, I cleared shades from Mom, Dad, Grandpa, Grandma Leigh, Aunt Mollie, and my sister Ann.

Thank You, Holy Spirit, for that clearing!

Feb 13, '08   Facilitator for Healing

Is the pressure in my head from Souls asking for help?

[| Yes, from living people and Souls on the other side. |]

For the last two weeks, I asked every day for angels to protect me from negative vibes from Souls asking for help, but the pressure hasn't let up. Is my Soul siphoning negativity out of family members? [| No. You are a "facilitator for healing" in the family. Your empathy allows the hurt to be transformed. The hurt is not sucking you under. It is being transformed into light. |]

Does being a facilitator for healing in the family mean that some of the emotions of family members will rise within or around me and get transmuted? [| Y |] Does that include My children and siblings? [| Y |] Does it include extended family, like spouses? [| N |]

FERN: Would Lorrie's being a facilitator for healing include her nieces and nephews? [| N |] Her parents? [| N |] Grandparents? [| N |] This may sound odd: Would Lorrie's being a facilitator for healing include the family as a whole? [| Y |]

Many years ago, the words "incest" and "incestiary" came to mind referring to our family. Does our family as a whole need deliverance from the spirit of incest? [| Y |]

Am I still meant to tell Joel that Aunt Mollie and Grandpa Leigh are his birth parents? [| Y |] Will it be beneficial for Joel to learn that because he is meant to help heal our family? [| Y |] When I meet with Joel and his wife Sara, would that be a good time for us to pray for clearing the spirit of incest? [| Y |]

May 4, '08   Key: No Judgment

Here I am, Father God, back from vacation. Bless You!
[| Well, Lorrie, you have typing to catch up on! I will help you sort your notes. You will have more enthusiasm now than you had a few weeks ago.

For a family to be healed, all situations in the family line, past and present, must be accepted without judgment. *By consciously choosing to be nonjudgmental about everything, you release fear and guilt from everyone in your family line back to your original ancestors. Your forgiveness for and full acceptance of your immediate forbears frees them to forgive and release their immediate forbears, and so on.*

Freedom and hope are available to everyone! Every person is

fully loved! Fully accepted! We are all in this together: I, your God, and you, My sons and daughters.

All graces and blessings are ultimately for everyone. All hope is yours. All love is yours. You can take in all the love you need and extend all the love you possibly can to everyone without love running out, for love is never-ending. []

Thank You for that encouragement, Father God!

I shared the above lesson with Fern, then asked: If even one person in a family is totally nonjudgmental about everything that occurred within their family, does that release all of those family members from judgment? [| Y |] Are even unkind actions that nobody else knows about released from judgment? [| Y |]

That is about the best news anybody could hear!

1-A: SEXUAL SLAVERY

Note: ^{JP} (Joel Prior life) is omitted after David and James, and ^{MP} (Me Prior life) after Rob and Richard in this section.

(Mar 26, '08)   THE BIG THING

First Lifetime

While Fern was listening to HayhouseRadio.com, a young man called in who had learned he had been a sex slave in a prior lifetime. The moderator told the young man he should write about it because very little has been written about sexual slavery.

Fern called to tell me about the experience she had. She said she got "goose bumps upon goose bumps" while the young man was speaking and *knew for certain that I had been a sex slave in a prior lifetime.*

I went to Fern's place so we could learn more about this. We learned from the Holy Spirit that in a previous lifetime, my brother Joel and I, twin brothers, were held as sexual slaves in a Poor Clare convent where the nuns were into "misguided" sexual practices. I will call us **David** (Joel) and **Rob** (me).

David and Rob didn't know who their parents were. A nun at that convent was their mother, but they grew up as "orphans" in the convent and lived their whole lives there. Several of the nuns used them for sexual activity. David and Rob didn't know what they were doing was wrong.

David had a daughter, **Rebecca**, by one of the nuns. Rebecca grew up in the convent, became a nun, and later had a male partner. Nobody told her who her parents were. Did David ever have sex with his daughter Rebecca? [| N |]

During that lifetime as sexual slaves, did David or Rob have sex with their birth mother? [| Both David and Rob did, not knowing it was their mother. |] Were some of the nuns who asked for sexual favors much older than David and Rob? [| Y |]

Did David have a love relationship with at least one of the nuns? [| Y |] Did Rob have a love relationship with at least one nun? [| Y |] I am glad for both of them.

Our Mom Picks Up the Spirit of Lust

Did sexual activity also occur between some of the nuns in that convent? [| Y |] Was our mother from this lifetime a nun there? [| Y |] Did she participate in sexual activity? [| Y |]

Did most of the nuns in that convent pick up the spirit of lust just by being a part of the group? [| They picked up the spirit of lust by their actions, not by being part of the group. |]

Were the Souls of our mother affected by the spirit of lust before that lifetime? [| N |] Did the spirit of lust from that lifetime carry forward with her into the recent lifetime in which she was our mother? [| Y |]

Did the spirit of lust within Mom carry a magnetic connection to other people, allowing that energy to enter the larger family? [| *Yes. That was the beginning of the spirit of lust in the Leigh family line.* |]

When people have the spirit of lust in one lifetime, and it doesn't get cleared, do they carry it into their next life? [| Y |]

Were David and Rob affected by the spirit of lust? [| N |] Has David's Soul gone to the light? [| N |] His daughter Rebecca's Soul?

[| N |] Is David waiting for Rebecca to go to the light with him? [| Y |] Will they be ready to go to the light soon? [| Y |]

Second Lifetime

Were Joel and I held as sexual slaves at a convent during another life? [| Yes. Again, you were both males. |] I will call us **James** (Joel) and **Richard** (me).

Did James have a child by a nun in that lifetime? [| Y |] Did Richard? [| Yes. He had triplet girls who were adopted out. He kept in touch with them for many years. |] Have those children all gone to the light? [| Y |]

Was our mom in this lifetime a nun there? [| Yes, but she wasn't involved in sexual activities with either of you. |] Was her Soul already affected by the spirit of lust before that second lifetime? [| Yes, from that prior lifetime when you and Joel (David and Rob) were sexual slaves at a Poor Clare convent where she was a nun and participated in sexual activities. |]

Did James and Richard manage to "escape" that convent? [| Yes. Both of them got married and had families. |]

Evening:

[| Lorrie, this is THE BIG THING that is opening up, another layer that you and Fern uncovered. There are not any more situations of this magnitude that need to be revealed. The rest will come easier after the aftereffects of these two lifetimes are cleared.

Your experiences during the lifetimes that you were a sexual slave at a convent still affect your health: the top of your head bothers you a lot, and you have elevated blood pressure. You are carrying cellular memories and tension from having been in those situations.

Within the next two weeks, do what you can to process repressed feelings and emotions connected with those lifetimes. Bless you, dear one! |]

Thank You, Father God!

(Apr 3, '08)   A FULLER PICTURE

I have been thinking about the two lifetimes in which Joel and I were sexual slaves. I'll write what comes to mind.

Worried (David). Watchful (Rob). Did they know that life could have been different for them if their dad hadn't hooked up with a nun? Oh, that's right, they didn't know who their parents were. As they got older, it might have been just the two of them to keep each other company. There was no TV, radio, or electricity, and it was likely very cold much of the winter. What a life!

Holy Spirit, does just knowing in general about the type of hurtful experiences one has had in a prior lifetime help to heal the effects of those experiences? [| Y |] That's good to know!

Relatives of Joel's and Mine in Those Lifetimes

Fern and I learned more by asking the Holy Spirit questions. David's and Rob's father in the first lifetime was Father Ken (our brother in this lifetime). Was "Ken" the son of a nun, also? [| Y |] Did he live most of that lifetime at the convent like David and Rob did? [| Y |] Had that pattern been ongoing for many years in that convent? [| Y |] More than 50? [| Y |] Wow!

In the second lifetime, which took place in a different convent, our brother Dean and his wife in this lifetime were our parents. For some reason, they couldn't take care of us and turned us over to the nuns. Aunt Mollie was Mother Superior In the second lifetime. Sexual play with us by the nuns started early in both lifetimes.

In both lifetimes, the nuns were Poor Clare nuns whose main work was caring for orphans. David and Rob (and James and Richard in their second lifetime as sexual slaves) worked in the garden and cared for the cows, chickens, etc. They were allowed to attend Mass and ate their meals with the nuns.

Were James and Richard affected by the spirit of lust in the second lifetime? [| Yes, but it was cleared later on. |]

Did the nuns use some birth control to prevent pregnancies? [| Y |] Did they sometimes induce abortions? [| Y |]

[| It was after the second lifetime, with both of you working with your Full Souls, that you and Joel decided to return to Earth to bring clearing for the family. |]

A Fairly Common Situation

Did other convents have similar situations in which boys (men) were held psychological captives and induced to satisfy the prurient desires of the nuns who lived there? [| Y |] Did a counterpart of that situation occur in monasteries, where the monks/brothers used some excuse to have one or more girls/women live there who ended up being sexual slaves of some monks? [| Y |]

Was denying the free will of the girls (women) and boys (men) the basic sin in those convents and monasteries? [| Y |]

Does God see all sexual relations that take place outside of marriage as being sinful? [| N |] Is the sinful part of any action that of somebody overriding another person's free will? [| Y |]

About Aunt Mollie and Joel

Hearing about those lifetimes makes me wonder about Joel's conception. Was he a love child of Mollie and Grandpa?

[| He was a love child of Grandpa Leigh but not of Mollie. |]

Fern and I learned earlier that Mollie had a child out of wedlock in an earlier lifetime that she wanted to be kept secret. Did she have a child in a lifetime when she was a nun? [| Y |]

(May 19, '08)   Healing for Mollie

> DREAM: Aunt Mollie was a nun in a convent. I was with her and many other nuns in a large room at the convent. I picked up hints that some of them had a man in their life.
>
> Next, I was in a room with some girls. I understood that a lot of sexual play was going on between them. END.

(At Fern's) Did that dream come from cellular memories of Aunt Mollie that I am carrying? [| N |] Was she trying to tell me about her experiences? [| Y |] I said lovingly:

> "Aunt Mollie, I am not judging you, and Fern isn't judging you for anything that took place in earlier lifetimes as a sister or in your recent lifetime. I believe the decisions we make as human

beings and the situations that result from them are meant to happen for us to learn who we are and to develop understanding and compassion for others.

"Children can't help it when they are taught to do things that others consider very wrong. I send love and compassion to you while in those situations.

"Bless you, Aunt Mollie, at every moment of every lifetime! Bless you in who you are and in who you are coming to be."

Do you understand, Aunt Mollie? [| Y |] Do you feel better now? [| Y |] I am glad! Bless you!

Holy Spirit, does Aunt Mollie need more healing?

[| Yes, especially for a lifetime when she was Mother Superior in a Poor Clare Convent. |]

(Mar 17, '14)   Healing For Joel and Me

Holy Spirit, I learned that 5-year-old Joel still feels animosity towards me for leaving him behind as we went from the chicken coop to the house when I was ten. Is another situation contributing to that animosity?

[| Yes. That animosity is rooted in Joel's and your second lifetime as sexual slaves in a convent. James (Joel) loved one of the nuns and had a child with her. Richard was (you were) attracted to that nun, too, and had sex with her specifically to hurt James. |] That was cruel!

(Jul 30, '14) It suddenly became clear that I have been very judgmental towards Joel and many others through the years. I also realized that when we judge someone, we also judge God, their Father-Mother-Creator. (Suddenly realizing one has sinned is called "being convicted by the Holy Spirit.")

The unresolved situation from the second "sexual slavery" lifetimes of mine and Joel's came to mind again: That I stole his girlfriend to hurt him in his lifetime as James. I determined to arrange to meet with Joel soon to get things settled.

(Aug 12, '14) On my invitation, Joel stopped in to see me. I told him about our previous lives as sexual slaves and that in his lifetime as James, I purposely had sex with the nun he loved to hurt him. I asked him to forgive me, and he said he did. He seemed to think the situation was funny, but I'm sure James didn't feel that way when it happened.

Holy Spirit, Joel said he forgives me, but does James'^{JP} Soul still feel like wanting to get even with me? [| Y |]

James, speaking for Richard and myself, I am very sorry for being so mean to you. Please forgive me. I flowed love and blessings to him for some time.

Father God, please help James work through the hurt and anger he still carries about that situation. Thank You!

End of 1-A: SEXUAL SLAVERY

1-B: PARENTAGE: TELLING MY SIBLINGS

(May 10, '08)   NOT EASY

Evening: I drove to Joel and Sara's place to tell them that Grandpa Leigh is my birth father and that Grandpa Leigh and Aunt Mollie are Joel's birth parents. After some small talk, I told them about the Holy Spirit guiding Fern and me in learning more about our family. I mentioned some minor things but didn't get any further.

Joel asked, "Who is this Fern?" I told him a little about her and that Father Ken had met her. Then Joel went into a spiel, almost like a sermon, "that the Holy Spirit leads us to the truth under the guidance of the Catholic Church."

Between times, Sara made pointed comments and asked questions. The atmosphere was tense. When I left, I felt determined never to try to share more with them.

I called Fern for support and to ask: Did Aunt Mollie have something to do with Joel's and Sara's resistance? [| Y |]

Father God, my nerves were already on edge before I went to Joel and Sara's place. They became more on edge while I was there. I tried to reason fear away by saying that Joel and Sara wouldn't hurt

261

me physically, that their words wouldn't hurt me, and that what they thought about me and my beliefs didn't matter. That helped some, but not enough. I place the situation in Your hands, Father. Thank You!

(Jun 7, '08)   The Junk Will Get Cleared

Fern and I learned earlier that Aunt Mollie was carrying a lot of painful cellular memories from previous lifetimes and junk from family members and that not much had been cleared. A lot of junk was put on me, too, but much of mine is cleared.

[| Junk that you are carrying will be cleared through this writing. The junk Mollie is carrying will be cleared through her son, Joel. |]

Is Mollie playing a part in clearing and healing the Leigh family line? [| Y |] A large part? [| No. You and Joel are doing most of the work. |] Is Mollie still willing for Joel to learn that she was his birth mother? [| Y |] Does she want him to learn that soon? [| Yes, and Joel is ready to learn about it. |]

Maybe I can meet alone with Joel.

[| Mollie isn't aware of who her birth father was. |]

Should I tell her in spirit that Uncle Mike is her birth father? [| Y |] I told Mollie later that day.

(Jul 5, '08)   The Status Quo

Are members of our family lines who are on the other side mostly healed? [| Y |] Are my living brothers and sisters mostly healed? [| Y |] Do their families need healing? [| Y |] Am I meant to pray for their family lines? [| N |]

For the curse of the spirit of lust to be cleared from the Leigh and Goerger family lines (the Goergers are affected through Mom), do my siblings need to be told about the parentage in the Leigh family? [| Yes, you can do that at any time. |]

Should I tell them in spirit? [| Yes. Tell them first about parentage in the Leigh family and then in the Goerger family. |]

(!!!) I haven't asked the men in the Leigh family for permission to share family secrets! Is Grandpa Leigh OK with me telling my siblings about parentage in the Leigh and Goerger families? [| Y |] Is

Great Uncle Mike OK with it? [| Y |] Mom's brother, Uncle Will? [| Yes. They are glad you thought about them. |]

I didn't note the exact dates, but sometime during the next six weeks, in spirit:

1. I told my brothers and sisters as a group about the parentage in the Leigh family,
2. I told each of those individually whose birth father is Grandpa Leigh, Great-Uncle Mike, or Uncle Will,
3. I told the rest of my siblings that information as a group.

Thank You, Holy Spirit, for helping me!

(Oct 22, '08) I already told Alice in spirit that Grandpa Leigh is her birth father. Does her Soul want her to learn about it in person, too? [| Yes. Plan on telling Alice next spring when she is back here. |]

(Nov 7, '08) The last 2 weeks, my systolic BP reading has been high. Holy Spirit, is Mollie's anxiety about me finally telling Joel in person that she was his birth mother one cause for that? [| Y |]

Is the spirit of lust still present in (overhanging) the Leigh, Goerger, and Jahner families?

[| Yes. You and Joel are to pray for deliverance for the family after he has learned more about the family background. |]

(Nov 18, '08)   NOW JOEL KNOWS

I met alone with Joel last evening to tell him the Holy Spirit wanted me to share some information with him. I told him about the parentage in the Leigh and Goerger families and that Aunt Mollie and Grandpa Leigh are his birth mother and father. I also told him I shared that information with Father Ken last July so Joel could feel free to discuss it with him.

Joel didn't react outwardly (he may repress his emotions). He said two things: He always thought of Aunt Mollie as this fancy woman who visited us now and then, and he usually likes to relate with God directly, not through another person.

He had a surprise for me, though. He gave me a copy of a prayer,

"Healing the Family Tree," that he got at a spiritual workshop recently. He said that ever since he got that prayer, God has strongly directed him to pray regularly and fervently for healing for our family lines, that he has the "mission" or "burden" to do that. That corroborates the understanding I received. I told him:

"That's why I was supposed to share the family parentage with you. Much healing has already taken place in the family. Further healing is meant to take place through you."

I am glad I finally had the chance to tell Joel these things! It's a weight off my shoulders. How he responds is up to him.

(Nov 21, '08)   Healing for Joel and Mollie

[| Lorrie, when you met with Joel, all that was intended for that time was accomplished. You are correct that he is holding himself aloof from his emotions. He will open to them fairly soon, but to help with that, please pray for releasing the spirits of religiosity and denominationalism from him and his immediate and extended family. Thank you for doing that.

Don't worry about Joel, yourself, or anybody. All is well! |]

Thank You, Father God. Bless You, to the utmost!

That evening, I prayed aloud to clear the spirits of religiosity and denominationalism from Joel and his family

(Dec 17, '08) While I was at Fern's place, she received a message from the Holy Spirit:

[| Mollie would like to hold Joel as a baby and as an adult and tell him she is sorry she couldn't care for him herself. |]

I could do that for her in spirit. At home, I held my doll to represent Joel as a baby and spoke for Aunt Mollie, *"Baby Joel, I love you! I am sorry that I couldn't raise you myself. You are a sweet baby, and I am proud to be your mother."*

Then, I spoke healing words for Mollie to Joel as an adult. Bless you, Aunt Mollie! Bless you, Joel!

End of 1-B: PARENTAGE: TELLING MY SIBLINGS

CHAPTER 2

WITCHCRAFT AND LUST

Dec 19, '08   FAMILY MEMBERS AFFECTED

Is the Leigh family line infested with the spirit of witchcraft? [| N |] Are some individuals (Souls) In the family line affected by the spirit of witchcraft? [| Y |]

(!!!) Was my brother Joel *a warlock* in one or more previous lifetimes? [| Y |] Then he needs clearing for witchcraft energies! I prayed for clearing witchcraft energies and contact points for witchcraft energy from Joel in this lifetime and in all previous lifetimes in which he was a warlock.

Dec 20, '08. Are witchcraft energies cleared from Joel? [| Y |] Are all contact points cleared? [| Y |] Wonderful!

Dec 26, '08   Clearing for Ann and Her Family

Are Carol and Susan, my sister Ann's daughters, being affected by witchcraft energies? [| Y |] Are Ann's granddaughters affected by them? [| N |] Are witchcraft energies in Ann's home? [| Y |]

Is there a spirit of lust in Ann's home? [| Y |] Are some of her granddaughters affected by it? [| Two of them are. |]

I told Ann about the clearing needed for her home, daughters, and granddaughters. I prayed with Ann to:

1. Clear witchcraft energies and the spirit of lust from Ann and her home,
2. Dissolve the root of witchcraft energies affecting Ann,
3. Clear witchcraft energies from Ann's daughters Carol and Susan and the spirit of lust from her granddaughters.

Is Ann's home cleared of witchcraft energies? [| Y |] Is it cleared of the spirit of lust? [| Y |] Are witchcraft energies cleared from Ann's daughter Carol in this lifetime? [| Y |] From Carol's previous lifetimes? [| Y |] Are witchcraft energies cleared from Ann's daughter Susan? [| N |] From Susan's previous lifetimes? [| N |] I will pray for her again.

I went to Ann's place that evening. We prayed for clearing and healing for her daughter Susan's family lines, mainly to clear the spirits of lust and witchcraft. We also prayed for clearing the spirit of lust from Ann's granddaughters.

Dec 29, '08. Is the spirit of lust cleared from Ann's daughter Susan in this lifetime? [| Y |] In previous lifetimes? [| Y |] Are Ann's granddaughters cleared of the spirit of lust? [| Y |]

Mission accomplished! Thank You, God!

Dec 30, '08   TAPROOT: WITCHCRAFT ENERGIES

Do the homes of others in the Leigh family need clearing for witchcraft energies? [| Y |] For the spirit of lust? [| Y |] Is being in their living quarters one way that the spirit of lust has been "hanging over" the Leigh family? [| Y |]

My systolic blood pressure has been high much of the time lately. Is that largely due to the effect of witchcraft energies on me? [| Y |] Do negative energies affect somebody more when asleep than when awake? [| Y |]

The "background clues" Father God gave 20 years ago hinted that something was affecting the family that was "like yeast." Father God, was the spirit of witchcraft the yeast You referred to? [| Y |] One of the clues was, "The taproot is the most important."
[| *Mollie was the catalyst for witchcraft energies entering the Leigh family line* back in her lifetimes as a nun when she and her pals used witchcraft against you and other nuns out of jealousy. There are other branches of witchcraft, but that was the beginning. The spirit of lust was connected with it, also. |]

Nov 22, '09   Clearing for Leigh, Goeger Families

The top of my head has been very uncomfortable again, which I learned is caused by negative energies.

(!!!) I haven't prayed yet for clearing the spirit of witchcraft that may be hanging over the Leigh and Goerger family! I immediately prayed to dissolve the roots of witchcraft and witchcraft energies from specific persons in the Leigh and Goerger families and the families as a group.

(!!!) If another person's Spirit can become incorporated in the cells in a child's or another person's body, maybe the spirit of witchcraft can, too, like if it is present in one's mother. It wouldn't do any harm to clear incorporation from cells in the bodies of family members, just in case.

I made the intention every day for the next two weeks for all living members of the Leigh and Goerger families whose Souls agreed to it that only that person's Soul might enter new cells as they are formed in their body, thus pushing negative spirits out. This is another breakthrough! Thank You, Father!

Mar 24, '10   For Mollie and Grandma Leigh

I have had a lot of sinus drainage lately. Aunt Mollie and Grandma Leigh both had that problem. Do one or both of them need prayer? [| Both of them do. |]

I began a 9-day Novena of prayers for them, and
1. Cleared enmeshment between Mollie's and Grandma's Souls and mine.
2. Cleared detrimental soul ties between Mollie, Grandma, all other people and Souls, and myself,
3. Cleared negative energies and outside Soul portions from Mollie and Grandma,
4. Invited portions of Mollie's and Grandma's Souls that are with other people (Souls) to return to them and prayed for healing.

Mar 27, '10. I had thick sinus drainage this morning, a sign that Mollie needs more prayer. I did a clearing for lust, witchcraft, anger, and other negative energies. Bless you, Mollie!

I had less sinus drainage that night. Is Mollie doing better?
[| Much better. Continue the Novena and other prayers as the Holy Spirit leads you. |] Are the portions of Mollie's Soul that had been with me reunited with her Soul now? [| Yes. You did very well in ministering that release. |]

Is Grandma Leigh doing better?
[| Somewhat. As you continue praying for her, you will come to some points that will bring about nothing short of a miracle. You have strong ties with her since she and you were originally part of the same Full Soul, and you were one Soul in the lifetime immediately before her lifetime as Mavis Leigh. You will feel much better when she feels better. |]

Does Grandma Leigh still need healing, though?
[| Yes. You might think that Grandma Leigh's brother-in-law, Mike, being the father of most of her children, should not have been that difficult for her to live with since Grandpa Leigh knew about their relationship, but it is hard for people to live a double life. In your Grandma's case, she had to pretend with her children that all was fine in the family. Thank you for praying for her. |]

Apr 4, '10   PRAYER FOR THE GOERGER FAMILY

I thought about Uncle Art, Dad's brother, having raped me at age 16. Did a portion of an unloving Soul enter my body at that time? [| Y |] Had it been hanging around Uncle Art? [| Y |]

Are unloving Souls attached to Uncle Art's Soul?
[| Not anymore. Forgiving Art and praying for clearing your Dad's family line helped clear unloving Souls from him, but he still needs prayer. |]

Are the portions of unloving Souls in my abdomen somewhat incorporated within cells in my body?

[| Yes. The infiltration lessened when you cleared the incorporation of Mollie's, Grandma Leigh's, and your Mom's Souls from cells in your body, but you should do that process again for at least ten days. |]

Do the portions of unloving Souls in my abdomen get irritated by certain foods I eat? [| No. They are irritated because they want to leave. |] I began the 10-day process of clearing Soul incorporation.

Would doing a clearing for the Goerger family help Uncle Art enough, or should I do a clearing individually for him?
[| Do clearing for Art's family lines for every lifetime of his, then do clearing for the Goerger family lines. |]

The next day, I did a clearing for Uncle Art's family lines and the Goerger family lines, then a clearing for the portions of unloving Souls that were in my abdomen and wherever else.

(Apr 26, '10) Holy Spirit, have all portions of unloving Souls been cleared from my abdomen and every part of me?
[| Yes, they have all been cleared! You can breathe a big sigh of relief in gratitude for that! I am happy for you, and so are Father-Mother God, the Holy Spirit, Jesus, and a swarm of relatives, friends, and angels! |]

Thank You, Holy Spirit, for guiding me as I did that clearing!

Apr 7, '10   PRAYER FOR THE LEIGH FAMILY

Is my son Chad's having Crohn's, an autoimmune disease that affects the digestive system, a sign that he or family members need clearing for stomach-related issues?
[| Yes. It is also a physical sign of the spirit of lust that had been present in the family line earlier and still is to some extent. When a negative spirit hovers over a family line, new shoots of that negative energy can appear after the original roots have been cleared. Weeds that spread through their root system are a good comparison. |]

I haven't prayed for clearing for my Souls in past lifetimes! When I do clearing for them, Should I include all of Mollie's Souls from previous lifetimes? [| The Holy Spirit suggests doing a separate clearing for your past lifetimes. That may take 20-30 minutes. It would be time well spent. |]

Are some people and Souls In the Leigh family still affected by the spirit of witchcraft? [| Yes. Mollie and her brother Will. |]

Would it work to pray for clearing for all lifetimes of Grandma and Grandpa Leigh and their children as a group?
[| The recommendation is for you to pray for Mollie and her lifetimes separately from the rest of her family because she had, and has, such a direct connection and influence with you. She was your baptismal sponsor and thought of you somewhat as her daughter. Praying for the rest of the Leigh family as one group will work out fine. |]

Apr 8, '10   Roses Connected to Witchcraft

I have a large mandala on my bedroom wall that has a white lotus blossom at the center. Does that blossom have witchcraft energy attached to it? [| Some. |] Did that energy get attached to it from Mandy when she did a Reading for me?
[| Some of it came by way of Mandy. But the witchcraft energies attached to it are tied back to an earlier lifetime of yours as a nun when other nuns directed witchcraft energies at you and used roses to continue those attacks. |]

Could I clear witchcraft energies from the blossom by having it in the large copper ring for three days? [| Y |] Does the rest of the mandala need clearing? [| N |]

Thank you, Fern! I am glad I can communicate with you! I put the mandala blossom in the copper ring immediately.

Apr 13, '10   For Mollie, The Leigh Family

Would doing a clearing for Aunt Mollie's family lines in every lifetime be a good way to help her become fully cleared?
[| Yes, pray for clearing for Mollie and bless her often "in who she is and in who she is coming to be at every moment of every lifetime and in between lifetimes." *(Blessing Prayer)*

Mollie had low self-esteem and suffered abuse in many lifetimes. Her Soul latched onto witchcraft energies as a way to have some power. Her inner child is very much in need of healing. Praying for healing for a person's inner child helps them in every lifetime, so you do not need to specify which lifetime you are asking to have healed.

Mollie is a powerful Soul with much potential for doing good. Father-Mother God and the whole universe will be grateful you are praying for her. []

Thank you, Fern, for helping me to hear clearly! Bless you!
[| Bless you, too, dear one! Good night! |]

I began blessing Mollie often and did a clearing for her family line in all of her previous lifetimes.

Apr 16, '10. I had a headache all night and a lot of sinus drainage. I take that as a sign that Mollie needs more clearing.

I prayed again for clearing unloving Souls, the spirits of witchcraft and lust, and all negative energies from Mollie. I dissolved any new roots of witchcraft and lust energies that may have developed and asked angels to pull up those roots from her family lines in every lifetime and dissolve them.

I spoke to Mollie's Soul from every lifetime, telling her that God does not see guilt in her. I cut detrimental soul ties between her and other Souls. In closing, I asked angels to minister to all of her Souls for an hour while I played soft music.

Apr 19, '10. Is Mollie's Soul from her recent lifetime as my Aunt Mollie cleared of witchcraft energies? [| Y |] Are Mollie's Souls from all other lifetimes cleared?
[| Not yet. One reason is that her brother Will's Soul is still affected by a spirit of witchcraft. Things will improve after you do clearing for unloving Souls, the spirit of witchcraft, and other negative energies from the Leigh family line. |]

Thank you, Fern! Bless you!

Apr 25, '10. I asked the 24 archangels, Jesus, Fern, Mom, Dad, and my brother Dean, to assist me in doing a clearing for Mollie's

Souls and the Leigh family lines. I had to cry as I thought about my Dad and asked him to hug me.

1. I cleared the enmeshment between my Soul and Mollie's and all other Souls from the Leigh family lines that were with me without permission. I told them to leave.
2. I asked the Holy Spirit to dissolve all non-beneficial soul ties between me and those Souls.
3. I ministered to Mollie's Souls and then to all other Souls from the Leigh family line:
   a. Did a clearing for the spirits of witchcraft, lust, and other negative energies,
   b. Sent blessings and love to Mollie's Souls that were unloving because of difficult circumstances during that lifetime to assist them in becoming loving,
   c. Asked angels to minister healing to Mollie's Souls and Souls in the Leigh family line. Thank you, angels!

Thank you, archangels, angels, Jesus, Mom, Dad, and Dean, for helping with this clearing! Thank You, Holy Spirit!

Holy Spirit, are my children affected by witchcraft energies that came through me and the Leigh family lines? [| N |]

I sensed that Father God might want to speak to me sometime. I told Him I would be willing to write during the night.

Apr 26, '10. 5:00 A.M. Good morning, Father God!
[| Good morning, Lorrie! I am very happy about the major clearing in your family line that you did yesterday. After doing major spiritual work like that, it is natural to feel aftereffects, so rest more today.

You do not need to analyze the clearings that take place. Follow My guidance. Major clearing and healing are in the offing. When and as it takes place, receive it and be simple, like a child.

I am glad for you and Fern that your receiving answers through her is going well. I will let you go back to sleep now. Good night, good morning, whichever you think fits! |]

Thank You, Father God! I do need more sleep.

7:00 P.M. Father, are all of Mollie's Souls from previous lifetimes cleared now of energies of witchcraft and lust?

[| They are cleared as much as can be at this point. Inclinations towards those energies that remain are for Mollie to deal with if and when other parts of her Full Soul choose to live a human life. You cannot imagine how grateful she is to you! |]

I am glad those witchcraft energies are cleared from Mollie. By the way, after I finished that clearing, I directed for any remaining witchcraft and lust energies to be encased with spiritual lead so they could no longer affect Mollie's Soul or others. Did they get encased with spiritual lead?

[| Yes. The Holy Spirit prompted you to ask for that. Mollie is grateful for that protective shield because she will now be relatively free of negative effects coming from those energies. The Holy Spirit will guide her on what to do about them now. It is no longer your concern.

The clearing that you did *was* your concern because you and your family were being affected by the situation. Well done, good and faithful servant! |]

Jun 25, '10   NOW ALICE KNOWS

My sister Alice, Ann's twin, is doing better health-wise and will be at Ann's place for a few days. I plan to go there to tell her and Ann that I learned from the Holy Spirit that Grandpa Leigh is my birth father and Alice's birth father.

[| <FERN> It is fine with the Holy Spirit for you to share that with Alice and Ann. Please bless them and all your other brothers and sisters because word about that will likely get around. Do not suggest to Alice what to do with the information. If she shares it with others, that is how things will be. Bless you, dear one! |]

Thank you, Fern! Bless you! Bless You, Father-Mother God! Jesus! Holy Spirit!

Jun 27, '10. Father God, is a portion of an outside Soul incorporated within cells in my right hip that is the main cause of the pain I have been having for six weeks? What comes to mind is that a "spinning ball of energy" moved in that is causing pain. I sense it is "red hot" and that a strand of energy is being pulled to it that keeps getting wrapped tighter.

[| You picked up correctly on that, Lorrie, and, yes, as you are wondering, this is something new. |]

Is that hot, spinning ball of energy connected with Mom's getting anxious about wanting to have Alice learn soon that Grandpa Leigh is her birth father?

[| You have the right idea, but it is not as you described. Your mother's, Grandpa Leigh's, and Alice's Souls want the tasks completed that their Full Soul assigned to them for this lifetime, and your Full Soul wants the same for you. Anxious pressure is being put on you by your Soul and by their Souls to tell Alice that Grandpa Leigh is her birth father. Peace! |]

Thank You, Father God!

Evening: I did a clearing for the ball of anxiety in my right hip. Father God, is it cleared?

[| Not yet. Instead of just blessing that energy and then commanding it to leave all at once, ask Cherub Angels to take hold of the outer strand of the anxiety and pull it gently as some other angels help rotate the ball so it can continue unrolling.

Picture in your mind that as the Cherub Angels carry the end of the strand into the astral plane, all of the fine strands of which it is composed sparkle a tiny bit and then disappear as they are converted back to the neutral energy they came from.

The word "allow" fits here. Allow the energy to be what it is at the moment. Then, invite it to be transmuted back to neutral energy. When love invites it, the anxious energy will gladly comply. You may ask for that process to begin as you sleep. Trust that the ball of anxiety will get cleared. |]

That is a great idea, Father God! Thank You!

Before I went to sleep, I asked Cherub Angels to carry the outer strand of the ball of anxiety and release it into the astral plane, where it can transmute to neutral energy as the ball unwinds. Thank You, Father!

Jul 4, '10. Is the ball of anxiety cleared from my right hip?

[| A small part remains. Some of the anxiety you allowed into yourself this week related to your health gravitated to that ball and added to it. Ask Cherub angels to continue unwinding the strands of anxiety and have it transmuted to neutral energy in the astral plane. They are doing a good job! |]

Thank you, Cherub Angels, for helping clear that anxiety. Thank you, Fern, Holy Spirit!

Jun 28, '10. I met with Alice and Ann this morning and told them about Grandpa Leigh being my birth father and Alice's birth father. Alice wasn't at all surprised and seemed grateful to learn about it. She said she had sensed/suspected for many years that she had a different father.

[| Speaking for your Mom's, Grandpa Leigh's, Alice's, and your Soul, thank you, Lorrie, for completing that part of their healing process. They are all praying for you. Good night! |]

Thank You, Father! I am relieved to have finally told Alice.

Aug 26, '10   Word of Encouragement

Thank you for regularly blessing your parents and everybody in the Leigh, Goerger, and Jahner family lines. It is helping everyone in those families and you more than you know.

Bless you, Lorrie, Fern, and everyone collaborating in bringing freeing messages from Spirit to the world and the whole universe! Enjoy the rest of your day now! |]

I will. Thank You, Father! Bless You, and bless All That Is!

2-A: SISTERS CECELIA[AP] AND GEMMA[AP]

Note: [AP] (Aunt Mollie Prior life) is omitted after Cecelia and Gemma in this section.

(May 8, '10)   CONNECTED ACROSS LIFETIMES

(!!!) I thought about MaryAnn, a candidate for becoming a nun two years ahead of me in high school at St Mary's Convent. She became a nun and is living here. I sense that she was affected by witchcraft energies back then and that those energies affected me. Is that correct, Holy Spirit?

[| Yes. It is becoming apparent to you, Lorrie, that when you "sense" that something is the case, the answer will be "Yes," that I am telling you that. |]

Was Sister MaryAnn one of the nuns in a prior lifetime who joined Aunt Mollie in directing witchcraft energies at my sisters Ann, Alice, and me when we were nuns in that convent?

[| Yes. Witchcraft energies carried forward with Sister MaryAnn to this lifetime and are still targeting the three of you through her. |]

Were the candidates Cora and Julie affected by witchcraft energies, also? [| Y |] They became nuns and also live here now. My sister Ann meets with them quite often for spiritual advice.

Are witchcraft energies attached to Sisters Cora and Julie?

[| They are cleared from Sisters Cora and Julie, but they both have a lot of witchcraft energy residue. That residue has a strong effect on Ann. |]

Is Ann clear of witchcraft energies?

[| Yes, but she also has witchcraft energy residue within her body, mind, and Spirit. Suggest that she clear negative residue from herself, her home, and family members every day for ten days and then do it weekly. |]

Were other negative energies attached to the nuns, the woodwork, and such at St. Mary's convent? [| Y |] Did the witchcraft and other negative energies cause the migraine headaches I began after becoming a novice?

[| They were one of the causes. Perhaps the main cause was that you were finding that life as a nun did not suit you. |]

(May 25, '10) I created a negative vortex outside to send the residue of witchcraft and other negative energies from Ann and Sisters MaryAnn, Cora, and Julie into if their Souls agree to it. Thank You, Father, for the clearing!

(May 25, '10)   MOLLIE: WITCHCRAFT LIFETIMES

I will call Mollie **Sister Cecelia** in the lifetime that she and her nun pals directed witchcraft energies at Ann, Alice, me, and other nuns. Is a part of Sister Cecelia's Soul with Sister MaryAnn now?

[| Yes, and it is somewhat incorporated within cells in Sister MaryAnn's body. They were good friends in that earlier lifetime, pretty much the kingpins in witchcraft activities. Please:

1.   Do clearing for that incorporation for nine days.
2.   After nine days, do clearing for the enmeshment between Sister Cecelia's and Sister MaryAnn's Souls.
3.   Ask the Holy Spirit to thin out and dissolve all detrimental soul ties between them.
4.   Clear witchcraft, other negative energies, curses, hexes, spells, and unloving Souls from Sister Cecelia's Soul.
5.   Ask Sister Cecelia and Sister MaryAnn to join you in canceling detrimental vows and promises.

When the clearing is completed, on a Sunday morning at church, invite Sister Cecelia's Soul and Mollie's Souls from other lifetimes to go to the light. What joy there will be on that day! You and your whole family will feel lighter. |]

[| <FERN> Lorrie, please invite me to be with you when you do clearings. I am as present now as when I was alive. You are not alone. *You and I are a healing team.* Bless you, dear one! |] (I had to cry.)

Will a clearing for Sister Cecelia clear much witchcraft energy from the Leigh and Goerger family lines?

[| <FERN> Yes, but the Holy Spirit still wants you to clear negative residue from your family lines after Sister Cecelia's Soul has been cleared and healed and to clear residue from your family lines on an ongoing basis. Monthly would be good. |]

I will do that. Thank you, Fern! Thank You, Holy Spirit!

The next day, I began the 9-day process of clearing the incorporation of Sister Cecelia's Soul from cells in Sister MaryAnn's body.

(Jun 6, '10) Holy Spirit, is the incorporation of Sister Cecelia's Soul cleared from the cells in Sister MaryAnn's body?

[| <FERN> Yes, it is. I am happy for you and your family! |]

Evening: I asked Sister Cecelia's and Sister MaryAnn's Souls to return portions of each other's Souls and prayed for healing for them. For Sister Cecelia: I dissolved the roots of witchcraft energy and cleared witchcraft energies.

Is Sister Cecelia's Soul clear of witchcraft energies?

[| Yes, but a residue of witchcraft energy is still attached. Please do clearing for it three more evenings. |]

I will gladly do that. (I did that clearing for three evenings.)

Are the witchcraft energies cleared that were overhanging the Leigh and Goerger families?

[| They are mostly cleared! We suggest that you ask for witchcraft residue to be cleared from family members at the same time as from Sister Cecelia's and Mollie's Souls from other lifetimes. Mollie is aware of the clearing and is most grateful! |]

(Sept 23, '10)   Affected by Sister Cecelia

DREAM: I was driving with some of my children and stopped at a house to visit even though I didn't know the people. Two young women wearing long dresses with a witchcraft symbol on the front came out of the house. My kids were affected by being there and by what the women said. I was about to leave when I woke up. END.

(!!!) Am I under attack by dark forces related to two of Mollie's Souls from lifetimes in which she was involved with witchcraft?

[| Y |] Have both of those Souls gone to the light?

[| They left the astral plane but are not in a happy place, so your Aunt Mollie's Soul cannot be fully happy yet. She is meant to be a powerful minister in helping people extricate themselves from the sticky web of witchcraft and sorcery, but that cannot come about until her Souls are free. |]

(Oct 5, '10) Holy Spirit, the top of my head has bothered me a lot lately. Are Mollie's Souls from lifetimes when she dabbled in witchcraft affecting me very strongly right now? [| Y |] Are portions of the Souls I dreamt about in my head?

[| Yes. A pathway was open from other Souls of Mollie's having been in your head earlier. |]

Are those Souls causing the sounds in my front car doors, which are louder lately?

[| Yes. They learned about that method of communication from Mollie's Soul, which had been there earlier. |]

Do they want clearing done specifically for them? [| Y |] I sense that my sister Ann should take part in that clearing.

[| Yes. You will be dealing with very low energy with those Souls. Until that energy has been cleared, ask for triple protection around yourself, Ann, and every person (Soul) in the Leigh, Goerger, and Jahner family lines who has a higher energy level than those Souls have. Your head will begin to feel somewhat better now that you have pinpointed the current cause of your discomfort. These are the steps that you and Ann should do:

1. Do the process of returning Soul portions between your Souls and Mollie's Souls in every lifetime of yours and between Mollie's Souls from every lifetime of hers.
2. Sever all detrimental soul ties between Mollie's and your Souls and between Mollie's Souls in every lifetime.
3. Ask for the aura of Mollie's Souls and your Souls to be sealed in every lifetime.
4. Ask for a Holy Spirit shower to clear negative residue from all of Mollie's Souls and your Souls.
5. Ask for a protective shield around Mollie's and your Souls to remain in effect until no longer needed. |]

Thank You, Holy Spirit!

Ann and I did those clearings a week later.

(Oct 7, '10) (!!!) Holy Spirit, did Mollie's Soul set up the plan with help from Heavenly advisors for her Soul to get caught up in witchcraft in two lifetimes so that after those Souls have been cleared of witchcraft and other negative energies, her Full Soul may be a strong force in dealing with witchcraft energies? [| Yes, that is the plan, and it is being implemented. |]

Does a Soul that was caught up with and suffered from a particular negative energy and was set free from it have special power over that energy? [| Yes, that is how things work. |]

As noted above, I am calling Mollie **Sister Cecelia** for one of her "witchcraft" lifetimes as a nun. I will call her **Sister Gemma** for the other one. Ann and I will use those names when we do clearing for Mollie's Souls. Is there something more I should do after we complete those steps?

[| Yes. Give thanks almost constantly for the clearing that has taken place by having a "singing Spirit"; being so grateful that thankfulness bubbles out of you no matter what you are doing.

For two weeks, bless Sister Cecelia's, Sister Gemma's, and Aunt Mollie's Souls every day and ask that they be filled with the crystalline white light of Christ and be well protected. That aftercare compares to the diligent care given to patients after surgery. Those Souls need to be kept free of negativity.

Ministering to those Souls of Mollie's will have added benefit for you and your sisters Ann and Alice: Your Souls from the lifetimes in which Mollie and her pals directed witchcraft energies at you will become much freer, enough that you might feel the difference. Good night! |]

Good night, Holy Spirit! Thank You!

I began blessing those Souls of Mollie's every day.

(Oct 11, '10) Ann and I prayed for clearing Sister Cecelia's, Sister Gemma's Souls, and all of Mollie's Souls from other lifetimes. Ann commanded the portions of Sister Cecelia's and Sister Gemma's Souls that were in my head to leave. The ministry went well. Thank You, God!

(Oct 13, '10)   Parts of Me Want Their Say

Holy Spirit, my head is bothering me a lot today. Are portions of Sister Cecelia's and Sister Gemma's Souls still in my head? [| Yes. Not all of them left. |]

(!!!) Are those Soul portions within a part of me? [| Y |] Is she, that part of me, willing to release them?

[| Not yet, because you did not discuss it with her. Nine-year-old Lorrie is split enough that she thinks of herself as a separate person. This is a new wrinkle. Most people do not have this type of situation to deal with, but those who do will be grateful for the example. |]

Thank You, Holy Spirit!

I talked with 9-year-olds Lorrie^MP and Sylvia^MP about needing to release the portions of Mollie's Souls. I went through the steps for clearing again with emphasis on clearing connections between Mollie's Souls and 9-year-olds Lorrie and Sylvia.

Thank you, archangels, Jesus, Fern, and family members, for helping with that clearing!

(Oct 21, '10) Father God, are portions of Sister Cecelia's or Sister Gemma's Souls still in my head?

[| There are still small portions of each of those Souls within 9-year-old Lorrie's and 9-year-old Sylvia's "head." They are fascinated by the process of clearing out other people's Souls.

To clear those Soul portions, ask young Lorrie and young Sylvia individually to say the words of clearing with you. To help them rejoin your Soul, invite them to say all of the prayers with you each day and explain things to them when you feel prompted. |]

Are the spirits of witchcraft and lust cleared from those portions of Sisters Cecilia's and Sister Gemma's Souls?

[| Yes, but there is a little residue of those negative spirits within their Souls and within you. Ask often for a Holy Spirit shower to flow through every part of you and every part of Sister Cecelia's and Sister Gemma's Souls.

The clearing is happening, and there is not much more to go! Keep the faith! Trust Me to bring about what I set out to do. |]

I trust You to complete the clearing, Father. Thank You!

(Nov 11, '10)   AFFECTED BY MOLLIE'S SOULS

Is the anxiety Mollie is feeling the main cause of my head discomfort? Is the increased sinus drainage I have had for several weeks connected to Mollie, also?

[| Yes, to both. "Family" for Mollie includes many people and Souls. She has a very caring Soul and would like help for people as soon as possible, but you are not meant to be on call to pray for every relative or friend of hers who needs prayer.

Please continue to keep her Soul out of your apartment and away from you, and ask for a protective shield around her to remain in place until no longer needed. |]

Holy Spirit, please keep a protective shield around all portions of Mollie's Soul until no longer needed. Thank You!

(Nov 16, '10) Father God, is the continuing discomfort in my head caused by the distress that Mollie's Souls are feeling?

[| It is caused by concerns that Mollie's, Sister Cecelia's, Sister Gemma's, and Corrie's[AP] Souls have. (Corrie: my mother in my lifetime as Corella[MP]). It is more difficult to block off the energies of one's parents, but things are OK. This, too, shall pass. |]

(Nov 23, '10) [| You wonder if it is spiritually wise to keep pictures of you and Mollie together. No, it is not wise to keep them, and I mean that literally. Dark energies are looking for every possible pathway to affect you negatively. |]

Both front doors of my car have a steady buzzing, tinny-type noise while I am driving. I blessed the energy and Souls that were in the doors, commanded them to leave, and asked for a Holy Spirit shower to free them, but nothing has worked. At times, it sounds impatient and almost angry. I wonder if portions of Mollie's Soul are making all that noise.

I sense that the answer to that is "Yes." Is Mollie holding a grudge against certain people? Against God? Against life?

[| Yes, Lorrie. Mollie is holding a grudge, not against anybody in particular, but against life for how things went for her in her recent lifetime and in several other lifetimes. A person (Soul) who was under the influence of a strong spirit of lust and permeated by the spirit of witchcraft for several lifetimes cannot count on getting cleared easily.

Clearing for Sisters Cecilia's and Gemma's Souls and Souls of Mollie's from other lifetimes "will take a while," put in earthly terms. You have done your part by following the guidance of the Holy Spirit regarding her. Now, I want you to have her just be a part of the larger family rather than singling her out for special blessings. As you know, saying someone's name creates a spiritual connection between them and you.

Also, yes, the sounds in your car doors are caused by Mollie's energy. Right now, I am informing her Soul from this recent lifetime and all her Souls from other lifetimes that they are to quit bothering you or risk facing the consequences.

You need to remove photographs of Mollie from your apartment. Destroy those in which she and you are together and put your photo negatives in the garage for now. Perhaps someday, you will have time to go through them and discard those with the two of you together.

Clear the soul ties that you have with Mollie. You learned earlier that she wished you had been her daughter and she was your baptismal sponsor. Ask the Holy Spirit to place a spiritual block in your baptismal bond with her. Bless you, Lorrie! Thank you, Fern, for helping with this! []

Thank You, Father God! Thank you, Fern!

I immediately said, "Holy Spirit, please place a spiritual block in my baptismal bond with Mollie. And please cut all detrimental soul ties between her Soul and mine in this lifetime and all previous lifetimes. Thank You!"

I discarded all photographs of Mollie and me together.

(!!!) Father, I have often felt peeved and somewhat ornery through the years without knowing why. Did some energies of the grudge against life that Aunt Mollie held remain with me when the incorporation of her Soul was cleared from cells in my body, and those portions of her Soul returned to her?

[| Traces of the grudge against life that Mollie held remained with you because it was attracted to the energy of the grudge against God, life, or whatever you carry. As with Mollie, your holding somewhat of a grudge relates to your present lifetime and several previous ones. |]

(Dec 1, '10)   Dark Forces Are Using Mollie

Father, a few days ago and just now, *nemesis* came to mind; that is some way Mollie is my nemesis. Have dark forces been using Mollie as a pathway to bring me down?

nemesis *n*. 2 b) one who imposes retribution (Web p. 965)

[| Yes, Lorrie. The Holy Spirit triggered that thought that, in some way, Mollie is your "nemesis." Besides being used as a term to denote a person who is a longstanding rival, *nemesis* is used in the sense that one needs to overcome one's nemesis. With the help of God, that can be done.

I am not saying Mollie was a bad person in this lifetime or previous ones. The energies of lust and witchcraft present early in her recent lifetime provided a pathway for dark energies to use that have been attempting to "throw you over."

Thank you for being patient. Please do not hesitate to cry when things get too much for you. Bless you, dear one! |]

Thank You, Father-Mother God!

End of 2-A: SISTERS CECELIA[AP] AND GEMMA[AP]

Nov 1, '10   NEW ROOTS?

It occurred to me that the overrun of yeast in my body may be a sign that the spirits of witchcraft and lust in the Leigh, Goerger, and Jahner families have gotten new roots. I prayed again for clearing those spirits from all three families.

Also, for a few weeks, I will not eat food that contains sugar. Father God asked me to "fast" in that way for the family when He gave the "Background Clues." I feel led to do that again.

Holy Spirit, is the overgrowth of yeast in my body a sign of family problems, a manifestation of family distress?
[| Yes, Lorrie. That is true for other people as well. |]

Dec 12, '10   Energies: Magnetic Connection

When people carry the same type of negative energy, such as anger, does that negative energy create a magnetic connection between those people? [| Y |] Is that connection similar to individuals having soul ties?
[| It is similar to a soul tie, but a tie of negativity between people is based on something extra within each of them, whereas soul ties come about through being related, having similar experiences, being good friends, lovers, and so on. |]

Suppose one has a particular negative energy within one's self, such as anger. Is there somewhat of a magnetic connection between that person and everyone else with the same or similar negative energy within them?
[| You hit the nail on the head, Lorrie! The understanding of this concept has been a long time coming. You know about the connection between every person (Soul) and all other people and Souls called the "network of love." Everything in the universe operates on the principle that everything is united. There is oneness between each love being and every other love being *and* between the bodies of negative energy.

When someone allows negative energy to be within or attached to them, they have an immediate magnetic connection with that type of negative energy wherever it is located. There are also weaker automatic connections with buddy energies that like to hang around with certain energies, such as spirits of revenge and murder, that are buddies of strong anger.

The attribute of the spiritual life that "like energies have direct connections to each other" is something that people will gradually become more aware of as the energy of Mother Earth and of every person and creature living on the planet continues to rise.

The time will come when people will be well advised to clear their Souls as a treatment method for physical problems. Clinics may even be set up that teach about the effects of negative energies on health and how to go about clearing them.

As you are guessing, Lorrie, the uncomfortable physical symptoms you are experiencing are directly attributable to magnetic connections with negative energies you meet up with in your day-to-day life. You already know how to disconnect yourself from them. Blessings as you go forward! Peace! []

Thank You, Father God! That is good news!

Jul 26, '11   GRANDMA LEIGH: SOUL HISTORY

Grandma Leigh and I used to be one Soul. Our Full Soul split into two Full Souls after our lifetime as Marie[GM]. I call those two parts **Marie**[1] and **Marie**[2]. Marie[1]'s lifetime and all lifetimes before that are previous lifetimes of Grandma Leigh's and mine (GM's lifetimes).

Were Grandma's-My Full Soul and Mollie's Full Soul originally one Soul? [| Y |] That means that all lifetimes *before that Full Soul splitting* are previous lifetimes of Mollie's, Grandma Leigh's, and mine: MGM's lifetimes. When I pray for Mollie's and Grandma Leigh's Souls from earlier lifetimes, *I am also praying for many of my Souls from earlier lifetimes.*

Aug 20, '11. Does Grandpa Leigh need a clearing and healing for his recent lifetime? [| Y |] For other lifetimes? [| N |] Am I being affected detrimentally by his not being healed? [| Y |]

I began blessing Grandpa daily, accepted him as my birth father, and prayed that he would know that God loves him.

Two months later. Does Grandpa Leigh need more prayer? [| N |] Thank You, Holy Spirit, for the healing that took place!

Aug 22, '11   Cleared Karma: Alice, Joel, and Me

Is the stomach distress I had been having related to a particular person? [| Y |] My sister Alice? [| Y |] Do I have karma with her that needs to be cleared? [| Y |]

Alice told me a few years ago about a painful memory regarding me (I don't recall the incident): She said when she was nine (and I was 19), I walked into the bedroom and "caught" her looking at her bare seat in the mirror. I said, "Shame on you!" She didn't say anything at the time but said she had been trying to check out a pimple. Even after hearing that explanation, I didn't apologize or ask Alice to forgive me for shaming her. I need to set things right!

I met with Alice this afternoon and asked her to please forgive me for shaming her for what was an innocent action on her part. She forgave me. I asked her if she would be willing to go through a process of forgiveness with me for our current lives and all previous lifetimes, which she did. Thank You, God!

(Sept 17, '11) Is the karma cleared between Alice and me related to that incident? [| Y |] Is there more karma that needs clearing between her and me? [| Y |]

(!!!) I need to ask Alice again to forgive me for molesting her as a baby when I was ten. In the spring of '93, I told her about recovering that memory and said I was sorry, but I sense that I need to deepen that. I also need to ask Joel again to forgive me for molesting him when he was 4-5 years old and I was 9-10. I will do it in spirit this time for both of them.

Alice, please forgive me for molesting you as a baby when I was ten years old. Thank you! May you be fully healed.

Joel, please forgive me for molesting you at ages 4-5 when I was 9-10. Thank you! May you be fully healed.

(Sept 19, '11) Is the karma between Alice and me all cleared that needs to be? [| Y |] Between Joel and me? [| Y |] Thank You, Holy Spirit!

Aug 23, '11   DIGESTIVE PROBLEMS IN FAMILY

Holy Spirit, I have had a lot of stomach discomfort for the last six weeks. Do I have inflammation throughout my body? [| Y |] Is it related to my sister Alice's health condition? [| Y |]

Are Alice's health problems related to some of her previous

lifetimes? [| Y |] Do I have a beginning of what Alice has: scleroderma, an autoimmune disorder? [| Y |]

Was a curse placed against one or more family members or the whole family in a previous lifetime that is causing serious stomach problems for my granddaughters Dana and Cindy? [| Y |] Do You want us to know who placed that curse against the family? [| Y |]

The next day, I prayed for clearing all curses from the Leigh, Goerger, and Jahner families and family lines.

Aug 23, '11. Is the curse cleared that caused digestive problems for my granddaughter Dana? [| N |] Is it cleared from Cindy? [| Y |] Thank You, Holy Spirit! (My ears became warm.)

Fern, do you want to say something?

[| <FERN> Lorrie, the scleroderma (that you recently learned has gotten a foothold within you) can be cleared after the curse behind the problem is cleared. It is very important that you fully believe and expect that.

I realize you need to head out to a family birthday celebration. I would be happy to go with you if you would like. []

Yes, please come with me. I appreciate it!

Sept 6, '11   Healing Is Taking Place

My head has been aching more than usual today. (My right ear is warm.) Father God, do You want to say something?

[| Lorrie, things are going well even though you feel miserable at the moment. Continue to strongly believe that your family lines, which include you, are in the process of getting some pretty serious things cleared. Take it easy when you need to.

You are wondering how your sister Alice fits into the family makeup. You received the understanding just now that Alice used to be part of the same Soul. That is correct. Her Soul split off from Grandma Leigh's Full Soul after her lifetime as Grandma Leigh. You do not need to know the reason for the split, but knowing that Alice is tied in with Mollie's and Grandma Leigh's energies as much as you are helps explain why she has so many health problems.

Please continue asking for a spirit of healing to hover over and flow through Alice and other relatives needing healing. The effort you and others in your family lines are exerting is worth the effort. Bless all of you! []

Sept 18, '11   Cleared Outside Souls from Joel

Holy Spirit, are portions of Mollie's Souls from several lifetimes with my brother Joel? [| Y |] Are any of them from a lifetime in which she practiced witchcraft? [| Y |] Are portions of Joel's Soul with him from a lifetime in which he was a warlock? [| Y |] I will call him **Cal**^JP in that lifetime.

Would You like me to do clearing for Joel for the portions of Mollie's Souls that are with him that are detrimental to him? [| Y |] For portions of Joel's Souls from other lifetimes that are with him that are detrimental for him? [| Y |]

Would You like me to clear detrimental soul ties between Joel and other people and Souls? [| Y |] Is there a detrimental soul tie between Joel and me? [| Y |]

I did a clearing for portions of Mollie's and Joel's Souls from other lifetimes that were with Joel that are detrimental to him, cleared detrimental soul ties between Joel and other people and Souls, and between Joel and me. Thank You, Holy Spirit!

(Sept 20, '11) Results of those prayers: Have all portions of Mollie's Souls that are detrimental to Joel been cleared from him? [| Y |] Have all portions of Joel's Souls from other lifetimes that are detrimental to him been cleared from him? [| Y |]

Have all detrimental soul ties between Joel and other people and Souls been cleared? [| Y |] Have all detrimental soul ties between Joel and me been cleared? [| Y |] It's like magic!

Sept 27, '11   Leigh Family Line: Clear Curses

I did a clearing for any curses that were hanging over GM's (Grandma/My) Souls and Mollie's Souls. When I finished, I asked: Holy Spirit, are all curses cleared from GM's Souls? [| N |] From Mollie's Souls? [| N |]

Some curses, "karmic curses," hang over a person because they placed a curse on others in their current or previous lifetime.

Speaking for all of GM's (Grandma/my) Souls, I said aloud:

"Everyone this applies to, please forgive me for any curses I placed against you and your family through my thoughts, words, or actions, whether unknowingly or on purpose, including and especially any that involved the use of witchcraft. Thank you for forgiving me!"

I invited Mollie's Souls to join me as I spoke aloud, asking everyone it applies to for forgiveness for having placed curses on them, ending with "Thank you for forgiving me!" I closed with, "Angels of the Violet Flame, please sweep through GM's and Mollie's Souls from every lifetime to clear the residue of negative energies. Thank you!"

Society has placed a stigma on illegitimate children. I cleared the thoughtform from the Leigh, Goerger, and Jahner families and family lines that children conceived outside marriage are bastards, "Not OK." Also, for every person (Soul) in those family lines, I replaced the erroneous imprinting of not being worthy of being loved with the truth that they are a child of God, a child of love.

Father-Mother God, do You have a comment?

[| Yes, Lorrie. Thank you, and bless you for your ministry this morning. Your family lines are much freer now than they were before those prayers. Each step you take brings more freedom and blessing to everyone in your family *and to everyone.*

While doing that praying, you wondered if you were asking for forgiveness, clearing curses, and clearing erroneous imprinting "correctly." There is no "correct way" to clear, pray for protection, healing, or whatever.

The main thing is to have the intention and ask for that to happen. That can be done out loud or internally, even without formulating it into words. It is, after all, the person's Spirit (Soul) praying. Blessings to all of you! |]

Thank You, Father-Mother God!

Oct 4, '11   Hang in There!

The top of my head is bothering me a lot again lately.

[| Lorrie, much healing has taken place and is taking place in Ron's and your family, the Leigh and Goerger families, and all of your family lines. If there were to have been very little or no healing that took place yet, you would be feeling much worse than you do. Remember, you have heightened sensitivity to negative energies compared to earlier. Bless you! |]

Thank You, Father!

Oct 12, '11. [| More breakthroughs will come that will be well worth however long you have waited for answers and relief. You are not alone in experiencing pain, discomfort, and concern. I am fully present with you. You have My strength to rely on, My arms to rest in, My love to sustain you, and My assurance that all is well to uplift you.

By the way, in this message and most times when you addressed Me as "Father God," you were conversing with Mother God and Me as one. Blessings and love to you and all from Us, the Godhead! May you have a wonderful day! |]

[| <FERN> Yes, Lorrie. Have a wonderful day! A host of angels and beautiful Souls are cheering you on. Bless you! |]

Thank you, Fern!

Oct 19, '11   Prayer for Joel

Father God, have portions of some outside Souls been with Joel from before birth?

[| Yes, some Soul portions strongly caught up with religiosity and denominationalism have been with him. |]

(!!!) Is there a Soul infestation in Joel's Soul? [| Y |]

Does he have a Type One Infestation, that of a loving Soul intermingled with his Soul? [| Yes. A portion of Mollie's Soul. |]

Does he also have a Type Two Infestation, that of one or more unloving Souls intermingled with his Soul? [| Y |]

I did steps 1-2 of clearing Type Two infestation from Joel:

1. Several times a day for the next week, I sent love and blessings to Joel early in his life, affirming that God is his Heavenly Father, that he is loved, and asked for a protective shield around his Soul.

2. Each day, I blessed outside Soul portions with Joel without permission and negative energies with or attached to him.

A week later I did steps 3, 4, and 5.

3. Cleared the incorporation of outside Souls and negative energies from within cells in Joel's body,

4. Cleared the enmeshment between Joel's Soul and outside Souls that were with him without permission and commanded them to leave,

5. Cleared the enmeshment between Joel's Soul and the negative energies and commanded them to leave.

Thank You, Holy Spirit, for the clearing that took place!

Oct 20, '11   Connected to Name Rose

Holy Spirit, is the curse cleared that caused (is causing) stomach problems for my granddaughter Dana? [| N |]

Dana recently went to the emergency room because of a severe migraine headache. Fern had that problem in the last year of her life. Is Dana a current lifetime of Fern's? [| Y |] Did Dana's Soul choose to have medical problems similar to Fern's, so the bottled-up anguish in Fern's Soul from her recent lifetime and earlier ones can be released through her? [| Y |] Wow!

Something else might be involved here, too. Is Dana's middle name, Rose, drawing negative energies to her? [| Y |] Is my daughter Patty's middle name, Rose, drawing negative energies to her? [| Y |] And is my name, Lorrie, drawing negative energies to me? [| N |] I use Rose in my User ID. Is using that name drawing negative energies to me? [| Y |]

(!!!) Is Aunt Rose, Mom's and Mollie's sister who died in an accident many years ago, in dire need of prayer? [| Y |] If she gets cleared, will that clear the attraction of negative energies to Dana, Patty, and me? [| Y |]

Maybe it will clear the "rose curse" from Dana as well!

(Nov 14, '11) I prayed for Aunt Rose in every lifetime and asked for the prayers to be applied to everyone in the Leigh family lines who needs healing:

1. Cleared erroneous imprinting from Aunt Rose (believing she is not worthy of being loved),
2. Cleared curses and negative energies from her
3. Invited unloving Souls of hers, if any, to choose to become loving,
4. Asked angels to minister to Aunt Rose's Souls from every lifetime for 45 minutes while I played soft music.

Holy Spirit, did that clearing help Aunt Rose?

[| She received some healing but needs more. She still has witchcraft energies that she picked up from Mollie. |]

Dec 13, '11   Ministering to Joel

While I was wondering what was causing increased discomfort in my head, *Lonnie*, a man from church who died several years ago, came to mind. Shortly after he died, I told Lonnie's Soul I did not want him near me.

Holy Spirit, is Lonnie asking for help for himself or his relatives? [| Y |] Does he have permission to do so? [| Y |]

(!!!) Was Lonnie another lifetime of Joel's? [| Y |] Is Joel in need of prayer? [| Y |] Does he need more clearing for Type Two Soul infestation, negative energies that intermingled with his Soul early on? [| Y |]

I prayed for clearing negative energies and outside Soul portions from Joel, then asked angels to minister healing to him and portions of Mollie's Souls that are with him.

Thank You, God, for the clearing and healing that took place! Did negative energies get cleared from Joel? [| Y |]

Have outside Souls been cleared that that were with Joel without permission?

[| Yes, including a portion of Mollie's Soul that intermingled with Joel's Soul before birth, Type One infestation. |] Wonderful!

Dec 15, '11. Holy Spirit, is another portion of an unloving Soul with Joel? [| Y |] Are there still negative energies with him, including the spirits of denominationalism and religiosity? [| Y |] Is Joel's need for prayer one thing that is affecting my blood pressure? [| Y |] Should I include his Soul from every lifetime when I pray for him? [| Y |]

I ministered to Joel in every lifetime of his:

1. Did clearing for all Souls, loving and unloving, that were with Joel without permission,
2. Extended love and blessing to Cal^{JP}, a portion of Joel's unloving Soul that was with him from a lifetime when Joel was a warlock. I invited Cal to become loving,
3. Cleared negative energies from Joel,
4. Asked angels to minister to Joel, to Joel's Souls from every lifetime, and to Joel's wife Sara for 45 minutes while I played quiet music.

Dec 17, '11. Did the portion of Cal's Soul that was with Joel from a lifetime in which Joel was a warlock choose to become loving? [| Y |] Did that portion of Cal's Soul rejoin the Soul it is a part of? [| Y |] That's good.

Did bits of energy of the spirit of denominationalism choose to become loving? [| Y |] Did some choose to become neutral? [| Y |] Is the spirit of denominationalism cleared? [| Y |]

Is the spirit of religiosity cleared? [| N |] Are those energies somewhat incorporated within cells in Joel's body? [| Y |]

At this time, are any portions of outside Souls within Joel's body? [| N |] Within his aura? [| N |] Attached to it? [| Y |]

Bless all you Soul portions that are attached to Joel's aura. I ask kindly and command all of you who are not meant to be with him to leave! Thank you!

Archangel Michael and Mighty Astrea, please help the Soul portions detach from Joel's aura that can't do it themselves. Guardian angels of those Souls, please take them to where they are meant to be. Thank you!

Holy Spirit, at this time, are any Soul portions attached to Joel's aura that are not meant to be with him? [| N |] That's wonderful!

Starting that day, I did a 9-day clearing of incorporation of the spirit of religiosity from within Joel.

Dec 26, '11. Jesus and Fern, please join me as I do clearing for the spirit of religiosity from Joel. I did that clearing. Is the spirit of religiosity cleared? [| Y |]

Thank you, Fern and Jesus, for helping with that clearing! Thank You, Holy Spirit, for all of the clearing and healing that has taken place for Joel in this lifetime and other lifetimes!

Dec 31, '11   Visiting Souls

I sensed that Souls might be present and asked the Holy Spirit about it. Grandpa and Grandma Leigh, Mom and Dad, and Mollie were present. I learned that Grandpa Leigh and his mother, my great-grandmother Leigh, are often with me. Bless all of you!

Apr 2, '12. After praying for healing for our family lines, I sensed a Soul was present. Holy Spirit, is a Soul of one of the Leigh family present? [| Y |] Mom's youngest brother? [| N |] Grandpa Leigh, my birth father? [| Y |] Does he want to thank me for being his daughter? [| Y |] And to bless me? [| Y |]

ME: Thank you, Grandpa, for being my father. You were meant to be for some reason. Do you have a comment?

Grandpa: Yes, Lorrie. I have been watchful for you your whole life. I am doing what I can to help heal the Leigh family line and the other family lines that are connected to it. I received the understanding that healing is coming about, so please don't give up on working toward that goal.

Also, your books will get published. Trust Father-Mother God, the Holy Spirit. You had the thought lately, "Everybody else is getting books published, so I can, too!" Hold onto that!

Bless you, Lorrie, at every moment in who you are and in who you are coming to be!

ME: Thank you, Grandpa, Dad! Bless you!

Aug 31, '12   More Curses Cleared

At the time that Marie's[GM] Soul split into Marie[1MP] and Marie[2GP], Marie[2] placed a curse against Marie[1] (me) to never find love. Is that curse still in effect? [| Y |] Is another curse hanging over me? [| Y |] Related to me telling our family story? [| Y |]

(!!!) Is the curse for me to die earlier than is planned by my Soul, by God, before I finish the writings? [| Y |]

Did Joel's Soul in this lifetime take part in making that curse? [| Y |] Is the main instigator of that curse a Soul of Joel's from a previous lifetime? [| N |] A Soul of Mollie's from a previous lifetime? [| Y |]

The next morning, I sensed that Souls were present. One was a Soul of Mollie's from a previous lifetime asking for help to release the curse she placed against me to die earlier than the plan for my Soul. I invited her to join me as I said:

"I cancel the curse I placed against Lorrie for her to die earlier than planned for her Soul. Please forgive me, Lorrie. God, please forgive me!"

The other Soul that was present was the portion of Marie[2]'s[GP] Soul that placed a curse against me to never find love. She, too, asked for help to release that curse. I invited her to join in as I spoke words of canceling the curse.

Holy Spirit, is the curse for me to die earlier than planned cleared? [| Y |] Is the curse of never finding love cleared? [| Y |] Thank You, Holy Spirit! That is temendously wonderful!

Nov 28, '12   Curse Using Roses Cleared

I sensed a Soul was present. It was a portion of Rose[MP] of Lima's Soul, a previous lifetime of mine. Holy Spirit, is there still a curse of attracting witchcraft energies hanging over Rose of Lima's Soul because her name is Rose? [| Y |] I wish that curse would be cleared.

I felt prompted to ask again: Holy Spirit, is the curse of attracting witchcraft energies because of her name cleared from Rose[MP] of Lima? [| Y |] Is it cleared from the name "Rose"? [| Y |]

(!!!) Did that curse get cleared just now by me wanting it to be cleared? [| Y |] I am overjoyed!

CHAPTER 3

DOWN TO THE NITTY-GRITTY

Healing for Prior Lifetimes: Joel, Mollie, Me: 1 Each

Mar 17, '11   AI DISORDERS RAMPANT

Many in the Goerger and Jahner families had or have autoimmune (AI) disorders: My sister Alice has Crest Syndrome; my son Chad, grandson Curt, and two nieces have Crohn's disease; Chad's son and daughter have a problem with dry eyes. His daughter also has Raynaud's disease. Several, including me, have fibromyalgia. Many have gluten intolerance, which is related to autoimmune disorders.[1]
[| <FERN> Lorrie, binding and dissolving the roots of autoimmune disease energies and directing that spirit to leave the family and transmute to neutral energy would help hold back the advancement of autoimmune diseases. After you have done that, ask for a Holy Spirit shower to flow through every person (Soul) in the family and through the family as a whole to clear residue. I'll let you do that now. Bless you, Lorrie! |]

Thank you, Fern, Holy Spirit!

I dissolved the roots of autoimmune disease energies in our family and family lines and did a clearing for those energies.

Apr 10, '11. I am having a lot of sinus drainage, which I have learned can be a sign that Mollie wants help with something.

To help Mollie's Soul and me feel better, I cleared the enmeshment between my Soul and Mollie's Souls from every lifetime. I placed a slip of paper with "sinus drainage and congestion" written on it in the large copper ring, asking for that condition to be cleared from everyone in the Leigh, Goerger, and Jahner family lines. Thank You, Holy Spirit!

Jun 8, '11. Father God, do our family lines need more clearing related to autoimmune disorders? Do we need clearing for *a spirit of fatalism,* that it is "our fate to be sick"? I sense that the answer to both questions is "Yes." I am concerned that I won't have enough energy to do the needed clearing.

[| Yes, your family lines need further clearing related to spirits of diseases, primarily autoimmune disorders. Also, the family is affected by a spirit of fatalism related to those disorders.

You can do much healing for yourself, others, and family lines in spirit while you sit quietly with your eyes closed. You can picture saying the words and prayers. Bless you! |]

Thank You, Father God!

Jul 19, '11   CURSES: UNDERLYING CAUSE

Holy Spirit, was a curse for the immune system to malfunction placed on our family lines? [| Y |]

(!!!) Is the malfunction of the immune system a side effect of the spirit of lust? [| Y |] So, is the spirit of lust in the family the underlying cause for many in the Leigh, Goerger, and Jahner families having autoimmune disorders? [| Y |] Is the spirit of lust mostly cleared from our family lines? [| Y |]

Is *Crohn's disease* in the family a specific result of the spirit of lust being (having been) in the family? [| Y |]

I did the first steps that Father God gave for clearing curses:

1. Prayed once a day for six days: "Loving Souls in our family lines, please join in sending a steady deluge of blessings and love to those who placed the curse of malfunction of the immune system on the family at the time the curse was put in place and ever since. Thank you!"
2. Prayed once a day for three days: "I ask that a steady Holy Spirit demagnetizing shower will have been flowing along

the pathways that the energies of that curse traveled on to reach our family ever since the curse was put in place. Thank You, Holy Spirit!"

Aug 2, '11. Holy Spirit, was *a curse of Crohn's disease* placed on the Goerger family? [| Y |] Is it connected with the spirit of lust being (having been) in the family? [| Y |] Is the spirit of lust present within some members of the Goerger and Jahner families holding that curse in place? [| Y |]

I did a clearing for the Leigh, Goerger, and Jahner families and family lines for the spirit of lust, the curse of autoimmune disorders, and the curse of Crohn's disease.

Aug 9, '11. Holy Spirit, is *the spirit of lust* cleared from the original Leigh family? [| Y |] The original Goerger family? [| Y |]

Note: The Holy Spirit said the "spirit of lust" is cleared, not "the curse of the spirit of lust."

Is the *curse for the immune system to malfunction* cleared from the Leigh, Goerger, and Jahner family lines? [| N |]

Is the *curse of Crohn's disease* cleared? [| Y |] Is it possible for those who have Crohn's to be healed now? [| Y |]

Aug 11, '11. [| Good morning, Lorrie! Getting the curse of Crohn's disease lifted from the family and prayers for clearing autoimmune disorders in the family lines were big steps in bringing about physical healing for many in the family, including your grandson Chris, who has a problem with dry eyes. I will guide you as to what else to do for Chris. Bless you! |]

Thank You, Father-Mother God. Holy Spirit!

Aug 14, '11. To help heal those with autoimmune disorders, I should ask for the restoration of the perfect original blueprint for every cell in their bodies!

I prayed individually for my grandson Chris and the other people in my family that I know of who have autoimmune issues. Then, I prayed for the rest of the family as a group.

"Chris [Name], I ask for a spirit of healing to hover over you and for healing love to flow through your veins. I ask for the perfect original blueprint to be restored for every cell in your body!" Thank You, Holy Spirit!

"Everyone in the Jahner family, I ask for a spirit of healing to hover over you and for healing love to flow through your veins. I ask for the perfect original blueprint to be restored for every cell in your body!" Thank You, Holy Spirit!

Has the perfect original blueprint been restored for every cell in Chris's body? [| N |] For some of the cells? [| N |] Are negative energies preventing him from being healed? [| Y |]

I asked about each of the others I prayed for. Restoration of the perfect original blueprint for all the cells in their body took place for each of them. Thank You, Holy Spirit! Did restoration of the perfect original blueprint for some of the cells in their body take place for some other family members as I prayed for them as a group? [| Y |] Wonderful!

Aug 19, '11   Connection: Chris and Mollie

Three years ago, I suddenly began having problems with my eyes being itchy. I asked the Holy Spirit several times if the itching problem was connected with Mollie, and each time, the answer was "Yes." My grandson Chris recently developed eye problems. That connects Chris and Mollie!

(!!!) **Holy Spirit, is Chris another lifetime of Mollie's?** [| Y |] Very likely, at least one of Mollie's Souls from a previous lifetime isn't cleared and healed! Also, if one or more of Grandma Leigh's or my Souls aren't at peace, that could be affecting Chris because, way back, Mollie, Grandma Leigh, and I were one Soul, and after that, Grandma Leigh and I were one Soul for however long.

(Jun 19, '14) I felt antsy and couldn't get to sleep. Other times when I felt that way, the cause was a portion of Grandma Leigh's Soul being with me. I asked the Holy about it.

A shade of Grandma's Soul is hanging over me, wanting to settle something. She is angry that I judged her when I learned that she and Great-Uncle Mike were lovers and that Mike was the father of all her children except the youngest. I apologized to her and asked her to leave. She left.

Aug 29, '11   Clearing for Mollie, Grandma, Me

To help Chris, I prayed for clearing negative energies from Mollie's and Grandma Leigh's Souls from every lifetime.

Holy Spirit, are all negative energies cleared from Mollie's Souls? [| N |] From Grandma Leigh's Souls? [| N |]

(!!!) Is Chris's fairly serious eye problem connected with a curse hanging over one of Mollie's Souls? [| Y |] Does something regarding me need to be cleared before Chris's eyes can be cleared and healed? [| Y |]

Does a curse that is hanging over Mollie need to be cleared from her for me to be cleared? [| Y |] Does that curse need to be cleared from me for Chris to be healed? [| Y |]

I did a clearing for all curses that are hanging over Mollie's Souls from all previous lifetimes of hers.

Holy Spirit, are all curses cleared from Mollie's Soul from all previous lifetimes? [| N |] From all current lifetimes? [| Y |] (That would include Chris.).

Sept 14, '11. I did a clearing for witchcraft and other negative (dark) energies from Mollie's, Grandma Leigh's, and my Souls from every lifetime.

Holy Spirit, are all of Mollie's Souls cleared of witchcraft energies? [| Y |] Cleared of other negative/dark energies? [| Y |]

Are all of Grandma Leigh's Souls cleared of witchcraft energies? [| Y |] Cleared of other negative/dark energies? [| Y |]

Are all of my Souls cleared of witchcraft energies? [| N |] Cleared of other negative (dark) energies? [| Y |] Do I and parts of me need clearing for witchcraft energies? [| Y |]

Sept 27, '11. I did clearing for witchcraft energies for myself and all parts of me. Holy Spirit, am I clear of witchcraft energies? [| Y |] Are all parts of me clear? [| Y |]

Do other people and Souls In the Leigh family line need clearing for witchcraft energies? [| N |] In the Goerger family line? [| N |] In the Jahner family line? [| N |] Wow! That's great!

Sept 8, '11   CHICKEN IS A LINK

Holy Spirit, I received the understanding a few years ago that the negative effects that family members experience from eating chicken are connected to the curse of the spirit of lust.

Was chicken used in some way in passing along autoimmune disorders in the Leigh family line? [| Y |] Was chicken used as a link between the spirit of lust and autoimmune disorders? [| Y |]

Nov 30, '11. Is chicken still linked to autoimmune disorders in the Leigh, Goerger, and Jahner families? [| Y |] Would we be protected from detrimental effects if we blessed the chicken before eating it? [| Y |]

Dec 3, '11   Clearing the Link to Chicken

Is an evil thoughtform keeping the connection between autoimmune diseases and chicken (poultry) in place? [| Y |] Clearing that evil thoughtform would clear that connection!

Steps came to mind for clearing the link between chicken and autoimmune disorders. I took those steps immediately:

1. I sent love and blessings to the evil thoughtform that links chicken and autoimmune disorders in our family lines and to the creators of that thoughtform.
2. I asked Angels of the Violet Flame to transmute the energy of that evil thoughtform and release it for good.
3. I asked Lord Sarcasian, Lord Melchizedek, and Archangel Haniel to clear all negative energies from the Leigh, Goerger, and Jahner families and family lines. (Starr pp. 62-63)
4. I said each day for three days: "My Soul, please ask every hour for a Holy Spirit demagnetizing shower to flow along the pathways by which those negative energies reach and affect our families. Thank you!"

Dec 15, '11. Is the connection between the curse of the spirit of lust and autoimmune disorders cleared for many people and Souls in the Leigh, Goerger, and Jahner families? [| Y |] Is it cleared for my grandson Chris? [| Y |]

Is the connection between chicken and autoimmune disorders cleared for many people and Souls in the Leigh, Goerger, and Jahner families? [| Y |] Is it cleared for Chris? [| N |]

If one would send love and blessing to all disease energies that are with every person connected to them by a spiritual umbilical cord, would that protect the person from ill effects from eating chicken? [| Y |] Can negative energies travel through a spiritual umbilical cord? [| Y |] Very likely through soul ties, too.

I sent blessings and love to all of the disease energies, germs, viruses, and other negative energies with people (Souls) with whom I have a spiritual umbilical cord or soul tie. I asked those energies not to travel to me through those connections and thanked them for respecting my wishes.

Holy Spirit, If I ask Chris's Soul for permission, would it be OK to make that request for him? [| Y |] I did that.

Aug 20, '12   MARIE[2]: CONNECTION TO CROHN'S

Holy Spirit, do I have a mild case of Crohn's? [| Y |] Is a spirit of Crohn's disease within me? [| Y |] Are the digestive issues I have been having lately related to Crohn's disease? [| Y |]

I learned from the Holy Spirit that a portion of Marie[2]'s[GP] Soul, enmeshed with the spirit of Crohn's disease, is with me. She is very angry at me and Marie[1MP]. An angry portion of Marie[2]'s Soul that is enmeshed with the spirit of Crohn's disease is within my younger son Pat. She would like to trigger Crohn's in him, to get at me through him. An angry portion of her Soul triggered Crohn's disease in my older son Chad years ago.

Holy Spirit, is a portion of Marie²'s Soul incorporated within cells in my body? [| Y |] Within my son Pat? [| Y |] Within my son Chad? [| Y |] Within my grandson Curt, who has Crohn's? [| Y |]

I began the 9-day process of clearing the incorporation of Marie²'s Soul from within Pat, Chad, Curt, and me.

(!!!) Holy Spirit, does the curse of Crohn's disease in the Goerger and Jahner families consist of portions of Marie²'s Soul, enmeshed with the spirit of Crohn's disease, being with many family members? [| Y |] Should I ask Lord Melchizedek to take charge of this? [| Y |] Thank You!

Lord Melchizedek, please take charge of the "Crohn's disease situation" in the Goerger and Jahner families and guide me as to what to do about it. Thank you!

Aug 31, '12   Clearing That Connection

Over the last ten days, I cleared the incorporation of Marie²'s^{GP} Soul and the spirit of Crohn's disease from cells in Chad's, Pat's, Chris's, and my body. Just now, I cleared enmeshment between Marie²'s Soul and each of our Souls and between the spirit of Crohn's disease and each of our Souls. I commanded all portions of Marie²'s Soul and the spirit of Crohn's disease to leave. I hope that helps.

Sept 1, '12. I began the process of clearing Soul incorporation from within other family members but soon realized it would be too taxing for me and too difficult to keep track of what has been cleared and from whom.

(!!!) I will ask Lord Melchizedek and his team to finish clearing the incorporation and enmeshment of portions of Marie²'s^{GP} Soul and the spirit of Crohn's disease while I sit quietly.

Lord Melchizedek, Archangel Haniel, and the Ministry Team, please clear the incorporation and enmeshment of Marie²'s Soul and the spirit of Crohn's disease from people and Souls in the Leigh, Goerger, and Jahner families and family lines while I sit quietly for 20 minutes. Thank You!

Afterward, I sensed that Souls were present. Portions of Marie¹^{MP} and Marie²^{GP} had come to ask me to clear enmeshment between their Souls and the spirit of Crohn's disease and between their Souls and people and Souls in our family lines where needed. I did that clearing.

Marie[1]'s guardian angel, please guide all portions of her Soul to the healing ring surrounding her Full Soul so they can receive healing. Thank you!

Marie[2]'s guardian angel, please guide all portions of her Soul to the healing ring surrounding her Full Soul so they can receive healing. Thank you!

Father God, please assist Marie[1]'s and Marie[2]'s Souls to reunite and return to being part of the same Full Soul if they are meant to. Thank You!

Holy Spirit, are all enmeshments cleared between those portions of Marie[1]'s and Marie[2]'s Souls, the spirit of Crohn's disease, and members of our three families? [| Y |]

Are those portions of their Souls cleared from everyone in our family lines? [| Y |] Are Marie[1]'s and Marie[2]'s Souls reunited? [| Y |] Another "miracle"! Thank You, God!

Sept 24, '12. Is the spirit of autoimmune disorders spread far and wide in our family lines? [| Y |] Should I place the task of clearing the spirit and curse of autoimmune disorders from our family lines in the hands of Lord Melchizedek, Archangel Haniel, and the rest of the Ministry Team? [| Y |] That will help!

Does Lord Melchizedek's plan for clearing our family lines of curses include clearing the whole network of dark energy centers and curses from the beginning on? [| Y |] Will that network of curses get completely cleared during my lifetime?

[| You won't see the curses completely cleared, but their roots will get uncovered, and the way to finally get them cleared will be made known to you. |]

Thank You, Father God!

3-A: UNLOVING SOULS IN FAMILY LINES

(Aug 24, '11)   OVERALL PICTURE

Are unloving Souls in the Leigh family line asking for help? [| Y |] In the Goerger family line? [| Y |] In the Jahner family line? [| Y |] Do some of those unloving Souls want help to go to the right place for unloving Souls? [| Y |]

Should I send blessings and love to all unloving Souls? [| N |] To the unloving Souls who are willing to receive them? [| Y |]

(Sept 22, '11) Holy Spirit, please place a protective valve that allows only love to pass through in all connections between me, parts of me, and unloving Souls. Thank You!

Should I ask that all unloving Souls that are with me or family members be encased with spiritual lead? [| Y |] Should I ask that all unloving Souls in the Leigh, Goerger, and Jahner family lines be encased with spiritual lead? [| Y |]

Holy Spirit, please encase all unloving Souls that are with me, with members of my family, and with Souls in our family lines with spiritual lead. Thank You!

Have all unloving Souls that are with me and with family members been encased with spiritual lead? [| N |] Have all unloving Souls in the Leigh family line been encased with spiritual lead? [| N |] In the Goerger family line? [| N |] In the Jahner family line? [| N |] Those answers puzzled me.

(!!!) Oh! Not all unloving Souls have been encased with spiritual lead because many may be unloving only because of having experienced painful circumstances or because of not having received enough love during their lifetime! Those Souls might want help to become loving!

Have all "actual" unloving Souls in the Leigh, Goerger, and Jahner family lines been encased with spiritual lead? [| Y |] Thank You, Holy Spirit!

Guides, please assist unloving Souls that have crossed over to go to the right place for unloving Souls. Thank you!

(Oct 18, '11)   Helping Souls Become Loving

"Loving Souls in the Leigh, Goerger, and Jahner family lines, please join me to help unloving Souls in our family lines become loving: 'I send a continuous flow of blessings and love to every Soul in the Leigh, Goerger, and Jahner family lines at the present moment and every moment of every lifetime of theirs to heal them and enable them to choose to become loving.'

"Thank you, everyone, for joining in."

(Oct 19, '11) Holy Spirit, did some unloving Souls from Mollie's lifetimes choose to become loving? [| Y |] From lifetimes of Grandma Leigh's? [| Y |] From lifetimes of Joel's? [| Y |] From lifetimes of mine? [| Y |] Have some of the Souls who chose to become loving already gone to the light? [| Y |] Wonderful! I can hardly believe how quickly prayers work!

(Dec 28, '11)   Helping Mollie's Souls

My head is very uncomfortable. Holy Spirit, did portions of unloving Souls from previous lifetimes of Mollie's that were in my head earlier return? [| Y |] With Your permission? [| Y |]

(!!!) Is an unloving portion of Mollie's Soul present from a lifetime when she was my Mother Superior when I was a nun? [| Y |] I will call Mollie **Sister Carmella**^{AP}in that lifetime.

Does Sister Carmella think the vow of obedience I made to her is still in place? [| Y |] I explained to her that vows are in effect only until the person who took the vow dies, and then I led her in releasing my Soul from that lifetime from the vow of obedience to her. I extended blessings and love to her and invited her to choose to become loving.

I cleared erroneous early imprinting from Sister Carmella and spoke for Father-Mother God in expressing Their love for her. I asked her to go to the place for visiting Souls surrounding her Full Soul and thanked her for doing so. Did she go to the place for visiting Souls? [| Y |]

(Dec 29, '11) My head doesn't feel any better than yesterday. Is there still a portion of an unloving Soul in my head from a prior

LORRIE LEIGH

lifetime of Mollie's? [| Yes, from a different lifetime in which she was your Mother Superior. |] (Here we go again.)

I will call Mollie **Sister Sara**[AP] in that lifetime. I went through steps of blessing, sending love, and doing a clearing for her like I did for Sister Carmella.

Holy Spirit, is the portion of Sister Carmella's Soul that had been in my head now loving? [| Y |] Is the portion of Sister Sara's Soul that had been in my head now loving? [| Y |]

Is the rest of Sister Carmella's Soul unloving?
[| Yes, and so is the rest of Sister Sara's Soul. |]

(!!!) Did those portions of Sister Carmella's and Sister Sara's Souls enter my head to receive help to become loving so they could help the rest of their Souls become loving? [| Y |]

(Dec 31, '11)   A CHANGE IN PERSPECTIVE

Note: I learned that portions of some of Mollie's Souls are unloving. I would guess they are unloving because of difficult circumstances during their lifetime.

My head is still very uncomfortable. Holy Spirit, are followers of Satan attacking me because I helped the portion of Sister Carmella's[AP] Soul that was in my head become loving? [| Y |]

(!!!) Was another unloving Soul of Mollie's from a previous lifetime order an attack on me? [| Y |] Should I order all of Mollie's Souls to leave and stay away from me? [| N |] Should I order all unloving Souls of Mollie's to stay away? [| N |]

(!!!) Have dark forces taken over some of Mollie's unloving Souls from other lifetimes and are using her energy and willpower to attack me? [| Y |] Is one of those unloving Souls from a lifetime when she was my Mother Superior? [| Y |]

(!!!) Are dark forces holding some of Mollie's loving Souls in bondage to force that unloving Soul of hers to attack me? [| Y |] If that unloving Soul would be free to do so, would it choose to become loving? [| Y |] Wow!

308

(!!!) Before a number of her lifetimes, did Mollie's Soul, under the direction of the Holy Spirit, choose to join the dark forces during that lifetime so she could work from within the group to sabotage it? [| Y |] That changes my perspective!

That day and the following week, I sent blessings and love often throughout the day to loving Souls of Mollie's being held captive by dark forces and to the portions of unloving Souls of hers being controlled by dark forces.

(Jan 1, '12)   MELCHIZEDEK COMES ON BOARD

While driving home from the store, I received the understanding from Father God that a lesson would come about "how to protect oneself from attack by dark forces and clear the dark energy centers that generate those attacks." After being home for a bit, I suddenly felt chillier than I ever had.

Father, is an outside Soul present? [| Y |] A Soul that will help us win against dark forces? [| Y |] **Melchizedek** came to mind.

Is Lord Melchizedek here (Gen 14:18)? [| Y |] Will he be taking charge of dealing with dark forces? [| Y |]

Are many Souls besides Mollie's being manipulated to do the bidding of the dark forces? [| Y |] When Lord Melchizedek puts his plan into action for clearing the dark energy center controlling Mollie's Soul, will dark energy centers controlling other Souls be cleared also? [| Y |]

Are many Souls set up as spies within the makeup of the dark forces who will work with Lord Melchizedek in the overall plan to defeat them? [| Y |]

(Jan 5, '12)   Helping An Unloving Soul of Mollie's

When I came home from work, I sensed a Soul was in my apartment. I went into my sewing (ministry) room and closed the door to ask about it.

Holy Spirit, are one or more Soul or Soul portions in my living

309

room? [| Yes, several Soul portions are present. |] With Your permission? [| N |]

Are they portions of the unloving Soul of Mollie's that is being pressured to attack me? [| Y |] Did those Soul portions think they had my permission to come here because of the love I expressed for them lately? [| Y |]

Are those Soul portions still under the control of the dark energy center? [| N |] Are they ready to receive blessings and love and become loving? [| Y |] (I had to cry.) This is a miracle of release from dark powers and of healing!

(!!!) Does Jesus want to do the clearing for those portions of Mollie's Soul and assist them to join their Home Soul? [| Y |]

Jesus, I sense you are advising me not to converse with the portions of Mollie's Soul that are present.
[| (JESUS) That is correct. |]

I sat quietly for 15 minutes, trusting Jesus to take care of the portions of Mollie's Soul in the living room. Thank you, Jesus, Father-Mother God, Holy Spirit, and whoever else helped with that clearing and healing! Bless you, Mollie!

(Evening) Hello, Father God! What a day! I am happy that Mollie's Soul received help but also very tired.
[| Yes, Lorrie, what a blessed day this has been! You played a major role in getting things to the point that those portions of Mollie's Souls could be freed. They will need extensive healing and rehabilitation, but there is plenty of "time" in eternity. Your Aunt Mollie's Soul is swelling with gratitude, and so is My heart and the "heart" of the universe. Bless you, dear one! |]

(Jan 6, '12) I sensed a Soul was in my apartment and understood from the Holy Spirit that Aunt Mollie had come to bless me. I sat quietly for a bit to give her time to bless me.

Holy Spirit, did Aunt Mollie's Soul leave?
[| Not yet. Mollie also wants to say she is sorry for any pain she caused you during her recent lifetime and previous ones. |]

I forgave Mollie for unresolved issues between her and me

during her recent and previous lifetimes, thanked her for coming, blessed her, and said she could leave. She left.

Thank You, Holy Spirit, for the healing that took place!

(Feb 17, '12)   Dark Forces at Work

Quite a few portions of unloving Souls entered my body and Soul through the years. Were many pressured to do so by dark forces to keep me from feeling well and too busy dealing with them to have time to work on the writing? [| Y |]

Are portions of some of my Souls from previous lifetimes being held prisoner to cause health problems for me? [| Y |] Are those Soul portions under the influence of High-Level Negatives (Starr pp. 62ff)? [| Y |]

End of 3-A: UNLOVING SOULS IN FAMILY LINES

3-B: DEALING WITH DARK ENERGY CENTERS

(Jan 1, '12)   HOW TO CLEAR THEM

My right ear became warm, and I felt very chilly. Father God, is a Soul present that isn't usually here?
[| Yes. Melchizedek is here. He wants to give you steps for clearing dark energy centers and for protecting you and members of your family from dark energy attacks.

1. Ask loving Souls in your family lines to join in sending a deluge of blessings and love to the dark energy centers that are beaming dark energies at individuals, families, and Souls in your family lines.

2. Ask for love and blessings to flow steadily to the Soul portions that are held captive in dark energy centers, the Souls and entities operating those centers, and the dark energies.

3. Ask for a Holy Spirit demagnetizing shower to have been flowing along the energy pathways those dark energies have traveled on ever since those pathways were set up. []

Thank You, Father! I will begin doing those steps every day. Thank you, Lord Melchizedek, for your help.

Lord Melchizedek: "You are very welcome, Lorrie! Thank you for all that you have done and are doing to help with this rather massive clearing and healing process that is taking place. Just remember that everything takes place a step at a time and, from your perspective, a moment at a time.

"I will leave now. Please do not hesitate to call on me for assistance as it seems fitting. Bless you, Lorrie!"

Bless you, as well!

(Jan 2, '12)   RECEIVER-TRANSMITTER CENTERS

Does a large dark energy center located in the spiritual plane collect negative (dark) energy from people and Souls in the Leigh, Goerger, and Jahner families and send a steady stream of that dark energy to power the spirit of lust and other negative spirits that are hanging over our families and affecting individuals in them? [| Y |]

Have the causes of my grandson Chris's eye problem been cleared? [| N |] Is *the curse of autoimmune disorders* cleared from the Leigh, Goerger, and Jahner family lines? [| N |] Is it being held in place by a dark energy center? [| Y |]

Lord Sarcasian, Lord Melchizedek, and Archangel Haniel, please clear the dark energy center that holds the curse of autoimmune disorders over the Leigh, Goerger, and Jahner family lines. Thank you!

(Feb 24, '12) Father God, is a spiritual ring on my head or above it that is a receiver for dark energies?

[| A dark energy center located above your head is causing the discomfort that you feel. |]

Does that energy center attract unloving Souls? [| Y |] Is it beaming dark energies at me? [| Y |] *It is both a receiver and a transmitter for dark energies.* [| Y |] Are many dark energy centers like that located within or near people and Souls in the Leigh, Goerger, and Jahner family lines? [| Y |]

If those dark energy centers were sealed with spiritual lead, would that prevent them from attracting unloving Souls and from picking up and sending out dark energies? [| Y |]

In the name of Jesus, I seal the dark energy center at the top of my head with spiritual lead. I seal the outer edge of all dark energy centers that are within or near people and Souls in the Leigh, Goeger, and Jahner family lines with spiritual lead.

I command all dark energies in those dark energy centers to leave, to go to where they are meant to be! Thank You, God!

(Feb 27, '12) Father God, are dark energies still being beamed at me from every direction?

[| Lorrie, you know the answer to that is "Yes." It is the same with dark energies as with countries or groups battling each other. The people, groups, or areas with the strongest resistance and weaponry are targeted the strongest.

Take cheer! Your efforts in following the steps given by Lord Melchizedek for clearing dark energy centers and protecting yourself and members of your family are already bringing about results. Love is powerful! |]

I ask for a Holy Spirit demagnetizing shower to flow through me all day and night to clear dark energy from the dark energy center above my head and clear contact points for dark energy from every part of me. Thank You, Holy Spirit!

(Feb 28, '12)   Clearing Is Progressing

Almost every day for the last two months, I did the steps Lord Melchizedek suggested for clearing dark energy centers from people and Souls in our family lines and myself.

Holy Spirit, did some of the dark energy in those centers choose to become neutral energy? (No answer.) Did some choose to become loving energy? (No answer.)

Did some of the dark energies choose to transmute to neutral energy *as they were sent out* to members of our families? [| Y |] Did some choose to transmute to loving energy *as they were sent out?* [| Y |] Did some of the Souls and entities running those centers choose to become loving? [| Y |] Great! We made progress!

(Mar 18, '12) Father God, is a steady stream of dark energies still being beamed at me?
[| Yes. Send love and blessings to those energies. |]

(!!!) Uh-oh! Each day, I have been asking for every part of my Full Soul to join me in flowing a deluge of love and blessings to the energy centers that are beaming dark energies at our families, the Souls and entities that operate those dark energy centers, and the dark energies. It isn't coming from love on my part, though, but from wanting to be protected and "make them go away."

I saw an image of what our person, our Soul, could and should be like. A bright glowing light emanating blessings and love out to the whole of creation, including dark energies and the beings (Souls) who are part of the dark forces.
[| Bless you, Lorrie! You are getting the picture of the ideal way to be. Remember, you and everyone are a work in progress. By being open to the Spirit, you will arrive at where and how you are meant to be. It behooves all of you to learn to accept yourselves with love as you are at every moment. Thank You for listening! Have a nice evening! |]

Thank You, Father! Thank you, Fern, for helping!

(Mar 22, '12)   IT HITS HOME

I have much discomfort at the top of my head. Holy Spirit, is the dark energy center at the top of my head sending dark energies against family members? [| Y |] Oh, dear!

(!!!) Are the entities operating that dark energy center unloving portions of my Soul from other lifetimes? [| Y |] Are one or more portions of my Soul from this lifetime helping operate it? [| Y |] Are those portions almost split off from the rest of my Soul? [| Y |] Are they crying out for love? [| Y |]

314

Are portions of many Souls of family members helping to operate dark energy centers? [| Y |] That sounds like the unloving Soul portions and the entities that operate dark energy centers are spread throughout our family lines. The unloving energy of those Soul portions draws negative (dark) energies from family members and dark forces to the dark energy center that those Soul portions are helping operate.

The understanding I am getting is that dark energy centers are operated by a conglomeration of Souls located throughout people's family lines: unloving Souls of people who are living and who have crossed over and loving Souls of people like me who ended up having a receiver-transmitter ring placed at the top of their head or elsewhere on or within their person.

Maybe my Soul and those other loving Souls stated their willingness before coming into this life to allow a receiving center to be placed upon or within them during that lifetime to become part of the clearing process for the family!

Father God, I sense that what I wrote just now is how things are. Do You have any comments or corrections?

[| Right on, Lorrie! Thank you for being willing to take the time to listen and receive. At the moment, I have no changes or corrections to make to what you wrote. A deeper understanding will open up as We proceed.

I am proud of you, as I am of all My children. Rest assured that you have the knowledge, love, and support of the universe at your disposal, as do all. I will sign off now. Bless you! |]

Thank You, Father God, for that encouragement!

(Mar 22, '12)   Spirit-Inspired Prayer

Lord Melchizedek, Archangel Haniel, and helpers, please minister to people and Souls in the Leigh, Goerger, and Jahner family lines while I meditate. Thank you! After I sat quietly for several minutes, the Holy Spirit prompted me to say aloud:

Dear Souls, God loves you to the fullest extent possible! You warm His heart. He says:

315

[| Bless you, My sons and daughters! Bless you, My little ones, aged ones, and all ages. Bless each of you at every moment in who you are and in who you are coming to be. My peace, I give to you. My love, I give to you. Receive and be healed.

Do not decide what to do based on what other people do or say you should do, not even based on what your church says or thinks you should do. Relationship with God is that of person to Person: The person of you to the Person of God. It is the most precious thing you can have. It is the most precious thing for Me, also.

Before you go to sleep, think of Me and choose to receive My love all night. You can receive healing and blessings while you sleep. Your Soul is more open to receiving while you are asleep. Shalom! |]

Father God, I lift myself to You along with all other people and Souls in our family lines who have had a receiver-transmitter for dark energies placed in their aura or within their person. I bless those people and Souls and everybody in our family lines. I pray that all of us will be open to the guidance of Your Spirit so the plan for freeing our families and family lines will come to completion. We trust that it will and are thankful for that! We choose to receive Your guidance, love, grace, and blessing. Thank You!

Thank you, Lord Melchizedek, for taking on the task of clearing our family lines of dark energies and curses. Thank you, Archangel Haniel, for helping with that clearing. Thank you to everyone in our family lines, the world, and the universe who is helping.

We pray that the clearing will come to completion for our families and family lines and, one by one, for thousands of other families and family lines until the healing for humankind (Souls) is complete. Shalom to everyone!

(Mar 23, '12)   Part of the Plan

During an earlier lifetime of mine, did somebody who practiced witchcraft put a receiver-transmitter for dark energy at the top of my head? [| Y |] Was it put in place during one of my lifetimes as a nun? [| Y |] Was it set to be triggered by a hypnotic suggestion? [| Y |]

Did Sister Mollie and other nuns who practiced witchcraft put it in place? (No answer.) Did they reach out to a High Negative within the dark forces to put it there? [| Y |]

(!!!) Was the High Negative who put that hypnotic suggestion in place Joel's Soul from a previous lifetime? [| Y |]

Was it part of the plan for bringing healing to our family lines for me to have a receiver-transmitter at the top of my head and for the Holy Spirit to open up understanding about dark energy centers and how to clear them? [| Y |]

Was it part of the plan, too, for Joel's Soul to place a curse of the spirit of lust on the Leigh family line? (No answer.)

(!!!) Was that curse already hanging over the Leigh family line because of actions of family members in previous lifetimes: sexual slavery and lust in the convent? [| Y |] Wow!

(Mar 26, '12)   Zeroing In

I asked the Holy Spirit before doing this: I extended love and blessings to the unloving Soul portions that are operating the dark energy center at the top of my head, invited them to receive love and become loving, and said that in a few minutes, I would send those away that haven't chosen to become loving.

Ten minutes later, I again invited those Soul portions to become loving, then, in the name of Jesus, commanded all of those who hadn't chosen to become loving. I asked Archangel Michael to help free any that needed help getting detached from my aura. I asked In-God-We-Trust Angels to come with their nets (Starr, Preface p. iv) and carry the unloving Soul portions that refused to leave to where they were meant to be.

Thank you, Archangel Michael and angels, for your help!

(Mar 31, '12) Holy Spirit, is the dark energy center at the top of my head still operating? [| Somewhat. |]

(!!!) Is that dark energy center composed of compressed Soul portions with dark energy? [| Y |] Are portions of my Soul from this lifetime in it? [| Y |] Portions of my Soul from other lifetimes? [| Y |] Portions of M-G-M's Souls (when Mollie, Grandma, and I were one Soul)? [| Y |]

Are portions of other people's Souls in it? [| Y |] Are all of the portions of outside Souls that are in that center enmeshed with the portions of my Soul that are in it? [| Y |] That sounds very complicated!

Evening: I cleared enmeshment between portions of my Soul and portions of other Souls that were in that dark energy center, extended love and blessings to them, and told them they were free to leave if they wanted to. Guardian angels of those Souls, please guide those that leave to where they are meant to be. Thank you!

Holy Spirit, please apply this clearing to all other dark energy centers operating within the Leigh, Goerger, and Jahner family lines. Thank You!

(Apr 13, '12) I asked the Holy Spirit about taking the following steps to help clear the dark energy center at the top of my head and those throughout our family lines. I received a "Yes" answer for each step:

1. Do a process of forgiveness between
   a. Those in our family lines who have been or are being affected by witchcraft energies and
   b. Those in our family lines and outside of them who directed witchcraft energies or placed curses against any individuals or families in our family lines.
2. Do a process of forgiveness between
   a. My Souls from other lifetimes that directed witchcraft energies against others and
   b. All individuals (Souls) in our family lines that were or are being affected by those witchcraft energies.
3. Invite every person (Soul) in our family lines to retract all judgments and curses they made, knowingly or unknowingly, against God, family members, and others.

(Apr 26, '12) I asked Lord Melchizedek and heavenly helpers to do clearing for our family lines while I sat quietly.

After a bit, I did the above steps to help clear dark energies from the dark energy center above my head and from centers throughout our family lines.

Holy Spirit, have the dark energies been cleared from some of those centers?

[| Yes, a number of them have been cleared. |] Wonderful!

(May 7, '12) Holy Spirit, if I seal the dark energy center above my head with triple-strength spiritual lead, would that prevent it from receiving and transmitting dark energies? [| Y |] I seal that dark energy center with triple-strength spiritual lead. (Pause)

Is that energy center still receiving or transmitting dark energies? [| N |] Holy Spirit, please seal all dark energy centers that are operating in the Leigh, Goerger, and Leigh family lines with triple-strength spiritual lead. Thank You!

Each day I have been asking my Full Soul and all loving Souls in our family lines to join in sending a deluge of blessings and love to the dark energy centers, the overseers of those centers, and the dark energies within them.

I will add to that: *Father God, I consecrate all dark energy centers and contact points for dark energy located within or near people and Souls in our family lines to be used for loving energy.*

(May 9, '12)   CONTACT POINTS FOR DARK ENERGY

A couple of times recently and just now, I felt a sharp pain in one of the vertebrae between my shoulders. Holy Spirit, are portions of unloving Souls attached to that vertebra?

[| No. A contact point for dark energy is there. |]

(!!!) Is a "contact point for dark energy" a small dark energy center with compressed Soul portions within it? [| Y |]

The side of my right hip and the left side of my neck have been quite sore on and off for years. Are contact points for dark energy located in those places, also? [| Y |] Are portions of unloving Souls from previous lifetimes of mine in one or more of those contact points? [| Y |] Are portions of *loving Souls of mine* in them? [| Y |]

Are portions of *unloving Souls of Mollie's from previous lifetimes* in one or more of those contact points? [| Y |] Are portions of *loving Souls of Mollie's* in them? [| Y |]

(!!!) Are some of the Soul portions in those dark energy centers somewhat incorporated within cells in my body? [| Y |] That helps explain why I haven't been able to get dark energy centers cleared! The incorporation of those Souls needs to be cleared before the Souls can leave. I immediately began the 9-day process of clearing Soul incorporation from within cells in my body.

I have cleared the incorporation of Souls from within cells in my body many times. I think the incorporation of Soul portions that were in dark energy centers didn't get cleared, so I realize that I should include clearing of incorporation as one of the steps to take in clearing energy centers.

(May 30, '12)   Centers Within Family Members

Holy Spirit, do many people and Souls in the Leigh family line have one or more dark energy centers within or attached to them? [| Y |] Many in the Goerger family line? [| Y |] Many in the Jahner family line? [| Y |]

(!!!) *Did most of the Souls in those dark energy centers have an autoimmune disease during their lifetime?* [| Y |] *Did all of them?* [| Y |] Should I ask for the restoration of the perfect original blueprint for every cell in their body for each of those people back in time when they were still living? [| Y |] At the time of their conception? [| Y |] Should I ask that for their parents, too? [| N |] For others in their family? [| N |]

Holy Spirit, are You telling me about these dark energy centers with compressed portions of the Souls of family members in them who had autoimmune diseases during their lifetimes to instruct me in how to clear the curses of autoimmune disorders and Crohn's disease from the family lines? [| Y |] Thank You!

End of 3-B: DEALING WITH DARK ENERGY CENTERS

320

Mar 25, '12   LORD, HAVE MERCY!

Lord Melchizedek and helpers, please minister to our families as I sit quietly. In a bit, I felt prompted to pray aloud:

"Lord God, have mercy on us, Your children! Many of us are lost and bewildered, searching for truth, love, and happiness in the wrong places. Many of us have greatly erred.

"Please clear the erroneous imprinting we received early on in the life of our Soul that we are not worthy of being loved. Place within each of us the truth that You love us dearly!

"Please forgive us for wrongdoing during our current lifetime and all other lifetimes. Please flow a Holy Spirit shower of love and a demagnetizing shower through each person (Soul) in our family lines to clear all traces of witchcraft energies and to help clear the spirit of witchcraft and the curses of the spirit of lust and autoimmune disorders. Thank You, Father!"

[| I flow My mercy and love through each of you. I forgive you for every moment that you were out of right order. I understand and see no sin. I see My hurting children.

My sons and daughters, come to Me in the depths of your Soul! Know that you are in Me. We are one. As you continue to be, you will realize that all is wiped away: All sin, degradation, and error. You are clean! You are free! You are healed!

The curses shall give way! Any onus that is hanging over you will be done away with in My good time and when you, My children, are ready. Shalom! |]

Thank You very much, Father God!

Apr 29, '12   AGREEMENT BY ALICE'S SOUL

My sister Alice is very sick. I felt prompted to clear the enmeshment between her Soul and outside Souls that are not meant to be with her.

(!!!) Holy Spirit, did Alice's Soul agree to carry the curse of the spirit of lust that is hanging over our family lines with her when she crosses over to clear it from the family? [| Y |] Did her Soul also agree to carry the curses of autoimmune disorders and Crohn's disease with her when she crosses over to clear them from the family? [| Y |] When she crosses over, will those curses be removed from the family? [| Y |] Wow!

Is the curse of the spirit of lust with Alice at this time? [| Y |] Is it encased with spiritual lead? [| Y |] Can it affect Alice? [| N |] Are the curses of autoimmune disorders and Crohn's disease encased with spiritual lead?

[| Yes, with triple-strength spiritual lead. **So you know what the situation is: The curse of Crohn's disease was specified against certain people in the family. It is a separate curse from the curse of autoimmune disorders.** |]

Holy Spirit, I ask an army of angels to always be with Alice until she arrives in Heaven. Thank You! I ask all negative energies to be cleared from Alice, her hospital room, and the doctors and staff who will be working with her. Thank You!

Apr 30, '12   MORE ROOTS UNCOVERED

I visited my sister Alice in the hospital. She said her daughters Callie and Wendy would visit her the next day and asked me to pray for them so they could have a better attitude toward her and not be judgmental.

Holy Spirit, does Alice's daughters' unkind attitude towards her stem from previous lifetimes of theirs? [| Y |] By asking "Yes" or "No" questions that came to mind, I learned that in an earlier lifetime, Callie and Wendy were nuns and dabbled in witchcraft in the convent where Mollie was.

"Sister Callie," "Sister Wendy," and some of the other nuns looked down on uneducated nuns, especially **Sister Agatha** (Alice), who did menial work. They picked her and a few other "lower-class" nuns as targets for witchcraft energy.

Surprise! Sister Agatha was spiritually powerful and was able to prevent the witchcraft energies from affecting her and the other targeted nuns. Some other nuns practicing witchcraft laughed at Sister Callie and Sister Wendy because a simple nun had foiled their efforts!

(!!!) Out of frustration and embarrassment, did Sister Callie ask Satan to strike Sister Agatha and her family line? [| Y |] Did Sister Wendy ask for that, also? [| Y |]

Asking Satan to strike someone and their family line places a curse on that person and on everyone in that family line is a serious issue. No wonder Alice has had so many health problems! And with Callie's and Wendy's Souls from that lifetime not being healed, it isn't surprising that they have an obnoxious attitude toward Alice in this lifetime.

The larger portion of Sister Agatha's Soul forgave Sister Callie and Sister Wendy back in that lifetime, but part of her Soul that couldn't forgive them is enmeshed with Alice's Soul and needs help to forgive them. A portion of "Sister Callie's" Soul is with Callie. Wendy has witchcraft energies attached to her.

(!!!) Dora (Alice's and my sister) has an attitude toward Alice almost identical to that of Callie and Wendy. Was she one of the nuns in that earlier lifetime who joined Sister Callie and Sister Wendy in directing witchcraft energies at Sister Agatha? [| Y |]

(!!!) Did "Sister Dora" also ask Satan to strike Sister Agatha and her family line? [| Y |] Is a portion of Sister Dora's Soul with Dora? [| No, but a shade of Sister Dora's Soul is with Alice. |]

May 1, '12   Prayer for Callie, Wendy, and Dora

For Alice's daughters Callie and Wendy and our sister Dora:

1. Cleared erroneous imprinting for their Souls,
2. Went through a process of forgiveness individually between Callie, Wendy, and Dora for all the lifetimes that they knew each other,
3. Extended love and blessing to all dark energies and unloving Souls that were with them and invited those energies and

Souls to choose to become neutral or loving; commanded all remaining dark energies and unloving Soul portions to leave Callie, Wendy, and Dora,

4. Asked that angels would minister healing to their Souls.

Results: Sister Callie and Sister Wendy forgave Sister Agatha for what they perceived as hurtful. Sister Dora still feels vengeful towards Sister Agatha but wants help to become loving. All three of them withdrew their request for Satan to attack Sister Agatha and her family line but have negative residue attached to their Soul from that action.

Sister Agatha's Soul forgave them back in that lifetime for directing witchcraft energy at her and asking Satan to attack her and her family line. Bless you, Sister Agatha!

The curses against Sister Agatha's family line that resulted from Sisters Callie, Wendy, and Dora asking Satan to strike Agatha and her family line are not cleared from people and Souls In Alice's family line. Alice's Soul will carry those curses away, also, when she crosses over.

May 2, '12. Do Alice's autoimmune disorders stem directly from Sisters Callie's, Wendy's, and Dora's wish for harm to come to Sister Agatha and her family line? [| Y |]

(!!!) **Is the curse of autoimmune disorders in our family lines a result of karma** related to Sisters Callie, Wendy, and Dora asking Satan to strike Sister Agatha and her family line; that the harm they wished on her and her family line came back on them and their family line? [| Y |] **Is it the same for the curse of Crohn's disease?** [| Y |] **Is that the origin of those curses?** [| **It is one of the roots**. |]

Many people and Souls In my (our) family lines have been affected by witchcraft energies. Are witchcraft energies affecting the family lines due to family members having practiced witchcraft in earlier lifetimes? Is that one of the roots of witchcraft energies? [| Y |]

May 29, '12. **Holy Spirit, Is the curse of the spirit of lust cleared from the Goerger family as a whole?** [| Y |] **From the Leigh family as a whole?** [| Y |] **From the Jahner family as a whole?** [| Y |] Is it still hanging over a few people in each of those families? [| Y |]

Jun 12, '12 **Is the curse of autoimmune disorders cleared from many in the Leigh family line?** [| Y |] **From many in the Goerger family line?** [| Y |] **From many in the Jahner family line?** [| Y |] That is wonderful news!

(!!!) Is the "curse of autoimmune disorders" called that because autoimmune disorders are "hanging over us" by being passed down in our DNA? [| Y |] Did somebody place a curse of autoimmune disorders on the family? [| N |]

Jun 16, '12   Nine-Day Healing Process

I asked the Holy Spirit individually about each person I know of in the family who has Crohn's disease: Is a shade of Aunt Mollie's Soul from her recent lifetime as our Aunt hanging over (Name)? The answer was "Yes" for all of those I asked about.

Is there a reason why a shade of Aunt Mollie's Soul is with each of those people?

[| Yes. Aunt Mollie is with them to help clear Crohn's disease. |]

Wow! Thank you, Aunt Mollie!

Holy Spirit, what can I do to help clear the spirit (energies) of Crohn's disease and other autoimmune disorders from our family lines and bring healing to those affected?

[| Please take these steps:

1. Write "Crohn's disease" and "all other autoimmune disorders" on slips of paper, tape them on purple paper, and put them in a large copper ring. (Purple is the color for transmuting and clearing.)

2. Place a spiritual copper ring around each person (Soul) in your family and family lines who had or has Crohn's disease or other autoimmune disorder. Ask the Souls of their birth parents to join them in the ring.

3. Ask the Souls from the prior lifetimes of each affected person to gather in a spiritual copper ring. Ask the Souls of their birth parents to join them in the ring.
4. For the affected persons, say each day for nine days:
    a. Angels, please minister healing, especially while they are sleeping, to all those who were and are affected by autoimmune disorders.
    b. Ask for a Holy Spirit demagnetizing shower to flow through those people and Souls for nine days.
    c. Ask for a spirit of healing to hover over each person (Soul) that is in a spiritual copper ring for healing Crohn's disease or other autoimmune disorders and for healing love to flow through them.
    d. Ask for restoration of the perfect original blueprint at the moment of their conception for all of the cells in the bodies of those who have (had) Crohn's disease or other autoimmune disorders.
    e. Play inspirational music for an hour daily to minister healing to those affected people and Souls. []

Thank You, Holy Spirit! Doing all those steps was a daunting task, but I started on it immediately.

Sept 30, '12. I have had digestive problems for a long while. Holy Spirit, does eating chicken act like a laxative for me?
[| Yes, when not filled with love. |]

The Holy Spirit prompted me to ask: **Is a contact point for dark energies being placed into chicken when I buy it?** [| Y |] **Do dark energies that are with me place those contact points into the chicken?** [| Y |] That is puzzling.

Dec 9, '12   CLEARING BY FAMILY GROUPS

Almost every day this past year, I asked Lord Melchizedek, Archangel Haniel, and the Ministry Team to minister to our family lines while I sat quietly for 15 minutes to:

1. Assist the dark energies in dark energy centers located throughout our family lines to become loving.
2. Clear the curses hanging over individuals, Souls, and families in our family lines.

Thank you, Lord Melchizedek and team, for your ministry!

Holy Spirit, for the most part, has the curse of Crohn's disease been lifted from the Leigh family line? [| Y |] From the Goerger family line? [| Y |] From the Jahner family line? [| Y |]

I understand that to mean that the "backbone" of the curse has been broken, but Crohn's can still show up here and there.

Feb 21, '13. I asked the Ministry Team to join me as I did a clearing for our family lines by groups for the spirits of Crohn's, Parkinson's, fibromyalgia, arthritis, all other autoimmune disorders, and all other negative spirits.

Family Groups:

1. Original Leigh family: Mom, her parents, and siblings
2. Original Goerger family: Dad, his parents, and siblings
3. The Goerger family: My parents, myself, my siblings, and their families
4. Jahner family: Ron's parents, Ron, Ron's siblings, and their families
5. The Ron and Lorrie Jahner family: Ron and me, our children and their families, and our grandchildren and their families.

Thank you, Ministry Team!

Mar 22, '13   DREW^{AP} IN THE PICTURE

I learned a while back that *my grandson Chris is a current lifetime of Mollie's.* He stayed at my place for four days last week. While he was here, I had much discomfort and a feeling of pressure in my head, a sign that portions of unloving Souls or dark energies were present. Also, my eyes began bothering me a lot.

Chris has had dry eye problems for several years. I learned a while back that an infestation of negative energies took place at the time of Chris's conception. I did a clearing for that, but Chris has continued to have problems with dry eyes.

I asked the Holy Spirit questions that came to mind and learned that *a portion of a Soul from a previous lifetime of Mollie's was with Chris.* I will call that Soul **Drew.**[AP] Energies of witchcraft and autoimmune disorders, including dry eye disease, are attached to that Soul. I began sending much love and blessings to Chris' and Drew's Souls.

Three days later. Holy Spirit, are the love and blessings I sent Drew's Soul helping him? [| Y |] Is a spirit of disease, including eye disease, hanging over Chris? [| Y |] Is a portion of Mollie's Soul with me from a lifetime when she had an eye disease? [| Y |]

May 14, '13. My eyes have continued to bother me. Holy Spirit, is a portion of Drew's Soul in my aura in the area of my eyes? [| Y |] Chris is continuing to have problems, especially with his left eye. Do one or more Souls from Mollie's (Chris's) prior lifetimes need clearing related to energies of eye disease? [| Y |]

(!!!) Is a portion of Drew's Soul within the left eye of Chris's astral body? [| Y |] Wow, again!

I invited Mollie and Chris and all of their Souls from other lifetimes to take part as I did a process of forgiveness between them and other people and Souls for everything they or the others felt hurt and offended by and for any curses that others placed against them or their families and that they placed against others or their families.

Holy Spirit, please apply that process of forgiveness for hurts and curses to everyone in our family lines, especially to those with eye problems. Thank You!

3-C: CAL, JP CALEBAP AND YEZZI MP

Note: JP (Joel Prior life) is omitted after Cal, AP (Aunt Mollie Prior life) after Caleb, and MP (Me Prior life) after Yezzi in this section.

(Mar 31, '12)   MORE SOUL HISTORY

(!!!) Is an outside Soul with dark energy overseeing the dark energy center at the top of my head? [| Y |] Is it a portion of **Cal's Soul** *(Joel's Soul from a prior lifetime as a warlock)?* [| Y |]

Is Cal also overseeing some of the other dark energy centers set up in the Leigh family line? [| Y |] In the Goerger family line? [| Y |] In the Jahner family line? [| N |]

Are other unloving Souls in the Leigh, Goerger, and Jahner family lines acting as overseers for dark energy centers? [| Y |]

(Apr 3, '12) Did Mollie live at the same time as Cal? [| Y |] Was she his mother? [| N |] Sister? [| N |] Brother? [| Y |] *Twin brother?* [| Y |] I will call him **Caleb.** Did Caleb become a warlock? [| Y |]

Is Caleb helping oversee some of the dark energy centers in our family lines? [| Y |] Would he like to stop being an overseer?
[| Yes, but Cal is controlling those portions of his Soul and wants him to stay there. Cal can control Caleb because many portions of their Souls are enmeshed. |]

Did I live a lifetime at the same time as Cal and Caleb? [| Yes. You were their younger cousin, a boy named **Yezzi.** |]

Did Cal plant the seeds of witchcraft within Yezzi? [| Y |] Does he have a lot of control over Yezzi? [| Y |]

By asking the Holy Spirit more questions, I learned that Cal and Caleb offered Yezzi as a spiritual sacrifice for the sake of witchcraft, allowing those who were practicing witchcraft to use his energy to carry out their attacks. Yezzi's energy being used in that way resulted in him dying in a long-drawn-out fashion. One could say that he died "at the hands of" Cal and Caleb.

Holy Spirit, might Cal's Soul become loving if he would be

accepted, blessed, and loved as he is, without judgment? [| Y |] Is a portion of his Soul enmeshed with Joel's Soul? [| N |]

Is a portion of Cal's Soul with Joel much of the time? [| Y |] Is that Soul portion unloving? [| It is at the edge between loving and unloving. |]

Am I meant to clear the enmeshment between Cal's and Caleb's Souls? [| Yes, but ask Jesus to do it with you. |]

Are portions of my Soul in this lifetime enmeshed with Yezzi's Soul? [| Y |] Is Yezzi with Cal much of the time? [| Y |] Cal and Yezzi spend much of the time with Joel.

(Apr 5, '12)   Ministering to Cal, Caleb, and Yezzi

I asked Jesus and Lord Melchizedek to join me in clearing the enmeshment between Cal's and Caleb's Souls, Cal's and Yezzi's Souls, and Yezzi's and my Souls. Thank you, Jesus and Lord Melchizedek! Angels, please minister healing to Cal, Caleb, and Yezzi. Thank you!

(Apr 17, '12) I sense that Yezzi's Soul feels lost and afraid, that he is trying to find a way to go where he is meant to be. Is that correct? [| Y |] Is he reaching out for love? [| Y |] Are portions of Yezzi's Soul enmeshed with my Soul? [| Y |] With adult me? [| N |] With young parts of me? [| Y |]

Are the portions of Yezzi's Soul that hang around Joel enmeshed with Joel's Soul? [| Y |] Is Joel's Soul somewhat like a child? [| Y |] Does he have blessed simplicity? [| Y |]

Is a part of Yezzi's Soul enmeshed with Caleb's Soul? [| N |] Is part of Yezzi's Soul enmeshed with Cal's Soul? (Slow answer) [| Y |] Is a shade of Yezzi's Soul enmeshed with Cal's Soul? [| Y |] Would a clearing for the spirit of control from Cal free Yezzi? [| Y |]

1. I cleared the enmeshment between Yezzi's Soul and all parts of me and between Yezzi's Soul and Joel.
2. I cleared the shade of Yezzi's Soul from Cal's Soul.
3. I cleared the spirit of control from Cal's Soul.

Results of those prayers: All of the above clearings occurred except that the enmeshment between Yezzi's Soul and parts of me is not fully cleared. Thank You, Holy Spirit!

(Jul 22, '12)   Healing for Cal

I sensed that a Soul was present. "Cal" came to mind. Holy Spirit, is Cal present? [| Y |] I sensed that Cal objects to my clearing of energy centers. Archangel Michael, please stand between me and Cal's Soul. Thank you!

Holy Spirit, does Cal's Soul want help to become loving? [| Part of it does. |] When a part of a Soul becomes loving, and the rest is somewhat unloving, can the unloving portions remain with that Soul? [| Y |] With protection around them? [| Y |]

(!!!) Is part of Cal's Soul in a spiritual copper ring right now? [| Y |] Is he starting to feel better? [| Y |] Does he want to say, "Thank you!" to me? [| Y |] (Wow!) Did Cal show up so I would have this "conversation" with him as encouragement that the spiritual copper rings work? [| Y |] Does he want to do his part in helping bring healing to the family? [| Y |] Wow, again!

Are portions of Cal's Soul and other Souls of Joel's from previous lifetimes still overseeing dark energy centers? [| Y |] Is the portion of Cal's Soul that is present trying to help those other Souls and Soul portions become loving? [| Y |] That is great! Thank You, Holy Spirit!

(Aug 3, '12)   Breakthrough for Caleb

I learned from the Holy Spirit that unloving portions of Caleb's Soul are with my son Chad, with his two children, and in their home, and portions of his Soul are in my home.

The top of my head is bothering me a lot. Holy Spirit, is the portion of Caleb's Soul in my brain? [| Y |] Does it want help to become loving? [| Y |]

(!!!) Do all portions of Caleb's Soul that are with family members and me want help to become loving? (No answer.) Would most of them like help to become loving? [| Y |]

I poured a deluge of love and blessings to all portions of Caleb's Soul, cleared erroneous imprinting for him, and asked his guardian angel to guide portions of his Soul to the healing ring surrounding his Full Soul.

Holy Spirit, did all portions of Caleb's Soul that were with Chad and his children and in their home choose to become loving? [| Y |] Did they go to the healing ring surrounding Caleb's Full Soul? [| Y |]

Did the portions of Caleb's Soul that were *in my brain* choose to become loving? [| Y |] Did they leave? [| Y |] That's great!

Did the portions of Caleb's Soul that were in my home choose to become loving? [| Most of them did. |] Did all of them leave? [| Only those left that chose to become loving. Some unloving portions are still in your home. |]

Instead of immediately commanding those unloving portions of Caleb's Soul to leave my home, I felt prompted to pour a deluge of love and blessings out to them and to all other portions of his Soul wherever they are for 24 hours before directing them to leave. I feel good about doing that!

The next day, I commanded all Souls (Soul portions) that were in my home without permission to leave.

Thank You, Holy Spirit, for teaching and guiding me!

(Jun 10, '13)   CLEARING A CURSE

(!!!) **Holy Spirit, did Cal and Caleb place a curse of having eye problems, including autoimmune eye disease, on Yezzi?** [| Y |] Is that curse still in effect? [| Y |] That means that a curse of autoimmune eye disease is hanging over me! [| Y |] Is it hanging as a karmic curse over Cal's Soul? [| Y |] Over Caleb's Soul and Souls from other lifetimes of Mollie's? [| Y |]

For three days, I sent love and blessings to Caleb, Cal, and whoever else was involved in placing that curse. I asked that a Holy Spirit demagnetizing shower flowed along that curse's energy pathways ever since the curse was put in place.

(Jun 14, '13) Holy Spirit, is the curse of having eye problems cleared that Cal and Caleb placed against Yezzi? [| Y |] Great!

I sensed that Souls were present. (!!!) Holy Spirit, are Cal and Caleb here? [| Y |] Do they want to ask Yezzi to forgive them for placing that curse against him and letting witchcraft practitioners use his energy to carry out their attacks? [| Y |]

Yezzi forgave them. Bless you, Yezzi! Way to go!

End of 3-C: CAL, CALEB AND YEZZI

CHAPTER 4

MAIN TAPROOT UNCOVERED
Healing for Prior Lifetimes: Joel, Mollie, Me: 1 Each

Jul 1, '13   CLEARING MOLLIE'S (MY) SOUL LINE

So many concerns have surfaced connected with Souls from lifetimes of Mollie's/Grandma Leigh's/mine that I decided to do clearing for our Soul line. I asked Lord Melchizedek, Archangel Haniel, and the Ministry Team to do the clearing, with me joining in. I did a clearing for:

1. Erroneous early imprinting for Souls in our Soul line.
2. Curses that our Souls placed against others and others placed against us, followed by forgiveness between the Souls involved.

As I finished those prayers, I saw an image of Souls in Mollie's (our) Soul line who need healing gathered in a large orb. The Souls who were mostly healed were in the outer portion of the orb, those who needed a little healing were in the next layer going towards the middle, those who needed somewhat more healing were in the next layer, and those who needed a great deal of healing were in the center.

Holy Spirit, does Heaven Hospital have a room where many Souls can gather like that? [| Y |] Should I call it a Healing Orb? [| N |] A Healing Ball? [| N |] *A Ball Room?* [| Y |] I had to laugh!

Jun 30, '13   Curse of Autoimmune Eye Disease

Holy Spirit, when Mollie was a nun and practiced witchcraft in one of her lifetimes, did she place a curse of autoimmune eye disease against Sister Agatha (my sister Alice)? [| Y |] I will call Mollie **Sister Pacifica**^AP in that lifetime.

If that curse is still in effect, a karmic curse of autoimmune eye disorders would be hanging over all of Mollie's Souls. Is that curse hanging over Chris, a lifetime of Mollie's? [| Y |]

Something caused a portion of an unloving Soul, **Pierre,** to fuse with the loving Soul of Sister Pacifica. It was the "Pierre portion" of her Soul that practiced witchcraft. That portion split off during that lifetime.

I learned from the Holy Spirit that the karmic curse of autoimmune eye disease is cleared from Sister Pacifica but not from Pierre. A portion of Pierre's Soul is in the sinus and eye areas of Chris's etheric body, and a portion is in the sinus areas of my physical body and the eye area of my etheric body.

Holy Spirit, are we close to uncovering the root cause for Chris's eye problem and my sinus and eye problems? [| Y |]

I sensed a Soul was present. It was a portion of Pierre's Soul enmeshed with a portion of Sister Pacifica's Soul. Pierre was asking for help for their Souls to be separated and for him to become loving.

I did a process of forgiveness between Sister Pacifica and Pierre and cleared enmeshment between their Souls. I invited Pierre to receive the love and blessings I flowed to him and to choose to become loving. Then, I directed him to leave.

Ministry Team, please do spiritual surgery to trim the remaining portions of Pierre's Soul from Sister Pacifica's Soul. Thank you!

Aug 7, '13   Curses Still with Alice

[| Lorrie, you have "turned a corner" in having cleared out Soul portions from yourself that were quite negative and controlling. Please direct every day for all outside Soul portions to leave that do not have permission from the Holy Spirit or your Full Soul to be with you.

You have been wondering whether the sealed-off curses are still with Alice's Soul for being transported away when she crosses over. Yes, all is going as planned regarding them. You do not need to know or understand what is taking place. Please continue to bless Alice, her family, and All That Is. Thank you!

Peace to your inmost being, Lorrie! Yes, the thought you just had is from Me, that it is good to be somewhat prepared for the unexpected so that difficult situations do not throw you too much off-kilter. Sayonara! Shalom! |]

Thank You, Father God! Good evening!

Sept 27, '13   Why Do I Keep On?

I learned from the Holy Spirit that a portion of Drew's[AP] Soul is with me that is enmeshed with a spirit of autoimmune eye disease. Portions of his Soul are incorporated within cells in my body and enmeshed with my Soul. A spirit of autoimmune eye disease is incorporated within cells in my grandson Chris's body.

I cleared the enmeshment between the portion of Drew's Soul that was with me and the spirit of autoimmune eye disease. Then I cleared the incorporation of his Soul from within cells in my body and the enmeshment of his Soul with mine. I commanded him to leave.

I cleared the incorporation of the spirit of autoimmune eye disease from within cells in Chris's body and the enmeshment between those energies and Chris's Soul. I commanded those energies to leave.

You might wonder if I have ever felt like giving up on doing clearing, praying for healing, and so on. Yes, it felt at times like it was too much, but,

1. God gave me the task of clearing our family lines.
2. I am being guided by Spirit every step of the way.
3. Father-Mother God, the Holy Spirit, often assured me that clearing for our family lines will take place.
4. We are gaining ground.

I see the prayers for healing and clearing for family members in this lifetime and previous lifetimes as steps on the way. Thank You, God, for guiding me and being with me!

Oct 19, '13   "I Am Here for You"

(My ears became very warm.) Good morning, Fern!

[| <FERN> Good morning, Lorrie! You have been thinking that you have nobody to share lessons with that you receive from Spirit and your experiences with Souls, but you do! One of the reasons I left my earthly life earlier than expected was so I could be a constant spiritual companion for you.

You can share anything with me, aloud or in your thoughts. I hear and empathize with you whenever you think, "I'm not feeling well today. It is so hard to go on like this." You are sharing your feelings with God at the same time, of course. Sometimes, I place my hand on your shoulder or head and pray with you.

The Holy Spirit wants you to know that your prayers to be protected and filled with the light of Christ do a great deal of good. You have an unspoken wish for everyone else to be protected at the same time. That prayer of your heart is heard and answered. You are connected with everyone through the Network of Love. All loving prayers are instantly applied.

Have a good day, dear one! Peace to you and all! |]

Thank you very much, Fern! Bless you!

Nov 25, '13   SINS OF THE FATHERS

CAME TO MIND: Sins of the fathers.

"You shall not bow down to them or worship them, for I, the Lord your God, am a jealous God, punishing the children for the sin of the parents to the third and fourth generation of those who hate me" (NIV Ex 20:5, see note on Ez 18:2).

"The one who sins is the one who will die. The child will not share the guilt of the parent nor will the parent share the guilt of the child" (NIV Ez 18:2a).

Note on Ez 18:2: "A proverb was circulating in Jerusalem and Babylon that the children were suffering for the sins of their fathers.

Although there are cumulative effects of sin the Lord here declares that each individual is accountable for his own sin."

Punishment for sins of one's ancestors is not passed down to later generations, but *the effects* of those sins are. Children who were abused tend to abuse as adults. Anger, promiscuity, alcoholism, and so on tend to run in families. As I wrote that, I saw an image of a spider web with many Souls in our family lines caught in it. I need to dissolve that web.

I feel led by the Holy Spirit to select and print portions of Psalms in which the psalmist asks God for mercy and forgiveness and thanks God for setting him free.

Nov 26, '13   Prayers to Clear "Sins of Our Fathers"

Father, if I understand correctly, You are guiding me to pray in the name of ancestors in our family lines and my Soul line in atonement for "the sins of the fathers." I plan to pray portions of Psalms of Affirmation and Petition, Praise and Thanksgiving, and Repentance for nine days. Will praying those Psalms help clear the "sins of our fathers"?

[| Yes, Lorrie, praying those Psalms will bring about much clearing and healing. Ask for clearing and healing *for all of the ancestors of everyone in your family lines,* including the ancestors of your in-laws and of your children's in-laws, back to the 4th generation. And you can add, "and further back than that if need be."

Good night from all of Us! Peace to your inmost being! |]

Thank You, Father-Mother God, Holy Spirit, and Heart!

Nov 30, '13. I prayed the Psalms of Affirmation and Petition, Praise and Thanksgiving, and Repentance in the name of ancestors in our family lines and my Soul line for the first time today. (I prayed those Psalms for eight more days.)

I went through a process of forgiveness between those people (Souls) and asked for a protective valve in all soul ties and spiritual umbilical cords between them and other people and Souls.

Thank You, God, for the healing that is taking place!

Note: Those psalms are included in *Healing Across Time III* (Ch. 3.D.13).

Dec 8, '13   Searching for Answers

I asked the Holy Spirit about what might be causing me to have indigestion for such a long stretch. This morning, *voodoo* came to mind. I called Beth to help with getting answers. There are voodoo energies in the apartment below mine. Some of those energies are attached to an object in the room below my bedroom, and a spirit of voodoo is attached to a person who visits the people in that apartment.

Beth said to ask the Holy Spirit to seal my apartment's floors, ceilings, and walls with spiritual lead and not to sleep in my bedroom for two weeks.

Holy Spirit, did the voodoo energies in the apartment below me cause the indigestion I have been having? [| Y |] Is a spirit of Crohn's disease in my body? [| Y |] Do I have Crohn's only because of the presence of those voodoo energies? [| Y |]

Do some parts of me have a curse of Crohn's disease hanging over them? [| Y |] I trust that doing the 9-day clearing for my Soul line and our family lines will take care of several issues affecting me and parts of me.

I slept in the other bedroom. For the next two weeks, I asked the Holy Spirit each day to flow a Holy Spirit demagnetizing shower through my apartment to clear all negative energies and to seal the outside walls, floors, ceilings, and windows with spiritual lead. Thank You, Holy Spirit!

Jan 1, '14   Chicken Still a Problem

I am learning from experience that I have stomach discomfort if I don't bless chicken and fill it with love before I eat it. Holy Spirit, is chicken still being used as a contact point for dark energies? [| Y |] Is a curse hanging over the Leigh, Goerger, and Jahner family lines for chickens to be a contact point for dark energies? [| Y |]

(!!!) Does meat carry the animal's emotions at the time of slaughter? [| Y |] People who are sensitive to energies could easily be affected by that emotional energy.

4-A: KOR^{MP}, MAVA^{AP}, AND JUVA^{JP}

Note: [MP] (Me Prior life) is omitted after Kor, [AP] (Aunt Mollie Prior life) after Mava, and [JP] (Joel Prior life) after Juva in this section.

(Jan 16, '14)   I AM THE CULPRIT

I asked the Holy Spirit about my digestive problems that seem to be at least partially connected with eating chicken. What I learned was almost mind-blowing!

The curse connected with chicken is this: *When members of our family lines eat chicken (poultry), we ourselves place a contact point into the meat that attracts energies of the digestive disorders of Crohn's disease, irritable bowel syndrome, and general malfunctioning of the immune system.* A powerful thoughtform set up by higher negatives is the driving force behind the curse. It is continuing to affect Souls on the other side, also.

Dark energies caused a change in the DNA of the first people against whom that curse was placed, and, of course, that defective DNA was passed down in the family lines. We need to ask for the restoration of the perfect original DNA back in time within the first people whose DNA was altered and clear the dark energy thoughtform that caused that alteration.

Mollie was the first person targeted by that curse in a previous lifetime in which she practiced witchcraft. I will call her **Mava.** A warlock in cahoots with other male witches placed it against her and her family line. **I was that warlock, Kor.** I recall one of Father God's clues: "Being in it gives the key to unlocking it." Joel was a warlock named **Juva** during that same lifetime. Mava, Kor, and Juva knew each other.

Jan 17, '14   Tremendous Breakthrough

[| Bless you, child! The dark secret from your past lifetime as Kor that surfaced yesterday is a tremendous breakthrough for you, your family lines, and your Soul line: that you are the one who cursed the Leigh family many years back to have digestive problems. That seemingly unexplainable situation of digestive problems showing up willy-nilly for you and your immediate and extended family members is set to be reversed. Healing is (will be) taking place across time in regard to this.

"As the bird by wandering, as the swallow by flying so the curse causeless shall not come" (KJV Pr 26:2).

"Like a fluttering sparrow or a darting swallow, an undeserved curse does not come to rest" (NIV Pr 26:2).

What we will be doing together is removing the cause for the curse of stomach ailments that have beleaguered your family line, even to the extent of coming down with a vengeance on one of your children (Chad has Crohn's disease).

The same type of opening up is waiting in the wings regarding the plethora of autoimmune disorders and diseases that bespeckle your immediate and extended family lines. Your task for the last lengthy time and for a while yet going into the future was, is, and will be to allow for and assist the tremendous opening up of the causes for the numerous stomach ailments, autoimmune diseases, and other diseases that run rampant in the Leigh, Goerger, and Jahner family lines.

You sometimes wonder how Jesus was able to heal people on the spot. Did he know what curses or karma had played a part in that person's having been born blind, having contracted leprosy, or whatever? Yes. He saw all of the predisposing factors – which negative spirits were playing a part and so on – and applied the remedy of love to clear up those situations in the present.

We will be bringing into the present the time of Kor's (your) placing a curse on the Leigh family and family lines for a contact point for dark energies to be placed in the meat of chickens and other poultry by family members themselves. The clearing and healing will take place in the present, and the rejoicing by all family members who have been affected or are being affected by that curse will take place in the present.

Throughout this time of clearing and healing, no blame is to be placed on anybody because nobody deserves to be blamed. Good evening, Lorrie and Fern! Bless you! |]

Thank You, Father God, Holy Spirit! Bless You!

(Jan 22, '14)   TAPROOT FOR AI DISORDERS

Father God, would You like to say something?

[| Yes. You recently came to a clearer understanding regarding the curse that was placed on the Leigh (Mollie's) family; that when they eat chicken (poultry), they themselves place a contact point into the partially digested meat that attracts dark energies, including and especially the energies of autoimmune disorders, such as Crohn's, irritable bowel disease, and rheumatoid arthritis, with that dark energy going through them into the meat.

Recently, you learned that **you** placed that curse on Mava during your lifetime as Kor. **That curse is the TAPROOT for Crohn's disease and the many other autoimmune disorders that members of your families and family lines have been dealing with.** |]

That curse directly affects the Leigh family because Mollie and Grandma Leigh are later lifetimes of Mava's. The Goergers and Jahners are connected to the Leighs through marriage.

[| The journey you have been taking in tracking down the side roots of why your family is plagued with autoimmune disorders and now uncovering the root cause is the main story you are meant to tell. The clues I gave you pertain directly to this issue of the family being under a curse for many years:

"Smoke: fire somewhere. Growth: a plant. A plant has roots. Taproot most important." (Dec 11, '07)

We will let you ponder these thoughts over the coming days. The picture will get clearer as time goes on.

We are happy that you have released some of the anxiety you were feeling about finishing this writing project. That responsibility is not on your shoulders. Your task is to write or edit whatever Spirit asks you to do for the day.

Bless you, Lorrie and Fern! I will let you sign off now. []
Thank You, Father-Mother God, Holy Spirit, Heart!

(Jan 24, '14)   Prayers for Clearing and Healing

Each day this week:

1. I asked all loving Souls in our family lines and my Soul line to join me in sending love and blessings to Kor^{MP} and any others who took part in placing the curse connected with eating chicken on the Leigh family.

2. I asked the Holy Spirit to flow a demagnetizing shower along the energy pathways that the dark energies of that curse traveled on in reaching members of our families through the years. Thank You, Holy Spirit!

(Jan 26, '14) I cleared erroneous early imprinting for Kor and his cohorts and for everyone in the Leigh, Goerger, and Jahner family lines back to the 4th generation.

(Jan 30, '14) Ministry Team, please begin clearing the dark energy thoughtform that keeps the connection in place in our family lines for dark energy contact points to be placed in chicken (poultry) by the individuals themselves. Thank you!

(Feb 2, '14) Holy Spirit, is a karmic curse hanging over Kor for placing the curse connected with eating chicken on Mava, her family lines, and his Soul line? [| Y |] Is that curse also hanging over all of Kor's (my) descendants? [| Y |]

Did some of Kor's pals join him in placing that curse? [| Yes. They used a pentagram. |]

Ministry Team, please join me: "I dissolve the pentagram that Kor and his pals used in placing that curse on Mava."

Angels of the Violet Flame, please sweep through to transmute the negative energy of that pentagram to neutral energy and to clear all negative residue from the area. Thank you!

Holy Spirit, is the pentagram dissolved? [| Y |] Are all energies of it cleared? [| Y |] Thank You very much!

Holy Spirit, did Kor repent for placing the curse connected with eating chicken on Mava and her family and Soul line?

[| Yes, but the curse is not yet dissolved. |]

(Feb 6, '14) I went through a process of forgiveness between Kor and his cohorts and everyone in the Leigh, Goerger, and Jahner families and family lines.

Holy Spirit, have Kor's pals repented for helping place that curse on Mava, her family lines, and Soul line in that previous lifetime? [| Y |] Has the evil thoughtform connected with that curse been dissolved? [| N |] Is it sealed off? [| Y |]

(!!!) Holy Spirit, after Kor[MP] used witchcraft energies to place a curse on Mava, her family lines, and Soul line for each person to place a contact point into chicken meat (poultry) for attracting energies of autoimmune disorders, did Mava[AP] use witchcraft energies to place the same curse on Kor, his family lines, and Soul line? [| Y |]

(Oct 25, '14)   HYPNOTIC IMPLANTS

From what I gather, Mava[AP], Juva[JP], and Kor[MP] were in competition with their witchcraft abilities. This next turn of events that I learned about is almost unbelievable: Kor placed a curse on Mava, her family lines, and her Soul line:

Curse #1: *For the persons themselves to place a contact point for dark energies into chicken meat (poultry) by a hypnotized portion of Mava's Soul being enmeshed with each of her Souls in later lifetimes that would be programmed by a hypnotic suggestion (implant) to follow those directions.*

Mava retaliated by placing that same curse on Kor, his family lines, and Soul line, plus she placed a second curse on him:

Curse #2: *The curse of the spirit of lust,* and

Curse #3: *The curse of autoimmune diseases.*

It ended up that Kor, Mava, and Juva each placed those three curses against the other two!

The hypnotized portions of their Souls that are with people and Souls in their family lines will remain hypnotized until Mava, Kor, and Juva cancel the curse they placed against each other that caused a hypnotized portion of that person's Soul to be with everyone in that person's family line and Soul line.

The hypnotized portion of Kor's Soul that is with me is causing problems with my digestion, even when I ask for my food to be filled with Divine love. Part of his Soul is incorporated within cells in my stomach. On top of that, a hypnotized portion of Kor's Soul is enmeshed with the portions of my Soul that are with my children and is placing a contact point for dark energies into the chicken (poultry) they buy and eat!

Holy Spirit, does Mava's Soul want help to become free? [| Y |] Does Juva's Soul? [| Y |] Does Kor's Soul? [| Y |]

Nov 21, '14. One at a time, I went through a process of forgiveness between Mava, Juva, and Kor for having placed those curses against each other, their family lines, and Soul line, and for any other curses they placed against each other or other people.

Then, I invited people and Souls in the Leigh, Goerger, and Jahner family lines who wanted to ask others for forgiveness to join me as I asked for forgiveness from others and extended forgiveness to them. Thank You, Holy Spirit

(Nov 25, '14) Holy Spirit, is the curse of autoimmune disorders lifted from our family lines? [| Yes, but it is still hanging over some individuals in those families. |]

I learned that a small portion of Mava's Soul was attached to each curse she placed against Juva and Kor. The same is true for Juva and Kor: A small portion of their Soul was attached to each curse they placed against the other two. That is the case with every curse somebody makes.

Evening: Portions of Mava's and Kor's Souls that have gone to the light were present. They came to help the portions of their Souls that haven't released the curses to forgive each other and be set free. I asked the Ministry Team to join me:

1. I again went through a process of forgiveness between Mava, Juva, and Kor for them to cancel the curses they placed against each other.

2. I cleared the hypnotic suggestion from the portion of Kor's Soul that was with me.

3. I did a retroactive clearing of incorporation of Mava's, Juva's, and Kor's Souls from within cells in my body

4. I cleared enmeshment between Mava's, Juva's, and Kor's Souls and my Soul and between each of their Souls.

5. Commanded all portions of their Souls that were with me without permission from the Holy Spirit to leave.

Holy Spirit, is the hypnotic suggestion cleared from the portion of Kor's Soul that was in my head? [| Y |] Did all portions of Mava's, Juva's, and Kor's Soul leave that were with me without permission? [| Y |] Thank You, Holy Spirit! Ministry Team!

Are there still hypnotized portions of Mava's, Kor's, and Juva's Souls within people and Souls In our family lines? [| Y |] I asked about various percentages and learned that hypnotized portions of Mava's, Juva's, and Kor's Souls are within about 90% of people's Souls in their family lines and Soul line. There is still much clearing to do!

(Mar 8, '15)   Ring of Negative Thoughtforms

There are sore spots in a circle at the top of my head. Holy Spirit, are those spots contact points for dark energies? [| Y |] By asking more questions, I learned that two of the sore spots are contact points for energies of autoimmune disorders that were put in place as a result of the curses Mava[AP] and Juva[JP] placed against me in my lifetime as Kor[MP] and two are a karmic result of Kor's placing the same curse against Mava and Juva.

Speaking for and with Kor, I again expressed sorrow to Mava and Juva for placing a curse on them, their family lines, and Soul line and asked for their forgiveness.

Holy Spirit, are negative thoughtforms with tiny Soul portions caught within them attached to those contact points? [| Y |] Are there many Soul portions in those thoughtforms from Mava's, Juva's, and Kor's Souls and family lines? [| Y |] I will ask the Ministry

Team to join me for nine days of clearing for those contact points and negative thoughtforms.

[| Yes, do that. |]

(Mar 19, '15) Each day for the last nine days, I asked the Ministry Team to join as I did a clearing for the dark energy contact points and the negative thoughtforms attached to them and prayed for healing for the Soul portions caught in those thoughtforms. I also asked again that the curse of autoimmune disorders that Mava, Juva, and Kor placed against each other and each other's family lines and Soul lines be cleared. Thank you, Ministry Team, for your assistance!

Has the curse of autoimmune disorders been cleared:
1. That Mava placed against Juva and Kor and their family lines and Soul line? [| Yes, for all who were willing. |]
2. That Juva placed against Mava and Kor and their family lines and Soul line? [| Yes, for all who were willing. |]
3. That Kor placed against Mava and Juva and their family lines and Soul line? [| Yes, for all who were willing. |]

Has the karmic curse of autoimmune disorders been cleared that rested on each of them for placing that curse against the others? [| Yes, for all three. |] Wonderful!

Have all the contact points at the top of my head related to the curse of autoimmune disorders been cleared? [| Y |] Wonderful! Thank You, Father-Mother God, Holy Spirit, and Heart! This is such good news! I can hardly believe it.

(Mar 22, '15)   Ring of Implants

The Holy Spirit said the contact points at the top of my head related to the curse of autoimmune disorders have been cleared, but I still have just as much discomfort, if not more.

(!!!) Holy Spirit, are there *implants* at the top of my head where the contact points had been? [| Y |] Should I ask the Ministry Team to clear those implants? [| N |] Should I ask the Medical Assistance Team to clear them? [| Y |]

Evening: I asked the Medical Assistance Team to clear the

implants at the top of my head while I lay on the couch for 30 minutes. Thank You, Medical Assistance Team!

Holy Spirit, are those implants cleared from my head? [| Y |] Should I ask the Medical Assistance Team to minister to me again for clearing and healing? [| Y |]

Two days later, I asked the Medical Assistance Team to minister to me for clearing and healing for whatever was needed. Thank you, Medical Assistance Team!

(Mar 23, '15) I learned from the Holy Spirit that a spirit of lust is in my astral body. Also, a spirit of lust is attached to several people and Souls In the Leigh, Goerger, and Jahner family lines. Ministry Team, please join me as I do a clearing for myself and my (our) family lines for the spirit of lust. Thank you!

I did a clearing for it.

Holy Spirit, is the spirit of lust cleared from my astral body? [| Y |] From all parts of me affected by it, if any? [| Y |]

Is the spirit of lust cleared from everyone in the Leigh family/ family lines who was willing to have it cleared? [| Y |]

Is the spirit of lust cleared from everyone in the Goerger family (family lines) who was willing to have it cleared? [| Y |]

Is the spirit of lust cleared from everyone in the Jahner family/ family lines who was willing to have it cleared?
[| No, some of those people and Souls need more prayer. |]

(Sept 3, '15)   Curse Using Chicken Still in Effect

Holy Spirit, I had digestive problems for the last six weeks. Is the curse that draws negative energies into chicken meat still in effect within me? [| Y |] (!!!) Is that because it isn't cleared from some of my Souls from other lifetimes? [| Y |]

Does the partially digested chicken in my digestive system attract witchcraft energies? [| Y |] If I ask the Holy Spirit to fill the chicken with love, will it be safe for me to eat it? [| Y |]

(May 1, '16) Holy Spirit, I have had digestive problems for the last several months. Is the curse connected with eating chicken that was placed against Kor, his family lines, and his Soul line still in effect within me? [| Y |] Is eating chicken the main cause for my stomach being upset? [| Yes. Also, there is a spirit of indigestion in your stomach. |]

I did another clearing for the curses connected with eating chicken that Mava and Juva placed against Kor, his family line, and his Soul line. I also did clearing for the spirit of indigestion. Thank You, Holy Spirit!

(Jun 6, '16) (!!!) Holy Spirit, is a karmic curse hanging over Mava's[AP], Juva's[JP], and Kor's[MP] Souls from other lifetimes related to their having placed those curses against each other? [| Y |] Do curses need to be cleared from every Soul in a person's Soul line? [| Y |] There is sure a lot to learn!

(Feb 4, '17)   INTRICATE ENMESHMENTS

My stomach has been very unsettled. Is it maybe trying to clear something out? I asked the Holy Spirit about it.

I learned that a portion of Joel's Soul, whose energy is incompatible with my energy, attached itself to me two days ago. Also, a portion of Juva's[JP] Soul is with me that is holding extreme hostility towards me and doesn't want to leave has been in my abdomen for a long time. It is enmeshed with the young boy and adult female parts of me but not with the main persona-me. Energies of condemnation and murder are attached to that portion of Juva's Soul. (Wow!)

Besides that, an unloving portion of Mava's[AP] Soul and other Souls with negative energy are enmeshed with the portion of Juva's Soul that is in my abdomen. *Those Soul portions are with parts of me that allowed them to enter.* Holy Spirit, is it time to send the parts of me away whose energy level is incompatible with mine? [| Y |]

(Feb 5, '17) I sealed all portions of Juva's and Mava's Souls that are with me with spiritual lead. I cleared enmeshment between Juva's and Mava's Souls and between their Souls and all parts of me. I asked Archangel Michael and Mighty Astrea to assist, then

349

commanded all portions of Juva's and Mava's Souls to leave along with all parts of my Soul that are enmeshed with their Souls, that refused to separate from them. Father God, I entrust those parts of my Soul into Your care. Thank You! (I coughed to assist with their leaving.)

Holy Spirit, did all portions of Juva's and Mava's Souls leave that had been with me? [| Y |] Did all parts of me leave that were enmeshed with Juva's and Mava's Souls? [| Y |]

Wonderful! Thank you, Holy Spirit, Archangel Michael, and Mighty Astrea!

(Feb 18, '17) I have an unusual aching in the top left of my head, and my stomach is unsettled. I learned from the Holy Spirit that a "part of me" that isn't a real part has been allowing Soul portions to enter without permission from the Holy Spirit. That "part" consists of *portions of Juva's and Mava's Souls that entered my Soul at the time of my conception* and have been with me ever since, enmeshed with portions of my Soul and incorporated within cells in my body.

Those portions of Juva's and Mava's Souls were unloving when they entered but are somewhat loving now. They want help to become more loving.

Holy Spirit, did those portions of Mava's and Juva's Souls have permission from the Holy Spirit to join with my Soul at the time of my conception so they would eventually have a chance to become loving? [| Y |] Wow!

Please place a protective valve in every connection between portions of Juva's and Mava's Souls and my Soul and between their Souls. Thank You, Holy Spirit!

I began placing a firewall around every part of me daily. (I don't know If I commanded Juva's and Mava's Souls to leave.)

(Apr 18, '18) As I was about to leave work today, I discovered that the Microsoft Outlook program and the Outlook files had disappeared from the computer. (A computer technician reinstalled it the next day and recovered our files.)

(!!!) Holy Spirit, did a portion of Juva's Soul cause the Outlook program to be deleted so I would ask about it and learn that he wants help to become loving? [| Y |] He is desperate!

Each day for the next two weeks, I asked my Full Soul and all loving Souls in my family lines and Soul line to join in sending love and blessings to Juva's, Mava's, and Kor's Souls and to every person (Soul) in our family lines and my Soul line who is asking for help. Bless all of you!

End of 4-A: KOR^{MP}, MAVA^{AP}, AND JUVA^{JP}

Jan 18, '14   LEARNING MORE

Circle of healing came to mind along with the understanding that as living family members learn to love and bless everyone, including their ancestors, their forgiveness, love, and blessing prompt those of their ancestors who are still holding resentments and curses against family members to drop the resentments and cancel the curses. As those ancestors are healed, healing flows down to their many descendants, wiping out diseases and helping reunite families. A big WOW! Thank You, Holy Spirit, for telling me that!

Feb 6, '14. Are tiny portions of the Souls of people in our families and family lines caught in the evil thoughtform that energizes dark energy contact points within members of our families? [| Y |] Is a portion of my Soul caught in it? [| Y |] Is a portion of the Soul of every person in our families (family lines) who had (has) autoimmune disease caught in it? [| Y |] Wow!

Are those Soul portions sealed so that no negative energy from that evil thoughtform can travel from them to that person (Soul)? [| N |] Holy Spirit, please place a protective shield around all Soul portions caught up in that evil thoughtform. Thank You!

Are those Soul portions protected now? [| Y |] Thank You!

Feb 11, '14. (!!!) Holy Spirit, besides the evil thoughtform keeping the connection between chicken (poultry) and autoimmune diseases in place, are other negative thoughtforms of autoimmune diseases hanging over the Leigh, Goerger, and Jahner families and family lines that we created by believing we cannot escape having autoimmune diseases because "they run in the family"? [| Y |]

Are tiny portions of the Souls of family members who had or have that disease (or are afraid they will get it) caught up in those thoughtforms [| Y |]

Ministry Team, please begin clearing the energies of autoimmune diseases from the negative thoughtforms hanging over individuals and families in our family lines and freeing the Soul portions caught in them. Thank you!

Feb 21, '14. My system acted like I had taken a laxative. Holy Spirit, were there negative energies in the chicken I ate last evening? [| Y |] Were the energies of fear and anguish that the chicken experienced when being slaughtered in the meat? [| Y |] No wonder my digestion has been acting up!

Would taking these steps before eating chicken clear negative energies that may be within or attached to it: Thank the chicken for being willing to have its body be food for people, bless it at every moment of its life, and ask God that the chicken's soul will have left its body shortly before being slaughtered so it will not have had to experience pain and fear? [| Y |]

I began taking those steps before eating chicken. Thank You, Holy Spirit, for telling me about this!

Apr 27, '14   Clearing For "Inherited" Diseases

Holy Spirit, I sense a method will open up for clearing the roots of inherited diseases. [| Y |] Does a person need to know which branches of their family lines need clearing? [| N |] When many people in a family are affected by the same disease(s), does that indicate that people (Souls) in their family lines may not be at peace? [| Y |]

Will placing disease energies in a copper ring be part of the process for clearing those energies from families (family lines)? [| Y |] I understand that another part of the process would be to ask to have a large spiritual copper ring placed around each family group, with many of the people and Souls In the family being present in two or more of the copper rings, such as with their birth family, with their spouse and children, and with their spouse's birth family. [| That is correct. |]

Will taking those steps for clearing disease energies and the roots of diseases follow various other clearings for family lines? [| Y |] Have I done enough clearing that it would be OK to ask for people and Souls In my (our) family lines to be ministered to in large spiritual copper rings? [| Y |]

I understand that I (we) should also have a ceremony in which we bless and extend love and recognition to everyone in our families and family lines, especially to those who did not feel loved and welcomed during their lifetime. [| Y |]

Is having the energies of an autoimmune disease in the marrow of their large bones one cause for somebody having that disease? [| Y |] Asking for the restoration of the perfect original blueprint for every cell in the person's body would clear those energies.

May 7, '14. Ministry Team, please join me as I do more clearing for our family lines. Thank you!

I intend for the energies of autoimmune disease to be cleared from every person (Soul) in our family lines, including from the Soul portions caught in dark energy thoughtforms hanging over some of the people and Souls In our families.

I placed slips of paper with the names of autoimmune disorders written on them in my large copper ring, including one that said, "All other autoimmune disorders." I left the slips of paper in the copper ring for two weeks.

Holy Spirit, please place a large spiritual copper ring around every family in the Leigh, Goerger, and Jahner family lines in which one or more family members: Had or have an autoimmune disease or have energies of autoimmune diseases in their DNA.

Please include families of grandparents and great-grandparents as far back as is necessary for clearing autoimmune diseases from individuals and families in our family lines. I ask for the spiritual copper rings to stay in place for as long as needed for those people and Souls to be cleared and healed. Thank You!

During my prayer time for the next two weeks, I asked the Ministry Team to join me in praying for the individuals and their families in the spiritual copper rings and to continue ministering to them for another 45 minutes afterward.

The praying and clearing that we did, in random order:

1. We went through a process of forgiveness between people and Souls in our three family lines as a group, focusing on canceling and asking forgiveness for curses they placed against others.
2. We did clearing of erroneous early imprinting.
3. We asked for the restoration of the perfect original blueprint for every cell in each person's body at the time of conception.
4. We asked for a spirit of healing to hover over each person, Soul, and family, for healing to flow through them.

Jun 21, '14. (!!!) Saying, "I am not OK as I am," could trigger one's body to attack itself through autoimmune disorders!

Holy Spirit, is the judging of ourselves and others that members of our families and I have done through the years *an additional primary root of the curse of autoimmune disorders* that has been (is) hanging over us? [| Y |]

Jul 7, '14   Contact Points for Dark Energy

Holy Spirit, is it true that a curse was placed on the Leigh family line that set it up that when we buy or eat chicken (poultry), we ourselves place a contact point for dark energies in it? [| Y |] When the meat gets digested, do those contact points cling to the walls of our esophagus, stomach, intestines, and bladder? [| Y |] Are many of the contact points for dark energies placed in chicken meat through the years still here and there throughout my body? [| Y |]

(!!!) Is a dark energy center in my right hip causing it to be continually sore? [| Y |] Does that energy center have several contact points for dark energy that settled in that area? [| Y |] Would a clearing for the contact points clear that energy center? [| Y |] That sounds promising!

Jul 14, '14. I met with Pastor Joyce for prayer to clear contact points for dark energy from within me and our family lines. I explained to her briefly about the curse connected to eating chicken placed on our family lines in the distant past and that I learned from the Holy Spirit that many such contact points have built up in my body through the years.

Pastor Joyce anointed me with Rose of Sharon oil and asked God to clear all contact points for dark energy from within me and everyone in our family lines.

Jul 17, '14. Holy Spirit, are all contact points for dark energies cleared from within me? [| Y |] Are they all cleared from everybody in our family lines? [| Y |] Did Pastor Joyce's prayer and the anointing with Rose of Sharon oil play a large part in that clearing? [| Y |] Thank You, God!

Nov 3, '16   Spirits of Death and Judgment

Holy Spirit, did a spirit of death enter me early in this lifetime? [| Y |] At the time of oral sexual abuse by Grandpa Leigh when I was three months old? [| Y |] By asking more questions, I learned that a spirit of judgment is enmeshed with that spirit of death. Some of those dark energies are in my brain.

Nov 7, '16. As I was thinking about a spirit of judgment being within me, I saw an image of a filmy mesh encompassing our family. I understood that if somebody clears the spirit of judgment from themselves, they quickly get filled with it again from the spirit of judgment that is with other family members.

Holy Spirit, is that how things work with a spirit of judgment and other negative energies? [| Y |] I sense it would be almost useless to try to clear a spirit of judgment or other negative energies from one person unless the family is included. Is that correct? [| Y |]

I did clearing for myself for the spirits of death and judgment and asked that those prayers be applied to every person and Soul in the Leigh, Goerger, and Jahner families and family lines. Thank You, Holy Spirit!

Nov 9, '16. Holy Spirit, is there a passageway for dark (negative) energies to enter me? [| Yes. Dark forces are trying to get at you in

every possible way. [] Are Souls that are above my head flowing as much negative energy into me as they can?
[| Yes, portions of Mava's[AP] and Juva's[JP] Souls. |]

Are those portions of their Souls being controlled by dark forces? [| N |] Did they join the dark forces? [| Y |]

Rhetorical question: What else is "coming down the pipe"?

Jul 25, '19   MAJOR CLEARING FOR OUR FAMILY LINES

I received directions from the Holy Spirit that it is time to do clearing for the combined spirits of lust and incest still hanging over the Leigh, Goerger, and Jahner families and family lines and that my sister Ann and I are to do that clearing. I will tell Ann about the situation and arrange a time for us to do the clearing. I will also tell her about my brother-in-law Lee being the father of several of my children. (That is OK with the Holy Spirit.)

Roots of the spirit of lust

A karmic curse of lust is hanging over Joel's Soul from the lifetime when he placed the curse of the spirit of lust against the Leigh family (but not over his Soul in this lifetime). The spirit of lust still hangs over the three family lines because of that karmic curse. There are *roots of the spirit of lust* within the Souls of family members who took part in lustful practices in convents and abbeys during previous lifetimes. There are other roots, as well.

I did more clearing during the last two weeks.

Aug 17, '19. Holy Spirit, has the curse of the spirit of lust been cleared from many individuals in our family lines? [| Y |] Great! My prayers for individuals and families *have* been doing some good!

Is a *spirit of incest* within or hanging over individuals and families in our family lines? [| Y |] Is it hanging over Ron's birth family? [| N |] Over his paternal grandparents' family? [| N |] Over his maternal grandparents' family?

[| Yes. Ron's Grandpa Conrad is a descendant of Mava's[AP] family, so he and his family are affected by the curses that Mava, Juva[JP], and Kor[MP] placed on each other and their descendants. |]

Holy Spirit, Is the aching in my lower back and the stiffness I have been having in my legs caused by energies of the curse of the spirit of lust and autoimmune disorders? (Strong:) [| Y |]

Aug 27, '19. I met with Ann to tell her about our families/family lines needing clearing for the spirits of lust and incest and that the Holy Spirit is asking the two of us to do it. I told her I would prepare a printout for us to follow and would meet with her again when I had it ready. I also told her about my brother-in-law Lee being the father of several of my children. She accepted that calmly without judging me. I have never sensed even a smidgeon of judgment from Ann about anything I have shared with her. Thank you, Ann! Bless you!

Sept 11, '19   Negative Energies in Family DNA

Holy Spirit, I have been thinking about the "contumely" that was dumped on me. You said my "gunky energy needs to be replaced with pure, clean energy." Are negative energies here and there throughout my body? [| Y |] Attached to my DNA? [| Y |] Are energies of the curses of the spirits of lust and autoimmune disorders within my body? [| Y |] Are those energies incorporated within cells in my body? [| Y |]

Are energies of the curses of the spirits of lust and autoimmune disorders within some of the cells in the bodies of family members? [| Y |] Are energies of those curses still hanging over (attached to) the Souls of some of the members of our family lines who have crossed over? [| Y |] Overall clearing is needed.

Was the "contumely story" a way of saying that junk was passed on to me and individuals in our family lines in our DNA? [| Y |] Would it lessen the effects of family distress on us if I (we) would seal all negative energy in the DNA of people in our family lines? [| Y |]

In the name of Jesus, I seal all negative energies within the DNA of everyone in the Leigh, Goerger, and Jahner family lines with triple-strength spiritual lead. Thank You, Holy Spirit!

Sept 28, '19. Ann and I went through the steps for clearing the curses of the spirits of lust and incest and other curses that are hanging over individuals and families in the Leigh, Goerger, and Jahner family lines and over the family lines themselves. I asked the Ministry Team and all loving Souls in our family lines to join us as we did the clearing.

I won't list all of the steps of clearing and healing that we did, but they included clearing negative energies, praying for the healing of each person (Soul) as needed, and, very importantly, a process of forgiveness between individuals and between families.

Thank You, Ministry Team and loving Souls in our family lines, for joining Ann and me as we prayed for clearing and healing for our family lines! Thank You, Holy Spirit!

Jan 1, '20   Making Progress

I learned that portions of Mava's[AP], Juva's[JP], Kor's[MP], and Yezzi's[MP] Souls are with me. Some of the curses they placed against each other have not been cleared. I reapplied all the prayers I said earlier to clear curses from them and the family lines. I did a brief process of forgiveness between Mava's, Juva's, Kor's, and Yezzi's Souls, cleared negative energies from them, did a retroactive clearing of incorporation of portions of their Souls from within cells in my body, cleared enmeshments between their Souls and my Soul and directed them to leave. They left. Thank You, Holy Spirit!

Jun 14, '20. I have been having a lot of stomach discomfort lately. Holy Spirit, is a hypnotized portion of Kor's Soul in my brain creating a contact point for dark energies within the chicken I eat? (No answer.) Is a hypnotized portion of Kor's Soul in the "astral brain" of some of my Souls from other lifetimes that has been creating a contact point for negative energies within my digestive system when I eat chicken? [| Y |]

(!!!) Is there a spiritual umbilical cord connection between my Soul and some of my Souls from other lifetimes? [| Y |] Does that connection allow the hypnotized portion of Kor's Soul within their astral brain to affect me? [| Y |] Is that the main cause of the stomach distress I have been having? [| Y |]

Holy Spirit, please seal with spiritual lead all of the Souls and bodies of those people who have a hypnotized portion of Kor's Soul within the brain of their physical or astral body that is programmed to create a contact point for negative energies in the chicken (poultry) that they eat. Thank You! Will that help me to have less stomach distress? [| Y |] Thank You!

Is the curse connected with eating chicken still hanging over the Goerger and Leigh family lines? [| Y |]

Aug 8, '21. (!!!) Holy Spirit, following the wish of my Higher Self, did my Soul agree to be a clearing point for clearing hypnotized portions of Kor's Soul from the astral bodies of Souls in our family lines? [| Y |] Learning that helps me feel better. It isn't that I have been failing to follow the leading of the Holy Spirit but that I wasn't meant to learn about this agreement earlier. I trust You, Holy Spirit!

Mar 1, '22. Is a portion of Kor's Soul with me? [| Y |] Is it unloving? [| Y |] Did his Soul come in unloving? [| N |] Is a *manic spirit* controlling that portion of Kor's Soul by a hypnotic spell? [| Y |] *Beelzebub?* [| Y |] Is Beelzebub an actual being? [| Y |]

Lord Melchizedek and the rest of the Ministry Team, please clear the hypnotic spell that Beelzebub placed on the unloving portion of Kor's Soul that is with me. Thank you!

Is the distress that I pick up from Souls, including Kor, Mava, and Juva, the main reason I am continuing to have an upset stomach? [| Y |] Thank You, Holy Spirit!

I called Beth to ask her to do long-distance clearing for me. She did a Holy Spirit vacuuming. Thank you, Beth!

May 1, '22   Clearing Snags

Holy Spirit, are some of the curses still in effect that were placed against me in earlier lifetimes? [| Y |] Are those that Juva[JP] placed against Kor[MP] and his family line still in effect? [| N |] Are those that Mava[AP] placed against Kor and his family line still in effect? [| Y |] Are those that Kor placed against Mava and her family line still in effect?

[| Y |] The curses placed by Kor and those placed against him are the ones that are not cleared.

Speaking with and as Kor, I repented for and canceled the curses that he made many times. (!!!) Is an unloving Soul with Kor that is preventing the curses from being canceled so I will eventually realize that his Soul wants help? [| Y |] By asking more questions, *I learned that an unloving Soul is with Kor – a portion of 9-year-old Lorrie! She is in the right place for unloving Souls and wants help to become loving so she can leave there.* A Soul named *Portia* is taking care of her. Thank you, Portia!

Loving Souls in my Soul and family lines, please join me in sending many blessings and love to that portion of 9-year-old Lorrie. Bless you, young Lorrie! I love you! We love you!

Mighty Astrea, Lord Melchizedek, and Jesus, please rescue 9-year-old Lorrie from the right place for unloving Souls. Young Lorrie's guardian angel, please assist her to go where she is meant to be. Thank all of you!

(The next day) Holy Spirit, has young Lorrie been rescued from the right place for unloving Souls? [| Y |] Good! Thank You!

Jul 28, '22. [| Lorrie, I reaffirm all the words of assurance and encouragement I spoke to you through the years. Your ministry to the family is uncovering and removing the causes of the curse of autoimmune disorders that have plagued the Leigh (your mother's birth) family line and the Goerger (your birth) family line through the years. Peace to you and all! |]

Thank You Father-Mother God! Bless You!

Oct 3, '22. My stomach has been quite sore all summer and fall despite having taken three 2-week courses of medication for an irritated stomach. Holy Spirit, are there contact points for negative energies in the lining of my stomach? [| Y |] Should I ask the Medical Assistance Team to do a clearing? [| Y |]

Later, I lay down for 30 minutes. Medical Assistance Team, please clear contact points for negative energies that are located within my digestive system or elsewhere. Thank you!

That night, I asked them to do more clearing.

The next day. Holy Spirit, are all contact points for negative energies cleared from my stomach lining and elsewhere in my digestive system? [| Y |] Wonderful! Thank You!

Oct 5, '22   Running a Race

I had to cry as I sat down for a time of quiet. I haven't been staying in touch with my emotions enough. A big part of feeling like crying is that it has been hard having my stomach hurting (irritated) for such a long while. I ask for healing for that, Father God! I ask that all curses that we (people and Souls) placed against others and thus against ourselves as a karmic curse be fully canceled and cleared. Lord, have mercy!

I received the understanding that I am "running a race," doing what I have come here, been called, to do. Father-Mother God, Holy Spirit, You often assured me that I am not alone in running this race. The Scripture comes to mind that those who complete the race are the ones who will receive the prize.

Once again, Father, I place my whole self and everything and everyone into Your hands. I place the clearing and healing for the Leigh, Goerger, and Jahner family lines in Your hands. Thank You that my brother Joel is a partner in this endeavor. I offer You these prayers along with all the unexpressed prayers in my heart and spirit and in the hearts of each and all of Your children.

I ask that every bit of condescension and judgment that remains within my mind and Soul in this lifetime and every lifetime be dissolved. Thank You for hearing my prayer!

[| Lorrie, dear one, I hear your prayers and the prayers of each of my children throughout time and eternity. Please remember that while you are living a human life, you are a "perfect imperfect human being." As you have pondered before, who would set the standards for perfection, anyway? Every person and Soul would have their own ideas.

I will let you go on with your day now. Peace! All is well! |]

Thank You, Father! You are a delight!

Nov 9, '22   More About Kor^{MP} and Mava^{AP}

(!!!) Holy Spirit, is there a pain implant in my brain? [| Y |] Does it trigger pain in my lower back and hips? [| Y |] Was it put in place by a Soul on the other side that was angry with me in an earlier lifetime? [| Y |]

By asking more questions, I learned from the Holy Spirit that Mava placed a pain implant within Kor's head during the lifetime they shared. It is *that implant* that is in my head. It had been with a portion of Kor's Soul in the astral plane, but the Holy Spirit allowed it to be transferred to me so it would get cleared. The persistent knocking sounds coming lately from my bathroom floor are signals from Kor asking for help. Mava's Soul is about one-third between unloving and loving.

That night, I asked the Medical Assistance Team to remove the pain implant from my brain while I slept. Thank you, Team!

Nov 12, '22. Holy Spirit, is the pain implant cleared from my brain? [| Y |] Is the portion of Mava's Soul that placed that pain implant within Kor's head now loving? [| Y |] That's wonderful!

Nov 30, '22   IT IS ACCOMPLISHED

I have done my best to follow the guidance of the Holy Spirit through the years as I prayed for clearing and healing for myself, members of the Leigh, Goerger, and Jahner families, and our family lines. I prayed for the same intentions many times, especially for clearing curses. You may have read or heard that one should pray about something only once and then give thanks. Is it OK to pray for the same intention many times? I say, "Yes."

"The original New Testament text...used the Greek present tense which implies continuous action...'Ask and keep on asking, and it shall be given you; seek and keep on seeking, and you shall find; knock and keep on knocking, and the door shall be opened to you'"(Lk 11:9 AMP).[2]

"The Master counseled persistency in his parable of the widow and the unjust judge. Jesus prayed three times for the same purpose in the garden of Gethsemane and did he not say that men, 'need to pray always and not to lose heart' (Lk 18:1)?" (Cady p. 7)

I learned about the importance of persistence in prayer from experiences Emilie Cady had that she tells about:

First Situation

Feeling led by God to do so, Emilie decided to quit sending bills to her clients and trust God to supply all of her needs. After two years of living in want "...she cried out to God, '...You told me in the vision that if I would...trust to You alone, You would prove to me Your sufficiency. Why have You failed to do it?'" She received the understanding that she needed to say the words, to declare: "God is supplying all of my needs." (Cady p. 9)

Second Situation

Emilie had been praying for five years that false charges against her elderly father would be dropped so he could return home, with no result. "One day she made an impassioned plea to God for his deliverance and was told that she, acting as God's agent, must declare his freedom." (To say, "My father is a free man.") She obeyed that direction, and her father was set free in a few days! (Cady p. 7)

(!!!) **Holy Spirit, do You want me to declare that the clearing and healing for our family lines that I am meant to be part of has been accomplished? [| Y |]**

I said aloud: "*I declare that the clearing and healing for the Leigh, Goerger, and Jahner family lines that I am meant to be part of has been accomplished!*"

Thank You, Father-Mother God, Holy Spirit, and Heart, for the healing and clearing that has taken place for individuals and families in the Leigh, Goerger, and Jahner family lines. Thank You for calling my brother Joel to be a partner in this endeavor. Please guide and uphold him as he continues to pray for our family and family lines. Thank You!

I will close off and say "Amen" to *Healing Across Time II*. Peace!

Dec 2, '22   SEE A DIFFERENT FUTURE

CAME TO MIND: Goof off. Nimbus. Nimble. Thimble. END.
[| Lorrie, even a thimbleful of hope is a great gift. Your writings will be, and even now are, offering many people thimblefuls and deep draughts of hope. Connection is ongoing between members of the Sonship and between Me and My sons and daughters, although much of it is on the spirit level and not consciously recognized by the vast majority of people who are yet living.

Many Souls in the astral plane are eagerly taking in the freeing messages coming forth and are on the watch for more, similar to how baby birds wait for the food the mother and father birds bring them. Believe this, Lorrie, even if your material were to stay in the form and at the stage it is at present, there has been and will continue to be much upliftment and freeing taking place within the Souls of your brothers and sisters in the Sonship because of it!

It is not just that a number of those Souls hear a message when it comes forth and receive further freeing. They pass the word along, with all Souls hearing that message instantaneously. That takes place as a message to understand with their mind and Spirit and as the spiritual essence of freedom, love, peace, joy, and hope for a better tomorrow flowing through them. The river of living water is flowing out to many! Thank you for being a channel for My Spirit! |]

You are welcome, Father-Mother God!
[| My sons and daughters, many of you are wondering: What is in the works? In the workings of the universe? Of your mind? Of Mother Earth? Situations that at one time appear almost certainly to be "in the works" can be changed by one's intention, by blessing Mother Nature and those involved in the situation, by seeing a different future. Even I cannot tell you what is in the works for you.

Your Higher Self, the Holy Spirit, has a plan and aspirations for you during this lifetime and for the future. The more closely you listen to your Higher Self, to the Holy Spirit, the more satisfying your life will be.

Love every part of your body and your life, past and present. Be open to life with the love of everything and everyone around you. Love yourself in every situation. Do not be afraid of twinges of fear you may feel when being asked to affirm what you believe or to step out to minister to others.

I am alive within you! I walk and work amongst you, My spirit children. Do not look or feel askance towards anyone, not even the ones that the "I know better" society considers "no-gooders." You will be blest in living in this manner. Look ahead with joy and know that the time is coming when you will begin to recognize Me in everyone you meet, minister to, and work with! This is real, My people! I am real within you! You are really and truly one with Me and with all!

What you believe is up to you. I will help shore up the belief in love and healing for everyone who asks, even if it is only by the tiniest glimmer of a wish you send out. I hear you! May you come to know Me as your loving Creator, Father-Mother, and All Being. Shalom! []

Signed in spirit,
Father-Mother God

IN SUMMARY

What can I say? I felt at times like I was going through a wringer or a dense forest as I learned about one after the other serious issue that I needed to deal with related to people (Souls) in the Leigh, Goerger, and Jahner family lines and in my Soul line. Thank God that a plan was in place!

I will end the story of my journey in bringing healing and clearing to our family lines and my Soul line with the phrase, "All's well that ends well." Thank God that all ended well!

May all go well and end well for you, your family, and your friends on your life's journey. When pain and difficult circumstances present themselves, know that "This, too, shall pass." May God be with you at every moment, and may you know that you are not alone. Blessings to everyone!

Signed with love,
Lorrie

APPENDIX

A. ASTRAL BODY – HUMAN ENERGY FIELD

Five Layers of the Human Energy Field

"The human body consists of five layers of energy. The first layer is the physical body, which has weight, shape, and volume. You can touch it, see it, and contemplate its reflection in the mirror. But there are four other energy fields surrounding the physical body that are not so easily seen and which are commonly referred to collectively as a person's aura. Together, these five layers, or energy bodies, comprise the human energy field. These layers are where our mental, physical, spiritual, and emotional characteristics are stored. They can be in balance or out of balance. Which is why energy medicine practitioners believe that it's not enough to just treat the physical body when people fall sick. The other four layers must be evaluated and treated as well."

Physical Energy "This is the layer that we generally think of as our physical selves. Although our physical bodies are a kind of package, consisting of flesh, skin, bone, organs, and blood, they are also energy, same as the other layers of the body that most people cannot see or sense."

Etheric Energy "The second, or etheric—from the word 'ether'—a layer of our energy body, is located approximately one quarter to one-half inch—but not more than an inch—from the physical body. Energy medicine practitioners who are adept at psychically sensing this layer have described it as feeling much like a spider web, sticky, even stretchy. It is also gray or gray-blue in color. The etheric energy body has also been referred to as the blueprint or holograph of the physical body."

Emotional Energy "The emotional layer of our energy body is the third layer. Centrally located among the five layers, this layer is where our feelings and fears reside. This layer can be quite volatile when we are experiencing extreme high or low emotions."

Mental Energy "This is the layer from which our ideas spring. Our belief systems are also stored here. This is where our thoughts are assimilated and sorted out, and it is where we house our personal truths, or, rather, our perceptions based on our experiences."

Spiritual Energy "The spiritual layer of the human energy field is the final layer. It is the place where our 'consciousness' or 'higher awareness' resides. This final layer ties us not only to our past lives but also to universal consciousness."

Disclaimer: *"The information contained on this site is intended for educational purposes only and is not a substitute for advice, diagnosis or treatment by a licensed physician. You should seek prompt medical care for any health issues and consult your doctor before using alternative medicine or making a change to your regimen."*[3]

A Study of the Human Energy Field
Karen O'Dell, Saybrook University, 2015

"The energy emitted by the body has also been found to change and vibrate in varying frequencies depending on the individual's physical and emotional state and permeates every cell within the body. Research shows that this field also flows outward and fills the space around the body and can be felt by other individuals as well." (Healing Touch Program Energy Magazine, pp. 39-43, excerpt)

B. NAMES: CURRENT AND PREVIOUS LIFETIMES (Partial List)

Current Lifetimes

Grandma Leigh – My grandmother on my Mom's side
Joel – My brother (5 years younger than me)

Kristen – Katherine's great- or great-great granddaughter
Lee – My former brother-in-law
Mia – Dual Soul that was with me in this lifetime
Mollie – My aunt (my mother's sister)
Ron – My former husband

Previous Lifetimes

Cal – Joel prior life as a warlock (knew Caleb and Yezzi)
Caleb – Mollie prior life (practiced witchcraft with Cal)
Cecelia – Mollie prior life (nun, directed witchcraft energies at me)
Corella – Me prior life (Corrie's daughter)
Corrie – Mollie prior life (Corella's mother)
Corrine – Me prior life (prostitute)
Darin – Lee prior life (married to Darla, sons Nate & Paulie)
Darin[2] – Lee prior life (had a low vibration energy level)
Darla – Me prior life (married To Darin, sons Nate & Paulie)
David – Joel prior life (sexual slave with James)
Erik – Me prior life (Kim & Tom were split-off portions of it)
Gemma – Mollie prior life (nun, directed witchcraft energies at me)
Harold – Lee prior life (Harold & Marie had a daughter-Kristen)
James – Joel prior life (sexual slave with David)
Juva – Joel prior life (witchcraft with Kor and Mava)
Katherine – Prior life: Marie's & Harold's daughter
Kor – Me prior life, warlock (witchcraft with Juva and Mava)
Marie – Grandma/Me prior life (married to Tony)
Marie[1] – Me prior life (my portion of Marie's Soul)
Marie[2] – Grandma Leigh prior life (her portion of Marie's Soul)
Mava – Mollie prior life (witchcraft with Kor and Juva)
Penelope – Me prior life (one of my earliest lifetimes)
Richard – Me prior life (sexual slave with Richard)
Rob – Me prior life (sexual slave with Rob)
Rose of Lima – Me prior life (nun)
Tony – Ron prior life (married to Marie)
Yezzi – Me prior life (knew Cal and Caleb)

BIBLIOGRAPHY

ACIM Preface quotes are from *A Course in Miracles* Combined Volume
Second Edition. Viking-Published by the Penguin Group, Penguin
Books USA Inc. 375 Hudson Street, New York, New York, 10014,
U.S.A. © Foundation for Inner Peace, c 1975, 1985, 1992, 1996.
Used with permission from the Foundation for Inner Peace (www.
acim.org andinfo@acim.org). All Rights Reserved

acim.org/acim/EN accessed July 2023 (At bottom of screen, click on
"Use Basic Cookies," click on magnifying glass to search for desired
text, copy, paste in your document. Citation is included.)

Bodine, Echo, *Echoes of the Soul: The Soul's Journey Beyond the Light*,
c 1999, New World Library

Cady, *Complete Works of H. Emilie Cady*, First Edition 1995; fourteenth
printing 2011, Unity Books

Emmanuel's Book: A manual for living comfortably in the cosmos,
compiled by Pat Rodegast and Judith Stanton, c 1989 Bantam

Emmanuel's Book II: The Choice for Love, compiled by Pat Rodegast and
Judith Stanton, c 1989, Bantam

Greene, Glenda, *Love Without End: Jesus Speaks*, 1998, Spiritis

Heart Song: Vibrating Heartlessness to Let Heart In, c. 1992, by Ceanne
DeRohan. Four Winds Publications

Hover-Kramer, Dorothea, *Healing Touch: A Guidebook for Practitioners*,
2 Ed., c 2001, Cengage Learning

KJV King James Version, Bible Gateway, www.biblegateway.com.
Accessed Jun 2020.

HAT I, Leigh, Lorrie, *Healing Across Time I: For Parts and All of Me*, c
2023, iUniverse

HAT III, Leigh, Lorrie, *Healing Across Time III: A Collection of Prayers for
All Purposes*, c 2023, iUniverse

Montessori, Maria, *The Absorbent Mind.*, c 1995, Henry Holt, NY

Original Cause: The Unseen Role of Denial, c 1986. Ceanne DeRohan. Four Winds Publications

Right Use of Will: Healing and Evolving the Emotional Body, c 2010. Ceanne DeRohan. Four Winds Publications

"Sedona Journal of Emergence," Light Technology Publishing

Starr, Aloa, *Prisoners of Earth: Psychic Possession and Its Release*, c 1987 Aloa Starr, 2nd Ed. Revised 1993, Light Technology

NIV New International Version, Bible Gateway, www.biblegateway. com. Accessed Jun 2023

Walsh, Sheila, *Honestly*, c 1996 by Sheila Walsh. Zondervan

Webster's New World Collegiate Dictionary 4th Edition, c 2004, Wiley

Wright, Machaelle Small, *MAP: The Co-Creative White Brotherhood Medical Assistance Program*, c 2006 Perelandra, Ltd

GLOSSARY

Disclaimer: I make no representation or warranty of any kind, express or implied, as to the accuracy of the non-referenced definitions given below. The understanding of spiritual realities is constantly evolving, and scientific and psychological research is ongoing. Lorrie Leigh

astral body – energy fields surrounding a person's body (See Appendix)

astral cord – an energy connection "made of astral and etheric energy [that] connect[s] two people's subtle bodies"[4]

cellular memory – "Body memory (BM) is a hypothesis that the body itself is capable of storing memories, as opposed to only the brain. ...there are currently no known means by which tissues other than the brain would be capable of storing memories. ...it has become relevant in treatment for PTSD." (Wikipedia) Also, see *Healing Across Time I*, Appendix C.

chakra – *n.,* in forms of yoga, any of the body centers, usually seven, that are considered sources of energy for psychic or spiritual power (Web p. 242)

contact point for negative energy – This writing: a connecting point for negative energy that is attached to or implanted within a person's body or aura that attracts similar energies; created and put in place by another person's strong intention or by use of witchcraft energies

copper ring (tensor ring) – made of two strands of twisted copper wire that clears negative energy. See *Healing Across Time III* Appendix A.

curse – *n.* 1. a calling on God or the gods to send evil or injury down on some person or thing (Web p. 356)

curse, karmic – a curse hanging over someone and their family as a result of that person or a family member having placed that curse on someone during their current lifetime or in a previous lifetime dark energy center – This writing: an energy-seeking center that has dark (negative) energies mixed in with Soul portions[5]

emotional body – one of the energy fields surrounding a person's body

erroneous early imprinting –This writing: the belief, picked up early on in the Soul's existence, that they are not worthy of being loved

energy-seeking center – This writing: a cluster of small portions of Souls that need clearing and healing that are magnetically attached to a Soul to receive healing

family distress – This writing: physical and emotional symptoms triggered within a person when loved ones and/or people (Souls) in their family lines or Soul line experience distress

family lines – This writing: a person's and their spouse's birth and adoptive parents, grandparents and great-grandparents (and spouses) going back to the beginning of their existence as Souls

Full Soul – This writing: the portion of a person's original Soul that is with God plus all portions of it that are currently living lifetimes, are with other people, in the astral plane, in Heaven, or elsewhere. Each portion of a Full Soul lives a human life only once.[5]

Full Soul, splitting – This writing: a Full Soul splits into two Full Souls when the energy level of parts of it gets too much out of sync

gatekeeper – an elemental (spiritual entity) which guards the psychic door at the base of the skull (Starr pp. 44, 51)

go to the light – a Soul going to its right place: Heaven or elsewhere

healing ring – This writing: a ring of love and light surrounding a Soul; a ring of love and light that we can ask to have surround ourselves (others) to be ministered to by angels[5]

healing touch – doing clearing and healing from within a person's aura (Hover-Kramer pp. 109-110)

Heart (capitalized) – the Son of God (Original, Introduction p. viii)

Heaven Hospital – This writing: a hospital in Heaven for Souls where people can be ministered to while still living (Bodine pp. 49-50)

Higher Self – This writing: one's Full Soul[5]

Holy Spirit Demagnetizing Shower – This writing: A flow of spiritual energy from the Holy Spirit that loosens the magnetic attraction between a Soul and negative energy and Soul residue

Home Soul – This writing: a person's Soul in their current lifetime ideal self – perfectionist ideals that somewhat control the person

implant – "a controlling device, generally of astral substance... implanted by psychic means [or] hypnosis." (Starr pp. 67, 74) A hypnotic suggestion could be implanted.

In-God-We-Trust Angels – a band of Angels one can call on to come with a net of golden light to carry entities away (Starr pp. 8, 28, 165)

in spirit – speaking to a person without them being present

inner healing – healing of emotions related to trauma

karma – Buddhism, Hinduism: the principle of cause and effect where an individual's intent and actions cause (influence) their future. (Wikipedia)

lost Will – a person's emotions that have been denied (repressed); Capitalized: Emotions that Mother God denied (repressed)

Medical Assistance Team (MAT) – a heavenly ministry team that is a function of "the Great Brotherhood of Light...The Sisterhood of Light...an organization of Ascended Masters, Angels, and Cosmic Beings united for the highest Service to God...includes Jesus the Christ, Gautama Buddha, Mother Teresa, Archangel Michael."[6]

Mighty Astrea – one of the Elohim (angels) of the seven rays[7]

negative energy, negative spirit – This writing: for each person, energy that has a lower-vibration rate than their energy has; energy that is lacking in positive character, such as anger or greed; energy that diminishes, deprives, or denies a person's energy

outside Soul – This writing: any Soul that is not part of a person's Soul in their current lifetime

Parent Soul – one's original Soul, a portion of which is with God in Heaven (Original, p. 69)

place for visiting Souls – This writing: one of several planes of existence located within a person's aura

Reading – a psychic studies a person's energy, makes observations

residue, energy – "tiny particles that got separated from the mass of energy that either float in the air or cling to people, animals or objects by static attraction"[5]

residue, Soul – small bits of the astral body of Souls that are separated from the Soul they are a part of

right place for unloving Souls – This writing: Home for unloving Souls shade – This writing: a portion of the astral body of a Soul

shalom – *n.* [Mod.Heb *shalom*, lit., peace] 1 hello 2 goodbye The traditional Jewish greeting or farewell (Web p. 1316)

Siamese identical twin Soul – This writing: the Soul of a person's identical twin that is still connected to the person's Soul because the Soul did not divide completely when the embryo divided

Siamese fraternal twin Soul – the incorporated and enmeshed Soul of the person's fraternal twin that did not survive

Soul, dual – This writing: a second Soul that is within a person's body because the person's Full Soul was connected to another Full Soul by a narrow strip of Soul essence at the time of conception, allowing a portion of the connected Full Soul to enter the baby's body along with their own Soul

Soul enmeshment – This writing: portions of Souls being mixed together

Soul incorporation – This writing: portions of an outside Soul that are enmeshed with a person's Soul being within some of the cells in that person's body, helping to sustain life

Soul infestation Type One – a portion of an outside loving Soul intermingling with a baby's Soul at conception or shortly afterward

Soul infestation Type Two – a portion of an unloving Soul intermingling with a baby's Soul at conception or shortly afterward

Soul infestation Type Three – negative energy intermingling with a baby's Soul at conception or shortly afterward

Soul line – This writing: A person's Souls from all previous lifetimes

Soul retrieval – assisting separated Soul portions to return to the Soul they are a part of

Soul, squatter – This writing: a Soul that is present as an infestation

soul tie – a spiritual/emotional connection between people

soul tie, carnal – a soul tie between people that is an aspect of the spirit of lust[5]

Soul, unloving – 1. A Soul that came forth unloving 2. A Soul that became unloving due to experiencing painful life circumstances.

Souls, intergrafted – This writing: A mother's protectiveness for herself can extend into her baby and somewhat "glue" a portion of her child's Soul to her Soul, creating a pathway between them.

supraphysical shell – calcified matter or shell attached to the astral
    body that was formed from "a habit, fear, or emotional behavior
    pattern that has been deeply imprinted in the etheric body" (Starr
    p. 102). It can be from a current or previous lifetime.
umbilical cord, spiritual – one type of astral cord
unloving Soul – This writing: A Soul that came forth unloving; a Soul
    that became unloving due to painful life circumstances.
violet flame – "...the coalesced spiritual energy of love, mercy, justice,
    freedom, and transmutation."[8]
vortex, negative – an area in which energy spirals counterclockwise,
    downward
vortex, positive – an area where energy spirals clockwise, upward
warlock – 1 a man who is thought to have magic power, as in practicing
    black magic; sorcerer or wizard; male witch (Web p. 1612)
Will – The four parts of God are Spirit, Will, Heart, and Body. Will is the
    emotional body, Mother God. (Original, Introduction p. xi)

OTHER BOOKS IN THE SET

HEALING ACROSS TIME I
Healing for Parts and All of Me

HEALING ACROSS TIME III
Prayers for Protection, Clearing, and Healing

REFERENCES

1 drsharonnorling.com/autoimmune-disease-and-gluten-sensitivity/
2 www1.cbn.com/questions/permissible-pray-more-than-once
3 www.learnreligions.com/layers-of-human-energy-field-1729677, by Phylameana Lila Desy. Updated on May 09, 2019.
4 https://www.alchemyrealm.com/cords.htm
5 Portion of a lesson received from Spirit between May 2008 and May 2012
6 www.Ascension-Research.org
7 www.ascension-research.org/astrea.html
8 https://www.violetflame.com/the-secret-of-the-violet-flame/

Printed in the United States
by Baker & Taylor Publisher Services